all the Clever Words on Pages

A portrait of my friendship with Aaron Weiss of mewithoutYou

Paul Matthew Harrison

PAUL DARRITON (signature)

CLEVER WORDS

Copyright © 2016 by Paul Matthew Harrison.

All rights reserved. No part of this book may be used or reproduced in any manner whatsoever without written permission except in the case of brief quotations embodied in critical articles and reviews.

ISBN: 978-0-692-73755-2 (paperback)

Second edition 2016

Publisher: CLEVER WORDS, Galena, IL
Cover design: Jimmy Wasion
Cover illustration: Michael Almquist
Proofreading and Formatting: Erin Keyser
Printed in Dubuque, IA, U.S.A.

The author can be contacted at:
paulmharrison1976@yahoo.com

Acknowledgements

Thanks to Erin Keyser for your help, encouragement, and guidance. You can find her books at erinkeyserhorn.com. To Jimmy Wasion for designing the cover. He can be found at jimmyanimation.com. To Michael Almquist for providing his drawing of Aaron for the cover. He can be found at mewithoutyou.com. To Vasily Kafanov for donating art for the cover that we didn't use. He can be found at kafanov.com. To Aaron Weiss for allowing me to objectify our friendship, put your disembodied floating cartoon head on the cover, and for letting me talk about you in public for fun and profit—also for enduring my endless questions and fact-checking over the years it took to write this book, and for enduring the unease of not knowing what from our personal conversations would be made public. To the guys in mewithoutYou for your relentless hard work and touring that allowed me to see Aaron over the years. I hope I represented the band accurately. Thank you, reader, for taking time to read my book. And thank you to everyone who gave me permission to quote their material in my book. Not everyone could be located for permission. Any concerns regarding this can be sent to paulmharrison1976@yahoo.com.

All the clever words on pages
Turn to fragments, circles, points, and lines
And we cover them like carpets
With graceful, meaningless ornamental designs

(Seven Sisters)

Table of Contents

Foreword
Introduction

1 Belief and Doubt   1
2 Christian Rock and the Tooth & Nail Revolution   7
3 JPUSA   15
4 Norma Jean   22
5 Weiss   25
6 The Operation   32
7 MewithoutYou   34
8 Crossroads   39
9 A to B Life   47
   3/28/03 Aaron Weiss Journal Entry   52
10 Renewed Faith   53
11 Natalie   57
12 MewithoutYou Cornerstone 2003   60
13 Aaron Weiss's Message: Cornerstone 2003   62
14 Fireside Bowl   67
15 Unrequited   71
   8/14/03 Aaron Weiss Journal Entry   74
   8/23/03 Aaron Weiss Journal Entry   78
16 Anabaptist   80
17 Metro 2004   90
18 Dark Night   91
19 Van Buren   94
20 Proposal   97
21 Catch for Us the Foxes   105
22 Alone to the Alone   115
23 Emergent   118
24 Cornerstone 2005   124
25 Aaron Weiss's Message: Cornerstone 2005   127
26 Crossed Paths   136
   7/7/05 Email to Aaron   138
   7/14/05 Email from Aaron   140

27 Homeless   141
28 Suicide   146
   11/24/05 Email to Aaron   149
   11/25/05 Email from Aaron   151
29 If You Can Someday Stop By   153
30 The New Monasticism   156
31 Beef 'n' Brandy   159
32 Upper Darby   164
33 Flower Shop   169
34 Carols   171
35 Dumpster Diving   173
36 Christmas Party   175
37 Thursday   177
38 Kensington   180
39 Bruderhof   182
40 Dumpster Diving (Pt. 2)   188
41 Conversations   190
42 Conflicted   194
43 Goodbye   196
44 Rocket Cat   198
45 Parting Reflections   201
46 Trinity of Desire   206
47 Drowning   208
48 Van Buren (Pt. 2)   210
   1/30/06 Email to Aaron   212
   2/02/06 Email from Aaron   213
   2/18/06 Email to Aaron   214
   2/18/06 Email from Aaron   215
49 April   216
50 Chicago   220
51 Elliott   221
52 House of Blues Chicago   223
   6/14/06 Email to Aaron   225
   6/21/06 Email from Aaron   227
53 Paradoxes   229
54 House Café   231
55 Nervous Breakdown   235

56 Cornerstone 2006   236
57 Aaron Weiss's Message: Cornerstone 2006   241
58 If She Comes Circling Back   256
   7/16/06 Email to Aaron   259
   7/19/06 Email from Aaron   260
   8/26/06 Email to Aaron   261
   8/27/06 Email from Aaron   262
   9/12/06 Email from Aaron   263
59 Brother, Sister   264
60 Mouse   269
61 The Sad Side of a Nowhere Town   271
62 New Atheism   273
63 Emily   275
   5/20/07 Email to Aaron   279
   5/25/07 Email from Aaron   280
64 Metro 2007   281
   8/30/07 Email from Aaron   283
   8/31/07 Email to Aaron   285
   9/12/07 Email from Aaron   291
65 Congress Theater   293
66 All the Clever Words on Pages   297
   3/10/08 Email from Aaron   299
67 Healing   300
   12/31/07 Journal Entry   302
   2/14/08 Valentine's Day Card from Emily   303
   4/20/08 Email from Aaron   304
68 Enigma   305
   5/28/08 Email from Aaron   306
69 Love   307
70 Wedding   313
71 Clearwater   314
   3/04/09 Email to Aaron   320
   3/21/09 Email from Aaron   321
72 Repudiations   322
73 It's All Crazy!   327
74 Metro 2009   344
   8/1/09 Email to Aaron   349

    9/5/09 Email from Aaron   350
75 Ashes   351
    January 2010 Email from Emily   357
76 Renfrew   358
    2/06/10 Email from Emily   361
    2/11/10 Email from Emily   362
    2/13/10 Email from Emily   363
    2/28/10 Email from Emily   365
    2/28/10 Email to Aaron   366
    3/13/10 Email from Aaron   468
    3/13/10 Email to Emily from Aaron   472
77 Wedding (Pt. 2)   373
78 Chicago (Pt. 2)   375
79 Earthen Vessels   381
    7/21/10 Email from Aaron   385
    7/21/10 Email to Aaron   386
80 All Our Dads Die   387
    8/4/10 Email to Aaron   389
    8/31/10 Email from Aaron   390
81 Old Habits Die Hard   391
    9/17/10 Email to Aaron   392
    11/11/10 Email from Aaron   393
82 Collapse   395
    12/20/10 Email to Aaron   397
    1/4/11 Email from Aaron   398
    1/4/11 Email to Aaron   399
    1/13/11 Email from Aaron   400
83 Thirty-Five   401
    4/21/11 Email to Aaron   403
    4/28/11 Email from Aaron   404
84 Galena   405
    11/12/11 Email to Aaron   409
    12/23/11 Email from Aaron   410
    12/24/11 Email to Aaron   411
    3/22/12 Email from Aaron   413
    3/30/12 Email to Aaron   415
    5/03/12 Email from Aaron   417

    4/20/12 Email to Aaron   418
    5/03/12 Email from Aaron   419
85 Cobain   420
86 Ten Stories   422
87 Wild Goose   434
88 Sometimes   436
89 Bottom Lounge 2012   440
    7/15/12 Email to Aaron   442
    7/31/12 Email in Aaron   444
    8/17/12 Email to Aaron   446
    8/30/12 Email from Aaron   447
90 Kaysha   448
91 Trinity of Desire (Pt. 2)   449
92 Upper Darby (Pt. 2)   551
93 The Fellowship   559
94 The Farm   563
95 The Dump   565
96 Sacred Harp   566
97 Temple   468
98 Linvilla Orchards   472
99 All Circles   474
    10/28/12 Email to Aaron   475
    10/31/12 Email from Aaron   476
    11/17/12 Email to Aaron   477
    11/19/12 Email from Aaron   478
100 Winter Trains   479
101 Ring   480
102 Bottom Lounge 2014   484
103 Idaho Courts   486
104 Foxes Anniversary Tour   490
105 Pale Horses   496
106 Fuck   507
107 Bad Christian   511
108 Birdie   514
    12/17/15 Note to Aaron   515
    12/17/15 Email from Aaron   516

Epilogue

Foreword

I first met Paul in the summer of 2000. It was my second time visiting a Christian community in Uptown Chicago called Jesus People USA (JPUSA). Paul was a new member of the community, which you will read about in much better detail later. I was enamored with JPUSA at the time due to my involvement with their annual music and arts festival, Cornerstone. I had recently joined the Christian metal band Living Sacrifice as a percussionist. We played Main Stage at the fest that year, taking the stage just before P.O.D., a band that used to open for Living Sacrifice but had just exploded into the mainstream.

Living Sacrifice was a veritable institution in the Christian metal scene by the time I joined. A decade into their career, they had played Cornerstone many times. Our album, *The Hammering Process*, was released soon after I met Paul, and I spent the next two years on tour. By the time 2002 rolled around and Living Sacrifice was preparing to record our sixth album, I was disillusioned with Christianity.

I first met Aaron Weiss around this time. MewithoutYou was a newer act on our label, Tooth & Nail, and they were gearing up to promote their debut album *[A→B] Life*. We played several shows and festivals together before my time with Living Sacrifice officially came to an end. Rocky Gray, our guitar player, had gone on to play drums for Evanescence. My brother Cory, who was in a band called Eso-Charis with me before I'd joined Living Sacrifice, filled in on guitar for Living Sacrifice's final shows in 2003 before he moved on to front Norma Jean. I also played in three other bands that toured with mewithoutYou over the corresponding years: Lovedrug, Unwed Sailor, and Bear Colony.

I have to be honest. I thought Aaron was a bit of a phony in the beginning. I felt like he had a shtick, an act, a portrayal of some higher idea of how he imagined himself to be that he put on for other people, almost like theatre.

The guys from mewithoutYou stayed at my house in 2003 as they were coming to the end of their touring cycle for *[A→B] Life*. Aaron asked to borrow my thesaurus and spent the remainder of the night reading and studying. While the rest of us were talking, catching up, and listening to music, Aaron had his head in a book. He seemed pretentiously obsessed with Bible study and other intellectual pursuits.

In August of 2003, after Living Sacrifice had just disbanded, I went on tour with Unwed Sailor. Joining us was a woman Aaron was interested in, so he took the Greyhound out to Washington D. C. to see her. Though he seemed crazy about her, and perhaps she gave him reason to believe she was crazy about him, she was actually dreading seeing him. She asked me to stay close to her so she wouldn't be alone with him.

When Aaron got to the show, we all shared a booth together. Aaron and I began to discuss philosophy and theology (because of course we did), but the woman Aaron came to see was totally disinterested in what we were talking about. I told Aaron during our conversation that I was no longer a Christian. It's the first time I had ever said that out loud to somebody. I seem to remember Aaron's face going into semi-shock and the conversation faltering. Soon after, we found ourselves in the van.

As we made our way to the next location that night, well over a hundred miles from Upper Darby where Aaron lived, knowing there was no romantic connection with the woman he came to see, Aaron suddenly asked to be let out on the side of the road. We tried to talk him out of it, but he was being all Aaron-y about it. She spent a moment with him and hugged him goodbye. He left her with a book of Rumi's poetry. As you'll read, Aaron swam across the Susquehanna River, stowed away on a flatbed truck, and hitched rides home.

My time spent traveling with Aaron and mewithoutYou corresponds directly with my impressions of him. As I met him again and again over the years, my opinion of him gradually changed. The more I got to know him, the more I was drawn to him and really began to like him. I think Aaron is a kind and gentle soul, an introspective person, critical of himself and always pursuing purer motivations and morals.

But my perception of Aaron is a big part of what I enjoyed when reading this book. Being deeply thoughtful means being exposed to self-damnation wrapped up in self-reflection. Aaron can be hard on himself. You see the self-abandonment, self-refusal, and even self-hate that makes listening to mewithoutYou such a cerebral experience. You also see some of the same qualities and characteristics reflected in Paul's personal journey.

I've known Aaron and Paul for over a decade. Apparently I introduced them at Cornerstone in 2003, a memory that escaped me until I read Paul's recollection. But this book is not a biography about Aaron—it's bigger than that. It serves as a memoir of the inherent difficulties in navigating the complicated landscape of faith, music, relationships, and morality.

I ran into Paul many times over the years while on tour with various bands. He always had a book to give me. But sometimes he would bring VHS tapes: everything from bands we both liked, my own performances, and even documentaries about everything from faith healing to televangelism. We had a kinship in our mutual disgust for religious charlatanism.

An author Paul and I explored mutually was John Shelby Spong, a retired bishop of the Episcopal Church and a liberal Christian theologian who denounced all things fundamentalist. I had always been interested in artists, authors, and literature that were considered taboo or "out there" by my Christian friends. This only became more pronounced and awkward as my time in Living Sacrifice rolled on. I was genuinely curious about getting to the heart of what I believed, and it wasn't anything I was doing artificially, but the questions I asked and the thoughts I entertained made my Christian friends uncomfortable. When I mentioned to my bandmates in the van one day that I no longer believed in the virgin birth of Jesus, some were hurt and deeply concerned for me. They thought I was reading too many books and talking to people who were corrupting me, but I had my own mind.

In the end, my mind went with my heart, and I walked away from Christianity and my association with the Christian music subculture. I wanted a deeper understanding of the world, but mostly I wanted a belief system that didn't rely on what I considered to be superstition. Fundamentalist Christianity didn't line up with anything I saw or experienced in the real world. I needed a faith that accepted the world around me, not one that asked me to deny it. I wasn't angry or resentful, but I was certainly disheartened by what I experienced during my time immersed in the Christian faith.

I was wrong about Aaron being insincere, in the same way that my friends and bandmates were wrong about me. One hallmark of my transition from Christianity to "other" was an inflated sense of self-importance about my journey. As you'll read, Paul thought God was speaking to him and calling him to "big things," and Aaron for some time fancied himself a spiritual guru, wanting to use his band as a vehicle to bring people to God, or to quit the band altogether and be a monk. I don't know what Paul and Aaron believe today, but we seem to be taking ourselves and our sense of importance in the world less seriously.

This is a story about feeling absolute confidence in your life's direction only to be confronted with its harsh realities, namely the battles that take place in your own mind. The realities of doubt, personal struggle, and suffering. It's the reality of *life in general*.

The thoughts and experiences presented here are easily relatable for any counter-culture youth group kid from the late 1990's and early 2000's, myself included. We recognize these struggles and relate to these anecdotes. We tried to find our way in life with the ideas and beliefs presented to us by the church, but we were stuck with ourselves at the end of the day. We were sold on a belief system that over-promised and under-delivered. But having walked away from certainties, we still find ourselves open to the transcendent in whatever form we find it.

Whether you came to this book as a fan of mewithoutYou, or out of love and curiosity about Aaron Weiss, or as a person who has lived through similar struggles with belief and doubt like me and Paul, you'll love this book.

Matthew Putman
(Eso-Charis, Living Sacrifice, Snailhuntr, Unwed Sailor, Lovedrug, Bear Colony, Chase Pagan)

Introduction

"How does it make you feel when a fan comes up to you to tell you that you've greatly affected and changed their life?"
"I usually think 'uh oh.'"[1]
—Aaron Weiss—

Aaron Weiss is best known as the strange and spiritually eclectic lyricist and frontman in the experimental indie rock band mewithoutYou. Aaron was infamous for being an anti-rock star, complaining that he cared little to nothing about the band he was in or its success. He swore year after year that he would quit, give away all of his possessions, and live without a home, like Jesus.

He was thought of as a hobo, a tramp, and a drifter for his penchant for train hopping and hitchhiking. He picked up the nickname "the scavenger" when he began to dumpster dive and frequent thrift stores for clothing and eat almost exclusively from the trash. This earned him the reputation of being a dirtbag. He became a war-protesting pacifist, a sometimes vegan, a somewhat environmental activist, and he experimented with communal living. A rumor circulated for years that he was autistic.

Spiritually, Aaron was raised Sufi—a form of mystical Islam influenced heavily by Eastern ideas—while being exposed to Judaism and Christianity in his childhood. He had given his life to Jesus in early adulthood but found it still didn't give him peace, take away his depression, or blunt his urge to kill himself. Only after a spiritual transformation in an Anabaptist community called the Bruderhof and in a community called The Simple Way at the end of 2003 did he find peace and hope.

Drawing from literary sources like the Bible, the Koran, the poet Rumi, Fyodor Dostoyevsky, and Soren Kierkegaard among others, Aaron delivered his poetic lyrics by shouting, screaming, and dancing spastically to spoken word, embodying passion, unrequited love, heartbreak, and spiritual longing.

---

[1] Brandon Herbel, "mewithoutYou – 09.12.06," *Absolutepunk.net*, 9/12/06.

With the band's popularity came a platform for Aaron to speak, mainly to an evangelical Christian audience, about his beliefs and practices. This would guarantee controversy with fans and frustrate bandmates who didn't always see eye-to-eye with him.

Fans began to praise Aaron for his writing genius and his spiritual devotion. Some began to look at him as a teacher, a guru, and a holy figure. Others saw him as a heretic.

Aaron, in his trademark self-abjection, repudiated all praise, calling himself a fraud, someone full of arrogance and love only for himself, warning that nothing he said or did should be listened to or followed by anyone. He reminded fans that he stole most of his lyrics and didn't have a creative bone in his body.

Everyone was trying to figure out Aaron Weiss, even Aaron.

He has also been my friend for the past ten years. What follows is the evolution of our friendship set to the backdrop of mewithoutYou's career. The emphasis of this memoir is primarily on our spiritual lives via conversations, emails, and books we've traded. We've supported each other through death, marriage, divorce, depression, mental illness, and constant spiritual shifts and life changes.

Although Aaron's beliefs heavily influence the band's lyrics, they don't represent the views of the other band members, all of whom have different beliefs.

It should also be noted that though the history of mewithoutYou is recounted here, this is in no way a proper band biography or an exhaustive interpretation of Aaron's lyrics.

Though Aaron is my friend, I still oftentimes stand back and allow myself to be a fan, to see him as a public figure. This allows me not only to see him as "my friend" but to appreciate him from a distance with everyone else. It also allows me to write about him both with a sense of intimacy and distance. Aaron said he would never write a memoir, so I have taken it upon myself to create at least a portrait of him based on our years together.

Aaron and I first exchanged contact information in the summer of 2005 amidst my own spiritual disillusionment and impending homelessness. I spent the year in nervous breakdown, finding it difficult to ward off the daily urge to kill myself. Aaron and his parents invited me to Philadelphia to stay with them that Christmas. Those few weeks saved my life.

In the upstairs office in Aaron's mom's house, next to his bedroom, I browsed his bookcases one autumn afternoon in 2012 while writing this book. There were obligatory books of Rumi's poetry, books by Bawa Muhaiyaddeen and Shane Claiborne, *The Myth of Sisyphus and Other Essays* by Albert Camus, philosophy books on theories of self and identity, and a copy of *The Journey to the East* by Hermann Hesse, among other books.

"Have you ever read that one?" Aaron asked of Hermann Hesse.

"No, I haven't."

"That's where I got the line for 'Seven Sisters' you used for the title of your book."

"Oh, really?"

"Yeah." He sat down on the couch downstairs, found the page, and read aloud:

> As I continued reading the manuscript, I had to cross out sentence after sentence, and as I crossed them out, they crumbled up on the paper, and the clear, sloping letters separated into assorted fragments, into strokes and points, into circles, small flowers and stars, and the pages were covered like carpets with graceful, meaningless, ornamental designs.[2]

He handed the book back to me, shaking his head and smirking. "More shameless theft. You can keep the book if you want it."

"Sure, thanks!" I said. "I thought of those lines in your song as a theologian carefully crafting doctrines and creeds only to realize he doesn't understand what he's talking about and has to go back to the drawing board. The words and ideas don't

---

[2] Hermann Hesse, *The Journey to the East*, (New York: Picador, 1956), 89-90.

represent anything but conjecture. But instead of giving up on that project and admitting we don't know what we're talking about, we make a fetish of the doctrines and creeds themselves—protecting them and defending them. I even envisioned ornamented pages from medieval prayer books, people astounded at their beauty without concern for whether or not the contents are true. It's as if we are finding peace and stability in our belief structures rather than in actually encountering God. But in a more tongue-in-cheek sense, I thought it would be a good title to describe all of our philosophical ponderings over the years while still coming up short of any clear answers."

"I apologize for taking myself so seriously that I thought I had any answers for you at all," Aaron said.

This book doesn't read like a dramatic narrative. It is a series of vignettes connected chronologically, sometimes moved along with standalone emails and journal entries.

The theological and philosophical misgivings and conjecture presented throughout the book are kept in place. They are not meant to be informative, but to be critiqued and carried forward in your own conversations.

Some names, locations, and identifying characteristics were changed by request. Though some unflattering details are told in some of these vignettes, my intention is not to purposefully hurt or harm anyone I write about, just to tell the events as I lived them.

I took the liberty to correct typos and clean up the grammar in transcribed speeches and email correspondence.

This is a completely rewritten edition of a book I self-published in 2007 under the same title. There is nothing of importance in that first edition that can't also be found here.

Thank you for reading.

Paul Matthew Harrison

1
Belief and Doubt

I was almost eight years old when my dad died of cancer at the age of thirty. I didn't cry when my mom woke my brother and me to tell us the news, nor did I cry at his memorial service. "Marty wouldn't want you to cry," my aunt assured me. I was glad he wasn't hurting anymore, and I believed he was in a better place. I spent my childhood wondering where he went and what happens after we die.

I grew up with my mom, Alicia, and my brother, Mark, on the south side of Chicago, in a working class, racially diverse neighborhood called Bridgeport. Though I was baptized Catholic and had attended catechism classes, we were a non-practicing, non-religious family.

I was interested in the paranormal: ghosts and poltergeists, haunted houses and demonic possessions. I wondered about Bigfoot and the Loch Ness Monster. Were UFOs and alien abductions real? What about psychics and mediums, tarot cards and astrology, astral projection and telekinesis? Were Nostradamus and other prophets real? Did Moses really part a sea and Jesus walk on water? Did saints really levitate and performs miracles?

Just before high school, I began asking ultimate questions about the meaning of life and how I was supposed to prepare for adulthood. I asked my grandmother for a Bible, but being the King James Version, I couldn't understand it, nor did I know how to read it.

My mom began dating and eventually married a man whose family was quite involved with church, some of them born-again Pentecostal Christians in ministry. On Thanksgiving of 1990, after asking one of them questions about Christianity and the Bible for an hour, I was asked if I would like to invite Jesus into my life and become born again. I said yes and we prayed together.

Being born again, I learned that all religions were false with the exception of Christianity, which was absolutely true in every aspect, and this could be proved to a certainty. Jesus was the only way to heaven and the only hope for mankind. The earth was less than ten thousand years old. Evolution was a hoax with no real scientific support and the methods we used to date the universe billions of years old were deeply flawed. There was a worldwide flood, as Genesis records, verified by science. The Bible was the only perfect book in existence, complete with fulfilled prophecy and other signs of having been supernaturally inspired by God. God was not just sitting in heaven watching, but was active in the world today, as was Satan. Miracles, faith healing, divine communication, answered prayer, occult powers, and demonic possession were real. Most importantly, the signs of the end of the world given in the Bible were so prevalent today that I needed to tell as many people as possible about Jesus before it was too late. I expected Jesus to return before I grew old and died.

I started attending a tongue-speaking Pentecostal Assemblies of God church. It was strange at first seeing a congregation of people shouting and yelling with their hands raised, dancing to worship music, rambling in tongues. Just as strange was seeing a rock-style worship band complete with a Neil Peart-influenced drummer. This was a far cry from what I remembered of the few times I visited a Catholic church as a child.

Dismissed downstairs to youth group after worship, I was met with a large library of books, movies, and CDs. Over foosball and pizza, after the mandatory Bible study, we took turns playing different Christian CDs. We had worship music and standard Christian pop, but we also had rap, dance, rock, and metal bands.

I found a video called *Hot Metal IV* in the youth group library and put it in the VCR. I was instantly hooked by three metal bands: Deliverance, Tourniquet, and Vengeance Rising. Completely bypassing hard rock and hair metal, I was taken with these Christian speed metal, thrash, and grindcore bands.

Between songs were short interviews with band members and fans, giving testimony of how they were brought closer to God through these bands. The musicians saw themselves as missionaries and evangelists. Their sole goal in playing metal was to tell people about Jesus and to provide a Christian alternative to mainstream metal bands that glorified sex, debauchery, and Satanism.

At the end of the video, a man with hair down to his waist introduced himself as Pastor Bob Beeman. He invited the viewer to call him any time at his heavy metal church, Sanctuary, in California.

I knew instantly that I wanted to be in a Christian metal band and reach the kids many churches didn't want in their youth groups—Satanists, occultists, and those isolated by abuse and depression. I would be a heavy metal evangelist.

My cousin took me to a Christian music store in Wheaton, Illinois called True Tunes. It was there that I found the legendary thrash punk band The Crucified; the technical thrash band Believer; a death metal band from Australia called Mortification, fronted by a youth pastor named Steve Rowe; and a death metal band called Living Sacrifice.

Besides *True Tunes News* and a music magazine for Christian pop artists called *CCM*, there was also Doug Van Pelt's *Heaven's Metal*, which would later become *HM Magazine*. His magazine covered the heavier bands I liked.

Mentors encouraged me to support only the bands that preached a clear gospel message at every concert and gave what was called an altar call, which is when the band preaches, then invites people forward to receive Jesus as if the concert were an evangelistic meeting. "If all you got from us tonight was lights and smoke and music, but you didn't get Jesus, then you didn't get anything from us at all tonight," they'd say. "Don't leave this place without Jesus."

Many of these bands played churches and church-sponsored ministry events where they either preached themselves or were used as bait before a minister came to the stage to preach. Ministry staff came forward to take all those present who received Christ at the altar call to another room in the venue to pray with them, give them literature like the Gospel of John, and help them find churches. It was our job as fans to pray that God used these bands and to bring our "unsaved" friends to these concerts to show them how cool and fun it was to be a Christian and expose them to the gospel message. Entertainment was a means of ministry.

Bands that played music without preaching or having an altar call were weeded out and held suspect as bands caring more about fame and ego than ministry. We would scour interviews and lyrics, looking for anything theologically aberrant, then "lovingly" correct them. If they didn't accept correction, we'd stop supporting them.

These bands needed to be accountable to a church or a pastor so they weren't out drinking, smoking, and having sex. It wasn't uncommon for Christian fans to randomly approach their favorite band members at concerts and ask them if they were struggling with temptations on the road or if they needed prayer. If they had a drink or a cigarette, used profanity, or wore a T-shirt of a secular band, we were gravely concerned for their spiritual health.

Back then, youth groups emphasized the need to be radical, on fire, extreme, and unashamed of Jesus. Our zeal was matched by our confidence that we had the truth, and everyone in the world needed to hear it. I was confident I would turn my entire high school upside down for Jesus.

I started my sophomore year with a Bible under my arm, a stack of apologetics books proving that Christianity was true, and Christian metal tapes to pass out to the Satanists, who back then were thought to be everywhere. Any kid wearing a Slayer, Deicide, or Cannibal Corpse shirt was a target.

My hair grew long and I wore T-shirts of my favorite Christian metal bands. I owned tough-guy Jesus shirts and even made my own that said: LIVE FOR CHRIST OR DIE FOR SATAN! Satan's hand was reaching from the flames. When a kid spit on me in the hallway, I bragged to my friends that I had been persecuted for Jesus.

My youth pastor taught me enough bass to play in the worship band at church and enough guitar to play heavy riffs and power chords for metal. All I needed now were musicians who shared my vision to start a metal band and for God to back me up.

Near the end of my sophomore year of high school, just as I was starting a Bible study group, I caught mononucleosis and had to spend the rest of the year at home in bed, too weak and tired even to sit up. When my strength never returned, I was diagnosed with chronic fatigue—a little understood and untreatable condition that left me with flu-like lethargy and weakness no matter how much rest or sleep I got. With a now-weakened immune system, it seemed I was sick with colds and in bed all the time. When I developed allergies and chronic widespread pain in my muscles, joints, and limbs, and the inability to concentrate became normal, I was diagnosed with fibromyalgia. Like chronic fatigue, little was known about the condition, and there was no cure or effective treatment. The prognosis was that I would live the rest of my life never recovering strength, never feeling good, and fighting the frustration and depression that would result from losing the life I once had and the future I hoped for.

I was certain this was merely an attack from Satan because I was intent on bringing Jesus to the kids he held in darkness. God would heal me and be glorified so I could continue to reach them. But all my praying, begging, believing, and visiting faith healers the next few years did no good. All the people praying for me, anointing me with healing oil, and commanding the sickness to go in the name of Jesus had no effect.

My time sick at home was spent on studying theology, philosophy, and apologetics with the intent of bolstering my confidence and being able to answer the tough questions asked by those I wanted to reach. Maybe God made me sick to give me this time to study for ministry rather than do schoolwork.

But the more I read, the more I realized just how weak Christian apologetics were in light of skeptical critique. In reading theological debates, rather than coming to a place of clarity, I saw that we couldn't agree on any one issue. How then could we be certain we had the truth? The more I read the Bible and books on how to resolve contradictions and difficulties in the text, the less confidence I had that the Bible was divinely inspired, or even true.

These intellectual problems were compounded by the fact that I couldn't detect God in my life at all. There was no guidance, communication, protection, answered prayer, healing, or anything to suggest that God cared about the details of my life.

I graduated high school in 1995, still sick and with my faith hanging by a thread, when my brother introduced me to the Internet. Looking up Christian apologetics, I was bombarded with skeptical critiques of Christianity. No longer able to sustain my faith, I wrote a thirty-page essay for my church leaders and family explaining why I could no longer be a Christian. I had become an agnostic.

Being as zealous and obsessed with Jesus as I was and certain of his presence and love in my life before everything went south, disbelieving was the most heartbreaking and terrifying thing I'd ever had to face. I spun into a deep depression, not knowing what to do with my life, especially now that the end of the world was most likely not imminent and my disability made it impossible for me to build a career. I continued to go to church and find every way I could to believe again, but it was all landing flat.

I found a part-time job at Family Bookstores after graduation, where I developed an immediate love for the corny, campy, Jesus kitsch we sold there. The more cringe-worthy, the better. There were Jesus fish for the car, bumper stickers with dire warnings on them, and T-shirts spoofing popular brand logos. We had Christian superheroes like Bibleman, a Christian Barney called Wally the Turtle, Testamints—the Christian breath mint, and little toy dinosaurs that said JESUS IS REX-ELLENT! on them. And who could forget purity rings and What Would Jesus Do bracelets?

We had our own subculture of Christian alternatives to everything in pop culture. It goes without saying that our shelves of music were filled with Christian versions of every conceivable mainstream artist.

As I understood it, Christians in the first century gave up this world and its comforts, including their wealth, homes, and possessions to live a life of suffering, preaching the gospel, and facing torture and death before the imminent return of Jesus. I wondered how it was that a multi-million dollar Christian pop culture entertainment industry where ministers could build lucrative careers emerged two thousand years later.

2
Christian Rock and the Tooth & Nail Revolution

Christian rock used to be called Jesus Music. In the late 1960s, hippies started coming to Jesus and flooding churches like Chuck Smith's Calvary Chapel in California. They began writing songs about Jesus to reach out to other hippies, burnouts, and runaways who were allowed to come to church with their long hair, blue jeans, and dirty bare feet. They hung out in Christian coffeehouses and passed out Christian pamphlets and newspapers on the streets.

Christian communes formed as hippies experimented with communal living. The compelling message these Christians preached was of Jesus as a counter-cultural revolutionary who hated religion and opposed systematic abuse and oppression. He was an anti-government pacifist who shared what he had and lived in community with others.

You could give up psychedelic drugs and Eastern mysticism and Jesus would be "a trip you'll never come down from." Using street drug dialect, they would say, "There's no high like the Most High," "Don't drop acid, drop Jesus," "Get turned on to Jesus," and "Experience Jesus." Some even got flack for saying they were "addicted to Jesus."

The evidence for Christianity was the love and peace you had in your heart after receiving Jesus. Jesus is not far or distant, but your buddy who is always with you. This message made Christianity simple and easy to spread.

The father of Christian rock is said to be Larry Norman, a strange figure with long blonde hair, beaming with charisma. As a member of the band People, he wanted to put out an album with Jesus on the cover called *We Need a Whole Lot More of Jesus and a Lot Less Rock and Roll*. Capitol said no, so Norman quit the band and released a solo album in 1969 deemed the first official Christian rock record: *Upon This Rock*.

In June of 1972 in Dallas, Texas, over 100,000 people showed up at the Cotton Bowl for a weeklong gathering called "Explo '72." It was masterminded by Bill Bright of Campus Crusade for Christ, an organization geared towards youth. He wanted people from all 50 states and over 100 countries to attend. Billy Graham preached and Andre Crouch, Larry Norman, Love Song, Johnny Cash, and others played at this event, exposing Jesus music to greater masses.

Resurrection Band formed in the early 1970s and began touring as other Jesus music bands did, leaving California and spreading across the country. After staying in Milwaukee for a short time, Resurrection Band settled in Chicago in 1972, founding a commune called Jesus People USA—one of the few remaining Jesus Movement communes still active today.

As the number of Christian bands grew from dozens into the hundreds through the 1970s, annual outdoor Christian festivals sprang up, drawing thousands of fans. Christian radio stations began covering middle-of-the-road Christian rock. In 1975, *Harmony* was published as the first Jesus music magazine. *Campus Crusade* and *Christianity Today* also covered Jesus rock bands. John Styll started *Contemporary Christian Music* magazine, later *CCM*, to cover these artists, coining the phrase "contemporary Christian music."

By 1977, Christian bookstores were making millions of dollars on Christian music and other products such as books, T-shirts, jewelry, and framed prints. Multiple labels spent lots of money promoting these artists. Variety-show televangelists had Christian musicians on as guests to perform their music, giving them a TV platform.

Up until this time, not much thought went into the production value of these artists because their goal was to evangelize, not to become pop stars. But moving into the 1980s, Jesus music was transformed into safe, non-controversial, polished entertainment for Christians. It created Christian pop stars who sang to the choir, losing their edge.

Some say Keith Green was the last prophetic voice of Jesus music, and after his death in an airplane crash in 1982 and the end of Bob Dylan's "Christian phase" in 1983, the torch was passed to U2.

Christian artists isolated themselves in a "ghetto" defined by lyrical content instead of musical style, then created what were essentially Christian versions of mainstream artists in every conceivable style. Critics began to lament that Christianity was once a leader in the creative arts but was now reduced to creating propaganda and copying popular culture in order to be a billboard for Jesus.

When I discovered Christian music in 1991, artists like Amy Grant and Michael W. Smith were being groomed for mainstream success. Tired of being in the ghetto, Christian musicians wanted greater exposure in the culture at large. The way they did this was by writing pop hits that were generally inspirational but ambiguous about Christianity. Amy Grant and Michael W. Smith were considered by many of their Christian fans to be compromisers, shunning Jesus to be mainstream pop stars with songs like "Baby, Baby" and "Place in This World."

Many Christian musicians were not given a platform in Christian circles unless they had explicit Christian lyrics and considered themselves ministers. That started to change when a man named Brandon Ebel came along.

In 1984, Jesus People USA started a festival in Illinois called Cornerstone. While many Christian festivals featured safe artists, Cornerstone was known for giving a platform to punk, metal, goth, rap, and underground Christian artists no one else was giving a chance. Eventually buying farmland in Bushnell, Illinois in 1991, Cornerstone became an annual Christian Woodstock, drawing thousands of people from all over the world for a week of camping, seminars, and events, with a couple hundred bands playing on multiple stages.

While attending Cornerstone Festival in 1991, an employee at Frontline records named Brandon Ebel was inspired to start his own label for underground punk, indie rock, and hardcore bands that other Christian labels weren't giving a chance. With Nirvana revolutionizing the musical landscape of the '90s and pop punk exploding with bands like Green Day, Christians playing underground music needed a home. In 1994, Brandon Ebel provided that home in Tooth & Nail records.

"Cornerstone is the number one reason Tooth & Nail was started," Ebel was quoted saying in *No New Kinda Story*. He signed Focused, Wish for Eden, Starflyer 59, the Blamed, Plankeye, and Blenderhead, then brought them all to Cornerstone to play in 1994. After making $10,000 at the merch table that year and seeing the positive crowd reception to his bands, he knew he was filling a niche. Brandon struck gold signing a high school punk band called MxPx who after releasing a couple of albums with explicit Christian lyrics soon found mainstream success singing about relationships and teenage problems in *Life in General*.

Tooth & Nail was caught between two subcultures. Some mainstream audiences thought their bands were too Christian, and some Christian audiences thought they weren't Christian enough.

While working at Family Bookstores, a woman returned an MxPx cassette to me. "I bought this for my granddaughter and Jesus is nowhere to be found in the lyrics. Why do you sell this here?"

Christian punk was a subgenre of a subgenre. Matt Diehl wrote in *My So-Called Punk: Green Day, Fall Out Boy, The Distillers, Bad Religion—How Neo-Punk Stage-Dived into the Mainstream*:

> Not every faction or permutation within punk was always tolerated, however. The first wave of Christian punk rock puzzled some of the punk's more traditionally dissident voices. Since then, however, Christian punk has become a massive movement, with religious bands like MxPx crossing over into mainstream sales charts—and winning the hearts and minds of nonreligious punk fans. In an ironic twist, the Christian punk artists were the ones who ultimately would embody what Greil Marcus called punk's "irreducible . . . desire to change the world," making converts of spiky-haired mavens one mosh pit at a time.[3]

---

[3] Matt Diehl, *My So-Called Punk: Green Day, Fall Out Boy, The Distillers, Bad Religion—How Neo-Punk Stage-Dived into the Mainstream*, (New York: St. Martin's Press, 2007), 35.

If punk meant having the freedom to stand up for your beliefs and say anything you want, then like the Christian hippies of the Jesus movement, Christian punks saw themselves as the ultimate rebels following the ultimate anti-establishment Rebel. They often found kinship with the straight edge bands who shunned drinking, smoking, drugs, and eating animals.

Tooth & Nail became a bridge between Christian music and the mainstream. When their bands moved to major labels, Tooth & Nail often took care of distribution to Christian markets. Christian bands found themselves much freer in the mainstream than among Christian fans or while playing in Christian venues. As music journalist Andrew Beaujon explains in *Body Piercing Saved My Life: Inside the Phenomenon of Christian Rock*:

> Christian bands have to worry about a lot of things that aren't, by popular standards, "normal": letting a cussword fly when they stub their toes onstage; defending their theology, their ministry, or their lack of theology or ministry; making their album artwork acceptable to Christian bookstores; having the number of times they do or don't mention Christ in their lyrics determine how much airplay they'll get; having to make a conscious decision whether to play shows in clubs, in churches, or in both; choosing their tourmates; deciding whether to do an "altar call."[4]

In *Apostles of Rock: The Splintered World of Contemporary Christian Music*, Howard and Streck separate Christian music into three general categories—separational, integrational, and transformational:

> The musicians of Separational CCM argue that music is designed to proselytize the nonbeliever, encourage the believer, or praise God. Integrational CCM counters that it is

---

[4] Andrew Beaujon, *Body Piercing Saved My Life: Inside the Phenomenon of Christian Rock*, (Cambridge: Da Capo Press, 2006), 60.

enough for the music to provide a wholesome alternative to the standard fare of the secular media and to give at least some voice to a Christian worldview within the larger marketplace of ideas. To this mix of reasons and rationales, Transformational CCM brings the claim that the purpose of Christian music is simply to exist; it is valuable because it is, not because it necessarily accomplishes some goal.[5]

Of these first two categories, Howard and Streck wrote:

In the end, God must solve all difficulties, reveal the meaning of suffering in the end, and/or point to some greater good. . . . The separational approach to Christ and culture suggests that CCM is to be always positive, always hopeful, and, apart from some tidy resolution, to never address one's own continuing failures and brokenness; such a topic might suggest that evangelical Christianity is ineffectual.[6]

They add:

It is argued that both separationists and integrationists, to borrow from Thomas Moore, have a tendency "to idealize and romanticize a story, winnowing out the darker elements of doubt, hopelessness, and emptiness." The intellect seeks summary meaning, Moore argues, "but the soul craves depth of reflection, many layers of meaning, nuances without end, references and allusions and prefigurations" that "enrich the texture of an image or story" and give the soul "food for rumination."[7]

Finally, transformational music says there is no distinction between sacred and secular, no separation between Christian and

---

[5] Jay R. Howard & John M. Streck. *Apostles of Rock: The Splintered World of Contemporary Christian Music*, (Lexington: The University Press of Kentucky, 1999), 144.
[6] Ibid, 214.
[7] Ibid, 210-11.

non-Christian, and that music is art for its own sake, not bait or propaganda. Many Tooth & Nail bands fit this category.

In contrast to the first two categories, transformational music rejects the formula that starts with a problem and ends with Jesus as the answer. Rather than having it all figured out and presenting a truth to the world, transformational artists don't have all the answers and their songs rarely have happy endings. Rather than romanticizing or idealizing the Christian life, they stay in darkness, doubt, struggle, and without resolve, acting often as a prophetic voice against both Christianity and mainstream culture:

> This approach argues that it is crucial to recognize the danger of mistaking one's own cultural understanding of the "nature of things" as God's law, accepting fleeting realities for transcendent truths. Given these assumptions, those working from this synthetic position tend to produce theologies and cosmologies that are both tentative—with any given moment potentially leading to circumstances that would demand a reworking of assumed truths—and fragmentary, since a complete understanding of God's "truth" is not possible.[8]

Suspicious of tidy answers, they wrestle with an unexplainable God "in terms that allow them to celebrate the mysteries, contradictions, and paradoxes rather than attempting to resolve them."[9]

Transformational artists are equally uncomfortable with the idea that Jesus is your friend and lover, that God is always there to comfort you like a cosmic daddy, and that he's waiting to meet your needs and make everything okay. Those messages, often found in songs on "safe for the whole family" Christian radio, are looked at as shallow idealism and escapism. Simply no one experiences Christianity the way it is portrayed in those songs.

These artists also opt for ambiguity, first-person storytelling, poetry, and metaphor in their delivery. They write about the

---

[8] Ibid, 117.
[9] Ibid, 118.

whole of human experience and some might even use profanity and paint explicit pictures of doubt and sexuality. Because of this, they are often neglected by Christian bookstores and the Christian entertainment subculture at large.[10]

I became a fan of many of these Tooth & Nail bands, and though I was unsure of my faith, I still wanted to start a Christian metal band, even if just to express my doubts and struggles.

---

[10] David Bazan of Pedro the Lion losing his faith album-by-album and using profanity and sexuality in his lyrics is a prime example of transformational music.

3
JPUSA

At the age of 24 in the year 2000, I was struggling to form a stable life. I still suffered daily pain and fatigue, and doctors were still lost for a treatment. I continued to lose part-time jobs because of my illness, and with that, apartments. I found myself moving home over and over again.

It was suggested that Jesus People USA on the north side of Chicago would be the perfect place for me if I liked art and writing and wanted to be involved with Christian music.

Growing my hair long, getting tattoos, and wanting to be fashionable for a band, I needed a job that didn't have a dress code. I found one at The Alley, a shop in Chicago that sold heavy metal band shirts, leather jackets, belt buckles, designer clothing, jewelry, and general counter-culture merchandise.

My first day there I met a girl with a lip piercing and a large colored mohawk. She was listening to a hardcore band on the stereo.

"That sounds great, who are they?" I asked.

"No Innocent Victim. They're a Christian band."

"Oh yeah, I've heard of them."

"Are you a Christian?" she asked.

"Yes."

"Ahhh!" She shrieked and threw her arms around me. "I am too! I've been praying for God to send another Christian here!"

As we talked more, she told me that she had lived a number of years at JPUSA and had recently moved out.

"It was suggested to me that I check that place out. Is it around here?"

"Yes, just a bus ride away. Do you want me to take you for a visit?"

"Sure!"

We took the bus to Uptown where the twin hotel-style buildings stood. The entrance led to the front desk and lobby area.

Besides a few offices, there was a fellowship room where church services could be held and a large common dining room next to the kitchen.

Everyone there seemed to be part of a scene. There were hippies with long beards and sandals; tattooed punks with mohawks and liberty spikes, buttons and patches on their jackets; hardcore kids with large plugs in their earlobes, sporting sleeves of tattoos; metal guys with their long hair, wearing old-school Christian band shirts; and gothic kids in full goth attire and make up. Pet rats were all the rage.

Being a commune, all of my practical needs would be met, and I'd have a home as long as I could do the required housekeeping. Jesus People ran a number of businesses and shelters, soup kitchens, and took care of the elderly.

The community also published books on Cornerstone Press, printed the long-running *Cornerstone Magazine*, had a healthy art community, and ran Belly Acres Designs, which made merchandise like T-shirts and stickers for just about every band I liked.

The president of JPUSA was Glenn Kaiser of Rez Band,[11] who was still making music. Bands like the Blamed, Ballydowse, and later, Headnoise were punk bands in residence. Folk and Celtic bands, such as Seeds and the Crossing, also lived there. These bands were signed to their in-house label, Grrr Records.

I could help run Cornerstone Festival and rub shoulders with other musicians. I might even meet that indie rock bohemian artist girl I'd always fantasized about, and she would marry me with no thought of how much money I had.

As I stood in the lobby at the end of my visit, I felt an urgency to quit my job and move in right away. I wondered if this was from God.

I'd learned enough about cults and communes by that time to be aware of their abuses: the charismatic leader who is practically worshipped and on whose word everyone hangs as he exploits them; having every aspect of your life controlled and

---

[11] Formerly Resurrection Band.

micromanaged by an abusive authoritarian structure; being overworked and seeing little benefit for yourself; the invalidation of the individual's needs, thoughts, and input; the demonization of the outside world; being kept from family and friends; and being threatened to believe you cannot make it on your own should you want to leave.

I looked into the history of JPUSA and found accounts of abuse from former members on ex-cult message boards. Dr. Ronald Enroth included a chapter on JPUSA in his 1994 book, *Recovering from Churches That Abuse*, which caused considerable public controversy. JPUSA responded to Enroth in their publication, *Cornerstone Magazine*, opening dialogue between them.

That May, I decided to move in, but before doing so I made a pact with myself that if I felt oppressed or taken advantage of in any way, I'd leave. I was going there to thrive and serve by using my gifts and talents.

"We recommend that you stay for a few months and see what it's like before committing to a contract to live here," the coordinator suggested as I stood in his office with a handful of my belongings. "It's not for everybody."

After a tour of the property and seeing the room I'd be sharing, I was left at the front desk in the main lobby to mingle and meet people.

Sitting behind the desk was a man named Johnathan Ford who was working on music for a project called Unwed Sailor. I didn't know that he'd been in Roadside Monument and Pedro the Lion.

A couple of his friends were visiting him from Arkansas. "Man, we're gonna sound so stinkin' heavy on Main Stage this year," the Filipino guy said.

"What band are you in?" I asked.

"Living Sacrifice."

He introduced himself as Arthur Green, who played bass in the band. His friend introduced himself as Matthew Putman, who had just joined Living Sacrifice as a standup percussionist. Matthew also toured playing drums with Unwed Sailor. Their wives Sara and Melissa were with them.

I had a moment of envy, seeing in front of me a picture of what I'd been dreaming about for years—being in a Christian metal band, traveling and meeting people, hanging out with friends, starting a sleeve of tattoos, and having a cute girl by my side.

"We recorded a couple of demo songs that we'll be giving away on cassette at our merch table at Cornerstone, but we have a CD here if you guys want to hear the new stuff," Matthew said.

Being a Living Sacrifice fan for the past decade, I didn't hesitate. "Yeah, absolutely!"[12]

The group of us went to the kitchen and found a stereo system where we heard demo versions of "Bloodwork" and "Burn the End." The tuned-down heavy guitar riffs, the guttural vocals, and Lance Garvin's insane drumming blew me away. Now I couldn't wait to see them at Cornerstone.

Matthew had a Bishop John Shelby Spong book with him. "Oh, you read Spong, too? I just discovered him last year while putting a pile of books together at a thrift store," I said.

Neither of us found fundamentalist Christianity quite adding up and were exploring authors taboo to the evangelical subculture we were in. Spong was an Episcopal bishop who denied the literal truth of every central tenant of the Christian faith. He was accused by his critics of being an atheist in the liberal and secular tradition, yet he still considered himself a Christian.

I agreed with Spong's deconstruction of fundamentalism, but found his liberal reconstruction of Christianity just as problematic. Over the next few years, Matthew and I traded Spong books at Living Sacrifice shows and discussed them.[13]

When it came time for Arthur and Matthew to leave the next day, I was so appreciative to have met them that I asked if I could

---

[12] I wrote their old vocalist D. J. back in 1991 and he called me on the phone to respond to my questions. "Call whenever you want to, just not past 9:00 P.M. or my mom will get mad." So metal!
[13] Some of Spong's title's we traded and discussed: *Rescuing the Bible from Fundamentalism; Living in Sin?; Born of a Woman; Resurrection: Myth or Reality?; Why Christianity Must Change or Die; and A New Christianity for a New World.*

pray them off. We all held hands in a circle by the front desk, and I thanked God for them, asking for their safe travels.

When July came around, I went to Cornerstone for the first time. Working the ticket booth at one of the gates, I got to meet many of the bands coming in. After seeing so many great bands, including Living Sacrifice on Main Stage with Tiki lamps, fog, red lighting, and their giant crown of thorns logo backdrop behind them, I knew I wanted to do this for the next decade. I went back to JPUSA determined to start a metal band.

But community life proved difficult for me. I was often asked to stay late for shifts on the dishes, even if it cut into my plans and personal time. I was told not to complain, but to work "unto the Lord." When I took the bus to visit my family just twenty minutes away on my day off, I was reprimanded. Others didn't get to visit their families, so it wasn't fair for me to visit mine. "This is your family. There are people you can spend time with here." If my family gave me money, I was chastised. The only income I was allowed was what was approved by the coordinators and worked for in the form of side jobs on top of my daily duties.

I worked two weeks on overnight phones at the front desk, which were twelve-hour shifts. Because the shift cuts into dinner time, you are paid $4.00 a night to go to the 24-hour hot dog stand down the block. A coordinator apologized for forgetting to pay me the previous two weeks and told me to go to the office and ask for the money when my shift ended. I asked for the money and was only given $16.00 and told to ask for the rest another time. When I complained that $4.00 a night wasn't even enough for the hotdog, fries, and drink down the block, I was told I would have to make due so the community's money wasn't wasted.

No one was allowed to leave the building without clearing it with a coordinator and taking a "buddy" with them. When a group of us wanted to walk down to the beach after a shift, we were told we couldn't go because we had an even number of eight people, which looked suspiciously like a group date. "Besides," the coordinator added, "there are women in bikinis at the beach that might cause you to lust."

Single men were not allowed to sit with or talk to single

women for longer than three minutes before someone came to break up the conversation. When I said hello to any girl walking by, most would stare at the ground and pass without a word. The truly rebellious smiled and said hello.

Dating was done by telling your family head—a person who oversees a small group you are assigned to—who you liked, and he would talk to her family head. They would determine if you were spiritually ready to date and a good match for each other. If so, you were allowed to court by letter-writing, eventually graduating to rules governing how much time you could spend together and how many kisses a day you were allowed.

When a youth group visited and one of the girls asked me questions about JPUSA during one of my shifts at the front desk in the crowded lobby, we were interrupted numerous times and told we couldn't talk. By her third day there, she was in tears, begging to go home. Suspicion, having her every move watched, and being micromanaged this way in a public setting humiliated her. All I could do was apologize and voice my own frustration with this ridiculous rule.

As warned by counter-cult ministries, I was overworked, micromanaged down to the books I read and who I talked to, kept from visiting my family, and kept from leaving the building at a coordinator's whim. My creativity, freedom, and spirit were killed by the feeling that I needed permission for every thought I had and action I took.

As I turned to others with my concerns, trying to find a way to endure staying there, I was warned that I would be kicked out for protesting too much, so I needed to keep my head down, keep working, and if I believed God led me there for a reason, I needed to stay and find out what God had in mind.

Others accused me of being negative merely for raising my concerns, adding that I was in no place to question the leadership God had placed over me. I was to obey without question or complaint. When one of these discussions turned into a heated argument over authority and obedience, someone present said, "You know what? *You* would make a good cult leader," and stormed away.

That night, I decided to leave. When I told my roommate I was leaving, he interrupted me. "Don't you go getting all negative on me or I swear I'll punch you right in the face." I packed my stuff the next day, called my mom, and moved back home with her. Once again, I felt utterly defeated.

My mom sat me down and explained that if I didn't apply for disability, I'd never have a life and would just keep moving home this way. At least on disability, I could afford an apartment, and if I wanted to start a band, I could do it as a hobby. Still flailing and floundering with establishing my life, I swallowed my pride, and with the help of a lawyer, won my disability case.

Because of income limits while on disability, this meant I had to learn to be poor and live simply.

4
Norma Jean

As soon as I retuned from JPUSA, I asked my friends Mark and Jay if they wanted to write songs with me and try to get a band off the ground. They said yes, and we went out and bought music equipment. We loved Tooth & Nail and Solid State bands, so we tuned down our guitars and created a hybrid of nu-metal and metalcore.

In June of 2001, Zao was headlining a show at Fireside Bowl in Chicago, supported by Living Sacrifice and Not Waving But Drowning. Matthew Putman emailed me: "Get here early, there's a band called Luti-Kriss opening. They're gonna blow you away."

Fronted by Josh Scogin, a kid fresh out of high school who didn't look at all like the frontman of a metal band, Luti-Kriss played a noisy and chaotic set. What they lacked in musical precision they made up for in stage presence—guitar slinging, headbanging, convulsing, and flailing themselves all over the stage.

After the show, Matthew ribbed me. "So you've been talking a lot about this band you're starting. When am I gonna hear some music?"

"Man, we're getting it together, we just need to find a drummer."

But before the year ended, both Mark and Jay's careers picked up, so they decided to forget about the band and focus on building their lives instead. We had written a total of almost one song.

After seeing a band called Skillet play a one-off local show, Jackie, the woman who brought them to town, said she was starting a ministry and would continue booking bands in various venues until she was able to find property and funding to open a coffeehouse venue.

"Would you like to come help book bands and run shows with us?" she asked.

"Well, I'm an agnostic, so I probably couldn't help on the

ministry end," I warned her.

"We don't judge here. It doesn't matter if you're an agnostic, we love everyone as they are."

I accepted, finding this the perfect opportunity to once again gain experience booking bands, running shows, meeting people in the industry, and rubbing shoulders with musicians who could be possible future bandmates.

We ran a pre-Cornerstone hardcore fest in the summer of 2001. Only a handful of the bands on the bill showed up to the muggy church basement, headlined by a metal band called Underoath. The ministry then took a group of teens to Cornerstone where I filmed my favorite bands for inspiration.

But by the end of summer, I was too fatigued to keep my part-time job at the zoo and volunteer with the ministry any longer. I quit both to rest.

Luti-Kriss, so as not to be confused with the rapper Ludacris, changed their name to Norma Jean and in early 2002 recorded the now classic metalcore album, *Bless the Marty and Kiss the Child*.

About the same time, a new band called mewithoutYou recorded their debut *[A→B] Life* for a June release. Tooth & Nail/Solid State released a split 7" vinyl that summer with two songs each from Norma Jean and mewithoutYou.

I went to Tooth & Nail's website and found mewithoutYou. A Beatles-esque picture appeared of four young guys with shaggy hair, donning a turtleneck and collared shirts and ties under dark buttoned-down jackets. They already stood out to me as something different.

On dialup, I listened to low-quality streaming mp3s of "Bullet to Binary" and "Gentlemen." MewithoutYou sounded to me like a garage punk band with their tuned down distorted guitars and gritty, shouting vocals.

What set them apart for me immediately was the literary and poetic nature of their lyrics—some delivered in French and spoken word by their vocalist Aaron Weiss—but being a metal fan, they weren't what I was looking for. Unable to attend Cornerstone in 2002, a friend took my video camera with her and videotaped Norma Jean's set for me. Though I didn't recognize who he was,

Aaron Weiss came out for his cameo in their song "Memphis Will Be Laid To Waste," taking the stage in a poor boy hat, his face framed with mutton chops reminiscent of a '70s John Lennon. He screamed and shouted his poetry as he spastically jerked and flailed and twirled, running into band members, embracing them, and throwing them to the ground.

I thought, "What a weirdo! Where did they find this guy?"

5
Weiss

Mike and Aaron Weiss were born to Elliott and Elizabeth Weiss and raised in Upper Darby, Pennsylvania—a racially-diverse, densely-populated working class township with a reputation for its many run-down and crime-ridden neighborhoods.

Elliott and Elizabeth met in Philadelphia at the Bawa Muhaiyaddeen Fellowship, a Sufi gathering named after the Sri Lankan former Hindu guru who founded it in 1971. Mike and Aaron were raised on Bawa's stories and teachings.

Elizabeth was once an Episcopalian Christian before adopting Sufism, partially due to the Eastern influence on the Beatles. Elliott identified as Jewish, but practiced an eclectic mix of Abrahamic religions. Aaron explained in an interview with *Busted Halo*, "They both converted to the Sufi faith, which is Islamic mysticism. So my dad was raised Jewish and became Sufi, but he still identifies himself as a Jew. My mom was raised Episcopalian and she converted thoroughly to Sufi Islam. I was raised hearing the stories and seeing my mom pray, but they never made me go to the mosque or forced me to accept what they believe. They were pretty hands off. They did tell me about God and taught me how to pray, but it wasn't regimented in any way."[15]

If there was one thing Elliott and Elizabeth were stern about with Mike and Aaron, it was that they never touch drugs. Both Elliott and Elizabeth had suffered serious mental illness and were hospitalized, their conditions exacerbated by taking psychedelic drugs when they were younger.

On being raised Sufi, Mike shared, "My parents met at this Sufi establishment, I guess you could call it. It's not really a church. It was a little embarrassing as a kid in a neighborhood

---

[15] Matt Fink, "Busted: me without You. Busted Halo talks conversion, pride, and holistic faith with the leader of indie rock's would-be revolutionaries," *Busted Halo*, 4/27/07.

where everybody's Catholic. You know, I just wanted to be Catholic, too. I didn't want to be different than anybody else. So it was a little embarrassing for a kid. I think I got a lot of great things from it, though. My parents always taught me to believe in God and that there is one God and, I don't know, stuff I still believe today."[16]

In an interview with *Jam Base*, Mike explained, "On Christmas we would go to my grandparents' house on my mom's side, and we would celebrate Hanukkah and Passover with my father's parents. Then there would be certain celebrations my mom would try to push on us, like I would witness her fasting for Ramadan. I've been exposed to the three major religions of the world pretty extensively. I think it always gave me a belief that there was a God, and that's been pretty strong, but not necessarily a specific religion or way to worship. Just going out into the world as an adolescent and seeing different friends of mine, some were Catholic or Jewish or Protestant, and it was very hard for me for a while to really latch onto any of them. But I really had a sense that there was something more than just what we perceive on a daily basis. Growing up in my house there was a strong sense of there being an ultimate moral truth. It wasn't just something we decided as individuals."[17]

Aaron was asked in a Tooth & Nail podcast to elaborate on who Bawa was. "Well, he's a teacher and a holy man who came to America before I was born and left the world many years ago, so I don't physically remember him, but there's tapes of him talking, and he said tell people to believe in God and to love God and to follow the prophets and Jesus. And my parents met while listening to his teachings, and that's how my brother and I were born, and he gave us our names and . . . he told the stories my parents would read us as children. He was telling us we should believe in God and to treat other lives like we treat our own life and to forgive people and that sort of thing. So it's all really simple, but very

---

[16] Racket Magazine, "mewithoutyou interview with RacketMag," *YouTube*, 9/7/09.
[17] Sarah Hagerman, "'There's a love that never changes/ No matter what you've done' – 'Allah, Allah, Allah' mewithoutYou," *Jam Base*, 2009.

deep and very powerful teachings that stuck with us, you know, our whole lives."[18]

Aaron described his childhood in an interview with *Lambgoat*: "Well, I guess my life growing up was really good. My parents really loved me and my brother a lot. I had friends around me. I was never real popular or confident or happy all throughout school. I felt like kind of a loser. I tried to do sports and I was never any good, so I was like, the manager of the basketball team. I didn't play on the basketball team, you know? Then I got kicked off the lacrosse team, and I'd go to the dances with my friends, like, a guy who I was friends with. I never really kissed any girls until pretty late in life, but even then, I was never happy."[19]

As a depressed teen feeling that he didn't fit in anywhere and thinking often of suicide, Aaron found great comfort in the poetry of the Sufi poet Rumi and found a home in the hardcore music scene, particularly straight edge. Soon he would be introduced to evangelical Christianity.

"I went to summer camp when I was younger, and I wasn't interested in what they were talking about," he told *Busted Halo*. "It was Episcopalian, from my mom's side of the family. They sent me there. I wasn't hostile; I just didn't care. Then, there was a sort of evangelical Christian organization in my high school called Young [Life], and they'd take people out to movies and go to fast food restaurants. It was just more of a social club, and they tried to keep it wholesome. It wasn't all about God. But then we went on a retreat and they started talking about God, like out in the woods, and I was like, 'Wait a minute. What's all this?' So around the end of high school is when I started attending a church and praying the language of Christianity."[20]

Aaron told Andrew Beaujon in *Body Piercing Saved My Life: Inside the Phenomenon of Christian Rock* that he started going to

---

[18] "Tooth & Nail Podcast 27: Emery, mewithoutYou, an Interview with Aaron Weiss & more," *Tooth & Nail*, 2009.
[19] Drew Ailes, "mewithoutYou interview," *Lambgoat*, 1/14/07.
[20] Matt Fink, "Busted: mewithoutYou. Busted Halo talks conversion, pride, and holistic faith with the leader of indie rock's would-be revolutionaries," *Busted Halo*, 4/27/07.

church with his friend, Greg Jehanian. "He would always tell me about Jesus: 'You know, people are gonna go to hell, and the only way not to go to hell is to accept Jesus as your savior, so you have to say this prayer.' So after a few times, I was like, 'Okay, I'll say this prayer.' But nothing really changed in my life."[21]

Aaron elaborated in an interview with Yoni Wolf: "I grew up Jewish. I thought of myself as a Jew when I was younger, and around the end of high school I joined a church for a couple of months. It wasn't very long, but it was enough for me to start identifying as a Christian. [Greg] was extremely convinced that Jesus was alive and real, and as far as I was concerned, he died thousands of years ago. But he was absolutely sure that wasn't true. He was raised in a, I guess I'd say, kind of evangelical family, and he kept his family's beliefs more or less. I remember one day we were in a donut shop and he told me, 'I'm even more sure that Jesus is alive than I am of the fact that you're sitting next to me.' And I basically trusted this guy. He was one of my best friends, and I just couldn't believe what he was saying. I was so shocked by that statement. How can that be? You're so sure about Jesus? I just equated God with morality."[22]

Aaron continued, "There was a whole group of my friends that started poking around at that church, and I think we were all searching for something to believe in, and we found this church and they were really accepting of us. I was really into straight edge and veganism and animal rights, and I was really intent on finding, I guess, a moral path. I was really intent on finding a good way to live, like being radically good. And that's something that's been with me ever since I was a little kid. My parents would read me stories about being a good son and being a good, faithful servant of God, or just good to my neighbor or whatever. It really resonated deeply with me. It still does. To me it was like one thing to the next, whether it was being straight edge to have a good, clean, pure lifestyle and be in control of my mind, or like, animal

---

[21] Andrew Beaujon, *Body Piercing Saved My Life: Inside the Phenomenon of Christian Rock*, (Cambridge, Da Capo Press, 2006), 261.
[22] Yoni Wolf, "Episode 74 – Aaron Weiss (mewithoutYou)," *The Wandering Wolf*, 9/24/14.

rights, to stand up for the little guy, and then Christianity was sort of, 'All right, I'm gonna take a leap into the eternal realm' at my friend's advice, 'cause he seemed so sure of it. I still remember, I got baptized, I said I don't understand what this is about, I don't feel a whole lot, but I want to go through whatever you guys are talking about and see if I feel the things you guys say you're feeling. And I never really did, I don't think, feel the kind of joy of a new life of a baptized believer or anything like that, but it definitely felt good to sing with my friends and to feel like we had a common goal and a common vision of reality, you know?"[23]

Busted Halo asked Aaron what his parents thought of his conversion to Christianity. "They were glad that I believed in God. But it was kind of a fundamentalist church, so I had some warnings from my family, like, 'Be careful of this spirit of self-righteousness.' They were sensing in me an arrogance that said, 'Now I have the truth and you don't. I'm going to tell you how it is.' Here I am seventeen years old and telling my parents, who are in their forties, everything about God and the Creator and the mysteries of the universe. It wasn't long until I fell off of that high horse and realized that maybe I don't know everything."[24]

Jeremy Enigk asked Aaron if his conversion strained his relationship with his parents. "It was difficult for a while, I think, especially after I started to go into a church building and read the Bible. There was this pressure from them that, 'No, you gotta believe what we believe,' and then I would try to convert them and, 'No, you gotta accept what I believe,' and this went on for quite a while until . . . I realized it wasn't my duty to convert anybody. It's my duty to love everybody and that God would bring about the conversion of one's heart if that's what needs to happen. But all the arguing stopped and all the fighting stopped and the disagreement. And rather than trying to convert each other, we've found a lot of common ground. And since, I've been able to go to my mom's mosque and worship the God that I

---

[23] Ibid
[24] Matt Fink, "Busted: me without You. Busted Halo talks conversion, pride, and holistic faith with the leader of indie rock's would-be revolutionaries," *Busted Halo*, 4/27/07.

believe in in that building, and both of my parents have come to worship services with my church and have sung songs to God with me in that context, and it's just been much, much more beautiful and free and alive. So I've just been tremendously grateful for that unity that God's been able to bring, even across the outer forms of different religions. And I'm not claiming that all religions are the same, but certainly that there is one God and that there is truth to be found anywhere you look."[25]

Only a few months after being baptized, Aaron was disillusioned. He and his friends would read the Bible and have questions about God not seeming very loving in either the Old or the New Testament. "There's some great stuff, and there's some confusing stuff, and then there's just some heinous sounding stuff. And I started to try to pick through that and question the stuff that sounded wrong."[26] But Aaron's questions were met with fear and hostility, which left a powerful impression on him. As far as questioning the Bible, "It wasn't allowed. It's like, if you raise any questions the whole edifice starts to crumble. If it's not the inerrant Word of God, all is lost."[27]

Aaron was put off, seeing institutionalized, fundamentalist Christianity as yet another form of self-righteous tribalism. "It was the same nonsense I ran into anywhere. This is just like the punk shows—the same politics, same games, and same rubbish. This isn't different, and again, it seems to be worse because it's in the name of something higher."[28]

John Vettese wrote that Aaron was enchanted by the teachings of love and compassion to all humanity in the Bible, but "soon became frustrated by the misapplication of those lessons in modern society: the disparity he saw in his own city between the wealthy and the poor, 'faith-based' government leaders thriving on intolerance and war, even the dubious multimillion-dollar

---

[25] Paul Harrison, "Aaron Weiss Jeremy Enigk Interview Synthesis 2008 mewithoutYou," *YouTube*, 6/24/14.
[26] Yoni Wolf, "Episode 74 – Aaron Weiss (mewithoutYou)," *The Wandering Wolf*, 9/24/14.
[27] Ibid
[28] John Vettese. "On This Rock. Local punks mewithoutYou play with a different kind of passion." *Philadelphia CityPaper*. 4/10/04.

industry surrounding Christian music. Quickly, the appeal of Bible study and Sunday services wore off."[29]

Aaron stopped attending church, realizing that his conversion was cruel and manipulative because it was based on threats of hell, but he continued his quest to find answers to ultimate questions.

Mike also attended the same church. "I was in a band called I Hate You, and I was trying to reconcile this newfound faith in Jesus with this band where we were talking about people beating the crap out of you if you're going to smoke a cigarette in front of me. But I was drawn to it because it was so fundamental. You know, you go around handing out tracts to people, making sure that they know that if they don't get right with God, the Rapture's going to come and they'll get left behind."[30]

Like Aaron, Mike would also abandon his fundamentalist zeal, but the two would soon find themselves playing music together.

---

[29] Ibid
[30] James Parker, "Sing to the Lord a New Song, Christian rock crosses over in the City of Brotherly Love," *The Atlantic*, 10/01/09.

6
The Operation

Mike and his friends used to skate and see punk and hardcore shows in Philadelphia—bands like Ink and Dagger and Crud. He started to play in bands in high school, so Aaron learned an instrument to join him. Aaron told Yoni Wolf, "I guess around tenth grade, I started playing drums. My brother was a bass player, and so I got a drum kit and played in a few kinda garage bands. You know, maybe a show at a bar here and there, recording a demo tape, but nothing that ever got into a proper studio or anything until maybe I was probably in college, maybe my second or third year in college."[31]

Not sure anything would come of it, Aaron and Mike enjoyed playing music together. "I love my brother and we've always been really close. It's a pleasure to have a relationship like that in stressful situations. Just to have someone to support me, I'm really lucky," Mike said. "I get to add that to the list of blessings."[32]

One of the bands Mike and Aaron joined was called the Operation. Fronted by their friend Greg Jehanian, the band first went by Sans Culottes. When the drummer quit, Greg called Aaron and asked him to try out. After a lousy audition, guitarist Marty Lunn said, "Well, we don't have any other choice."

"I wasn't flattered," Aaron recalls, "but I got the job."

Mike Weiss and Chris Kleinberg joined on guitars and Derek Turnbaugh played bass.

The Operation was an indie rock band with explicitly Christian lyrics. Some could have passed for worship songs.

After putting out an EP called *Invisible Man EP* in 1999, the Operation followed with a full-length release in 2001 called *There is Hope for a Tree Cut Down* on Chad Johnson's Takehold Records.

---

[31] Yoni Wolf, "Episode 74 – Aaron Weiss (mewithoutYou)," *The Wandering Wolf*, 9/24/14.
[32] Meghan Groth, "Bellowed Blessings and Drastic Dynamics: mewithoutYou headlines the Radio Takeover Tour in Buffal," *The Spectrum*, 11/15/04.

When asked in an interview how the label got its name, Chad answered, "Actually the name comes from a verse in II Timothy. In a nutshell it talks about being generous with what God gives you and to always strive for what lies ahead. In essence, taking hold of what God gives us and sharing whatever that is with those around us."[33]

Chad's vision was "to produce quality indie recordings for up-and-coming bands and to serve as a vehicle of spiritual stimulation in both a creative and original format" geared towards metal, hardcore, indie, emo, and pop.[34]

Aaron wasn't content behind the drum set. "I felt kinda confined as a drummer with the energy that I had, and I wanted to dance more. I was never a good drummer technically or anything, but I really, really loved to play, and I would really give it my all. Super sloppy, but it was definitely a full body workout. And I felt like, man, if I didn't have this stool here and this big ol' lunky instrument, I could have more fun performing."[35]

Yoni asked Aaron how he transitioned from drummer to frontman. "Actually, it was almost a mistake, but my friend and I recorded a Christmas present for his sister. It was like a joke kinda hardcore song. We were just screaming something about—I don't remember—something about Christmas, but I listened to it and thought, you know what, that sounds kinda cool, you know? There's potential there! I never screamed before, it's kind of an awkward thing to do for the first time. You gotta just jump off the cliff and see how it sounds, and I did, and I thought, 'Oh, this is kinda nice.'"[36]

With Aaron on vocals and Mike and Chris on guitars, they started a side project called Me Without You.

---

[33] Nate Bailey, "Takehold Records, Birmingham, AL, www.takehold.com," *Decapolis*, 2001.
[34] Ibid
[35] Yoni Wolf, "Episode 74 – Aaron Weiss (mewithoutYou)," *The Wandering Wolf*, 9/24/14.
[36] Ibid

7
MewithoutYou

"Well, Mike's my brother, the guitar player, and Chris Kleinberg has been my best friend for years. We've played in all kinds of crappy bands and never really did anything. We knew Rick Mazzotta and that he was a drummer, and Daniel Pishock, our bass player, didn't actually even play the bass until we asked him to join the band. I was the bass player before,"[37] Aaron told Vanessa Chalmers.

In the very beginning, Ray Taddeo brought his songs to the project and Me Without You recorded them on a demo in 2000 called *Blood Enough For Us All*. Only 75 copies were made. The cover art is a simple drawing from the children's book *The Giving Tree*—an old man sitting alone on a tree stump with his hat on the ground next to him. The songs were a mix of punk and hardcore, backing guttural, distorted vocals in the style of Nirvana's "Endless, Nameless," recorded in raw basement quality. The lyrics, for the most part, are impossible to decipher.

When I discovered it, I told Aaron I loved the garage band quality of the demo. "You mean the gar-bage band quality," he countered. "I can get behind everything else we've done. That's the only thing we've put out that I'm not proud of. Those were Ray Taddeo's songs and he did half of the vocals on the recording."[38]

Mike told Jonathan Bautts, "The guy who wrote most of the music for that ended up quitting. Those songs weren't even mewithoutYou songs, really. It's kind of hard to explain. They were written for another band and then it became mewithoutYou. It's a long story . . . ultimately, what I'm getting at is that EP wasn't really the band, even at that time. When we were selling

---

[37] Vanessa Chalmers, "mewithoutYou interview," *San Diego Punk*, 12/03/04.
[38] Ray Taddeo went on to release an impressive 6-song hip hop EP in 2005 on Makebreak Records called Bella Futuro, *Empire of Hope*. Aaron rapped on a song called "70 x 7."

that CD at shows, it wasn't really the idea we had behind mewithoutYou. We were still trying to have something to sell and we were playing those songs. The idea behind those songs and the person who wrote them weren't a major part of what the band was supposed to be. Anyway, the record we did after that, *I Never Said That I Was Brave*, I always kind of consider that our first one."[39]

Aaron told Yoni Wolf, "It just felt like a series of accidents, you know, it wasn't something I was very determined to do. None of us were determined in it, and none of us ever had any plans to see it through or to do it for a living, it was just kinda something we were doing on the side. I don't want to say it was a joke because it wasn't meant to be funny, but it was very low pressure."[40]

Aaron told Vanessa Chalmers, "We were playing really heavy, thrashy, noisy music and none of us even liked it, but then somehow from that came music we kind of, sort of liked."[41]

I Never Said That I Was Brave—the title taken from a Leonard Cohen song called "So Long, Marianne"—was recorded in early 2001. The band's name was now one word, stylized as mewithoutYou.

The cover art was done in 3D by Max Morresi, a friend in Mike's class in Upper Darby High School. It features two robots, one with a large brain in a transparent dome and the other apparently having its head blown up. Max created similar computer-generated images and displayed them at an art show where he handed out 3D glasses to viewers. MewithoutYou sold their EP with 3D glasses as well.

These songs were more polished than the demo, but still heavy enough to be considered post-hardcore. Although Aaron screamed every song, his vocals were now decipherable. The standout song and early fan favorite was "Flamethrower." Aside from Cohen, there were nods in the lyrics to The Smiths, Neutral

---

[39] Jonathan Bautts, "mewithoutYou," *Mammoth Press*, 6/05/09.
[40] Yoni Wolf, "Episode 74 – Aaron Weiss (mewithoutYou)," *The Wandering Wolf*, 9/24/14.
[41] Vanessa Chalmers, "mewithoutYou interview," San Diego Punk, 12/03/04.

Milk Hotel, and Fugazi.

On choosing mewithoutYou as the band's name, Aaron told Vanessa Chalmers, "My friend suggested it years ago for a different band and I was like 'No, that's lame,' 'cause it sounded too fluffy and emotional. Then when our band started getting real noisy we thought it'd be nice to have a fluffy sounding name for a noisy, kind of obnoxious band."[42]

In 2002, Aaron told *HM Magazine* that the band's name is about the rift between God and man. "The songs being as negative and painful as they are only make sense in that context. Like, 'This is the pain I've subjected myself to without God, this is the mess that I've made for myself on my own' . . . I hope ultimately through the sadness and everything, most people will be able to see at the end—this is the answer—Jesus died on the cross, and because of that, we have life eternally. We have forgiveness for our sins. We have a beautiful friend, a lover—a Father. It's an excitingly romantic and beautiful thing, but I guess I sometimes focus on the things that are hard about life, rather than the things that are wonderful about God."[43]

Though mewithoutYou was never considered an emo band, the post-hardcore scene was cultivating eccentric and charismatic vocalists spilling their hearts out about God and girls, such as Jeremy Enigk of Sunny Day Real Estate and Chris Simpson of Mineral.

In the book *Nothing Feels Good: Punk Rock, Teenagers, and Emo*, Andy Greenwald placed the origins of emo in the punk and hardcore scene of 1985 with a band called Rites of Spring. In a scene with bands like Black Flag and Minor Threat taking punk into hardcore and spouting political messages and anger at the establishment, Rites of Spring added melody and personal, introspective lyrics to their songs. Experimental post-hardcore bands like Fugazi, Mineral, Jawbreaker, Drive Like Jehu, and Sunny Day Real Estate were considered proto-emo bands.

---

[42] Vanessa Chalmers, "mewithoutYou interview," *San Diego Punk*, 12/03/04.
[43] David Pogge, "The Pain of Separation," *HM Magazine* , #97, Sept/Oct 2002, 24.

Critics of emo see it as immature and self-obsessed; men wanting to get their hearts broken and display the pain for its own sake, to create drama with no resolution, to pick at scars and display them like trophies. Emo idealizes heartbreak, and as Jessica Hopper notes, it, "keeps women on a pedestal or on our backs. It relegates us to the role of muse or heartbreaker, an object of either misery or desire. Emo just builds a cathedral of man pain and then celebrates its validation."[44]

By 2002, Dashboard Confessional became the poster band for emo. Greenwald says Chris Carrabba's songwriting is "fearless, a willingness to throw himself into any lyric, melody, or sentiment, no matter how bombastic, traumatic, or corny."[45] Mineral's "If I Could" is described as either a "guileless, innocent romantic, or a creepy, self-defeating stalker prone to indulgent poetry."[46] Greenwald adds that emo takes pride in "an arrogance derived from superior humility."[47] In short, the lyrics and delivery in emo are histrionic—exaggerated victimization for the sake of performance drama.

But this same catharsis took place in a spiritual context. Of Mineral, Greenwald wrote, "Chris Simpson's gloriously ecstatic and defeatist visions of the world are so soaked in religious imagery that it's impossible to tell if he's venerating a high school crush or Jesus Christ."[48]

Of Jeremy Enigk, former frontman of Sunny Day Real Estate, he wrote that Enigk sang desperately about losing himself, subsuming himself in something larger. Jonathan Poneman, co-founder of Sub Pop, said the band fell apart partly because Enigk became a born again Christian. "He'll get very introspective and down on himself and then he'll reach out and seize onto something. It's a vaguely manic-depressive cycle—to go from so down to grabbing onto something that will inspire and uplift him

---

[44] Andy Greenwald, *Nothing Feels Good: Punk Rock, Teenagers, and Emo*, (New York: St. Martin's Press, 2003), 133-34.
[45] Ibid, 209
[46] Ibid, 42.
[47] Ibid
[48] Ibid, 41.

and make him incredibly productive. After the first record, the thing he seized was Christianity. He became kind of an overbearing zealot and made a lot of proclamations that bummed out the other members of the band."[49]

These descriptions of eccentric, emotionally intense, obsessed, depressed, self-loathing charismatic frontmen bleeding from heartbreak, writing creepy self-indulgent poetry, and moving their focus towards God with enough neurotic zeal to bum out their bandmates could not be a better prototype of Aaron Weiss.

The scene was ripe for mewithoutYou to emerge.

---

[49] Ibid, 33.

8
Crossroads

A storm had muddied the dirt roads and camping grounds at Cornerstone 2001. The festival was now experiencing power outages. With so many fans and industry people present, bands not on the official festival schedule showed up to play on generator stages with the hopes of getting noticed and possibly signed to a label.

Every few hundred feet down a given path you could find bands playing on plywood platforms run on generators or car batteries with a small gathering of spectators surrounding them. To gain an audience, these bands plastered flyers on tent poles, porta-potties, or anything else nailed down. Mostly comprised of untalented high school kids ripping off their favorite signed metal bands, every now and then you'd find a gem.

Just as the power went out again and the festival stages went silent, mewithoutYou began playing on a generator stage. With no other bands to see, a crowd began to gather.

Their gimmick was to wear suits and turtlenecks, even on dusty roads in the middle of July, while playing heavy music. Though musically raw and unpolished, they managed to "somewhat play their songs" as Aaron Weiss put it, making a spectacle of themselves.

They caught the attention of Adam MacKinnon of Tooth & Nail, who thought mewithoutYou had a Drive Like Jehu vibe—a band known for its distinct post-hardcore and proto-emo noise. Adam brought a man named Greg Patterson to see their next performance. Adam and Greg went back to Seattle and convinced Brandon Ebel to sign them to a four-record deal with Tooth & Nail.

Brandon wasn't impressed with The Operation, but he was impressed with the lyrics, charisma, and antics of Aaron Weiss as a frontman for mewithoutYou.

MewithoutYou was the side project of a Christian band that

was signed to a Christian label. They were discovered at a Christian festival and signed by another Christian label. For these reasons, and because Aaron was vocal about his faith in interviews, mewithoutYou began with the reputation of being a Christian band. But this association was reluctant.

When Chad Johnson signed The Operation to Takehold, he said, "I distinctly recall Aaron sharing with me by phone that they were going to begin a side project comprised of the majority of The Operation and heard several of those demos as well. It wasn't until Cornerstone where I saw mewithoutYou's first generator show under a tree that I really caught the vision and realized what a wild frenzy they'd fallen into. I was already moving toward a deal with Tooth & Nail when Aaron told me about mewithoutYou. So, instead of competing for their attention and future albums, I encouraged them to join me at Tooth & Nail."[50]

Chad further recalls, "One of my favorite, fondest memories of the guys was during a meeting at the old T&N offices in Magnolia, a suburb of Seattle. Around an executive meeting table, they expressed their concerns with the Christian music industry and how maybe I was sent from God 'to be swallowed by the beast only to slay it from the inside.' We laughed hysterically, but that comment summed up the challenges both they and I were having with the idea of Christianity—or lack thereof—within a music industry bubble. I'm grateful for the opportunities to have worked with both The Operation and mewithoutYou. All of it was grace and none of it was deserved."[51]

Aaron understood that people "could infer that we were somehow affiliated with Christianity if not explicitly a Christian band at any point. It was close enough."[52]

He explained to Yoni Wolf, "When we were talking about signing with [Tooth & Nail], when we had no other options, there were zero other offers on the table, so we were warned, you know, this is gonna come with some religious baggage and kinda

---

[50] Email, 7/31/15.
[51] Ibid
[52] Yoni Wolf, "Episode 74 – Aaron Weiss (mewithoutYou)," *The Wandering Wolf*, 9/24/14.

Christian expectations, and we said, 'Oh, we'll be fine.'" Still, "We tried to kind of push against it from the beginning."[53]

Johnathan Ford of Unwed Sailor advised mewithoutYou, "If you want to, you're at a stage in your career where you could go either way. If you start playing churches and Christian festivals and Christian venues, there's a lot of money there 'cause people will just give; they'll kinda give their tithe money to support the arts."[54]

"For me at the beginning, I'm a little bit ashamed to say, I wasn't very sensitive to it," Aaron continued. "I thought, well, I felt a little weird, but I didn't have any strong beliefs about it. And to their credit, I'll say, it was a few other guys in the band. Our bass player at the time had really strong convictions about not selling anything inside a church, he thought, because of the scripture about the market and the marketplace. And he said, 'If we have merchandise and we play a church we have to set it up outside or I'm not playing.' And, in hindsight I respect him for it. At the time I just thought he was a pain in the neck. It's like, 'Aw, come on, why are you so uptight?'"[55]

Aaron continued, "But I do remember one show in particular we played and . . . it felt like a youth group kind of event where it was family-friendly and parents were there, and in between bands someone would get up and kinda talk. You know, it felt like they were trying to get people to believe something, and at some point the rubber hit the road and they're saying, 'We're here to let you know about Jesus Christ' and all these things and I was little taken aback, like, 'Oh, I didn't expect that.' It was a little much. It felt like a kind of a bait and switch. But at the same time, I wasn't that upset about it. . . . Our drummer—after that show, we went back to the hotel room—was just weeping, just weeping and weeping and weeping. 'I can't do this, I can't do this,' you know? I didn't understand why it affected him so much at the time because I think I was a little bit desensitized to that whole world. It felt weird, but not necessarily anything wrong. I just thought, 'Aw,

---

[53] Ibid
[54] Ibid
[55] Ibid

that's just the way they want to go about things.' And to some extent I still believe that. But the point is, for us there was a deciding moment, or a deciding season or period where we had to really ask ourselves, 'Do we want to plug into this circuit and start making connections in this world and portray ourselves as a church-friendly, family-friendly Christian kind of band, or do we want to go and play bars and the secular route . . . places that are not asking you what you believe?' So that was something we decided, I think, with relative unanimity early on."[56]

Aaron said Rickie "was raised Catholic. I don't know where his beliefs are—were at that point or are today—but I got the impression that he was more sensitive to the manipulative nature of what was being said and to what, now when I look back, was something at the very least fishy, if not outright objectionable. I look back, man, I would never want to play and support and draw people into something like that and then have a guy get up onstage and give them the sales pitch at the end. It's just not something I'd want anything to do with. And he felt that earlier than I did. I think he was more instrumental in steering us towards the secular route."[57]

Feeling a strong kinship with JPUSA and Cornerstone, they still played the fest and a few other Christian-affiliated festivals, "but for the most part we just tried to steer clear of it 'cause it felt like people were just going to listen to us because we were affirming their beliefs, and not because they cared about the art we were making or about anything that we were trying to say that might have been challenging to their beliefs. It was almost like they were looking to just filter out anything that conflicted and just find the stuff that reinforced where they were already at."[58]

Luke Kruse of *Decapolis* wrote, "Outside of playing a few music festivals connected to the Christian music industry, mewithoutYou has made an effort to primarily play in secular venues and not limit themselves to the Christian subculture. Richard admitted how easy it would be to go play churches and

---

[56] Ibid
[57] Ibid
[58] Ibid

make '$5,000 a night, but it's not something we want to do. Playing up on sanctuaries is just strange in general. It was hard at first trying to play bars and having 15-20 people a night, but we consciously tried to do things and have a booking agent.'"[59]

Andrew Beaujon asked Aaron if mewithoutYou was a Christian band. "I don't think so. I don't know, we've never been clear on that one."[60] Andrew followed, asking why the band signed to a Christian label and played Christian festivals. Aaron clarified that they don't play churches. Cornerstone and Purple Door were the only Christian fests they played. "Like Dave Bazan, Weiss considers mewithoutYou's ventures into the Christian world almost as missionary ventures."[61]

"I don't feel very comfortable in the Christian subculture environment," Aaron continued. "I don't feel a lot of authenticity. I don't connect with a lot of people. Not that I'm authentic and they're not, but somewhere in my heart is longing for something honest and eternal, and all I see is fads and corny T-shirts and young kids who were mostly raised and taught what they should think and haven't had a chance to question it.... The main reason I can try to justify even being in a band is to communicate to the people who are gonna come to these kinds of gatherings or listen to our band just because we're on Tooth & Nail Records and say to them, 'You know what Jesus called us to do is to come and die, suffer and sacrifice, lay down our lives for other people. Not to try to live the most comfortable life we can or have a whole lot of fun or look a certain way.'"[62]

This question of whether or not mewithoutYou is a Christian band became difficult to answer as Aaron became more vocal about his own faith. Aaron's views were often mistaken as the beliefs and mission of the band as a whole.

"At times this is scary," Rickie told *HM Magazine* in 2004 concerning Aaron's beliefs. "I don't always agree with everything

---

[59] Luke Kruse, "mewithoutYou interview," *Decapolis*, 4/27/05.
[60] Andrew Beaujon, *Body Piercing Saved My Life: Inside the Phenomenon of Christian Rock*, (Cambridge: Da Capo Press, 2006), 262.
[61] Ibid, 263.
[62] Ibid 263-4.

he says onstage or offstage or in a song or an interview, so it is tough to fully back him up . . . his lyrics don't represent everyone in the band and I think it is hard for people who see us to separate the two."[63]

In 2008, music journalist Steven Wells wrote, "Aaron Weiss says he's been on an intense spiritual journey, which can be hard work for the rest of the band. Drummer Rickie Mazzotta, a lapsed Catholic, isn't even sure he believes in God. Of Aaron, he says, 'I just want my friend back.' By which he means the crazy kid who laughs and jokes and is said to have once thrown a burning squirrel corpse at a rival band. 'Maybe heaven is being buried underground and being eaten by a maggot and that maggot turns into a fly and the fly is eaten by something else,' says Mazzotta. He says he thinks about the possibility there might not be a God almost every day."[64]

When asked about Aaron's beliefs, Rickie said, "To be honest, I don't know what Aaron is. I know he's a very spiritual dude. He can be caught in his bunk reading the Koran or reading the Bible. I think he's really fascinated with life and death and how God particularly, in this instance, a Christian God plays a part into the passing on."[65]

He went on, "I don't like to consider us a Christian band. But I know some people would. . . . It could definitely become a divisive thing. To me, any kind of music with an underlying agenda . . . I get turned off by unless the band is good. I don't really care to know what people have going on in their personal lives. It's like a catch-22, being in the band. . . . Aaron is so full of life and wants to just share all of the experiences with people. But, at the same time, I just want it to be a straight-up rock band."[66] Rickie told Luke Kruse at *Decapolis* that it's best to talk to him about band stuff, "as Aaron has the tendency to get sidetracked

---

[63] David Allen, "Me Without You," *HM Magazine*, #109, September/October 2004, 35.
[64] Steven Wells, "Oh, Sweet Jesus," *Philadelphia Weekly*, 9/24/08.
[65] John Benson, "Amen, Brother. mewithoutYou argues that it's neither emo nor Christian rock," *Colorado Springs Independent*, 11/09/06.
[66] Ibid

and 'go off' about spiritual matters."[67]

Rickie added, "I like the idea of searching for answers. That's kind of where I'm at with the spiritual aspects. It can't hurt to explore your options, even if you find there is nothing at all. I think that's exciting—the idea that nobody knows what's going on when you die."[68]

Mike said, "When we talk about religion, we're talking about organized specific groups of people, usually in vast numbers and organized in some sort of structure or hierarchy with doctrine that gets written. Examples of religion would be Islam, Catholicism, and Judaism. Religion doesn't really influence our music at all. But I would say there's a certain sense of spirituality in terms of Aaron's lyrics. For Aaron, I think he's motivated by a sense of there being more to this world than what we can see with our eyes, that there's a lot of mystery in that unknown question mark of what created all this. Who created all this? What are we supposed to do with our lives? How can we live our lives to the fullest, in terms of being of service to other people? He definitely reads the Bible, but that's not all he's inspired by. There's an ancient mystical poet named Rumi that I think Aaron is influenced by, along with books that he's read. Possibly stuff from the Quran and the Bhagavad Gita. There's definitely that aspect of his songwriting. I think Aaron is writing songs to express his curiosity and fascination with wanting to be devoted to something that is greater than all of us.[69]

As mewithoutYou embarked on their tour in 2002 with Norma Jean and Beloved, Aaron shared his own views on the matter. "Well, I think God wants me to tell people some things that he's told me. And he's revealed it to me in my life, the Bible, and I think with his Holy Spirit, and they're pretty clear and pretty obvious things. But I think we have a way of avoiding the obvious for the sake of doing whatever we feel like doing at the moment. So, yeah, I guess the short and skinny of it is that there's a lot of things wrong that God wants to make right and hopefully he can

---
[67] Luke Kruse, "mewithoutYou interview," *Decapolis*, 4/27/05.
[68] Ibid
[69] "mewithoutYou is never alone," *The Triangle*, 11/03/06.

use our band as a vessel to share his love with people. And not just in a fruity kind of, like, 'God loves everybody, everything's all right' kind of way, but if God loves me and I say I'm gonna try to love God, what does that mean in my life? It puts a lot of demands on your life. Jesus said if you love me you'll obey my commands, and a lot of people say they love God or claim to be Christians and, I don't know, the way the Bible says to live and the way most of us live is as different as the east and west. So I feel like the best I can do is just be a willing vessel, and if God wants to say something in it, our generation obviously likes music, you know. They'll listen to me more if I'm in a band playing music than if I just wander around with a sandwich board and a soapbox and the Bible. Or maybe one day I'll do that. So you'll see me with wild hair, dressed in camel skins, eating locusts and honey, living in the desert. Who knows?"[70]

---

[70] Cody Grace, "Aaron Weiss," *YouTube*, 3/10/14.

9
A to B Life

In the summer of 2002, mewithoutYou released their debut album *[A→B] Life*. According to Aaron, the title of the album means, "We're all going to die and our life is a vapor and a shadow."[71]

After seeing Vasily Kafanov's artwork on the Smashing Pumpkins *Machina* EP, they liked it so much they picked his art for their debut and every album they would release after.

MewithoutYou started out dressing up in suits, but this brought comparisons to The Hives. "We're just not like them so we decided to shed that idea and just dress nice instead,"[72] Aaron said, opting for turtlenecks and pea coats.

Aaron was asked in 2007 if he remembered those early days, when the band toured in their suits and turtlenecks. "Boy, I'm trying to forget," he said. "I've prayed for a bad memory, because that's gone. And I don't want to think about that anymore. Yeah, we wore wool coats in the summertime, and it was a gimmick."[73]

Luke Kruse at *Decapolis* wrote, "The first time I saw mewithoutYou was at Cornerstone Festival 2002 . . . and it proved to be one of the most memorable shows I've ever seen. The band went up on stage in the mid-afternoon 90 degree weather in winter parkas. Flowers were strewn about the stage, vocalist Aaron Weiss threw himself around with no regard for his safety, and the crowd stood in awe. I suddenly had a new favorite band."[74]

Amanda Thumper saw the same show and wrote in *HM Magazine*, "The performance that sticks out in my mind the most is MEWITHOUTYOU. Their music is full of personality. The band was wearing turtlenecks on a hot day, for crying out loud. Only

---

[71] Brandon Herbel, "MewithoutYou – 09.12.06," *Absolute Punk*, 9/12/06.
[72] Bob Glass, "MEWITHOUTYOU makes Council Bluffs stop on 'strange' tour," *The Gateway*, 10/08/02.
[73] zao24, "Cornerstone '07 Part 29: Aaron Weiss discussion part 1 of 4," *YouTube*, 7/27/08.
[74] Luke Kruse, "mewithoutYou interview," *Decapolis*, 4/27/05.

the drummer seemed to be affected by the heat, since he stripped off items of clothing between songs. What an interesting band. I think the singer is autistic."[75]

Fans began discussing this rumor on message boards, mistaking for autism Aaron's social anxiety, nervous fidgeting, and his sometimes awkward manner and disjointed thoughts when talking between songs.[76]

When asked about it, Aaron responded, "For me, yeah, it's almost just like a curiosity. It's sort of funny. I laughed when I heard that. People have asked me, 'So I heard you're autistic,' and I'm like, '. . . No?' It's funny that people would say that without knowing. Obviously, it's not true whereever they got it from. It just goes to show that you can't believe everything you hear or read."[77]

David Pogge described mewithoutYou's sound as "dark, dirty, and beautifully painful"[78] Musically, *[A→B] Life* is considered a post-hardcore album. They kept the heavy, distorted guitars featured on their EP but incorporated more of Chris Kleinberg's spacey shoegazer-style guitar sounds. Aaron's screaming was more controlled and intelligible, balanced with spoken-word. Mike added punk rock shouting to songs like "We Know Who Our Enemies Are," while Dan contributed melody with clean vocals on an acoustic version of "I Never Said That I Was Brave." Though compared to bands like Fugazi, mewithoutYou was unique and hard to define. The same would prove true with each successive album.

Behind Aaron's cathartic screaming were lyrics about sordid jealousy, unrequited love, neurotic obsession, insecurity, loss, and loneliness—half-plagiarized from other musicians, poets, and writers such as the Sufi poet Rumi, Leonard Cohen, Kurt

---

[75] Amanda Thumper, *HM Magazine*, #97, Sept/Oct 2002, 22.
[76] I discovered the *HM Magazine* blurb in 2012 and sent it to Aaron. He responded, "Thank you for the note right around my birthday. You cleared up a perpetual mystery in my life—that ever-so-frequent autism question, at last explained!" Email, 3/22/12.
[77] Drew Ailes, "mewithoutYou interview," *Lambgoat*, 1/14/07.
[78] David Pogge, "The Pain of Separation," *HM Magazine* , #97, Sept/Oct 2002, 24.

Vonnegut, John Donne, Neutral Milk Hotel, and The Smiths. These emotions were contrasted with seeking peace and fulfillment in God. This intense melodrama, inner-conflict, and ambivalence were perfect lyrical fodder for the grittiness of the music.

Justin Style wrote, "Some would argue that *[A→B] Life* is a record that the Christian market isn't ready for. There's no CCM image-posing here. Aaron spits out each word like it might just be his last, and his confessional lyrics range from struggles with lust to boldly confronting God in a body of work that at times is embarrassingly honest."[79]

"It's all very silly, you know?" Aaron said. "It's all half tongue-in-cheek, melodramatic, and really over the top sometimes. It's a really funny record, I think. I don't know if people are going to get it, but I hope they do . . . I hope they get the joke, the great joke that is Me Without You."[80]

"Recording the first record, I didn't care what I was saying for the most part. I just wanted to be cool and make out with girls," Aaron said.[81] He further told *HM Magazine*, "Not only can I not sing or play an instrument, I've also stolen all the lyrics I pretend to have written. So what does qualify me to be on this stage?"[82]

He told Yoni Wolf, "I was writing words in the studio. I remember one song, I was like, 'I only wrote half of the required amount of lyrics for this part. I'm gonna go upstairs and write the other half,' and just jotted something down and came down and sang it. It was like, oh, who cares, it's not going anywhere."[83]

"The theme when I look back at the lyrics seems to be 'I'm a screwball, we need each other, God is beautiful and good,'" he said in an *Absolute Punk* interview.[84] He told Vanessa Chalmers

---

[79] Justin Style, "Mewithoutyou: Kerrang! magazine were impressed by the Philly Godcore band," *Cross Rhythms*, 12/24/03.
[80] Ibid
[81] "mewithoutYou's Aaron Weiss," *Yahoo Voices*, 5/24/10.
[82] David Allen, "Me Without You," *HM Magazine*, #109, September/October 2004, 35.
[83] Yoni Wolf, "Episode 74 – Aaron Weiss (mewithoutYou)," *The Wandering Wolf*, 9/24/14.
[84] Brandon Herbel, "mewithoutYou – 09.12.06," *Absolutepunk.net*, 9/12/06.

they were about "mainly faith and lack of faith. Relationships—that's everything, everything of value is a relationship in some way, whether it's to God or another person."[85] Another time he answered, "For me, the songs are mostly about trying to find faith in God and figure out why I exist and what my responsibilities are as a human being. So, simple questions everybody asks themselves. What's gone so wrong and how do we make it right?"[86]

Though Aaron drew from his own feelings and relationship experiences with his on-and-off girlfriend, Amanda, the lyrics are only slightly autobiographical. The real Aaron and Amanda bear only some resemblance to the characters in the lyrics and their exaggerated drama.

"I'm usually pretty open about what's going on in my life. I don't hide a lot, you know," Aaron told *Godcore*. "But some of the stuff I steal from other people so it's not exactly . . . it's not written by me, let alone about me. But you know, it'll always be something that I can apply to my life in some way. It's not just taking stuff that sounds cool or trying to confuse people. I try to make a pretty straightforward story or idea come out clearly and have it be about something that I really have experienced and not just speculation."[87]

As Aaron began writing for the next album, he took his platform more seriously. "At first I didn't care, I wanted to be in a band. But when I started to realize that I was going to die someday I thought, 'I don't have a single day to waste. I don't have a single hour I can spend dancing around on stage for my own glory.'"[88]

Instead of just being an entertainer, he felt he should be serving Jesus. While at times wanting to use the band to talk about Jesus, he balked at using the band as a ministry tool as time went on. "We could say that we are going to do this for God, when in

---

[85] Vanessa Chalmers, "mewithoutYou interview," *San Diego Punk*, 12/03/04.
[86] "Mewithoutyou artist of the day interview," *YouTube*, 2007.
[87] Godcore.com interview, 5/05/2005.
[88] Vanessa Chalmers, "mewithoutYou interview," *San Diego Punk*, 12/03/04.

reality all of this is selfish ambition. It's better to say we are just a band, and pray in our hearts that God will be glorified."[89]

Aaron was still trying to write more hopeful lyrics that focused on God, but he had not experienced much peace. One source of unrest in his life was his on-and-off relationship with Amanda. To put an end to that, Aaron asked Amanda to marry him.

---

[89] Justin Style, "Mewithoutyou: Kerrang! magazine were impressed by the Philly Godcore band," *Cross Rhythms*, 12/24/03.

3/28/03
Aaron Weiss Journal Entry

I asked Amanda to marry me on Sunday at church. We were all singing "I Need Thee Every Hour," which is a song I've always liked. So I gave her this ring I'd bought, a tiny pearl surrounded by lavender amethyst gems on pink gold. See, she wasn't even my girlfriend so she was very surprised. She cried and said yes.

The next night, she called and she was crying again, but the sad crying, and when I asked if everything was alright she said no, it wasn't. We talked and she said she doesn't want to marry me right now. Good reasons I won't bore you with, but ah, it's been a confusing sort of week.

There's a Bible verse somewhere, says "it is well with my soul," but I wonder where this wellness of mine comes from. Detachment is one thing, but I'm afraid sometimes that maybe I don't care about a thing in all the world but myself.

Maybe you could keep me and her in your prayers, if you do that sort of thing? One thing is certain, and my brothers and sisters sang it all around as I either made a step toward God or another awful mistake: "Oh bless me now my Savior, I come to Thee I need Thee every hour, Thou most Holy One oh make me Thine indeed, Thou Blessed Son."

-ajw

10
Renewed Faith

I was sitting in my bedroom one January evening in 2003. I had been working with Borders books and music and living with my brother. My life had finally stabilized.

My brother decided at the end of 2002 to move out and live with his fiancé, so I could no longer afford rent on my own, nor could I afford a security deposit to move. Having had a bad roommate experience in the past, I wasn't up for that option. I feared I'd have to quit my job and move home once again.

"All I ever wanted was for you to exist, to love me, to have a plan for my life, and to have a wife to share it with, but I can't make you exist," I prayed in tears, exasperated by how difficult my life was.

A response came in the form of a thought: "Who said I didn't exist?"

Knowing this was my imagination, I played along and developed an inner dialogue over the next hour with "God." He told me that all I had to do was listen for his guidance and obey him when he spoke to me, and he could restore my life. I didn't have to believe Christianity was true, I didn't have to have my doctrinal ducks in a row, I didn't have to believe the Bible was the word of God, and if he led me to a church, I didn't have to agree with everything happening in that church. I simply needed to acknowledge that God was with me and give testimony of what he was doing in my life. What was paramount was that I obey when he speaks. I would have the rest of my life to struggle with theology and never come to a perfect understanding, he encouraged me.

I told him I still wanted to work with bands and youth in a Christian coffeehouse setting like I did a couple of years back, perhaps even still start a band.

"Did I miss my calling?" I asked.

"No," God said.

The next night, Jackie called. I hadn't talked to her in over a year, when I stopped volunteering for the ministry. "We found property for a coffeehouse. God put it on my heart to ask you to come back and book bands for us," she said. I wondered if maybe I did have a conversation with God after all.

As an appendix to my dialogue with God the previous night, he made an odd and random request. He asked me to find Mariah, a girl I'd had a conversation with a year-and-a-half previous on the way home from Cornerstone, and to share my story with her, that he was speaking to me and bringing me back to him. During the only conversation we'd ever had, Mariah said she was giving up on God and church.

"Lord, I've only spoken to her once and I have no idea where to find her. You'll have to cross our paths somehow," I said.

Three months later, I put in my two-week notice at Borders and planned to move home again as my health took a dive and I could no longer keep my hours. I left the hiring manager's desk and bumped into a girl on the way out.

"Hey, remember me? I drove you home from Cornerstone a couple years ago." Mariah came out of a room where she'd just finished watching a training video. She'd just been hired.

"Yes!" I said. "I need to share something with you."

Before leaving that day, I left a long note in her mailbox, sharing with her that God had brought me back to him, was restoring my faith, and had specifically told me to share my story with her. She wasn't ready to give her life back to God, but she said I wasn't the first person God sent to her to encourage her to come back to him.

With the content of my inner dialogue that night in January playing out in my external circumstances, I wondered if this was what some around me talked about when they said you could have a personal, intimate, conversational relationship with God. I'd begun to have spontaneous convictions, see visions accompanied by words in my mind, and just know things intuitively.

I looked into some Christian books on hearing God's voice to see if anyone else was having experiences like this. It turns out they were.

I bought *Experiencing God: Knowing and Doing the Will of God* and *Hearing God's Voice* by Henry Blackaby; *Hearing God: Developing a Conversational Relationship with God* by Dallas Willard; and *Knowing God's Will: Finding Guidance for Personal Decisions* by M. Blaine Smith as guides to explain what I was experiencing. These books spoke of having a conversational relationship with God where you not only talk to God, but you also listen for and journal the response you get.

Encouraged that God was present and communicating with me, I now had a revival of faith and a newfound hope. A light had turned on inside of me. I no longer felt lost, wandering, or alone. A path was unfolding before me as God was guiding my life. With the promise of guidance and the restoration of my life, including a promise to heal me of my crippling pain and fatigue, God assured me that I would never know despair again.

Getting the coffee house up and running was taking time, so we couldn't book bands right away. As spring turned to summer, the building was still not ready for shows, and my health was still poor.

With the ministry moving at snail's pace, I made plans to move to Florida in hopes that the warmer climate would help me function better. Once there, I would look for musicians to start a metal project—a concept album called *The Funeral of God*. I wanted to contrast the meaninglessness of my life without God with the purpose that comes from a God who loves me and knows my name.[90]

As July approached, I packed most of my stuff, taped up the boxes, and made arrangements to stay with family in Florida. I printed one hundred flyers containing my *Funeral of God* poem:

I have attended the funeral of God
And the universe went silent
A flame extinguished

---

[90] I had been listening to and reading a Christian apologist named Ravi Zacharias who gave a message quoting Nietzsche's parable of the madman on the death of God. This was my jumping off point.

And I was free
To wander
With tears unending
Lost to chase the wind
To mourn the loss of meaning
And to realize that God's funeral
Was my own

I meant to post the flyers on the fest grounds and hand them out, looking for interested musicians. Once I returned home from the fest, I would drive to Florida to start my new life.

Jackie was putting a leadership team together for the ministry and wanted me to stay and be a youth leader. "There is a girl named Natalie who is joining our team. Like you, she is coming out of the world and just started living for God again. You have to meet her, she's awesome."

"Sure, I'd be glad to meet her," I said. But I was still moving to Florida right after Cornerstone.[91]

---

[91] The full story of my time with Natalie will be told in another memoir called "God Told Me to Marry You."

11
Natalie

The first day of the fest, I headed over to Living Sacrifice's merch table to see if Arthur and Matthew were there. Living Sacrifice was breaking up, so I wanted to make sure I had Arthur's contact information since they wouldn't be coming through town on tour anymore.

Matthew was at the table, just heading out, and invited me to get something to eat with him in the food court. On the way out, we passed a shirt that said: SATAN IS A NERD! Matthew flicked it and smirked. "This place is a glorified youth group."

As we made our way to the food court, a couple of guys passed us on the way. "Man, I heard you guys absolutely owned the fest last night. Everyone is talking about how amazing your set was," Matthew said. They smiled and said thank you.

Matthew introduced me to his friends, and after making small talk, we moved on.

"Who were those guys?" I asked.

"They're in mewithoutYou. You should check them out when you get a chance."

When we got to the food court and sat down, we continued our conversation. "I'm so tired of being in a metal band," Matthew said, getting bored with heavy music. Being a fan of Radiohead, indie rock, and experimental music, he wanted to do something else. He invited me to see Unwed Sailor as he was drumming for them at the fest that year.

"I'm really happy Living Sacrifice is over and I don't have to play fests like this anymore," he continued. "This isn't real. It's like we're rock stars here and everyone wants an autograph, but as soon as we leave, we're playing in dinky bars and clubs where nobody cares who we are."

Later in the fest, Arthur and I had lunch. He confided in me that he was going through a divorce and was hurting, so we exchanged emails and I promised to check in on him.

At 4:00 on Wednesday afternoon, I stood under the tent covering the Underground Stage on which a band called Dead Poetic was about to play. As I was loading a tape into my video camera, Jackie tapped me on my back and gave me a big hug.

"Oh my goodness, how did you find me here?" I asked, incredulous that she would run into me at a fest that size.

"Oh, I knew you liked Dead Poetic and that I would probably find you here."

After hugging me, she introduced me to the tall, thin, Italian brunette standing next to her.

"Paul, this is Natalie. She's the woman I've been telling you about."

"Hi, I'm Paul."

I reached out my hand to shake hers. As soon as our hands met I heard God say, "Stay and help her walk with me." This was accompanied by a vision of us standing shoulder-to-shoulder as partners on a ministry team, youth leaders surrounded by teens. This happened in a flash, before I could let her hand go. I was taken aback but tried not to let it show.

"Natalie is only staying one day, so she's leaving tonight, but we're going to meet in the Asylum around 1:00 A.M. to have coffee and chat. You're welcome to join us."

"Okay, sounds great," I said. They left as Dead Poetic took the stage. I hit the record button on my camera, trying to shake off the weight of what I'd just experienced. *I'm not staying here. I'm going to Florida.*

I ran into them again later that afternoon in the store, and again that evening on the main path. "We're walking Natalie back to her car," Jackie said. "She's decided to go home early—it's a four-hour drive. Listen, we're having worship at Natalie's apartment next Friday. You should come, it's gonna be awesome! You can give her your number, and she'll call you with the details."

I reluctantly wrote my number down for her with every intention of not going. "Well, it was really nice meeting you."

"You too," she said, hugging me goodbye.

I headed over to one of the Encore tents to see Zao close the night, then ran into their drummer Jesse at their merch table the next day. "Hey man, I videotaped your set last night. If you want me to send you a copy, just give me your address or an email, or you can contact me here." I pulled out one of my few remaining *Funeral of God* flyers and gave it to him.

When I got home from the fest, I avoided calling Natalie, happy to have a flat tire as an excuse not to make it to worship at her place that Friday.

12
MewithoutYou Cornerstone 2003

While trading videos online, I found a person who had videotaped both mewithoutYou sets at Cornerstone as well as a message Aaron had given. Watching the video, I understood why there was so much hype surrounding them at the fest. During their first set, there were flower petals strewn across the stage and bouquets tied to the microphones. A man proposed to a woman onstage and she accepted, Aaron showering them with stems and flowers.

Mid-set, Aaron announced that he would be speaking and sharing some thoughts at the Underground Stage Thursday or Friday. "There's a prayer tent, it always seems suspiciously empty—even my own presence very much not to be found there, so maybe I'll see you there this year for a change."

During the second set, Aaron said, "I'm sorry to all of you for singing songs about my own problems, that you've been duped into—some of you, at least—listening and even singing along with the words. But I pray God's glorified in some backwards way. And speaking of God . . ." Aaron asked them to attend a Bible study the next day at 3:15 P.M. at the Underground Stage. The crowd cheered and Aaron thought it strange. "It's not a pep rally, it's a Bible study."

Just before the final song of their set, Aaron apologized for trying to be fashionable and looking so cool onstage when earlier that day he wore an Elton John, Billy Joel extra-large tour T-shirt. "I hope you'll forgive me and forgive us our shortcomings. We're trying to love you guys, in a way, and I don't know how we can love you, you, and you," he pointed to individuals in the crowd. "We've only just met. But my name is Aaron, and hopefully we'll spend some more time together tomorrow if I won't have completely lost my voice."

"I love you, Aaron!" someone yelled from the audience.

"I don't love you guys, but God does, and uh, that means

more than my affection, that's for sure. So, the last song is, uh, it's ripped off from some old poem I read, like most of my lyrics."

They ended their set with "Everything Was Beautiful and Nothing Hurt." The title is a line from Kurt Vonnegut, the lyrics containing lines from John Donne's "A Valediction: Forbidding Mourning."

13
Aaron Weiss's Message: Cornerstone 2003

I put in the second video and watched the message Aaron gave at the Underground Stage. He stood bearded in a white T-shirt and shorts, opening in prayer, asking that the Holy Spirit be there to soften hearts and open ears, hoping the dialogue and discussion they were having would please God.

He was nervous, having never spoken to a big crowd before. He didn't know exactly what to say, so he started reading from loose notes he'd taken on disjointed topics. Aware of the responsibility of being a teacher and the Bible saying teachers will be judged more harshly, he let the audience know that he didn't presume to be able to teach them anything at all.

"It's sort of been an overwhelming week for me. And you're all at the same festival as I am, we're at Cornerstone Festival, and it's supposed to be a time of worshipping God. Now for me, I've read my Bible less in these past three or four days than I'm accustomed to reading it when I'm at home. I've also prayed less probably than I ever do, really, except for when somebody else suggests we pray. I don't take time aside and I don't find quiet time with God and this is because of the tremendous amount of activity around us. And you probably know what I mean. You see so many people you probably don't see otherwise. And maybe it's overwhelming for you, too." Aaron prayed that everyone there would find some peace, quiet, and stillness.

"I don't want to just start tearing down things about this festival. I can tell my experience, and it's been draining, and I've had a difficult time. And my friends and I have been joking, calling it sort of a Leviathan or a monster of some sort that takes over. I'm in a band, and we played the other day. I'm certainly not plugging the band, quite the opposite. I'm telling you that we played and people came and applauded and sang some of the words. I'm the singer in the band, and this makes me feel like, wow, look at that, people know I'm the singer and they care about me and they like me and there's an acceptance that comes with that, and it's very satisfying in a way. In fact, when I first started playing with this band, it was about two years ago at this very festival, and we got signed to a label that morning. And people were saying, 'I like you guys.' I mean, I grew up with like, buck teeth and was white trash and kinda not really liked by many people, and girls never liked me and everything . . . I had very low self-esteem. So then when I come here and people like my band, I'm like, 'I'm the greatest guy in the world!' So it's very dangerous because all throughout the Bible you can read these repeated warnings . . . you know, blessed are you who weep, blessed are you when people say bad things about you, blessed are you who mourn, the poor in spirit, and woe to you who laugh and woe to you when people are saying good things about you."

Aaron found this praise dangerous because he wanted to bring Jesus to anyone who came to see the band or to see him speak. But instead of blessing people and praising God, "in reality I walk around to see people and to be seen by people. And I'm concerned with what people think of me and who I'm seen with. My gosh, just yesterday I did that myself. I saw somebody in a band that I really like, and I thought, I'll go say hi. Maybe I could be talking to him, people would see me with this fella and they'd say, 'Well, Aaron's in with that guy, he must be pretty cool!' So you see what an idiot I can be."

Tired of talking about himself, he asked fans about their lives, and as they poured out their stories of heartbreak, Aaron lamented that he was looking over their shoulder for someone more important to be seen with.

"Well, we're not a successful band, the band I'm in, by most standards, but by some, we are. And it has not been satisfying in any way, in any good way or lasting way. In fact, it's made me want to shoot myself." Miserable, Aaron feared he would quit the band and break it up.

"And there was a girl that I was engaged to, and things went sour and I hit sort of rock bottom with that. And I started to see these scriptures of grieve and mourn and wail and wash your hands ye double minded and ye sinners, humble yourself before

God and he will lift you up, and I started to grieve and mourn and wail. And this is not self-pity, because I am not telling you what the world has done to me or what the devil has done to me or what other people have done to me. I'm telling you what I've done to myself by accepting a lie. I exchanged the truth of God for a lie, because I knew that Jesus died on a cross and that that was real and that that was eternal. And I know that there are bands that sell a whole lot of CDs and are popular, and that is not real. This whole world that's around you, the people that you see and talk to, the outfits that you wear, how you come across to people, people's opinion of you, or how many units you sell as a band, is all very much an illusion."

He apologized again for the audacity of getting onstage and thinking he knew what anyone needed. "I'm not pretending to love you or care about you in the least bit. Sometimes I wonder if I even love my mom and my dad the way I yell at them and take them for granted. But then I'll come here and if there's somebody at a show that can help my band's career, well I'm the friendliest guy in the world. So what about my mom and my dad? Why can't I love them and the people around me? Well, I think maybe that's what I should say to you guys: go home and love your mom and your dad. It's simple enough, you can't really argue with me," he said, laughing.

Aaron encouraged the audience to love people, expecting no benefit in return. "These people all around you who don't offer you anything, these are Jesus. These people are Christ himself. He said, of course, whatever you do to the least of my brothers, you've done to me. And I've walked by people in the street who are starving, and I've walked by people who are lying in the cold in Philadelphia without a blanket. And did I come back with a blanket? Certainly not. So what did I do to Jesus there?"

Aaron was upset with himself that he didn't go to the Compassion International booth to help starving children while at the fest. "Maybe hold me accountable and ask me later today, 'Did you make it over to that tent with the booth with the children who are starving?' See, I don't even know what it's called. You know, I certainly know my favorite bands and where their merch table is.

But do I know about the people needing help who have nothing to offer me? Help me, is what I'm asking you, because I'm in a bad place, you know?"

He highly recommended a book called *The Way of the Pilgrim*. "It doesn't have an author, it's written anonymously by an eighteenth century Russian peasant with this shriveled up hand and a knapsack and some breadcrumbs and a Bible. And he walked around loving people, and that's it. And what are we doing? We're gonna go home to our television sets and our CD players with the merch that we bought, and with our stories about the cool bands that we saw. But man, I was over at the prayer tent. I went there only because I said something the first night like, 'How come none of you are at the prayer tent?' And then I thought two days later, 'I still haven't gone to the prayer tent.' So, for the sole purpose of not being a blatant hypocrite, I went to the prayer tent. No interest in praying whatsoever. I'd much rather see and be seen in the busy and lovely food court."

Aaron continued, "Well, I guess what I'm asking you to do is maybe to start thinking about things eternal and set your eyes on Jesus, truly, not this Christian festival, certainly not the bands that are playing, though they can glorify God. I'm not saying there's no place for entertainment." He paused. "Maybe I'm saying there's no place for entertainment."

Aaron had been trying to follow Jesus for the past two years and at first had a hard time reading the Bible and praying, but he encouraged the audience to press through and make that a habit in their lives, as doing this transformed his life.

Weary of the idea that Jesus is your personal buddy, Aaron reminded the audience that Jesus is their authority, someone to submit to and obey, to do what he taught and follow his commands. Though you are saved by grace, all that will remain in your life is the eternal works you've done for the kingdom of God. "It's to God's glory that I believe in Jesus, despite American Christianity and not because of it."

Aaron recommended reading the Danish thinker Soren Kierkegaard and Russian novelists like Fyodor Dostoyevsky and Leo Tolstoy, who were insightful thinkers that engaged their

Christian faith in a much deeper way than the American evangelical Christian subculture appeared to.

"I think all you need is God, the God of the Bible, and his Son, Jesus, and his Holy Spirit. And that's all I got for you, really."

Aaron's message brought to the forefront in me a concern I had since my days in youth group. I knew I liked our church pizza parties, entertaining worship bands, working at the Christian bookstore, and contemplating a career in ministry. I wanted to enjoy life, and to ask God for blessings in the way of health, marriage, and a good middle class existence. I wanted nothing to do with helping the poor, giving people shelter, visiting people in jail, helping widows, or standing up for the oppressed. These things depressed and overwhelmed me.

I knew that I couldn't live the life that Jesus called his disciples to: to give up their homes, possessions, families, livelihoods, and safety to follow him in a life of hardship, suffering, torture, and death. I reasoned that some were called to that life and I simply wasn't. I'd always feared that I was not truly following Jesus. Instead, I was just an evangelical Christian enjoying my life. I appreciated that at a festival like Cornerstone, a bastion of pop-culture entertainment and fun where Jesus is commoditized as ministry, Aaron reminded us to look for something deeper.

14
Fireside Bowl

As I shared a journal of my week at the fest on the Project 86 message boards, an online friend named Russ asked if I caught mewithoutYou. "No, man, but they were the talk of the fest." Russ lived in Canada, so he was upset that he missed them at a previous festival he attended in the United States.

When I saw that mewithoutYou would be playing at Fireside Bowl right in the neighborhood, I made plans to go and see what all of the hype was about.

Russ asked that I pick up a T-shirt and send it to him in the mail. I asked him what his favorite song was, wanting to surprise him with a video of the set. "Gentlemen" was his favorite.

I found mewithoutYou's merchandise table before the show and introduced myself to the man setting up.

"Hi, my name is Paul. Are you in the band?"

"Hi, I'm Aaron." He shook my hand. "Yes, I'm in the band."

"What do you do?"

"I'm the singer."

He had a very gentle demeanor and perfectly pointed, well manicured sideburns.

"Do you do dedications?" I asked.

"Sure."

I handed him a card that said "Russ from Canada" on it.

"Russ missed you guys play at a previous festival and is kicking himself for it. He couldn't make it to Cornerstone and he lives in Canada, so I thought it would be nice to send him a video of the set with his favorite song dedicated to him. He likes 'Gentlemen.'"

Aaron took the card and kindly agreed to do it.

"Thank you very much!" I picked a spot to videotape.

Mike, opened the set with the guitar intro to a new song called "Disaster Tourism." With a nervous smile, Aaron said, "Here it goes," and clenched his navy coat closed, as if he wanted to hide behind it. He approached the microphone with the left side of his face, hands in his pockets, with eyes closed, as if sneaking up on it.

As the song built, his spoken word turned to yells and screams of angst, his body in fits and jerks, arms and coat flailing. Soon he was slamming into the wall, spinning, and bouncing off of other band members.

"Now for another one," Aaron said, once again with a nervous smile as they moved into "Nice and Blue." Rickie looked like he was dancing behind the drum kit, slamming the symbols in fury. As everyone in the band became more active onstage, Aaron continued to spin, hit the ground, bounce off the wall, and run into his bandmates.

"It means a lot for me to see a few here, especially a few of you." Aaron tried to catch his breath after the song. "Sorry to Dan, whose bass I knocked out of tune being careless in that previous song." With nervous laughter, playing with the microphone cord, he continued, "I'm not much of a dancer, naturally, but heaven knows that I'm trying. And sometimes a limb here, a head there, those bass tuning pegs get in the way. We're called mewithoutYou, from Philadelphia, and we're gonna do quite a few more."

"Gentlemen" was the third song in the set. Aaron remembered the dedication. "I'm supposed to send one out for Russ, I think, a fella in Canada, who I don't even know, Russ. I mean, you didn't even come to the show—the guy with the video camera asked me to do this—and sure, I'll say Russ, yeah this song's for you, but between me and you guys, it's not for Russ at all. I got no love for Russ. Number one, he's not at the show. Number two, Canada? Come on Russ! Not that America is anything special, but Canada?"

After the song, Aaron continued, "So I have a lot of friends from this Jesus People USA which is right in the neighborhood. You like them? Some of you know them, some of you might not. I don't know much about them, to be honest, but they seem like a decent group of guys. Well anyhow, I'd like to thank you guys for coming out. So maybe after the show we can go out for some ice cream, some of you? I don't know what there is to do in this town. Is that good? There's a place? Maybe you could show us. So we're called mewithoutYou. I told you that, didn't I?" Aaron sighed. "We're gonna do a few more songs."

There was an anxiousness and nervousness about Aaron. When he talked, he trembled and stumbled over his words. He also exuded an innocent boyishness and a charming quirkiness.

They played "We Know Who Our Enemies Are" and dedicated it to friends and family at the show. During an instrumental song before "Silencer," Aaron came offstage into the crowd to hug family and friends before finishing the song.

Twice throughout the set he spoke of the emptiness he still felt. "So we have a lot of friends here, man, it's really, really kind of you. It's because we're a long way from home. We've been traveling for so long, and it gets very tiring and very old, of course, for us playing these same songs and doing these same dances. I mean, it's the same thing, just a different city. You know, we always used to think, 'Well, if we could be in a rock band and we'd come around and play . . . well, that would be the greatest, we'd play these songs.' And then we started doing that and it wasn't so great anymore. So we said, 'Well, if we could just get on this label or that and then we'd be happy.' Well, then we got on a record label. And then we said, 'If we could just get on tour with this band.' Well, the point is that every time we'd set these goals, it would be achieved, and it's still miserable every time. I mean nothing has made me happy with this lousy band. Sorry, guys, you're good friends and all but the music is just kind of, uh, fickle."

He went on to say, "I'm a very content person, thanks be to God, and a lot of these songs are about God, but it's more about, um—it's more than I care to get into right now because I don't feel like talking about God, really. I haven't been thinking much about God so there's not much for me to say right now except even when I'm not thinking much about him, he still somehow manages to take care of me and love me. So this one is about him and this girl. Don't you applaud, because it's more about the girl than God, and she's no good, all right? She's all right, but man." He sighed.

"Bullet to Binary" began.

Before the set ended he reminded everyone, "We're playing tomorrow in La Crosse, Wisconsin, then we go back home for a week and tour and then write and then record, etcetera, etcetera. It might not terribly interest you. It doesn't even interest me anymore. I don't even care what we do, but it's nice to be here."

Trying to banter before the final song of the set, Aaron's discomfort showed and he interrupted himself, turning to his bandmates. "I'm ready when you guys are, honestly. I'm floundering around up here. I don't need to talk. One of you guys can talk." He spoke through his nervous smile and stepped back from the microphone, putting his hands into his pockets.

After all of the angst of rejection and unrequited love in the songs, they fittingly finished the set with "The Cure for Pain," ending with the line, *Jesus, have mercy on us.*

I found Aaron after the show and thanked him for the dedication.

"I tried to make it fun. I hope it's what you were looking for."

15
Unrequited

Before I could head off to Florida, Jackie offered me a salaried youth pastor position and an apartment if I stayed with the ministry and trained for six months first. She had a barbeque at her house for the team to discuss the vision for the ministry. This was my first time seeing Natalie since Cornerstone. Eager to investigate the gravity I couldn't shake upon meeting her, I spent most of my time there talking with her and getting to know her.

By the end of the afternoon, I knew it wasn't attraction or infatuation I felt, but a deep care for her, like I'd known her my entire life. I didn't want to leave her side.

As I walked her to her car, I told her I was deciding between Florida and Jackie's offer to stay. "You're not going anywhere," she teased in a sultry voice, then offered to help find me an apartment in her neighborhood.

There was no response to my flyers to start a band in Florida, so I took Jackie and Natalie up on their offers.

Over coffee one evening, Natalie and I confided in one another that we both knew from the day we met that God had placed us in one another's lives for a reason, but neither of us felt a green light to date.

As I prayed about it, God said he wanted her to seal her heart so it belonged only to him. She was trying to end a dysfunctional on-and-off relationship and start a new life when a woman praying over her at a retreat in Arkansas told her the same: "God wants you to seal your heart."

"I don't get any creepy vibes from you, which is nice. Let's just take it a day at a time and see what God is doing," she suggested in the car after coffee. The next morning, she helped me move into the studio we found together.

I finally made it to Natalie's apartment for worship that week and sat next to her, holding the sheet music while she played flute. After a wonderful evening with everyone, she hugged me goodbye, saying, "We're neighbors, it's gonna be great!" I realized at this point that I was attracted to her.

The following week, we planned breakfast and she didn't return my call. When I checked in on her, she told me she had gotten back together with her ex, Tony, and hoped that she wasn't breaking my heart.

I reminded her about God wanting her to stay single, seal her heart, and leave her past behind. I didn't want to see her hurt, and I felt this was the reason God placed me in her life—to help her walk with him.

For the next few months, our friendship was strained. Whenever we spent time together, Natalie was visibly uncomfortable with me. When people surrounding us told us we looked great together and asked if we were a couple, she became irritated.

I continued to pray for Natalie when one evening God told me that he revealed to her that I was placed in her life to be her husband, and that her harsh treatment towards me and discomfort around me was the result of her not wanting this path. He told me to wait for her and not to feel rejected or take any of this personally. She wouldn't reject me forever. "She is your wife."

If what I heard was true, God told her I was to be her husband before he told me she was to be my wife. I didn't tell her what I heard, I waited to see if she would say something first.

Natalie, through tears over breakfast, said she knew I was placed in her life by God and that he kept speaking to her about me whenever she prayed about Tony, but she wanted him instead of me. In fact, the thought that she would have to marry me—a man she didn't get a "husband vibe" from and could never imagine having sex with—felt like punishment to her. She got so upset with God that she determined this was either Satan deceiving her or that I had somehow manipulated, brainwashed, or placed a curse her, causing her to feel drawn to me against her will.

When I asked her if she was willing to pray about what was happening to see if this might be from God, she said no, she just wanted this to stop. When I sent her books to consider the stories of others who had gone through something similar, she refused to read them.

By November, she left the ministry for a number of reasons and asked me not to contact her. I felt like I had completely failed in my role in her life. God told me this wasn't the end of his plan for us and to keep waiting for her.

At the same time, Jackie determined that there would be no youth pastor position or ministry team due to the "pride" leadership positions were causing. Rather than a church, we would just be a coffeehouse. She retracted her offer of the salaried youth pastor position and apartment. The following month, she changed her mind and decided to start a church after all and gave the position to someone else.

By the year's end, Natalie was gone, no shows were being booked, I wasn't going to be a youth pastor, I didn't move to Florida and start my band, and still sick, I was about to lose my job and apartment and move home again. If this was God's idea of restoring my life as I followed his guidance, he was doing a terrible job.

While my life felt like it was coming undone and I was starting to lose faith in the final months of 2003, Aaron's faith was being revolutionized, but not before a bit of girl troubles of his own.

8/14/03
Aaron Weiss Journal Entry

Without much planning I bought a one-way Greyhound ticket to Washington, D.C. where Unwed Sailor was playing. After a long ride and a long walk to the club, well I missed their show, and though I'd planned on spending the night with them afterwards, I felt a strong compulsion to be alone, so they reluctantly let me out on the capital belt loop that surrounds the city and I put out my thumb. This, at maybe 1:00 A.M.

After a few hours of walking on the shoulder and no rides, I tried the onramp and it worked much better. A Middle Eastern fellow gave me a short ride, then a few more hours of walking and a sweet southern trucker picked me up, mumbling incoherently under his mustache. He dropped me at a truck stop, but after one or two hours there and no takers I walked back to the highway and got picked up by an old stoner who said all the religions of the world are united and consistent with science, and he also called black folks monkeys. I was speechless, and expressionless, wondering, is there a right way for me to respond?

He left me on 95 along Baltimore and I walked a while on high bridges that shook when the real big trucks rumbled by, I mean the very concrete shaking up and down. I was scared until finally a work zone gave me room to walk, and get this: the onramp there had a stop sign, and I waited there looking people in the eye real pathetic for some pity, covered in my own sweat ten times over at this point, but no one would even look at me.

So this one flatbed with a tread caterpillar one-man forklift chained to the back stopped there and I took my chance, hopping on the back and hoping no one else would see, and they didn't. So I laid down on that flatbed and I zoomed north through the NO HAZMAT tunnel headfirst out of stinking hot Baltimore, laying my body between the treads of the tractor and hiding my face under my book bag from traffic alongside so they couldn't see me laughing out loud and thinking, now this is living! But the truck left the highway before long, and I hopped off when it slowed down just enough.

I got another ride so fast I couldn't believe it, the fellow so happy to stop for me he almost got rear ended. The son and the grandson of preachers, we talked about the Bible. Where he left me, I walked a ways just north of Aberdeen and finally a state trooper stopped and gave me a hard time. He frisked me and warned me and put me in the car and said I couldn't walk on the freeway, especially because of the bridge coming up, how there's no room to walk. He drove me a few miles away, to a lousy business road that runs along 95 where no one's going anywhere far like Philadelphia, and tells me to walk along there.

Man, this is after about 10 hours and I'm still seventy miles from home, so I walked and got a short ride back to 95 and kept on walking north, but brother, that bridge! With me afraid of heights and it was maybe a mile long, no space to walk, cars ripping by and death or worse if I fell, it was so high, the trooper was totally right.

Well I climbed down to the Susquehanna riverbank and in one of my more severe fits of stupidity, I thought maybe I could build a raft to float my stuff and swim across. I found some logs and a long strip of vinyl trash and strapped them together, and they floated on the water level, so I put some old 2x4's on top and then took off my clothes and put them and my books in these plastic bags, wrapped them in an old raincoat I found and set them on the 2x4's. Then I found some rope that someone had used to tie up mystery animal bones to a tree, maybe in some sort of ritual, and I untied it and took the skull for good measure. I tied the skull to the raft and the raft to the rope and the rope to my neck and started the swim.

Not even one tenth of the way there I start cramping up from all the walking I'd done, and I got scared and grabbed onto some fixed driftwood and waved down this fishing boat. Half out of the water and only in my underwear, a yellow bundle floating ten feet away on a makeshift raft fastened to my neck, I started, "I know how this must look."

He said I was unsafe, but he wouldn't give me a lift maybe

cause it was all too weird, so he insisted I turn back, and I said I'm going on with or without him, so he sped off and I got back to swimming and praying out loud. I did the backstroke, so the prayer sounded funny in my head 'cause my ears were underwater and I trusted God and thought what a funny story this would all make. Then I would turn over and swim the breaststroke with the rope between my teeth. Switching back and forth like that for over an hour, I made it maybe two-thirds the way across and finally waved down some real nice water-ski family who picked me up and fed me a bologna and cheese sandwich and dropped me on the north shore.

I took off what little I had on and on a lonely old rock lay down in the sun next to a rotten fish skeleton. The distant roar of factory machines, the steady rush of cars and trucks going where they're going much faster than me, a big spider web blowing around above me and the warm wash of sun all put me to sleep, but I jumped up after maybe a minute, disoriented and paranoid and naked, sensing the fallen tree trunks and dead leaves and close flying dragonfly were conspiring against me. It made sense at the time, that's how tired I was.

Back on 95 only a few minutes before encountering another trooper. The same routine, hands where I can see 'em. He found the skull in my bag and it put him on edge. When he ran my ID and came back, he said, "Weren't you warned about walking along this road?" "Yes sir," I said. "Then what the fuck are you doing here?" (It was a reasonable question.) I told him the truth, I was just trying to get home, and when I told him my raft story he lightened up a lot.

Ah, it was about 21 hours in all and I made it home, but the rest of the story's downhill. Except, I got picked up by this fellow who says he's a Pulitzer Prize winner, PhD, published poet, songwriter for Alicia Keys and all this other stuff. I tried to be very impressed because those are the most impressive things a person can do, in a sense. I'm not trying to come down on the guy, that's how we all are, I think. 'Cause look, can I ask your forgiveness for something? In saying all this, all I'm really trying to do is make myself out to be adventurous and cool.

-ajw

8/23/03
Aaron Weiss Journal Entry

People seem entertained by my last journal entry, which was a lot of the idea really, but a girl the other night said how that story was a display of my trust in God's hand of protection, which made me immediately embarrassed and regretful, as the truth is, I know my own heart at least enough to recognize when I'm just showing off. And should I really be so proud of that sort of behavior?

I'm reminded of the story of the man who walked up and down the railroad tracks repeating "Jesus will protect me," right up until the moment the train killed him. The idea is not that Jesus won't protect us, but that maybe his protection is less like stopping speeding trains (or lifting us out from rivers) and more like giving us the intelligence to stay out of senseless danger. I don't at all mean to say our ultimate goal is to prolong our life on earth! Christ calls us beyond petty risks—even to lay down our lives for the sake of God's kingdom. No, we shouldn't fear death, but to put ourselves in harm's way for the sake of mere exhilaration is foolishness.

Maybe the worst thing about my trying to come across to you (whoever is reading this, and for whatever reason) as some wonderful, spontaneous, free-spirited Jack Kerouac type is that I know very well who I truly am. And in case I've misled you up 'till now, maybe I should set something straight. Would you care to know?

My name is Aaron. I'm almost 25 years old and I live with my parents. My dad does my dishes and my mom does my laundry and a few months ago I wet my bed. That's who I am. Do you want to know who else I am? I abandoned duty and loyalty to Jesus and to the girl of my life for the sake of an exciting, vulgar new world of fantasy and egomania. That's who I am. Do you want to know what else? I am full of sadness and confusion and shame, and despite my knowing the beautiful truth about the mercy and peace of the God of Love, my actions only prove that I don't care about anyone in the entire universe but myself. That's who I am. Pleasure to meet you.

-ajw

16
Anabaptist

Aaron attended a church in Philadelphia called Circle of Hope, which was located above the Circle Thrift store. Pastored by Joshua Grace, it was described as a hip, young, vibrant, progressive church with a bend towards social justice issues.

Steven Wells wrote, "The Circle of Hope meeting here in Fishtown isn't much of a rock 'n' roll experience . . . But you couldn't spit in this room without hitting a crazy, out-there, commune-living, sedition-spewing radical troublemaker, out to shake American Christianity out of its complacent materialist coma." He added, "Anarcho-Christianity is alive and kicking in Philadelphia."[92]

A man named Shane Claiborne, who started an intentional community called the Simple Way with a group of friends in 1998, came to speak at Circle of Hope. Shane was part of the Christian Peacemaker Teams where he spent time in Iraq and also worked in Calcutta with Mother Teresa.

Aaron approached Shane after the service and asked him how he could join their community. After meeting over dinner, Aaron moved in that October. He stayed until the end of the year, then moved back into his parents' house in January when mewithoutYou started their tour in 2004.

A few members from the Bruderhof, an Anabaptist community in upstate New York, came to help the Simple Way fix up houses. They invited Aaron to visit and he accepted. By the time he returned, his experience and understanding of Christianity was revolutionized and his life drastically changed.

Aaron came to identify more with the Radical Reformers and Anabaptists—the Amish, Mennonites, Hutterites, and Quakers—and their emphasis on pacifism. He contrasted the communal

---

[92] Steven Wells, "Oh, Sweet Jesus: Philadelphia is either home to the most genuinely Christian movement in America or it's a festering spiritual slum. All depends on how you look at it," *Philadelphia Weekly*, 9-24-08.

Anabaptist ideals—based on Acts 2 and 4, in which believers sold all they owned and put it in a common pot so everyone's needs were met, and living by the Sermon on the Mount in which Jesus warns us to shun wealth, power, ego, and pride—with conservative evangelical Christianity in America, which seemed so far from those ideals. More and more, he saw American Christian pop culture as an idol sheltering us from the teachings of Jesus rather than putting them into practice.

Influenced by the Anabaptists, a man named Eberhard Arnold left his upper class upbringing in Germany and made it his goal to work among the destitute. Once married to Emmy, they opened their house to those who needed shelter.

Intent on forming a community, Emmy writes in *Torches Together: The story of the Bruderhof Communities–their life, together, sharing all things in common* that they were influenced by the writings of St. Francis of Assisi, Soren Kierkegaard, and George Fox of the Quakers. She adds that Leo Tolstoy and Fyodor Dostoyevsky "spoke to our condition through their writings."[93]

Though Tolstoy didn't accept the supernatural doctrines of Christianity, his life was turned around by following the ethical teachings of Jesus. Late in his life, many of his writings became religious in nature, such as *The Kingdom of God is Within You*. He had finally left his estate and his family to wander as a hermit before getting sick and dying.

Tolstoyan groups formed, disciples following his teachings, which he disparaged, telling them he had no teaching and that groups devoted to him should instead follow the teachings of Jesus and their own conscience.

Eberhard and Emmy met with the German Youth and Tolstoyan groups on Thursdays, sometimes up to one hundred people of every stripe and background—"members of the various branches of the youth movement, young people from Christian groups, anarchists, atheists, Quakers, Baptists, artists, and also

---

[93] Emmy Arnold, *Torches Together: The story of the Bruderhof Communities–their life, together, sharing all things in common*, (Rifton: Plough Publishing House, 1964, 1971), 24.

representatives of the revivalist movement"[94]—for deep conversations into the night. They gathered in nature to sing folk songs, form drum circles, and dance to a God bigger than their understanding. Everyone brought food for a potluck.

Arnold anchored everything he taught in the Sermon on the Mount. He even adopted the costume of the German Youth to show his break from the middle class and his new identification with the poor.

They discussed the many hardships and impracticalities of being pacifists who lived in community and followed the teachings of Jesus. They wanted to live in poverty, share in suffering, and give their possessions away.

One Christmas Eve at Sannerz, the community decorated a tree in the forest with candles, circled it, and sang Christmas carols. "After the Christmas message had been proclaimed, everyone took a lighted candle from the tree and we walked down the Albing Mountain in procession. Each one would protect his candle from the wind, and if one was blown out, it would be rekindled from another. This for us was a symbol of brotherly life."[95]

They decided to become one with the Hutterites. Eberhard announced this among lit torches at night. "When only two torches remained alight, Eberhard went to the middle of the circle and leaned them together so that they blazed twice as brightly..."[96]

Emmy wrote that the "bondage of capitalism and career" and the individualism of middle-class life called many away from the community, among other hardships. She spoke of "ambition and arrogance" being enemies of communal life. They couldn't suffer with the poor if they themselves weren't poor and couldn't live for the other without crucifying the self.

They knew they were imperfect and were always in process. "We were aware that our own movement came from the youth movement, religious socialism, the worker movement, and

---

[94] Ibid
[95] Ibid, 53.
[96] Markus Baum, *Against the Wind: Eberhard Arnold and the Bruderhof*, (Farmington: Plough Publishing House, 1996), 204.

Protestant and Catholic movements, which as products of the times also have their defects and do not have eternal meaning in all aspects."[97]

As war-protesting anarchists who opposed nationalism, they could not salute Hitler as savior and could not support German National Socialism. Because of this, they felt persecution was near. They came to America in 1954 where they settled in Rifton, New York. It was this community—Woodcrest—that Aaron visited.

During his visit to the Bruderhof, Aaron had a life-changing experience. "I remember being up one night and the wind was blowing outside, and I thought if I went out I would see an angel outside. There was a stuffed gorilla in the room. I was ready for it to start talking to me. And the way the shadows were falling on the curtains by the window, everything seemed alive. And I realized that what I wanted all along was not the Christian religion, but was God Almighty."[98]

Instead of being hopeless and thinking about suicide every day, Aaron now had hope and thought about quitting the band to become anonymous and serve Jesus.

"Every day, I'd probably think about killing myself fifty times a day. It's all I could think about. I didn't really think I had any purpose," Aaron shared in an interview. "I went to live in the Simple Way, and then I visited the Bruderhof. I had the most powerful experience I've ever had in my life by such a huge margin that there was never any close second. It was just the knocking off of the donkey and redirection of my life. And ever since then everything became really clear, really simple, in that it all came back to love, that's all any of it was, that's all any of it is to me anymore . . . It was all I felt like I needed, and all I felt like I was called to provide for anybody, in anything I do, it was just the love of Christ. So everything has continued to be fairly simple for me since then."[99]

---

[97] Emmy Arnold, *Torches Together: The story of the Bruderhof Communities – their life, together, sharing all things in common*, (Rifton: Plough Publishing House, 1964, 1971), 130.
[98] Ibid
[99] Haylolz, "Aaron Weiss talks about life," *YouTube*, 10/23/06

Aaron describes the Simple Way as "a house, an organization of people, friends of mine, that live in North Philadelphia and try to follow Jesus by sharing their lives together, sharing their possessions, and serving their neighbors. It's just a handful of people that take the teachings of Jesus more seriously than most groups, and the Spirit of God is strong and clear. A group of people that I'm very grateful for, and I hope to always be united with them in some way."[100]

In 2006, he told *HM Magazine*, "I suppose the God I believe in comes from the Gospel and the teachings of Jesus, and particularly there's a verse in one of the letters written by John that made its way into the Bible that said if anyone loves, he knows God, because God is love, but if you don't love then you don't know God. Even after becoming a Christian and accepting the Christian religion, I didn't feel much of a change in that. Then just shy of three years ago, I had a sort of encounter where I felt like Paul in the Bible when he was knocked off his donkey and blinded, and then all of the sudden everything was different. The only thing that changed was this simple idea of love and this reality of love."[101]

Aaron told Luke Kruse at *Decapolis*, "These experiences were so different than my church experiences, where I wasn't seeing any of that love for each other and sacrifice. Most churches I see don't take that seriously enough."[102]

He expounded more in an interview with *Lambgoat*. "I went to visit this community and saw people who loved each other, and I realized that was all I ever needed. It wasn't to be popular, or to be accepted, or to be successful, or to get married . . . any of the things I tried to do and failed, in some respect. I realized all I've gotta do is love people, and if I find my contentment in serving people, and giving, and loving—then it's not dependent on what people's response is. You know? You don't say, 'She's gotta love

---

[100] Manuel Enrique Garcia, "MewithoutYou Interview – September 29th, 2006," *Driven Far Off*, 10/02/06.
[101] Doug Van Pelt, "mewithoutYou interview," *HM Magazine*, #121, September/October 2006.
[102] Luke Kruse, "mewithoutYou interview," *Decapolis*, 4/27/05.

me back or else I can't be happy,' or 'She's gotta marry me,' or 'We've gotta sell this many records or I can't be happy,' or 'I've gotta have this kind of house or I can't be happy.' It's more like, no, I've gotta love people. And I've gotta love God. And that's always possible."[103]

"I've come to feel the peace which surpasses all understanding, not to say that I've got it locked down, but, boy, I'm happy," he told *Today's Christian Videos* in 2004. "It was fairly recently, a couple of months ago. But something hit me that was the simplicity of the Gospel: Just love the Lord your God with your mind, heart, soul, and strength, and love your neighbor as yourself, and realizing I could do this wherever I am, on the road or at home. If Paul could do this on a deserted island or in a jail cell and still continue to praise God . . ."[104]

He continued, "It's clear as can be. Woe to you who laugh. Blessed are you who weep. The Beatitudes turn everything upside down. You're trying to get ahead of everybody else, you're trying to rule the world with political might or with force or with manipulation or with money and sex or whatever tools people use to try to overcome you or have other people do their bidding. But Jesus taught us to submit, and Paul said why not rather be wronged, why not rather be cheated? That's like Christ. Of course he could have come and said I could have legions of angels at my disposal, you know? He tells Peter, put away your sword. We don't need to win that way, we're gonna lose. 'Woe to you who are well fed, you've already received your comfort.' It's very clear, it's everywhere, it's everywhere, but we ignore that. Then we choose instead—well the American church will pick don't smoke, don't drink, don't curse, don't have sex, then you're a Christian. You know, we have these, like, four things. But never mind the entire message of the cross, the Suffering Servant, and no servant being greater than his master. And if Jesus is our master, we see ourselves as greater than him. Well, we go in palaces, myself, too. I have a house, and I have a bus I ride around in. I eat better than

---

[103] Drew Ailes, "mewithoutYou interview," *Lambgoat*, 1/14/07.
[104] Eternal Rock, "Mewithoutyou interview from 2004," *YouTube*, 7/16/07.

Jesus did, and I'm more comfortable than he was. Foxes have holes, and birds of the air have nests, and I got a nice house, and Jesus had no place to rest his head, so I'm wondering, when are we gonna really be serious about this? Jesus said this is how the world will know you are my disciples, that you love one another, you know? Because people who love one another would gladly give away their stuff if it means feeding each other, give away their excess, their luxury, if it meant providing for the necessities of life for others, you know? Really, the church in Acts 2 and 4. They sold all they had to give to the poor, houses and land set at the feet of the disciples, and said distribute it as there is need, you know, they said they didn't consider any of their possessions their own but shared everything they had. This, again, completely counter to the American paradigm."[105]

Aaron began reading *Rich Christians in an Age of Hunger* by Ron Sider and became vocal about issues relating to politics, social justice, wealth and poverty, and war and pacifism.

In an interview with *Busted Halo*, he explained further, "Jesus said to love your neighbor as yourself and love God—these are central teachings and central focuses of our life as Christians—not a belief in a doctrine of Christianity or an acceptance of a religious form but a life lived of love. And that's going to play out as community. If you have a problem, and I love you, that's my problem. If you have a joy, and I love you, that's going to bring me joy. And we share it. We share everything. We share our struggles and our triumphs and our money and possessions. We share our faith and our hopes and our fears and struggle together and try to help other people around us who maybe don't agree with us or have anything to offer us in return. Just living a life of service—that's what I got out of the communal life that I tasted there. It's just a simple life of love that I believe everyone is called to. It's going to look different ways, but for me that was the realization that Jesus didn't call me to a belief more abundant or a doctrine more precise. He called me to a life more abundant. He called me to a life where there's fruit that you can taste and see and touch

---

[105] Ibid

and smell and feel—tangible reality. 'The kingdom come on Earth as it is in Heaven.' That was something where I'd read the words before, but it had never penetrated my heart before that the Gospel has social implications and an immediate relevance. That was tremendously liberating from this obsession with the purely spiritualized version of Christianity. When it talks about setting free the captives, that's spiritual. When it talks about 'blessed are the hungry and the poor,' that's spiritual. Spiritually hungry and spiritually poor—that's in there. But so is the tangible stuff. People need food and they need shelter and they need freedom, both economically and politically."[106]

Aaron was asked if he found this transition difficult.

"I wouldn't say so, because it's so bankrupt, the notion of just living for your own desires and pursuing your every whim and trying to ensure financial security. To store up money so that one day you can retire and have 15 years of relaxing until you die—has that worked for anybody? Has that given anybody eternal peace? Has that given anybody that sense of 'I know why I'm here. I know the purpose of my life'? I look around and I see the failed American dream. People that are trying to claw their way to the top of the corporate ladder or some social group, and you realize that there's no real contentment at the top. Whatever little ways that I've tried with the band—like, 'Oh, we need to get on this label'—you end up wanting something else. Then you get on this radio station, and you want something else. You get in this magazine, and then you want something else. You get on this television station, and then what else? What else? What else? It's never enough. Jesus calls us to less and less. He calls us to a simpler and humbler and more broken and emptied out lifestyle of service. To me, the moment that I realized that, it all made sense. It was perfectly clear. Everyone is called to that, and there's room down there for everybody. But there's only room at the top for one person. That would be a sad world, if our only purpose was to be the most successful or the world champion or the richest man

---

[106] Matt Fink, "Busted: me without You. Busted Halo talks conversion, pride, and holistic faith with the leader of indie rock's would-be revolutionaries," *Busted Halo*, 4/27/07.

alive."[107]

Aaron began to think about where our food, clothing, and other goods came from, wondering who was oppressed in producing these goods. He didn't want to be complicit in the "rich oppressors" who take advantage of others for profit, whether from sweatshop labor or underpaid farmers.

"For example, if someone is throwing out a bunch of tomatoes that are bruised or about to expire, I feel like if I go and pick those up out of a dumpster and cook those, I'm still benefiting from that in some way, but I'm not supporting a system that I feel is oppressing people. It's kind of a temporary fix."[108]

Aaron wanted to "bring into reality that possible Kingdom that we talk about, where no one would go hungry while somebody else has extra, where no one person would have two coats where someone else doesn't have any. You see the Scriptures are calling for that redistribution. If you've got two coats, give one away. If you have extra, supply for those in need. Everybody shares everything in common. Everyone's needs are met, but not through selfishness, but through sharing and community. For me, it's just a more beautiful way to live, and it has given me so much peace. There's no question in my mind that God gives us those directions not to restrict us or as rules, but because that's the life more abundant. That's the way we're meant to operate, so it's the way we live peacefully."[109]

Aaron was interviewed for Shane Claiborne's *Another World is Possible* film on poverty. "I grew up right here in Philadelphia, but for the first twenty-four years or so of my life, I didn't think a whole lot about a lot of the poverty that I saw. Abandoned factories I would drive by, it sorta became part of the landscape. And I never gave much thought to what exactly caused all the poverty or where all the jobs went or why the factories were closed down. When I came to live in Kensington with the Simple Way October of 2003, I only lived there for three months, but in that short amount of time I went on a reality tour myself. And being

---
[107] Ibid
[108] Ibid
[109] Ibid

able to look at the landscape of the city and hearing some of the causes, it made it a lot more real than, well, in the past I heard about globalization and evils of multinational corporations, and these were just words to me at the time. When I came and saw the effects of some of these ideas in reality, it was very powerful and it made me rethink a lot of things. It was kinda the beginning of a huge transformation in my life that's still going on. The first thing I thought was I gotta get my friends over here to show them some of this, to work through some of this together. I still don't understand all of the depths of the problem or what causes the sort of poverty that I see, but my relatively simple and naïve understanding of it is that it's greed: greed for power or for more profit and a lack of respect and care for human life and a lack of compassion. To recognize the part I played in that and to try to see that the evil in the world is not something outside that I can look to and say, well, it's this government or this religion or this corporation or this group of people. But to say, well, where is the greed that I have in my heart, where's the lack of compassion that I have, where's my indifference, my selfishness? I'm trying to correct myself. And then maybe if I can change and start to live better, somebody will see that and want to live better. And that's how I hope to teach people, not necessarily pointing at them and saying this is why you're wrong and everything else is wrong, but it's to try to do better myself, you know?"[110]

Aaron's radical transformation—his newfound beliefs, values, and practices—would take place in his lyrics, interviews, speaking engagements, and among his friends, family, and bandmates. But not everyone would appreciate his spiritual trajectory.

---

[110] Shane Claiborne, "Another World is Possible: Vol 2 – Poverty," *Jamie Moffett Media Design & Production*, 2005.

17
Metro 2004

In February of 2004, the Tooth & Nail Tour brought mewithoutYou to Metro in Chicago with Anberlin, Watashi Wa, Emery, and Ace Troubleshooter. MewithoutYou took the stage wearing winter coats and included in their set five new songs from their upcoming sophomore release *Catch for Us the Foxes*. Aaron was overwhelmed playing the venue where the Smashing Pumpkins got their start and joked that our sports teams were almost as good as the ones in Philadelphia.

From the balcony, I watched the band spin, twirl, and throw themselves around the stage in high energy. When not running into bandmates, Aaron was curled up on the floor, rocking back and forth by Rickie's floor tom. Rickie's drumming was sharp and heavy, thundering through the floors, rattling the bar upstairs, vibrating straight through my chest.

This was not the corner of an old bowling alley. I was seeing mewithoutYou on a large stage in an iconic venue, playing through a professional sound system. That night, I heard them at their best and eagerly anticipated their new album.

18
Dark Night

I wrote Natalie in January and told her I missed her, hoping we could somehow reconnect. We went out for coffee, and she apologized for mistreating me. "I know God wouldn't want me to treat you that way. For some reason, you're still on my mind. Maybe he's just trying to show me the kind of guy I should be looking for."

Still, every time we made plans and got together, it was strained. "Now this is just coffee, it's not a date," she would remind me.

There was always pain in her eyes, and it seemed she was always crying. Anytime she entered a room, I couldn't pay attention to anything else. Friends saw my discomfort around her and advised me to avoid her and go to church elsewhere, even to leave the state for a while. But I wanted to stay where God called me.

In June, Natalie told me she didn't need guy friends in her life, and that we weren't really friends anyway, so she didn't want me to call her and see how she was doing, and when I saw her at church, she wanted our interaction to be little more than the social politeness of "hello" and "goodbye." We had been getting along since January, so this was a shock to me.

I set up a meeting with Natalie, the pastor, and a member of the leadership team to try to find out why she was so uncomfortable with me and put her at ease. The meeting was a total disaster. I took their advice and decided to leave the ministry and move to another state.

"You are in a dark night of the soul period," a friend suggested. She recommended that I read Catholic mystics like St. John of the Cross, Teresa of Avila, and Madame Guyon.

In this dark night of the soul—or desert period—God arrives in your life in an overwhelmingly supernatural way. You hear his voice, sense his presence, and feel the nurture, hope, and comfort of being close to him. It seems prayers are answered and blessings come easily. God gives you a calling and makes promises to you about great things happening in your future.

Then suddenly, he turns the lights out. You can no longer sense his presence or hear his voice, worship feels empty, and prayers bounce off the ceiling. You feel absolutely forsaken. Whatever God promised, you have to let go as the opposite occurs in your life.

Tragedy and sickness, betrayal and hardship, testing and purifying, and dying to all sense of self result from this period of suffering, which could last a decade or more. If I endured and let God complete this work in me, he could trust me with the destiny he had planned for me. I would sense his presence in my life like never before and see his promises to me fulfilled. Nothing in the world could shake my faith after that.

The more I suffered and felt that I was losing my faith, the more I was supposed to get excited about what God was doing. "God doesn't do this with nominal Christians. There's a big calling on your life," someone at church suggested.

Others prayed over me and prophesied messages from God about the grand calling he had for me that involved traveling, speaking to youth, seeing the supernatural, and that he would heal me completely of my illness. By all accounts, Natalie was supposed to be my partner in this calling and our marriage used for higher purposes. In letting her go and letting that promise die, I was told God could then "resurrect" the promise in his time and in his way.

I had been talking regularly with Arthur since Living Sacrifice ended. He suggested moving in with him and working on the music project I hoped to start before I met Natalie. With nothing left for me in Chicago, I took Arthur up on his offer and made plans to put the year behind me and move in with him the first week of July.

I asked Natalie if she'd like to meet me for a final dinner to make sure we parted on good terms. Though we weren't speaking, she was happy to.

"I'm sorry for any awkwardness or discomfort I put you

through in all of this. I really believed God brought us together and had a plan for us. I just wanted to see God's will for our lives come about," I said as we sat in a booth at J C Georges.

"I didn't mean to be so rude to you, but I felt that I had to be stern. I just didn't want to do something I never felt completely comfortable doing," she responded.

"Tony is out of my life and my relationship with God has never been stronger, so you have no need to worry about me anymore."

We made our way to the parking lot after dinner. "The only reason I stayed in Chicago was because of you. I love you so much," I said, hugging her goodbye.

"Maybe when you come back, this will all be behind us and we can be friends," she said.

"No, I'm not ever coming back." I was certain.

"Oh, you'll be back," she teased in her trademark sultry voice before getting in her car and driving away.

The first week of July, I packed my car and headed for Van Buren, Arkansas.

19
Van Buren

The night I arrived in Van Buren, Arthur said he was eager to start writing and practicing a few times a week. But before I could even get unpacked, Zao released their Ferret debut, *The Funeral of God*, which like the vision for my project, was a concept album.

"Arthur, they stole my idea!" I said, remembering that I had given their drummer Jesse a flyer with my poem on it after filming Zao's set at Cornerstone the previous year.

When I calmed down, I reasoned that I had no patent on the concept, and my band never got off the ground anyway. I had no real evidence Zao used the idea from my flyer. Either way, we would be accused of copying them, so I had to scrap the project and had no other ideas.

"Well, get settled in and we'll come up with something else. There's no rush," Arthur suggested. Besides, he was preoccupied with the divorce, spending time with his son, and seeing a girl he'd met.

Josh Scogin left Norma Jean in the summer of 2002 and was coming to Fort Smith with a project he had in the works called The Chariot. They were playing a venue called The Gate, run by Bradley Hathaway, whom I recognized as a roadie in Living Sacrifice from their *Processed* home video.

Upon meeting Bradley, I connected with him instantly. He announced before the show that night that he was closing down The Gate because his spoken word poetry performances were taking off. He'd just been asked to go on tour with mewithoutYou and Blindside.

He asked me if I wanted to take over The Gate and keep running shows in town. All he requested was that I change the name of the venue. Arthur and I agreed to do that. We would paint, renovate, and open a shop on one side of the building to sell T-shirts and accessories, and we'd have shows on the other side. The final day of The Gate was an all-day festival of bands, but the fire department came to shut it down for fire code violations.

When Bradley gave me the number to the property owner to work out rent and other details, she apologized. "I didn't know he was having bands play there. That building isn't zoned for concerts and will never pass inspections, I'm sorry."

With the band on hold and The Gate falling through, I had no idea what I was doing in Van Buren.

After getting my new apartment set up two weeks after I arrived, I spent a day praying and once again, after a long dry spell, God spoke. He told me he didn't want me to start a band, but that he brought me to Arkansas to protect me because the ministry back home was about to endure a painful collapse and a lot of people would be hurt. He warned me that when it happened, Jackie would call and ask me to come back, offering me a youth pastor position and an apartment again. I was to say no. He did say, however, that he would bring me back to Natalie at the right time to marry her, so my stay in Arkansas would be temporary. I was to use my time there as a time of healing.

The next month, I got a phone call. It was Jackie, offering me an apartment and asking me to come back and pastor because there had been a split, and the pastor she hired had resigned. Having guidance from God, I said no.

I wrote to Natalie's mom, asking how Natalie was doing. She said she was really hurt by the split and didn't quite know who to trust because she was close to both parties. I sent Natalie a video tour of my new town and a message I hoped would encourage her.

She called to say thank you, and we had a great talk. She even asked to visit and bring one of her friends. "My eyes have really been open to some things lately," she said.

The same day Natalie called, my friend Lauren called from California and said she had been praying for us. "God told me Natalie's eyes are open now and you're gonna be a very happy man this winter."

In September, I woke up one morning and heard God say, "I'm healing you for what I'm calling you to do." Over the next few weeks, the many symptoms of chronic fatigue and fibromyalgia that had crippled me for more than a decade began to dissipate until I found myself completely healthy by October.

I didn't know what God was calling me to do, but one afternoon I felt a burden to pray that was so heavy I couldn't do anything else. As I prayed and listened, God said, "Sell everything you own, move back home, buy a ring, and propose to Natalie. I promise you she'll say yes."

Natalie didn't visit after all, but we were on good terms now. I had a dream that I went home to propose to her and Tony was back. I woke up crying, but God comforted me. "Trust me when I tell you he's gone and she's ready for you. Don't worry."

I asked Natalie's mom for a ring size so I could follow through, but she said I was premature on the ring and should wait until I spent some time with Natalie first. If she said it was okay, then she'd give me a ring size.

I took a deep breath, sold all of my furniture and appliances, took only what fit in my car, and drove home to Chicago that October with $800 in my pocket and a promise from God, excited to see what was about to unfold in our lives.

"What are you going to do if you sell everything you own and propose to her and she says no, then you find yourself homeless and have to start all over?" my friend Brandon asked.

"I won't regret it. She could always look back and see that someone loved her enough to do this, and I could look back and say I trusted and obeyed God."

My dark night was about to be over, and every time I looked at Natalie's face, I would no longer see pain but be reminded that God exists and is good to us, and we could give that hope to others.

20
Proposal

My mom and her husband moved to Galena, Illinois, so the flat that I grew up in upstairs from my grandmother and uncle was open. I was allowed to stay there until after Christmas. Almost instantly, I found a job at a Christian bookstore. I worked and saved more money for the ring and to get an apartment after Christmas.

I called Natalie and left a voicemail, saying I was in town for a week if she'd like to get a bite to eat. I didn't want to scare her off by telling her I moved back. Two weeks went by and she hadn't called back, but I wasn't going to push. Lauren—the girl who called from California to tell me I'd be a very happy man this winter—said she would pray about this to find insight from God.

As Thanksgiving approached, I started to worry that this was all in my head and that God hadn't really spoken to me. I was about to be embarrassed in front of my whole family. Still, daily, I ran my hands over my body and marveled that I had no pain or fatigue and that my mind was sharp. I couldn't explain this other than God healing me, just as he said.

I spent the day in prayer and listened for God's voice. "Natalie will call you in December and invite you to her parents' house for Christmas where you will get a ring size, and she will accept your proposal. She'll help you look for an apartment again, and when the time is right, you'll marry and she'll live there with you. I'll give you the next step after that. Things are about to move fast, be excited!"

But I wasn't. I was terrified that when this fell apart, I would lose my faith. "Just so I know this isn't my imagination, can you confirm what you just said to me through Lauren? I'm so scared this isn't you and the rug is going to be pulled from beneath me."

"Son, I would never do that to you. I'm your Father and I love you," God assured me.

Mentors noted that I never referred to God in endearing

terms, encouraging me to learn that he is my Father, that his love for me is deep, and that he cares about the details of my life. God never called me "son" before, so the feeling of God's love, protection, and guidance in this moment was significant. I needed to trust him.

I fell asleep on the floor crying with my journal and cell phone next to me. My phone rang, waking me an hour later. It was Lauren. Without even saying hello, she started, "God said don't worry, she'll call you."

"I was praying and just heard God tell me Natalie would call me in December and not to worry. I asked him to confirm that through you so I knew it wasn't me talking to myself. Did you just hear this from God, too?"

"No, he told me last week, but said to hang onto it until the right time. He said to call you now."

This couldn't be coincidence.

With my hope renewed, I was overjoyed. I recorded everything that was happening so I could write a book about the amazing way God had brought Natalie and me together and give it away at our wedding.

But before the night ended, God had one last thing to say. "You're gonna see something you're not gonna like. Remember to keep your eyes on my promise and not on your circumstances."[111]

"What am I gonna see that I'm not gonna like?" I asked. There was no response.

The next day, Natalie's friend called. "Hey, I heard you were back in town. I told Natalie you were back, but she gets upset whenever I bring you up. She's spending time with Tony again, but they're just friends."

After the initial punch in my chest, I caught my breath, knowing God warned me I'd see something I wouldn't like. But he also encouraged me not to worry. Natalie would say yes to my proposal. I knew they were hooking up again, but Tony or no Tony, I was going to propose.

---

[111] When God said he was healing me in Arkansas, he first had me repeat that I would not be moved by what I see, think, or feel, but only by what he tells me. Now he was asking me to put it in practice.

I sent Natalie and her parents Christmas gifts through her friend, but still had not heard from her. My heart sank more and more as Christmas approached. After opening gifts with my family on Christmas Eve, it was clear that she wasn't going to call and invite me to her parents' house for Christmas to get a ring size. I crossed my fingers that maybe she'd call Christmas Day. I got ready for bed and checked my phone near midnight. There was one missed call and a voicemail.

It was Natalie.

Taking a deep breath, I checked the message. She thanked me for the Christmas gifts, but rather than being happy about them, she thought it was inappropriate of me to send them and wanted to send them back. "You know what, just call me."

I dialed Natalie's number. She answered the phone, crying.

"Hey, are you okay?"

"No. God told me not to invite Tony back into my life and I did. We reconnected and have fallen back into old habits, but we're not together. Now I'll have to heal my heart and get over him all over again. I know I don't want to marry him.

"As soon as you called saying you were in town and left that voicemail, I deleted your number. I did nothing to invite you back into my life. I thought all of this finally went away, and here you are infiltrating my life again."

"The last time we spoke, you wanted to visit me in Arkansas, and we were on good terms. What happened between then and now?"

"I just wanted to take a road trip with my friend. My dad told me it might give you the wrong idea and lead you on, so I didn't come.

"You got my mom that framed print for Christmas, and she really likes it. Now she is going to ask me why I'm not spending time with you. I feel like you're going behind my back to get my parents to accept you. My dad doesn't like you one bit. He thinks you're a total manipulator.

"I know why you called, and I'm begging God that it's not you, but I can feel you praying against me. My pastor said you're using charismatic witchcraft on me."

I had no clue what charismatic witchcraft was.[112]

"Natalie, I'm just trying to follow God's guidance in my life. He told me your ex was gone, you were ready for me, and to come home and propose to you."

She was still crying.

"Are you okay? Do you want me to come over?" I asked.

"No, not even a little bit. I don't see a need for us to be friends given what you believe about us."

"Well, you know, I came home to put a ring on your finger." I tried sheepishly one more time, my proposal having been rejected preemptively.

"Yeah, you already said that." She was cold. "Who knows, maybe God will cross our paths again one day. But I have a headache now. I should go."

I told her it was good to hear her voice again.

I didn't want to hang up, knowing it meant the end of my faith. I took the silver flip phone from my ear and held it in front of me to close it, but realized I wasn't looking at my hand. Like everything else in the room, it was a foreign object that moved on its own. I couldn't feel my own weight, and terrifyingly, couldn't locate myself in my body. I had turned into a ghost and disconnected from everything around me.

I wrote Natalie a note of apology, saying I was wrong about everything and obviously not hearing from God. I encouraged her to move on and date and marry whomever she wanted, assuring her I was not praying against her or using witchcraft on her.

In the meantime, I had to figure out how I would bounce back and save my faith, if there was anything to be salvaged. I felt like I had been dropped off a cliff and left for dead.

Natalie called a few days later and left a voicemail, letting me know that she got my letter and didn't want to hurt God or me or ruin our lives. She would fast and pray for a couple of weeks and

---

[112] In Pentecostal circles, charismatic witchcraft happens when a person spiritually manipulates, intimidates, or controls someone in the spirit realm so they feel an almost irresistible compulsion to do something they don't really want to do. In this case, Natalie felt drawn and connected to me though she didn't want to be, as if a spell was on her.

get back to me, but I wasn't to contact her in the meantime.

When I didn't hear from her after two weeks, I wrote her a forty-page book detailing everything that had happened in my life concerning her—every sign, my healing, everything God had spoken, the messages others gave to me from God, and all that had convinced me to a certainty that God wanted us to marry. It was the book I had hoped to write when we married. Perhaps this would give her some understanding of my motivations.

Natalie received the book in the mail and was upset by it. She finally invited me over to tell me she still didn't have any clarity from God after praying about us.

"I understand why you thought God wanted us to be together, but I let Tony read your book and he thought you fell in love with me just like he did and it has nothing to do with God. He wanted to burn the book with me, but I said no because your heart was in it. Tony and I are having the most delightfully lustful relationship. I don't mean to hurt you, but I can never imagine having sex with you."

I asked her if she was positive about this, because once I've grieved and emptied her out of my heart, there was no way I could ever open to this again. She was sure, adding, "I'm doing everything I can to make this irreparable."

She reiterated that she couldn't see us being friends, so this was goodbye again.

I respected her wishes, and like before, asked if she wanted to have a final lunch with me and part on good terms. We ate at the Italian restaurant by the tracks near her apartment. All I remember is the pain in her eyes and the frown on her face while I sat numb, chewing on garlic bread, still unable to believe she was rejecting me.[113]

I went home and wrote furiously over the next couple of weeks, emptying into three books everything I ever wanted to say

---

[113] Natalie was always smiling and had a bubbly personality, but there was always pain in her eyes. Some of Aaron's lyrics reminded me of her: *She put on happiness like a loose dress over pain I'll never know* in "Silencer" and *she wore that phony smile on her face, I guess like a bandage on a wounded place* in "My Exit, Unfair!"

to Natalie to get her completely out of my system. I added a card with my picture in it, asking her to remember me. I left everything in a box with her roommate. With that, she was now out of my life.

Feeling lost, I woke up and prayed. "Lord, you've been speaking to me and guiding me for two years and I've been in the center of your will, doing everything you said. Now I feel completely lost and without a map. You promised me Natalie would say yes. What went wrong? How could she say no? You said she was ready and that her ex was out of the picture. You told me not to worry. You promised me that the rug wouldn't get pulled this way. You confirmed it. Do I get an apartment now with this ring money? Do I go back to Arkansas? Do I wait longer for Natalie? I need you to speak again and put me back on the map, because now I doubt you exist at all."

I went to work that afternoon and a customer followed me in, grabbed three books, and came to the counter immediately.

"Hey, Ravi Zacharias. He's one on my favorite authors," I said.

"Brother," he slapped the top of the books. "Sometimes we need to stay on the plan God gives us."

"Oh wow, I just had to let go of a plan God gave me," I said, and told him of my proposal turned bad.

As we talked, it was revealed that this man attended church with Natalie and knew who she was. He got excited and clapped his hand.

"Brother, I don't know if you know this, but I'm prophetic. I have given Natalie words from God before, and she always balks. I came in here this morning and picked out these books, and God told me to put them back and buy them later. I went down to Old Country Buffet and ate with my friends, but after they left, God told me just to sit and wait. Finally he told me to go back and buy these books. Now I know why he had me wait. I want to encourage you, brother. You did not miss God, you did not miss God, you did not miss God. Natalie is rebelling against God and spiting him, sabotaging this on purpose."

He went on to tell me that I needed to keep waiting for her, that God had a plan for our marriage, and it was for the kingdom of God. I needed to follow my calling until he dealt with her and she was finally ready.

"The only plan I had from God was to propose to her, and after we married, he would give us the next step. I have no idea what the next step is."

He said he saw us on a platform in front of a multitude of youth and that we were set apart for God's kingdom. Our calling depended on our partnership.

I tried to walk away from Natalie several times, and every time, someone came along and gave me a word from God not to. I couldn't get out of this, and Natalie wouldn't let me in. I felt trapped in hell.

After work, I told Natalie's mom about this guy I'd never seen before coming into the bookstore and saying God sent him there to encourage me to wait for Natalie. "I don't know what to say," she responded, "but I think you'd better move on and find someone who loves you and treats you well."

A pastor friend who went through this situation with me from the beginning advised that I avoid "parking lot prophets" like this. He thought this guy was more likely to be from Satan to put me back on a painful path with Natalie.

"I thought it was Satan all along," his wife said. "Natalie had not once come out of the world and let go of her sinful lifestyle. All she did was hurt you these past two years and your faith has been shipwrecked. We can't remember the last time you were happy. You've just been obsessed with her. We look at the fruit of this and there is no peace, no life, you're both constantly hurting, and your relationships with God are strained. I don't see how any of this could possibly be from God."

When I asked Natalie about this prophet during our final conversation at her apartment, she said he was a troublemaker in her church and should be ignored; that he had gotten reprimanded for giving prophecy to congregants while the pastor was not present to oversee it.

I wondered what kind of Twilight Zone I had fallen into where it seemed friends and strangers alike had messages from God for me, seemingly confirmed by uncanny coincidences, but these messages led me either into frustration or off of a cliff. In the end, nothing worked out. We couldn't even tell what was from God or what was from Satan.

"No more!" I begged God. "No more intuitions. No more inner dialogue. No more prophets or dreams or visions. No more of this 'guidance' or these coincidences. I'm losing my sanity."

And just like that, it all stopped.

Now spring, I was more hollow and lost than ever. I fell into a nervous breakdown and couldn't function at work. God remained silent and nowhere to be found. The world became a terrifying and overwhelming place to be alive. I felt myself descending into despair, not wanting to live anymore, and I could do nothing to stop it.

I felt victimized by a cosmic joke, wondering who was behind the scenes molesting and destroying my life from the inside out. It felt as if there was a conspiracy to attack and destroy me from the spirit realm. But why? This was all so absurd I couldn't believe it was really happening, even while it happened.

I started to agree with the existentialists: life is absurd and full of struggle.

"You better cut it out or you're gonna miss the rapture," an elderly woman at church warned me. "You don't believe in Jesus anymore?"

"I'm an existentialist these days," I said.

"What's an existentialist?"

"It's the belief that life is ultimately absurd and meaningless, so you have to create your own purpose to get through a miserable existence. It's the feeling of being cosmically alienated, orphaned, and alone in the world."

"Well no wonder you don't have any friends." She scowled.

Somehow in that exchange she added that Sean Connery could put his slippers under her bed any day. Unlike me, at least she had something to live for.

21
Catch for Us the Foxes

As I moved home to Chicago to propose to Natalie in October of 2004, mewithoutYou released their sophomore album, *Catch for Us the Foxes*.

Musically, *Catch for Us the Foxes* was a deliberate maturation from *[A→B] Life*. "I think we did some exploration on the current record, and it turned out better than any of us could have hoped," Mike said.[114]

Mike spoke of the difficulties of recording the album. "I think we were all left feeling a bit drab about the response that *[A→B] Life* got on many different levels, and we wanted to really calculate our way into writing our masterpiece (I don't now, nor did I ever believe that it was a masterpiece). The result was painstaking sessions with each other, writing and writing and analyzing and arguing and arguing and analyzing. It took us a few months to write two songs, maybe longer. On top of that, Aaron was on the verge of giving up altogether. I think that maybe if it wasn't for Brad Wood, he would have quit right in the middle of recording vocals. That was a very intense time for everyone involved. I think the difficulty in really doing a band full-time is grossly underestimated by many. It's definitely my dream come true, but it hasn't been without its seemingly impossible moments."[115]

Though Aaron wasn't pleased initially with his vocal performance on the album, Mike thought Aaron's style made the band unique. "My brother's vocals set us apart, he's got a very unique style all to his own. I'll listen to a generic instrumental version of one of our songs, but when his vocals come into the equation, they set us apart from anything else. They're so vivid, all

---

[114] Jeremy Ritch , "An Interview with Mewithoutyou," *Buzzgrinder*, 2/03/05.
[115] "MewithoutYou plays Trocadero for record release show," *Examiner*, 5/16/09.

of our originality stems right from there."[116]

On mewithoutYou's musical evolution, Aaron recalls, "Fortunately, I like it better. It's not too different. Rather than starting off with a guitar riff, a lot of the songs would start with the drums or the bass and it would form the foundation of the song, and the guitars would kind of be layered on top of it. Some of the songs have a lot stronger rhythm section. The record is more experimental. Dancier beats and some British pop sounding stuff. I think it might turn some people off. I don't know. Some people won't think we're as heavy as we used to be or that this record is more diverse. Maybe some people will like it better. There are still some songs that are just as heavy as the older stuff that we've done, but on some of it there's more singing and more melody."[117]

He continued, "The way it was structured around the drum and bass coming together first was sort of an intentional change because when we wrote the majority of the songs on the last record, we didn't have our bass player, Daniel. We were a four piece with no bass player. I was playing bass, but I didn't want to be because I'm not a bass player. My brother, Mike, who plays guitar in the band, wrote most of the bass lines on the first record. We tried out a bunch of guys before Dan, but it never seemed to work out. As soon as Dan joined, we all knew immediately that he was the guy that we were looking for. The last record was almost entirely put together by my brother. He would come with a guitar riff a lot of the time. He would write Chris' guitar. He would sometimes even tell Ricky what to play. It was more of a collaboration, but it was more Mike than anyone else. With this record, we all pulled our own weight. Ricky and Dan collaborated together on the drum and bass. Chris did his thing and Mike did his thing. Understandably, it turned out more colorful than the last one that was mainly one guy's idea."[118]

Lyrically, Aaron moved away from the pain, anger, and

---
[116] Meghan Groth, "Bellowed Blessings and Drastic Dynamics: mewithoutYou headlines the Radio Takeover Tour in Buffalo," *The Spectrum*, 11/15/04.
[117] Kevin, "Aaron Weiss Interview," *Acclaimed Punk*, 2004.
[118] Ibid

sadness of the first album, along with his relationship problems, and focused more on God and the hope he now had. "When you can confess to people without being judged and vice versa and say, 'God have mercy on us,' it's really good. That is where I have been relieved of all the pain I sing about. I still sing about it because people can relate, but I don't hurt anymore."[119]

Aaron told *Decapolis* that girl troubles occupied a lot of his time and that it's sometimes challenging to deal with memories from the stage, but at other times he felt no connection to his lyrics and was just putting on a show. "I should hope that singing to God doesn't get old. Sometimes it is a challenge to pay attention to every word I say and really make it a prayer, not just go up there and dance around."[120]

Writing lyrics for this album was also a challenge. "It was kind of a stressful time for me. We had about a month and a half before the recording and very little written, so we decided not to play any shows and stay home and write like it was a full time job. The guys got a lot of their writing done during that period, but I didn't come up with too much, so by the time we went out to actually record the album, there was still a lot unfinished on my end. While they were tracking their instruments or going out at night hanging around the city, I was pretty much set up alone in my room trying to finish the words. For a while I didn't think I was going to get it done, and the other guys didn't think that I would either. They were kind of stressed out because I hadn't shown them any of what I've been doing. I wanted to wait till I was finished, but there we were at the studio and I wasn't finished. My procrastination kind of made us all a little on edge, but it all worked out."[121]

Looking back on these first two releases a decade later, Aaron said, "I have a soft spot for the older ones too like *Catch for Us the Foxes* where I can look at a darker time of my life where I was completely depressed and hopeless, and another half of the songs were written with incredible hope. I was pretty much close to a

---

[119] Jeremy Ritch, "An Interview with Mewithoutyou," *Buzzgrinder*, 2/03/05.
[120] Luke Kruse, "mewithoutYou interview," *Decapolis*, 4/27/05.
[121] Kevin, "Aaron Weiss Interview," *Acclaimed Punk*, 2004.

mental breakdown during it where I called my mom, crying, saying, 'I can't do this, mom, this is horrible.' The first one, I can only look back and say it took ten days and we did it. It's raw and got us on the road and to where we are now. I don't begrudge it, regret it, or listen to it either." Of the first album, Aaron added, "It was a fairly crude time of songwriting in terms of drop D power chords which, musically, is something we are not terribly proud of . . ."[122]

Still looking back, he reflected, "I could say I wish I wasn't so hung up on this girl, or I wish I wasn't so self-absorbed where I would be so overly dramatic about my problems, or I wish I wasn't so vain and arrogant about trying to come across in a certain way to impress someone, but at the same time, I was 22/23. I wish I wasn't so hung up on spiritual beliefs and on my ideas. I wish I wasn't so trusting in my own conceptions, but it seems valuable to experience that mode of thinking and being."[123]

At the end of 2004, Dan announced his departure from the band on the mewithoutYou's website: "I have come to a point in my life that I feel that I have done all that I possibly can with mewithoutYou, and I am ready to move on to pursue another adventure. I was with the band for over three years and I'm so thankful for all the opportunities and blessings that were given to me during this time period."

"I think Dan was thinking it was time to move on to something else, I mean what can ya say? It's cool; he gave us three years and brought so much to the band," Aaron said. "He was just so talented and so good. He wasn't even a bass player when he joined—he was a guitarist and played piano and just picked up the bass and got his own thing and we all appreciate it. I mean seriously, not in a 'Here's your gold watch retirement' kind of way. He is just a talented dude and a good friend and I feel not having him in the band anymore is cool because we can still relate as friends."[124]

---

[122] Jon Ableson, "Ten Years On: mewithoutYou - [A→B] Life," *Alter the Press*, 7/9/12.
[123] Ibid
[124] Jeremy Ritch , "An Interview with Mewithoutyou," *Buzzgrinder*, 2/03/05.

Replacing Dan was their old friend and bandmate in the Operation, Greg Jehanian. "Those are big shoes to fill," Greg said. "I'm excited to see where it goes. The chemistry is definitely there."[125]

"Greg's really laid back. Super fun guy to have around. Friendly," Aaron said. "But at the same time he doesn't have the same work ethic that our old bass player did. Dan, I think, was a little harder to work with because he had stronger opinions, but that same intensity made him good to have around because he was very determined to have exactly the right sound, exactly the specific drum part to go along with his bass line. He was very intentional about everything he did. Yeah, just very serious about music. Whereas Greg is very gifted. Music comes very naturally to him. From the time we first started playing in bands together, he was cranking out pop-punk songs and I was the drummer, and he was the singer. Right off the top of his head he can just come up with something good. But at the same time he doesn't know about different pedals or different amps, or doesn't really . . . know too much about getting just the right sound. But he writes good parts. That's the most important. I mean, well, and our friendship, I guess, is the most important thing. We spend so much time together not on stage. We have to all gel. But we all got along with Dan, too, so in that respect we're all friends."[126]

When Rickie was asked how it was working out with Greg, he said, "It's taken a little while to get used to him. Dan had a really defined sound, and it's been kind of hard to capture that because Dan was like a pedal god. We've kind of had to replicate his setup, but things are going well."[127] After touring together, the band decided to make Greg a full-time member of mewithoutYou.

Focused on touring full time, the band "bought a 1985 MCI bus on eBay and converted it to run on used vegetable oil, which all diesel engines can run on so don't believe the lies," Chris told MTV. "But with used vegetable oil you have to go out back at restaurants. You stick a hose in the dumpster—a grease

---

[125] Ibid
[126] Drew Ailes, "mewithoutYou interview," *Lambgoat*, 1/14/07.
[127] Luke Kruse, "mewithoutYou interview," *Decapolis*, 4/27/05.

dumpster—and you pump it out through filters and it's a whole lot of messy work. It's environmentally cleaner, and it's fun, and we save an assload of money."[128]

They gutted the seats and rebuilt the interior, bunks and all. While being able to drive on vegetable oil at fifteen to twenty cents a gallon, the maintenance was never-ending. "We've basically become mechanics first and musicians second," Chris said. "There have been many, many nights where we've been under the bus trying to fix something, and a lot of times, it's been like, 'Ok, time to play.' So you just wipe the grease off your hands and pick up your guitar."[129]

"Yeah, it runs on vegetable oil, which we get from restaurants when they're done frying food in it," Aaron explained. "We collect it, and then we filter it and heat it, and we put it through our diesel engine, which is what the diesel engine is built for. Right now, most of them run off petroleum-based diesel, of course, and we know that that's running out. And, also, we hear that there are wars being fought over who has control of oil, and that's another thing that I don't want to be a part of. At present, I don't think there are any wars being fought over waste vegetable oil. But, of course, who knows what's going to happen? But, right now, I think a more sustainable answer is not relying on automobiles as much as we do. If we're a band playing locally, maybe we can ride our bikes and travel around. Maybe we can play acoustically. It doesn't have to look like this, where we go on a full U.S. tour and have big amps and all this merchandise. We're still fitting into this pattern of what bands do, and I'm kind of uncomfortable with that, but at the same time, we're so steeped in that. We came out of that."[130]

When this bus finally broke down, they replaced it in 2007 with another one, which they also gutted, rebuilt, and rigged to

---

[128] MTV Interview, 2005.
[129] James Montgomery, "Mewithoutyou: Not Your Average Christian, Vegetable-Oil-Fueled, Flower-Flinging Rockers. Philadelphia band's eccentricity has worked in its favor," *MTV News*, 11/21/05.
[130] Matt Fink, "Busted: me without You. Busted Halo talks conversion, pride, and holistic faith with the leader of indie rock's would-be revolutionaries," *Busted Halo*, 4/27/07.

run on vegetable grease.

As mewithoutYou toured, they encouraged fans to bring food for potlucks so they could encourage one another.

"Before the shows we had potlucks where we encouraged friends and fans to bring food and make homemade meals so it's not just like we're the band and you're just the audience," Chris said. "We try to make it something bigger than that."[131]

"With Mewithoutyou the community thing goes further than the band, they are trying to extend that into their friendships and community. Every Wednesday they hold a community meal in which anyone is invited to hangout, eat, and just spend some quality time with each other," wrote Jeremy Ritch.[132]

"I'd much rather talk about this than any band stuff," Aaron told Ritch. "It extends to not just the band or my family but to anyone who is searching or hurting in whatever way. Jesus taught us to love each other as ourselves and to love God above all, and those two things make up the entire message. I think the life of Jesus is a perfect example of doing this. If you want to get along with people, especially those different from you, you must lay down your life, pride, comfort, money, luxury, and desires. So if you are actually going to love someone as you love yourself, it's going to hurt. People are really hurting in the world, so we started coming together. It's been going on about a year now and it is not just a dinner, we are getting together for all kinds of reasons. You should come by, actually anyone reading this should come by, or better yet get together with your own friends and talk about things that are real life. Do you believe in God? Why are people suffering? What can we do about it?"[133]

Once fashionable, Aaron now dressed like a hobo, finding his clothes in dumpsters and thrift stores. He began eating almost exclusively from the trash.

"Actually, Aaron made a conscious effort in trying not to be fashionable. He was caring so much about what he wore and not enough about people in the crowd. So basically, he decided to

---

[131] MTV Interview, 2005.
[132] Jeremy Ritch , "An Interview with Mewithoutyou," *Buzzgrinder*, 2/03/05.
[133] Ibid

become a scumbag. I don't even know if he brought another change of clothes on tour," Rickie shared with *Decapolis*. "Aaron is a very unique individual, borderline homeless."[134]

Rickie explained that Aaron earned the nickname "scavenger" because he ate from dumpsters. Hoping to dispel the "misconception that we're scumbags," he added that he has never been in a dumpster in his life. "I don't understand Aaron. God bless him. I just hope he doesn't get sick."[135]

In the same interview, Aaron shared, "We're never going to be as beautiful as a flower God made. We should be beautiful in the way that Sarah in the Old Testament was, with a quiet spirit. I got tired of trying to look hip and sexy and whatever. I want my beauty to come from a gentle spirit. In our weird little scene we have some influence, and I don't want to put myself up there to be a fashion model."[136]

As Aaron wrestled more and more with living like Jesus and identifying with the poor and the lowly, trying to live up to the Hebrew characters tattooed on his wrists—BLESSED ARE THE POOR IN SPIRIT and FOR THEIRS IS THE KINGDOM OF GOD—it became increasingly difficult for him to stay in the band.

"There's going to come a day where nobody cares about our band, or who we are, or what we've done," he said. "For the most part, today, most people now don't care what we're doing, but there will come a time when nobody cares and our efforts musically won't have come to anything."[137]

Speaking with *HM Magazine*, he said, "Sometimes I think my only responsibility as a Christian musician is to quit being a Christian musician."[138] He questioned whether the band was glorifying God or just a way of glorifying himself.

"I don't know about all this," he told *Kaffeine Buzz*. "I don't know about being in a band, having all of our expensive

---

[134] Luke Kruse, "mewithoutYou interview," *Decapolis*, 4/27/05.
[135] Ibid
[136] Ibid
[137] Kevin, "Aaron Weiss Interview," *Acclaimed Punk*, 2004.
[138] David Allen, "Me Without You," *HM Magazine*, #109, September/October 2004, 35.

equipment, and our big bus, and driving around and having people clap, and say, 'Good job, you guys are doing a good thing,' when I see the early church was getting killed for their faith. I can talk until I'm blue in the face about poverty, but as long as I'm still living in comfort, you might as well throw away the tape you're recording this with, because I don't live by it. The only reason I mention it is because this is what I'm thinking about, and I see that my life doesn't correspond with my ideas. It's like, 'What now?'"[139]

As Aaron's focus turned towards The Sermon on the Mount and his criticism of conservative evangelical Christianity grew louder, he began ruffling the feathers of the average consumer of Christian music—whether it was denying the inerrancy of the Bible, saying that hell wasn't a literal place of fire for those who refused to accept Jesus, or for criticizing George W. Bush, the Republican Party, and the Iraq War. He took up traditionally leftist causes such as environmentalism, animal rights, the redistribution of wealth, and critiqued capitalism, corporate greed, and typical right wing stances on homosexuality, American exceptionalism, and Islam, all while being clear that his criticisms were based on Christian values, not leftist values. He put no hope in political parties, political philosophies, or economic theories.

"Anyone that makes a living pleasing people, accepting bribes, doing the popular thing, invading countries, murdering, stealing resources, is far from what Jesus would want. Any sort of the rhetoric the Bush administration used to justify the Iraqi war is sickening. Bush using Christianity to justify war is idolatry and nationalism. Committing violence and brutality and theft in the name of Jesus is the worst of anything. If you're a Christian you have to lay that stuff down—love your enemies, turn the other cheek. When faith and power mix together, the results are troubling. When people say, 'When you reject the Republican Party you're rejecting God,' well, that just has to be one of the biggest tricks the Devil has pulled. God is forever, the Republican Party is not. The people who say God is a Republican, well, you've got a very, very strange Christian. He's not a Democrat either, but

---

[139] Sarah Jaffe, "MewithoutYou interview," Kaffeine Buzz, 2/19/04.

he's definitely not a Republican. Jesus did not come to build up a political party. He came to bring Truth. America is just gluttonous, wicked, and frankly probably in line for God's wrath. Christians don't want to hear about that. They want to hear 'God Bless America, go to church on Sunday, and all is well.' We are not fooling God."[140]

Aaron wasn't pulling any punches. In *Rapture Ready! Adventures in the Parallel Universe of Christian Pop Culture*, Aaron told Daniel Radosh, "Jesus never mentioned homosexuality once. How has it become such an issue? Strange. Strange how all the things that Jesus actually did talk about fail to become issues. I really do continually expect Christians to be the most willing to accept pacifism, peacemaking, or redistribution of wealth, and care for the poor, and rethinking our prison systems and all that. But we end up being the most belligerent and hard-hearted and self-righteous and all the rest. Scary."[141]

None of these issues were close to my heart or on my radar. I was heartbroken, alone, and afraid. Desperate for God and for answers, I was trying not to kill myself. Fortunately for me, these were the themes Aaron wrote about in *Catch for Us the Foxes*.

---

[140] Luke Kruse, "mewithoutYou interview," *Decapolis*, 4/27/05.
[141] Daniel Radosh, "Rapture Ready! Adventures in the Parallel Universe of Christian Pop Culture," (Berkely: Soft Skull Press, 2010), 198.

22
Alone to the Alone

Now March of 2005, I saw *Catch for Us the Foxes* at Best Buy and bought it. What I noticed upon playing it in the car on the way home was that the drums were pulled back in the mix, there was far less distortion on the guitars, and Aaron's vocal delivery was not as aggressive as on their debut. The songs were more complex and melodic and less gritty. The polish didn't grab me.

I played it on repeat, sitting in the bathtub with the flu, hoping the album would grow on me. I heard a line about a *whispering in my ear, soft but getting stronger, telling me the only purpose for my being here is to stay a bit longer*. Then, something about a bicycle crashing and coming apart with the back wheel *aimlessly drifting around*. It was such a good description of my life at that moment, I got out of the tub to check the track number. The song was called "Four-Word Letter (Pt. 2)".

Aaron went on in the song to sing about fashion, vanity, doubt, his dad's unimaginable loneliness, and the excuses we make to keep ourselves from coming together and giving ourselves totally to God. He implored the listener, like the old hymn, to join him in going down in the dirt, down by the river to pray. He invites everyone, including his mama, his nana, and his ex-girlfriend Amanda to be *utterly changed into fire. To sacrifice the shadow and the mist of a brief life you never much liked*.

As if pulling the sentiment right from my chest, Aaron ended the song, *We hunger, but though all that we eat brings us little relief, we don't know quite what else to do, we have all our beliefs, but we don't want our beliefs, God of peace, we want you*.

Backing these lines was the guttural cry of Scott Krueger from The Pslaters. Scott said, "'On Four-Word Letter (Pt. 2)' the chant is a cry to God to meet us broken, lonely, friends, family, foes as we go to the river. It is a cry, a prayer, and a proclamation that despite our wandering eyes we really want to want our First Love, our Hope, our Pillar of Fire."

The song moved me so deeply that I sat with the lyric books to both mewithoutYou albums and pored over every line.

Starting with *[A→B] Life*, a picture was painted of a man's obsession with a girl who refused to return his love. She was rude, cold, and indifferent to his affection and advances. In "The Ghost" she says *it's the devil, I suppose. But it doesn't matter much to me.* Her indifference is painted wonderfully with descriptions of him feeling the breath from her nose on his neck as it blows by: *the warmth passed me like her love did.* In "Gentleman," she is silent, arms folded, looking down as he passes by.

As if taking a page from my dynamic with Natalie, the character is rejected, but returns in a long walk home. *I said I'd not come back, but I'm coming back. And you'd better be alone.*

Like my perseverance and waiting for Natalie, Aaron's character in "Nice and Blue" waits *for six years on* and has only just begun. In all of his imploring her to receive his love and surrender to God, being rejected and coming back, he is exasperated in "Silencer," asking God how much longer he has to endure this and how much more he has to pretend to be strong. In "The Ghost" he says he's too strong to surrender, but far too frail to fight.

The character tries to find peace in God, not this woman, and implores her to do the same. In "Be Still Child" he encourages her to stop running, hiding, and being afraid of God. He gives up his illusion that he can find peace and comfort in her, so finds it in God instead. In "Nice and Blue" he tells her he was once the wine and she was the wine glass that held him, but *God became the glass. All things left were emptiness.*

The album ends with "The Cure For Pain." He assures this woman that her surrender to God will only make the softest sound *like sugar pouring into tea. Darling let your Self pour down and dissolve into the Love who revealed himself there quietly to me.* The song ends: *Jesus have mercy on us.*

Moving on to *Catch for Us the Foxes*, "Tie Me Up! Untie Me!" resonated as the character is lost and wandering, looking for God, but he can't find him. *My sweetheart moved away, swept off like garbage in the alleyway—I need more grace than I thought. Brother, I'm far away from everything good!*

He complains that all of this wishing he was dead is getting old. In "Carousels," he wants to jump in front of the passing cars and in his weariness of life tells Jesus he's ready for him to come back.

In "My Exit, Unfair!" Aaron writes: *But until I let you go I didn't know, you were never mine at all. But now I spend my days in ever-increasingly complicated ways, convincing myself of the rightness of each word I say.*

This is exactly where I was, trying to let go of a woman I'd never been on a single date with, yet was absolutely certain we would be married, and now I kept retracing the trail that led me to propose, adamant that I wasn't wrong about this.

In the midst of writing these lyrics, Aaron's transformation and newfound hope emerged. One theme throughout the album was to let go of your individual needs and problems and to be subsumed in something larger than yourself: loving God and others in community. In "Torches Together," Aaron asks why we should be sad, poor, and lonely when we can be torches together. He uses illustrations of wheat being ground into grain, grapes being crushed into wine, and playing chords instead of single notes as examples of unity throughout the album.

At the end of "Tie Me Up, Untie Me" Aaron finally finds God. *And now I haven't even thought about killing myself in almost five months.*

Knowing mewithoutYou would be at Cornerstone, I made it a priority to meet Aaron and ask him how he went from wanting to kill himself to finding God and having hope. I thought if anyone in the world could understand what I was going through, it was him.

23
Emergent

I put in my nine-to-five at the bookstore and paid my rent, but this wasn't why I'd come back to Chicago. Still going through each day in a haze, all I cared about was trying to understand what had happened the past few years and why God seemed so absent. I started giving my hours away to other employees as social anxiety increased and it became difficult to look people in the eyes.

I contrasted my desperation for God with the platitudes, simplicity, and certainty of the "inspirational" Christian products we sold at the bookstore. With my faith hanging by a thread, I wondered if there was a space for me to struggle with all of these doubts and where I wouldn't be led to the same pat answers that didn't resonate.

I went down to the old Borders bookstore I used to work in and thumbed through the books, looking for critiques of Christian pop culture. Almost immediately, *The Christian Culture Survival Guide: The Misadventures of an Outsider on the Inside* by Matthew Paul Turner stood out. The cover featured a boy wearing a JESUS IS MY BOSS trucker cap, surrounded by a *What Would Jesus Drink?* mug, a button that said JESUSAVES with the emphasis on USA, a Jesus fish, and a TV set with a red X over it—because good Baptists don't let their kids watch TV.

This book was published by Relevant. I scanned the shelves for anything else I could find by that publisher. There were books on the spiritual lives of mainstream artists: *Walk On: The Spiritual Journey of U2* by Steve Stockman, *Restless Pilgrim: The Spiritual Journey of Bob Dylan* by Scott M. Marshall, and a collection called *Spiritual Journeys: How Faith Has Influenced 12 Music Icons*.

There were memoirs by Christian musicians, like Andrew Schwab's *It's All Downhill from Here: On the Road with Project 86* and *Simplicity* by Mark Salomon of The Crucified and Stavesacre fame. Later that year, they put out Bradley Hathaway's book, *All the Hits*

So Far But Don't Expect Too Much: Poetry, Prose & Other Sundry Items. A red label adorned the upper right corner of the cover: "As seen on tour with Blindside, mewithoutYou, the Chariot and others."

Everything with the Relevant logo on the spine had a certain style that appealed to me. Their books were mostly memoirs of doubt and struggle in living the Christian life. *Authentic, transparent,* and *spiritual journey* were buzzwords and phrases that kept appearing, this to contrast the suffocation many Christians felt from being unable to express their doubts and struggles in their church environments.

Relevant also had a magazine with the tagline: *God, life, and progressive culture.*[142] Its goal was to keep Christianity fresh and relevant to people in their 20s and 30s, ages when many people leave the church and never return. Relevant also became the primary voice for emerging church authors.

The emerging church was a growing trend among young Christians from all denominations to have a safe space to doubt, question, and explore alternative Christian doctrines and practices. It brought back liturgy, icons, and religious art removed by megachurches. In a backlash to fundamentalist certainty, it distrusted institution, authority, and systematic theology, opting instead for poetry, storytelling, paradox, mystery, and mysticism. These Christians were often politically liberal and had no problem with drinking, smoking, or using profanity. They listened to secular music and watched R-rated movies—often holding their meetings in wine bars—and found themselves welcoming atheists, Buddhists, and others into their fold comfortably without trying to convert them. Instead, they tried to listen to and learn from people of other faiths and worldviews. "Belonging before believing" was a common catchphrase.

The emphasis in these communities was less on what people believed doctrinally—orthodoxy—and more on what they did for others in practice—orthopraxy.

I happened upon a stack of titles by Brian McLaren,

---

[142] It's now: *Faith, Culture, and Intentional Living.*

eventually buying everything with his name on it. The book that got most of the attention and generated a good amount of controversy was *A Generous Orthodoxy: Why I am a missional + evangelical + post/protestant + liberal/conservative + mystical/poetic + biblical + charismatic/contemplative + fundamentalist/Calvinist + Anabaptist/Anglican + Methodist + catholic + green + incarnational + depressed-yet-hopeful + emergent + unfinished Christian.*

Though the emerging church claimed not to have leaders, and it considered itself a "conversation" rather than a movement, McLaren was the most influential writer among the group.

In his ten books or so at the time, McLaren asked readers to consider that perhaps evolution happened and that the Genesis account of creation might not be literal. Maybe Satan isn't a real, invisible, diabolical being, and hell is not an actual place sinners go to burn forever after they die. Perhaps the end times isn't about giving up on the world and waiting for the rapture, but bringing the kingdom of God to earth through social justice, meeting people's practical needs, pacifism, and taking care of the environment. Maybe saying the Bible is God-inspired doesn't mean it is absolutely true and without error. Perhaps there is room for Christians to be liberals and Democrats, or at least not conservatives and Republicans. Perhaps salvation isn't about my individual soul being saved and getting to heaven, but about us making a difference for everyone on earth. Perhaps Jesus didn't die on the cross as a blood sacrifice to appease an angry God. God might, in fact, be with people of other faiths, and maybe just loving everyone without an agenda is better than trying to convert them to Christianity. And maybe we have this all wrong—the idea that Christianity is a system of doctrine and theology we have to prove through apologetics and defend rationally, making converts to this system by some formula or prayer to make them born again. For those struggling to hang on to faith because they couldn't hold their conventional beliefs, McLaren wrote that there was hope in the "perhaps" and even in letting go and saying we simply don't know.

In many of the emerging church books, God is portrayed as wild, untamable, uncontrollable, and impossible to box and define.

He can be found anywhere and everywhere—especially in the music of U2 and in movies like Braveheart, The Matrix, and The Lord of the Rings. He could be found in a brothel, in the gutter, in the eyes of the poor. Begrudgingly, they also admitted that God could be found in the conservative Protestant evangelical tradition they abandoned.

There was no one true Christianity spanning history, but all expressions of it were culturally relative. So what could we emphasize from the past and utilize creatively in the present? What new expression of Christianity could we envision for the future? This dynamic of borrowing from the old to create something new became known as ancient-future faith. A church might use icons and meditation from past traditions and mix that with club-worthy dance worship music.

The emphasis in emerging church writings was on creating a kind of Christianity relevant to postmodern culture—a culture where people no longer believed in truth as established through arguments and evidences, so they focused more on people's personal stories and experiences. The most effective way to communicate in this dynamic was through storytelling: creative nonfiction, biography, and memoir.

Alongside these books lampooning Christian pop culture and expressing these emerging values were popular spiritual memoirs such as *Blue Like Jazz: Nonreligious Thoughts on Christian Spirituality* and *Searching for God Knows What* by Donald Miller, *Girl Meets God* by Lauren Winner, and *Traveling Mercies: Some Thoughts on Faith* by Anne Lamott. These books framed the Christian life through self-depreciating humor, doubt, depression, and the messiness of everyday life.

Still browsing the Christian section at Borders that day, my stack now a dozen deep, I found many others, including *The Myth of Certainty: The Reflective Christian & the Risk of Commitment* by Daniel Taylor. I took my stack up to the café, ordered a latte, and spent hours skimming and taking notes.

The Myth of Certainty said that certainty is impossible not only for Christians, but for people of any belief system. This book was written for reflective, question-asking Christians who felt trapped between two worlds, finding a home neither in secularism nor in anti-intellectual fundamentalism where people were not allowed to ask real questions or search outside of the allowed "safe" sources:

> The reflective Christian not only wants to ask real questions, with a sense that something is at stake, he or she also wants to broaden the range of allowable evidence in this trial of what one can believe and live for. The subculture wants only to allow approved evidence from within its own experience and tradition . . . A reflective Christian wonders why certain writers are to be read and seen, if at all, only with a hostile, defensive, error-sniffing attitude.[143]

One book that caught my eye was a hardcover biography called *Wounded Prophet: A Portrait of Henri J. M. Nouwen* by Michael Ford. The flap on the jacket said Nouwen was a Dutch Roman Catholic priest whose writings were in the caliber of C. S. Lewis and Thomas Merton. For a man with such spiritual influence, he was described as authentic, transparent, and revealing, a man who struggled with doubt, anxiety, insecurity, and loneliness. Given my current descent into despair, I was drawn to stories of similar faith struggles.

Reading spiritual memoirs and biographies inspired me to begin writing my own. It was the perfect medium to explore the events in my life and tell them without having tidy answers, resolution, or redeeming messages to justify them.

Soren Kierkegaard and Fyodor Dostoyevsky were popular among emergent types. Kierkegaard was a nineteenth century Danish thinker and a devout Christian who is thought to be the father of existentialism, which focuses on the individual living authentically. He felt that people who called themselves Christians—merely because they were baptized, believed certain doctrines, or were Christians by birth and culture—were not truly

---

[143] Daniel Taylor, *The Myth of Certainty: The Reflective Christian & the Risk of Commitment*, (Downers Grove: Inter Varsity Press, 1986, 1992), 37.

Christians. People needed to face the reality of despair in their lives, then seek an authentic encounter with God. He exposed the limits of reason and science to present a unified and total truth, positing that Christianity is absurd and cannot be proved with reason and science, putting the emphasis on truth as a life-changing encounter with Jesus, not a system of thought.

Dostoyevsky was a famous Russian novelist whose characters often struggled with belief and doubt and moral responsibility. A Russian Orthodox Christian, he struggled with gambling, affairs, epilepsy, and had quite a difficult life. His *Notes from Underground* is thought to be the first existentialist novel.

I read *The Seven Storey Mountain* by Thomas Merton, a man who became a hermit monk. I began to fantasize leaving the world behind and having nothing but God. Monks and mystics often spoke of ecstatic and blissful encounters with God. I wanted this more than anything else in the world.

In June, I quit my job and moved out of my apartment. I was going to devote all of my time to seeking God, and if it was the case that he didn't exist, I was going to kill myself. I couldn't see spending the rest of my life heartbroken, hopeless, dissociated, and in despair. I had struggled long enough.

Before leaving Arkansas to move home and propose to Natalie, I met Barry and Sarah, a pastor and his wife, who were starting a church called Mt. Olive in Van Buren. I decided to move back there and join them, hoping I would find God somewhere on the journey.

I moved out of my apartment, put in my notice at work, and packed my car with what was left of my belongings.

Now July, Cornerstone was upon me. The only items on my agenda were to find Brian McLaren, who was speaking that year, and Aaron Weiss, to see if they could make sense of my journey, then follow Arthur back to Arkansas after the fest and try to rebuild my life and my faith in Van Buren.

24
Cornerstone 2005

Brian McLaren was giving a lecture in one of the morning seminars at Cornerstone, so I made sure to get there early. Without any regard for proper manners, I approached him as he was setting up at the podium to speak and asked for a moment of his time.

"I heard an interview with D. A. Carson on the radio on the way over. I guess he wrote a book called *Becoming Conversant with the Emergent Church*. He said your views were heretical and unorthodox. I was wondering if you have been in conversation with him."

McLaren said Carson hadn't contacted him and was perplexed that such a brilliant mind would write a book that so blatantly misrepresented him. "I don't recognize my views in what he says I believe."

McLaren opened his message saying he'd just viewed another website calling him a wolf and a dangerous heretic, so whether we were there to get something from his message or there to hunt for heresy, he hoped we'd all find what we came for.

During the question and answer session following his message, I raised my hand and he called upon me. I said, "I was an agnostic for many years, but before that time, I depended heavily on the apologetics of guys like Ravi Zacharias and Norman Geisler, who I am sure you are familiar with." He affirmed that he knew who they were. "Well, I realized the limitation of apologetics and theology and found it impossible to be certain that Christianity is true. As an agnostic, God came to me in a supernatural encounter and through that experience, I began to hear his voice and sense his presence, even being healed of a twelve-year-long disability. I was terribly disillusioned when the guidance I got from God didn't pan out and I could no longer trust these personal encounters. My Christian friends seem to be taking shots in the dark for answers just like me, so I can't trust them either. I cannot trust the Bible, theology, apologetics, experience, encounters, or community to support my faith. What do I base my faith on?"

Brian began his answer, saying the pursuit of propositional truth and certainty through reason, theology, and apologetics is a failed attempt of modernism called foundationalism. The other extreme is to be a relativist and a mystic, depending fully upon subjective mystical experiences and supernatural encounters. "The balance, I believe, is to follow Jesus. Jesus said, 'When you obey me, *then* you will know that what I say is true.' Simply practice the teachings of Jesus and their truth becomes self-evident."

While riding around with Arthur on his golf cart, we saw a homeless looking guy with long hair, a full beard, and tattered clothes. He was digging through the trash cans in the food court, eating what he found. "Is that Aaron Weiss?" Arthur asked. We drove up, and sure enough, it was.

The last time I saw him, he was clean cut and sharply dressed. Now I could hardly recognize him. I was concerned by how he was dressed and disgusted that he was eating food from the trash.

"It's amazing what some people will throw away," Aaron said. He had a Pizza Hut breadstick and some packets of sauce in his hand. A girl approached him and gave him a breadstick someone had left behind on a picnic table nearby. Soon after, he found a half-eaten funnel cake on a paper plate.

Arthur introduced me to Aaron and we shook hands. I didn't know how to begin, so I came right out and told him I was in a bad place. "I've had a hard time finding God after what seemed to be two years of supernatural communication with him. I lost everything trying to follow God's leading. I proposed to a girl and she said no. I just couldn't settle for working in a bookstore and maintaining an apartment, so I quit my job and moved out to devote my time to seeking God. Now I have to decide whether or not to go back to Arkansas with Arthur or stay in Chicago and take my job back. I'm kinda lost and have been suicidal lately."

He listened intently, but his face was bright with hope. "I stayed with this community in Philadelphia for three months called the Simple Way, and it absolutely revolutionized how I see

Christianity," he said. "We are called to come together and love God and others, giving up our own lives and our own problems. I used to want to kill myself ten times a day, but when I looked at the world as a harvest, ripe with people needing love, and learned we are simply called to love others, I've had a hope in my heart that I can't contain ever since."

Not wanting to keep him longer, already embarrassed to have shared as much as I did, I thanked him for his time. "I appreciate you talking with me and for writing those lyrics that resonated so much with me. I thought if anyone could understand where I was, it would be you."

"I appreciate you too," he said, making me feel like I was the only person in the busy food court.

The next day as I was wandering through the merchandise tents, I ran into Aaron again. "Hello, Paul," he said, introducing me to the person he was talking to. I was astounded that he remembered my name.

Before mewithoutYou's midnight set in the Encore tent, they noticed a girl at the fest—Timbre Cierpke—carting a harp around, so they invited her onstage to open their set and accompany some of their songs. They played *Catch for Us the Foxes* straight through to a humid, packed tent, which reeked of sweat and straw and mud, their trademark flower bouquets tied to the microphone stands. Aaron wore a Chinese pointed peasant hat and suspenders, throwing flower stems into the crowd throughout the set as we sang along.

25
Aaron Weiss's Message: Cornerstone 2005

"Me? I'm alright. I've been better. I've been worse. Nice to see you guys here. My name is Aaron. Can you hear me in the back? No? Then how did you know what I asked?"

So began Aaron's message on the final night of the fest as a couple hundred people gathered to watch him speak. He didn't have a sermon or Bible study prepared. He wanted to have an open discussion where people could raise their hands and share their doubts, struggles, testimonies, and topics they wanted to discuss.

Aaron opened his message with the Lord's Prayer. "That's the best I got. In a lot of ways I don't have anything for you. I'm reminded of my inability to help anybody in any way."

Aaron lamented that even more people showed up to see the band the previous night, but there was less time to communicate with everyone. "We're here to play these songs, but I have something to communicate, something in my heart, which is hope. I have hope that I want people to have. I see people who are sad and confused and afraid and I say, 'Man, I wish they can feel this comfort and this hope that I have, but how can I do that? I don't know."

Following up on a discussion he had with fans after mewithoutYou's set the previous night, Aaron wanted to talk about what it meant to be a Christian, because the word meant so many things to different people, and his views were changing all the time.

If there were people present who were confused, full of doubt, or didn't believe in God at all, Aaron said he somewhat wanted to encourage them to stay on that path and to avoid the path of certainty. He told the story from John 9 in which Jesus healed a man who was born blind. The Pharisees investigated it, saying Jesus was a sinner for healing on the Sabbath, so God couldn't have healed the man through Jesus. Jesus said to the

Pharisees, "For judgment I have come into this world, so that the blind will see and those who see will become blind." Some Pharisees asked, "What? Are we blind too?" Jesus answered, "If you were blind, you would not be guilty of sin; but now that you claim you can see, your guilt remains."

In retrospect, Aaron says, the Pharisees were the bad guys, but they were respected religious leaders and teachers who prayed and kept the law, "probably the kind of people that we would consider the best Christians now." Just as they couldn't see God because of their Jewishness, Aaron worried that modern Christians couldn't see Christ because of their Christianity. Somehow God favored the screwballs who didn't have it all worked out, but came to God with a contrite heart over those who looked like they had it all together and had all the answers.

"So I have a particular concern for people at this festival, myself included," Aaron continued, "who mostly would say, 'I'm a Christian,' mostly live in America, mostly have access to or possess an incredible unheard of amount of convenience and luxury and wealth and power, far more than the people of Jesus' day that were rich and powerful, the kind of things that we have access to. So when you read in the Scriptures about the dangers of wealth and Jesus warning those who have and those who are comfortable, and then I look around at a church with all of this, I have to really be concerned, you know, I'm really, really concerned."

Aaron had been thinking for a few years about what it really means to follow Jesus. "I was talking to a fella last night who said, 'You know, I'm sort of an agnostic, I don't know if I trust God,' and I said, 'You know, I am too.' *Agnostic* is just a word. *Christian* is just a word. *America* is just a word, but I use it." There are people who call themselves Christians but don't live it, and people who say they don't know what they believe but live Christianly. He went on to explain that these labels are exterior postures when it is our hearts that matter.

Aaron used to believe that preaching the gospel meant converting people to Christianity. "For a long time, I bought it. 'Okay, that's my purpose, it's to convert people to what I am.' I thought, 'I'm not happy. I don't want people to be like I am. I don't want people to want to kill themselves. I don't want people to feel like they're lying every day when they look at other people or when they go to church or when they read the Bible.' So now, I suppose something has changed in me."

Aaron wanted to convert all of the Christians there by inspiring them to leave behind the religion, organization, bureaucracy, institution, and politics in Christianity, and instead, simply follow Jesus. We could strip down Christianity and try to get back to the law of God written on our hearts, the Holy Spirit in us, and the wisdom and power of God revealed in nature, leaving behind traditions, doctrines, and theologies that "divide and cause factions."

For those who claim they are already there, he warned of the dangers of claiming to see and encouraged the audience to be continually blind. When the blind receive sight, how long before they become the Pharisees and start judging the people who are blind, so God has to make them blind again? Our posture should be "almost like a blind groping, or just reaching up with our hands, or crying out for someone to help . . . saying the One who loves me, whoever you are, the One who is Truth, the One who is Light, the One who brings healing, the One who brings sanity, the One who creates order. You know? And the word *God* is what represents all that, but of course we can say *God*. People have used God to justify a lot of really, really, really nasty things, so I don't believe in the word *God*. I have no faith in the word *God*. I have no faith in the word *Christianity* or in the name—the verbiage—of *Jesus*."

He lamented the abuse of Christianity, like those who use the name of Jesus like rubbing a magic lamp to heal a friend's hemorrhoids or the way televangelists use his name to get a Mercedes or to run a parlor show.

"The blindness wouldn't be like 'there is no truth' or 'there no God,' because atheism is of course its own sort of dogmatic religious tradition, and a fixedness and a sight that claims to have this knowledge that's impossible to have. And we understand truly that God is so much greater than our comprehension. May he bring us all to a sort of blindness where we are in a constant state of wonder."

Aaron explained, "What changed in me was just realizing that Jesus said my purpose was not to convert people to Christianity. My purpose is to love God with all of my heart, my mind, my soul, and my strength, and to love my neighbor as myself. Now that may end up converting people to follow Jesus and love him. In fact, I think it will. But I think we are sorta putting our cart before the horse, you know, if we thought it was our mission to convert people. Because then we'll try all sorts of business tactics and have giant flashy signs and put ads in newspapers and big glass cathedrals and make all kinds of statues and big ways of making Jesus attractive and trying to get people into our building—'Don't go to that building, go to my building,'—and all these forms of craziness to me. They come from a desire to convert people rather than of simply loving them and serving them."

What does it mean to love your neighbor? "Man, you know, you know what your needs are. Maybe we don't. Maybe we don't know what it means to be hungry, or to be thirsty, or to be in prison, or to be alone, or to be mentally ill, or maybe we do. I mean, you guys have been through a lot different stuff than me, but I suppose I want to simply encourage you guys to try to love people, especially those who are in the most need."

Aaron used the illustration that we were individual grapes on a vine that must be crushed to make wine, or individual stalks of wheat that must be crushed and ground into grain to make bread, so that in unity we suffer together. Now together, we love our neighbor as ourselves. "I believe in oneness between Jesus and the Father in a sense, and I believe in oneness between us in a sense, but I don't see it, you know? And so I guess what I'm really longing for is for what we say we believe to become a reality."

Aaron reminded the audience that Jesus said not everyone who calls him Lord will enter into the kingdom of heaven. Those who not only hear, but put his words into practice have built their houses on a strong foundation. Don't be like the Pharisees and call yourself good for obeying, because only God is good. If Jesus said only his Father in heaven is good when he was called a good teacher, how much more should we think of God all the time?

"In your suffering, try to draw close to God. In your pleasure, be careful, because we have more than anybody has ever had. And the Bible always, always, always, always warns the rich. Over 30,000 children are dying every single day of starvation or preventable disease, and we're buying iPods and cell phones. I simply think it's a form of craziness or a real, real, real intense trickery of the mind or hard-heartedness that allows us all to be complicit in this, like, 'Let's just go ahead with it.' We know this is wrong, we all have this feeling like, 'I don't need this. These people need food. I should give them my stuff. But everybody else has got one, so I'm normal.' But Christians should not follow what everybody else is doing. We should be the ones who are following Jesus, that's all, and the world will do what it will. But for us, we'll be recognized as the disciples of Jesus, and not by our T-shirts or the festivals we attend, or the church buildings we visit or the Bibles we read, or any of the other ways in which we identify ourselves as Christians. Not by the language we use . . . Jesus said by our love for each other. So shucks, if we don't have that, if that love isn't a reality, again, I know God is not fooled by the letter. But we were told to live by the spirit, not by the letter . . . "

He clarified that what he was saying was very simple, but because we're so overloaded with philosophy and information, it's hard to just simplify it to saying yes or no to Jesus about giving away possessions, turning the other cheek, not resisting evildoers, and loving our enemies. Instead of changing the teachings of Jesus, just admit they are too difficult to follow. He complained that instead of following Jesus, we look for timbers of the ark or argue about creationism and evolution. Isn't it much more important to ask if Jesus really meant what he said? They weren't suggestions, but commands.

"I see Greg over there oozing, 'It's God's grace, it's God's grace,' so I don't want to become a works man. We don't have to do all these things. We have to love God, and we have to love our neighbor as ourselves."

He continued, "I at least want to come to you as an honest

voice and say, 'We're not doing it.' I'll tell you this much—I'm not doing it. And when I have people say, 'Man, you're really doing it,' I'm like, 'What? How is everyone else living that by comparison I look like I'm taking this seriously?' Because I'm a screwball. I'm not there. I'm not there at all."

"I'm giving, if anything, a message of hope. I know it's simple, but before, I used to want to kill myself. I don't now. So it's very good news for me, because I used to think, 'When am I gonna die, any day now?' And now I think, 'The harvest is plentiful. Look at all of this. Everywhere there's somebody to love. Everywhere there's somebody who's hungry, everywhere there is somebody who's lonely or somebody else wants to die, somebody who just needs a friend, somebody who just needs a hug.' I could live a hundred lifetimes and never fulfill all of the purpose that there is, that God would have me do. We should never be bored and just pop in a movie to kill some time."

Aaron wished he could live up to his message. "I'm struggling. I'm really struggling. So forgive me for even standing up here. It's a very audacious thing for me to sit up here because of how I know things have gone so wrong. And I can only say, boy, I know God has used some really, really, really bad people, so I'm a little bit comforted by that, but still, I am only up here because somebody's gotta say something. Somebody's gotta say this isn't alright. We can't keep doing this because it's not making anybody happy."

At this point, someone named Sam addressed Aaron from the audience. Aaron repeated his comments for the audience. "He says, 'I don't believe in God. I used to be a Christian and believed it firmly but since then have come to believe that we have sort of a ship in a storm, and we take any harbor we can, to grab onto something.' And for him he says that his lack of faith or his belief in no God has helped him, made him feel set free, gave him something to cling to. And I think, yeah, that makes sense. I guess I already said that I kinda view atheism as similar to the dogmatic Christianity of, 'I have my understanding of things and I actively, avowedly, disbelieve in an intelligent designer of all of this.' That's a hard thing to say. I don't know many people that come out and say it because of how small we are."

After speaking of the vastness of the universe and the improbability of life existing without God having created it, he continued, "No, God is probable. I don't ever want to argue with you and say, 'God exists,' because again, I'm more and more convinced that *gah* as it comes out of my throat—like starts with a *guh* and goes into an *ah* and ends with a *duh*—is just that. I'm just saying a word. And the truth behind that word is light. The Bible says, Scripture records this thing: 'God is light.' It also says, 'God is love.' There are some clues into the nature of that power that that syllable represents. Light and love to me are good things, and I want light in my life. Don't hide your sins in darkness, confess them and bring them to light.

"You can say that you're an atheist, but if you want the light to come in, if you want to be set free of all that is untrue and all that is illusory and all that is so temporary, I said we were closer in belief than we might think because of the language we use. I don't know, of course, the state of your heart."

Aaron said the parable of the sheep and the goats in Matthew 25 was an essential portion of Scripture for his conversion experience. In it, Jesus returns to earth and all the nations are gathered to him, then he will separate everyone to the left and the right, the way a shepherd separates the sheep from the goats.

The sheep on the right enter paradise, Jesus says, "'For I was hungry and you gave me something to eat, I was thirsty and you gave me something to drink, I was a stranger and you invited me in, I needed clothes and you clothed me, I was sick and you looked after me, I was in prison and you came to visit me.'

Surprised, they asked when they had done these things for him. Jesus replied, 'Truly I tell you, whatever you did for one of the least of these brothers and sisters of mine, you did for me.'

He then turned to the goats on the left and sent them into eternal fire. "'For I was hungry and you gave me nothing to eat, I was thirsty and you gave me nothing to drink, I was a stranger and you did not invite me in, I needed clothes and you did not clothe me, I was sick and in prison and you did not look after me."

Like the sheep, the goats were also surprised, asking when

they had done these things to him. Jesus' answer was the same. "Truly I tell you, whatever you did not do for one of the least of these, you did not do for me."

"Both parties were surprised is what I mean," Aaron continued. "So I don't want to kick some new doctrine or say anything too caustic or subversive, but again, in my blindness, I certainly wouldn't be surprised if there were people who used the word atheist to define themselves, but in their spirit knew God, and they saw that light and love and followed after that, but could find it impossible to connect with the word 'Christian.'"

Aaron began fumbling here, trying to be very careful. He knew on one hand that many think if we just believe or say the right thing, that if we believe correct dogma and theology, we'll be saved. But on the other hand, there was a call to action: forgive and you'll be forgiven. As opposed to believing certain dogmas, he found freedom in trying to practice love, forgiveness, humility, mercy, grace, brokenness, patience, hope, kindness, gentleness, self-control, and faithfulness.

"To me there is a tremendous pride in both sides, of atheism and in dogmatic religion, saying, 'No, I have it,' and when someone says something opposing that, they see it through the lens of what they've already established. And they're not seeking truth, and they're not seeking light, and they're not seeking for healing or anything, to me, that God represents, but they're seeking to affirm what they already believe. That's a real concern of mine, when I get here and say, 'Jesus this' or 'Jesus that,' and whoever is out there in the crowd is like, 'He said Jesus! I like him!' because they have their belief in Jesus, but it's a different Jesus. This is the deepest, darkest, danger for me of idolatry, of having other gods before the true God."

Aaron called on one last person, a man named Larry, who admonished the audience to read their Bibles carefully and consider the words of Jesus. He warned Aaron that he was leading people astray. "No matter what the rock star says, if it lines up with Scripture it's right, if it doesn't it's wrong. Don't let anybody, don't let *anybody* lie to you or mislead you about the importance of the words of Jesus Christ who said in the Scripture, I am *the* way, *the* truth, and *the* life. Read your Bible, that is where you will get solid information about what it means to be a servant of God."

Aaron responded, "Thank you, Larry. I think somebody had a similar problem with what I was saying last year. I started to stumble upon some of these ideas, and they came up afterwards and said, 'You know, Jesus said if you would lead someone astray, it would be better to tie a millstone around your neck and be drowned in the sea,' because someone asked about the Bible and they didn't like my response. Someone asked my opinion of Jesus and didn't like my response. It didn't line up with what they believe, so they essentially told me, 'You'd be better off killing yourself than to keep on saying what you're saying.' And I agree that if I am leading people astray and intentionally deceiving people and hurting people and dragging them down into a place of darkness, that I would be better off dead, because this is a very, very serious thing we're talking about. That's why I do so reluctantly. However, my response to them was, 'Yeah, you're right, and you too, be very, very careful. Be very careful what you're dragging people into or what you are trying to convince people of.'"

Aaron ended his message: "My mom's teacher has something he says that he likes. He says, 'The truth comes from God, the mistakes are mine.' I reiterate that from my perspective. Please forgive me for all of my many mistakes. Not just here as to what I said, but what I write in my songs, what I do every day when I walk around that hurts others, please forgive me for that. Give your trust and your love to the one who created you. May peace be with you."

26
Crossed Paths

Arthur told me to meet him at his car near midnight the final night of the fest if I wanted to drive back to the hotel and follow him to Van Buren in the morning. I arrived to find his roommate waiting for him at the car as well. We chatted until an hour-and-a-half went by. Arthur was still nowhere to be found.

I walked back to the Asylum and helped them take their tent down. Soon it was past 3:00 A.M., and I started to walk the empty fest grounds praying for guidance. Large tents where bands played and where merchandise was kept were now empty and littered. I looked up at the moon and asked God if he existed or if he could hear me at all. I asked if I should try to find Arthur and follow him home, or if I should return to Chicago, take my job back at the bookstore, and stabilize myself again.

"Lord, I would love to see Aaron one more time to pray over him and send him off in peace. If he's still here, could you cross our paths?"

Just after I finished that prayer, I wandered down a path into a large empty tent. Walking in the other side at the very same time was Aaron with a small group of people collecting glass and plastic into boxes and cleaning up the fest grounds. I said nothing. I simply thrust my arm into piles of wet garbage and began pulling out plastic bottles with them, quietly thanking God for crossing our paths.

"I videotaped mewithoutYou's set if you want a copy. I tried to videotape your message, but there was so much noise I couldn't hear you. If you want me to send you a copy, just give me an address to send it to."

"If the sound quality is any good, MTV wants to use footage from the fest for a feature on the band."

"I'll listen to it when I get back and let you know, but it's open air and the crowd is singing loudly."

Aaron picked up a flyer from the grass and in black Sharpie

wrote down his address, phone number, and email.

"Have you decided where you are going next?" he asked.

"No, I'm still kinda lost. I haven't decided yet. But I appreciate you taking the time to talk with me. Would you mind if I prayed you off?"

"Not at all."

He looked worn out, so I placed my hand on his forehead and asked God to give him rest for his weary and ever-ruminating mind, then hugged him goodbye.

I went back to my car and slept in the back seat until the sun came up. I decided to head back to Chicago and take my old job back. As I worked and saved money for an apartment, I would live in my car for three months to try to empathize with the poor.

7/7/05
Email to Aaron

Hello Aaron,

I'm sorry to say that the video I was going to send doesn't have top quality sound. The sound isn't bad, but everyone is singing along so they are just as loud as you. It's good for my memory, but not for MTV2. I hope you get the audio you are looking for. I can send it anyway if you'd like.

I wanted to quickly thank you for your example at Cornerstone this year. When Arthur and I saw you in the trash cans at the food court on that first day and drove up on the golf cart to say hello, I was very much moved by that. I don't know why exactly, except that I have been living a middle-class Christianity for the most part and have always neglected the downcast and have strived to move from middle-class to upper-middle-class. The Christianity there abhors me however, especially in America.

So my heart was challenged the entire time at the fest. I didn't buy one shirt or CD, just a few books to give away. I quit my job managing a Christian bookstore and moved out of my apartment last month because I want to be out touching lives, so I became voluntarily homeless. I was going to move to Arkansas with Arthur after the fest but I am in Chicago, living out of my car, and putting all of the money I make into writing and publishing.

On the very last night of the fest, I wandered the grounds at 3:30 A.M. in restless prayer, asking God for guidance. I asked him for an opportunity to pray with you and send you off safely. I wandered down this path and decided to walk into this big empty tent, when you walked in at the same time. I know better now than to seek signs, but pulling plastic bottles with you and that small group of people—getting my hands dirty with you—gave me a sense of community I have not felt in all of my church gatherings and Bible studies. So Aaron, you have indirectly inspired me to stay homeless until I am broken and caring for the forgotten. It is such an amazing gift, and my heart still burns.

Thank you again for your kindness. I am keeping you in prayer,

Paul

7/14/05
Email from Aaron

Paul,
Very good to hear from you my friend! Your email made me smile very big, and I am very encouraged and inspired. I wish I were so willing to follow my convictions so immediately as you seem to be, and I hope to have the courage to keep going lower, lower and lower still! God's love for the 'unimportant' people of the world is so clear in the Gospels (all over the scriptures, really), but it is hard not to see people in terms of 'what do they have to offer me?', to see God's infinite value in the world's worthless.

God protect you my friend! I hope all is well—
Peace & Love,

Aaron

27
Homeless

Deciding to experiment with homelessness, almost serendipitously, I found a lone copy of new release faced on a shelf at the bookstore called *Under the Overpass: A Journey of Faith on the Streets of America* by Mike Yankoski. Mike and his friend Sam Purvis decided to give up their comfortable middle class lives and live as homeless people in six large American cities.

Like me, Mike wanted to learn what it meant to have to trust God daily to provide for him, as Jesus taught when he said not to work, save money, and trust in your nest egg. Mike wanted to follow Jesus into the call of hardship and suffering, and like Paul the Apostle, learn to be content in all situations—whether in need or with plenty, well fed or hungry, jailed or free.

They lived on the streets with alcoholics, addicts, mentally ill people, and criminals, learning how to get food from the trash, to take it from restaurant tables before it gets thrown away, and they learned how to panhandle and use dumpsters as toilets. They also learned what it was like to spend your whole day invisible in plain sight as most passed by without making eye contact.

In the end, Mike and Sam hoped to empathize and identify with the poor to learn better how to help them. When I returned from Cornerstone, my boss said he'd be opening a new store in August and could give me hours then. In the meantime, I would live in my car and try to understand what if felt like to have no home. I allowed myself to eat on $5.00 a day to avoid dumpster diving, and if I needed to shower every few days, I'd ask a friend. Once a week, I would try to spend the night at someone's place.

I thrive in order and stability. I wanted to see if I could thrive in chaos, on the fly, living out of my car. I made my base the parking lot of the Brookfield police station next to Kiwani's Park, where I could wander the park at night or sit by Salt Creek.

I mastered the art of washing up, shampooing my hair, and brushing my teeth with bottled water and using public washrooms to change clothes.

Most nights, I pulled my front seat back and slept under a sheet in my car. The nights I didn't want to sleep in my car or at the park, I went to the 24-hour Dunkin' Donuts to read and write. This particular location was run by Indian Americans with bindis between their eyes, red dots representing the third eye in Hinduism.

A customer came in one night, a young Arab woman, wearing a head scarf. In boring American English, she ordered the same thing I did, a vanilla sprinkled donut and coffee. Above her, The Simpsons was playing on TV. We all laughed together, eating our donuts. I realized that despite the religious and cultural differences of everyone in the room, we all liked cartoons and donuts with sprinkles.

I drew in small, lined notepads, wrote terrible poetry, and worked on guitar chords in my downtime in case I needed to panhandle. I also wrote an autobiography in spiral notebooks. I went back to childhood and tried to remember year-by-year every major influence in my life to understand how I had gotten to this point and what changes I needed to make going forward.

Reflecting on my own behavior, I paid particular attention to becoming born again as a teen and to all of the mentors, teachers, books, philosophies, and theologies that influenced me.

I compared myself to my brother. He is stable, practical, and responsible, going to work every day and building his career. In contrast, I find the practical life he leads insufferably boring. I long for God, heaven, the spiritual realm, intangibles like philosophy and theology, and I need large, passionate missions of eternal significance. I'm prone to idealism and magical thinking. But if I didn't learn how to be practical, stable, and grounded like my brother, I was going to end up ruining my life this way again and again.

With my newfound health, I got off disability in January when I took the management position at the bookstore, so my income was now running low. I looked forward to the prospect of managing another bookstore and getting a place again, ready to finally stabilize. But the bookstore location fell through, so I'd now have to wait until September. This meant living in my car into the crisp autumn. I started to panic. This experiment might lead to actual homelessness.

Some nights, I pushed a picnic bench into the bushes at the park and lay on my back staring at the night sky. "Where are you, Lord? Why have you abandoned me like this? I did everything you said. You can't just leave me here like this." The silence was deafening. The more ignored I felt, the angrier I became. "Answer me!" I began crying. "Answer me!" I repeated, choking on tears, until I lost my voice.

I lay there with my arms outstretched in total surrender. "Take my life and put me anywhere you want. Do anything you want with me. Just answer me." I begged for guidance, the blissful sense of his presence, the inner-peace that surpasses all understanding that Paul the Apostle wrote of, but none of that came. In almost direct proportion to my prayers, my anxiety, breakdown, and nightmares increased.

The urge to kill myself became all-consuming. There was a small wooded area in the park next to the creek that was pitch black at night. I walked to the edge of the creek. "If there was ever a time you needed to show up, it's now," I prayed.

"Paul, all you have to do is walk in, lay back, and inhale. You can do this." I took a deep breath, but I still couldn't move. An image flashed in my mind of children—playing baseball on the fields in the park and eating ice cream with their families—becoming sad from news of the body being fished out of Salt Creek. With nowhere to go in the day, I sometimes sat and watched these little kids play baseball and have fun with their families, realizing I was so far away from their simple lives that it seemed as if I was watching it on a movie screen. I imagined the phone call my mom would get and her crying for the rest of her life.

As I tried to walk forward, a rush of adrenaline snapped me out of my numbness. I went back to the picnic bench in the bushes and continued to lash out at God in anger, wondering where he was and why he wasn't answering me.

My boss gave me a handful of hours in September while

opening the new store, but his partner convinced him not to give me a management position. "Let him live in his car until he learns his lesson and never does something this stupid again," he said.

My boss took me out for lunch after a shift of loading boxes from the warehouse and unloading them at the bookstore. "You make me angry," he said. "You could get a loan, go to college, and open bookstores like I'm doing. You're so smart and you're wasting your life doing this."

My mom gave me the same lecture. "If I were in your place, I would be working my butt off and doing everything I could to get on my feet again. I would get two or three jobs." But my answer to both of them was the same. I was in such a breakdown that I couldn't function emotionally to take care of myself.

At the end of October, I found work at a shoe store in Yorktown mall for just over $6.00 an hour, plus commissions. My grandmother reluctantly allowed me to stay in the empty flat upstairs again for two months. It looked like things were finally coming together and I'd be on my feet again.

"Grandma says you have to leave. She doesn't want you up there." My mom called, just as I got settled in. I asked my grandma why I couldn't stay. "I never said that, of course you can stay." She was puzzled.

The following week, my mom called again. "Uncle Bob called me and said Grandma wants you out again." She was sick, and being up there, I was causing her stress.

I came home from work one night near midnight to find the doors locked and bolted so I couldn't get in with my key. I woke my grandma and she angrily let me in. Once upstairs, I found all of my appliances unplugged. She said she was turning the heat off and suggested that I put my mattress in the back seat of my car.

Confused and angry, I packed my stuff in my car and left the key on the stairs with a note for my grandma and uncle, telling them they weren't true family if they would just kick me out this way. I got on the expressway and accelerated, looking for anything concrete to slam into. I parked on the street in Brookfield and cried myself to sleep again under a light blue bed sheet.

I went to work the next day. My manager at the store offered to let me stay on his couch if I just gave him money for utilities. I accepted. I put on my khakis and polo shirt and pretended to be interested in Uggs and Birkenstocks, but spent much of my time at work holding back tears and trying not to look customers in the eyes. I took breaks to the food court where I sat and watched all the people pass. Christmas music filled the mall, families shopped, kids played, but I watched it all as if behind a glass looking into an inaccessible world.

I didn't want to return to the store. I wanted to find somewhere to die. I got back to the store and called a friend. "I can't go an hour without wanting to kill myself. I wanted to drive through an intersection on the way to work today, but I pulled over and cried instead."

"Then you'd better get to a hospital and get medicated immediately," she implored me. "Do I need to call an ambulance?"

But no hospital or pill would give me back my relationship with God or sense of hope. I didn't want to be kept alive. I wanted to be brought back to life.

28
Suicide

MewithoutYou came through town on tour in October with Coheed and Cambria, Blood Brothers, and Dredge. Aaron invited me to come along with them on the bus, but I refused on the grounds of needing to keep working and get established.

In November, mewithoutYou attended mtvU's Woodie Awards ceremony and won a Left Field award, beating out Saul Williams, M.I.A., Matisyahu, and Arcade Fire. The award was for the band that came out of left field and made an impact by being so creative they defied classification in one genre.

Under the heading: "Mewithoutyou: Not Your Average Christian, Vegetable-Oil-Fueled, Flower-Flinging Rockers," MTV reported, "Philadelphia band's eccentricity has worked in its favor." They won the award because "they're overtly Christian, they drive a van that runs on vegetable oil and they often shower the stage in flowers during their spastic live sets. They hold potluck dinners before each show, sport scraggly, unkempt beards and exude a vaguely culty, hippie-dippie vibe that's way more off-putting than they probably realize. Yet despite all that (or maybe because of it), Mewithoutyou have managed to carve out their own little niche on the indie scene, and have achieved a level of success that most bands in their position would kill for.[144]

On MTV's website, a feature was done on mewithoutYou that contained footage of the band's Cornerstone performance and sound bites from the band, along with energetic live performances of "Paper Hanger," "Four-Word Letter (pt. 2)," and "Tie Me Up, Untie Me," filmed on a flower-strewn, in-studio stage. Aaron had cut his hair and trimmed his beard, wearing a flannel shirt and shorts, looking far less unkempt than he had a few months back at Cornerstone.

---

[144] James Montgomery, "Mewithoutyou: Not Your Average Christian, Vegetable-Oil-Fueled, Flower-Flinging Rockers. Philadelphia band's eccentricity has worked in its favor," *MTV*, 11/21/05.

Meanwhile, I spent November on my boss's couch. My experiment in homelessness didn't help me identify with the poor in the least. Instead, it solidified my desire for a stable middle-class life.

Now Thanksgiving, my mom called and suggested that I call my grandma and uncle and wish them a happy Thanksgiving. I told her no, they weren't family to me. This began a four-hour tearful conversation.

Having completed my autobiography, my history was fresh on my mind, so I began to pour out everything I didn't like about our family, especially its lack of communication, depth, and connection.

"Your childhood was great. How could you and your brother grow up in the same home and turn out so different?" my mom asked. "You were always a strange kid and hard to connect with. When you were twelve you were fun to be around, then you went off the deep end with that goofy born again stuff and came home speaking in tongues and everything was so serious. I thought, 'there he goes again.'"

She thought I was too deep and heavy. I obsessed too much on ultimate questions about God and the meaning of life. I was a religious fanatic with my head in the clouds and no common sense.

My grandmother used to tell me no one knows how we got here, what the purpose of life is, or what happens when we die, so it's a complete waste of time to think about it or worry about it. "You're gonna drive yourself crazy," she'd say. "Stop worrying about the whole world and just take care of yourself and your family." Her life was marked by the simplicity of waking up every day and going to the bakery, cutting her grass, cleaning her house, and cooking for family.

I tried to explain to my mom that once you encounter God or the supernatural, there is no way to return to a "normal" life. I was miraculously healed, and God told me to propose to Natalie. My current despair came from trying to understand why she said no and why God seemed to have left me in the dark ever since.

"Sometimes fibromyalgia just goes into remission naturally,

Paul. And yeah, I'm sure God told you to sell everything you own and propose to a woman who doesn't love you and who you've never even been with on a single date. God wanted to ruin your life. That makes sense, Paul." She had no more patience for this.

"Get away from all of those crazy churches and crazy people you hang around with, stop reading all of those books, and just be normal. You're gonna be thirty years old, you're healthy, and you had a job and an apartment, but you screwed all of that up and decided to live in your car. Now you want to blame everyone else. Just keep working, find an apartment, and be normal. Everyone is tired of worrying about you."

She was right. I was crazy, I had no clue how to live a practical life, and there was probably no God who ever spoke to me. Knowing that this loss was too big and a lifetime was not long enough to heal from this despair and heartbreak, I hung up sick with dread and nausea. I needed to end my life that night. I called Lauren in California and asked her if she thought I was crazy. She said I sounded despondent and was worried about me.

I wrote Aaron a rambling, stream-of-consciousness email, but so as not to alarm him, gave the impression that I hadn't given up yet. After sending the email I fell asleep, hoping the nausea would pass and I wouldn't go through with killing myself. When I woke up a few hours later to a migraine and a nervous system on fire, a response was waiting from Aaron.

11/24/05
Email to Aaron

Aaron,

Hello there, this is Paul in Chicago again. I hope you are enjoying your Thanksgiving and are unwinding from all of the travel. May you get all of the rest you need in spirit, mind, and body.

I couldn't see you guys this time around due to not having any money, but I did see you on MTV after reading the news section and was glad to see you there.

Without sounding too alarming, I have desperately been trying not to take my life in recent months. Not for trivial reasons, Aaron, but for lifelong despair, collapse, suffering, and failure.

Since we last talked, I have lost my family. Not that they are out of my life—we are all polite to one another—but there has never been connection.

I have been part time in a shoe store at the mall and am living on my manager's couch. The alienation, rejection, fear, collapse, and struggle have been more than I can bear, with even the simplest of things collapsing. Now I am stuck in the mundane, losing all sense of mission, calling, passion, and gifting.

God, of course, is impossible to figure out, and I only frustrate Christian friends who offer me safe and dogmatic answers. I have always swayed in and out of unbelief, seeing God as friend, lover, and enemy. It's just that I have these passions that I am told to put away for the sake of working a nine-to-five and liking it. I would rather die.

I have no idea where I will end up next, but your recent journal entry has caused me to wonder if I should sell my car and use the money for my passions—art, music, poetry, and writing. My passions have always gotten me in trouble. Too deep, too honest, too weird, too eccentric, too transparent. The people saying this to me are living very apathetic, passionless, boring lives. I will probably be homeless by Christmas and asking God to guide my footsteps from there.

I'd love to have a heart-to-heart with you one of these days. God willing, we'll get together and have something to offer one another. Thanks for inviting me along on tour, Aaron. Maybe next time I can come along and help out.

Paul

11/25/05
Email from Aaron

Paul,

Brother, I am saddened by your letter but not without hope. For many years I thought every day about killing myself and then it was a simple revelation that I was not here to find happiness but to serve others (though it so happens that in the little I've done that I've found tremendous happiness). But I don't want to talk lightly about these things, certainly not type about it and send it on a computer.

If you are overwhelmed by rejection, try to set Jesus before your eyes, who was rejected and mocked and beaten and killed. If we follow him, sometimes I think we can expect no better than this, and sometimes in my momentary sufferings I thank G-d for the chance to experience what he did.

You mentioned your calling and purpose in life. Do you see this to be pursuing your passions, art, music, writing, poetry? I don't think you should put those away (and I'm definitely am not suggesting a 9-5 job), but what I'm getting at is that I have been thinking about our calling and purpose in life if we follow Jesus is to feed the hungry, clothe the naked, stand up for the rights of the oppressed, forgive and teach and learn and pray and fast and worship, etc. What do you think?

Are you a pacifist?

If you can come out to Philadelphia, I will find places for you to stay. If you don't have the money for gas, I'll send you the money. There is a community of faith and love here where people look out for one another and are trying to meet each other's needs. There is a community in upstate New York called the Bruderhof that you have to come with me to visit. I used to think about killing myself every day, and two years ago to the day I was there visiting them and the trip changed my life COMPLETELY. Have you visited JPUSA out in Chicago? How about Reba Place Fellowship? What city are you in nowadays?

I would much rather talk to you in person. Phone would be a decent compromise, so call me if you have a phone. I connect with you brother, though I hardly know you, feel a deep care for you, maybe from G-d, maybe just 'cause I can relate to what you're saying so well.

You're not crazy, the world is crazy, and you are feeling alienated from it and that is a good thing—in a sense an absolutely necessary thing (be MORE honest, weird, transparent, eccentric!), but don't despair. Have hope, be patient (not the patience like waiting for the elevator but the deeper lifelong patience), forgive everyone who's ever hurt you (easier typed than done, I know, and I'm sorry), pray to G-d for me and I will remember to pray for you. May our Mother Hen gather you under his wing and protect you.

Peace, peace, peace to your heart,

Aaron

P.S. Tell me what to do and I'll do it.

29
If You Can Someday Stop By

The next afternoon, I called Aaron. He patiently listened to the entire saga that brought me to this point in my life. I knew how crazy it all sounded and kept apologizing.

"Am I crazy?" I asked.

"No, you are not crazy, the world is crazy," he reassured me.

"Everyone keeps asking me why I can't be normal, but their lives look so boring to me. They go to work, pay the bills, entertain themselves, have nothing interesting to say. I had a calling from God that was all consuming. Now I have nothing to live for."

"Well, Jesus said not to toil and labor and store up, nor to run after possessions and to create a stable life. He had nowhere to lay his head and received daily bread from his Father without any care for his reputation, life, or safety. There is a certain kind of mental illness that results in spending your whole life trying to create stability and security in this world."

Aaron couldn't relate to the more supernatural elements of my story—God speaking to me, healing me, and guiding me with signs concerning my calling and Natalie. His faith didn't exactly develop in a fundamentalist stream.

"This is as close to supernatural as I'm ever gonna get on you," he began. "There was a girl I was talking with a couple years ago, and every time I came to her town I would get dressed up and try to impress her with my sense of fashion. I bought these $180 handmade leather shoes that looked like alligator skin. I got them on sale for $135, but to put this in perspective, I spent that much money on what are essentially foot covers.

"This girl was so pretty, but whenever I talked about God or spiritual things, she became disinterested and looked around the room, bored. When I talked about music, fashion, and things I was mildly interested in, she was right there with me. I stared at her across the table, when suddenly her face turned haggard right before my eyes. Her skin wrinkled like a raisin and sagged over her skull. This immediately snapped me out of the trance of being taken by her beauty and charm, which Proverbs said is fleeting and vain."

This was the night in 2003 that Aaron went to see Unwed Sailor and visit this girl. After realizing there was no connection, he wanted to be alone, so asked to be let out of the van and swam across the Susquehanna while hitchhiking home. "I remember all of the grasshoppers jumping around, keeping me company as I lay in the grass and walked along the road on the other side of the river, so I mentioned them in 'January 1979.'"

Our conversation was interrupted. "My dad just said to invite you to our Christmas Eve party. He has a big party every year, and he said you're welcome to come."

I was warmed by the thought, but I also wondered what kind of family invites suicidal strangers into their home from hundreds of miles away to spend Christmas with them.

Aaron reiterated what he said to me at Cornerstone. "Brother, I was suicidal for such a long time. Ten times a day, day after day, I would think, 'Today's the day I do it.' Everything I did was a distraction from wanting to kill myself. Then I went to live with this community called The Simple Way for three months and spent a week at a place called the Bruderhof, and man, I haven't been the same since. I saw people loving one another in such a beautiful way. Instead of seeing the world as a place of suffering that I wanted to escape, I saw it as a field ready to be harvested. Look at all of the lost, broken, hungry, forgotten, and unimportant who need to be loved and taken care of. Ever since I realized this, that the message of Jesus and the kingdom of God was simply about coming together and loving others, I haven't wanted to kill myself—almost two years to the day now."

Aaron was looking for repossessed properties at auction, hoping to start an intentional community. "If you can make it to Philadelphia, there is a community of people here who will care for you. We live simply, dumpster dive, feed the homeless, and pray for one another, but I don't want to give the impression that that's all we do."

"I told my friends that I met you while you were eating out of the trash cans at Cornerstone, and they joked that I should invite you over and they'll take you to the buffet—they'll just drive down the alley."

"Friends here bust my chops all the time too. Why would I pay full price for bananas when people throw perfectly good ones in the garbage every day? I don't like seeing food go to waste. I'll admit, I'm obsessed with it to a fault."

Before I knew it, three hours had gone by. "Well, my mom is baking some cookies so I should join her. We just got back from tour so I should spend some time with my parents. I'm visiting the Bruderhof for their New Year celebration. Promise me you won't take your life before visiting with me."

"I promise. I applied for a position at Borders. If they don't hire me, I'll come to Philadelphia and be a part of your community. I apologize for burdening you and spilling out all of my problems on you, a virtual stranger." I was embarrassed.

"No man, I think it's beautiful that you can be that transparent with someone you hardly know. It's much better than hearing 'Your band rocks,' or 'Will you sign my T-shirt?' like I am used to hearing. It would be great to have you here. There aren't many people I can discuss these things with. A lot of people just want to invite me to parties and I'm bored with that. I don't want to count my chickens before they hatch, but I'm stoked that you're coming!"

"Thank you for talking to me today, I really appreciate it."

"May God—not the Trinity, the deity of Christ, or some formulation, but the God of peace, truth, light, and love, the Father and the Mother Hen, whoever he or she is—protect you," Aaron finished.

Somehow, Aaron made me feel like the benefit would be all his if I came to stay with him.

30
The New Monasticism

As Aaron and I discussed communal living ideas, I sent him information from counter-cult websites about JPUSA and the Bruderhof, emphasizing that in communes, freedom is lost, spirit is crushed, and people become little more than workers who are used, controlled, and subjugated. Abuse is covered up and suppressed to make the commune look good. I suggested that we just work, get a place together as roommates, and then share what we have with open hearts. I emphasized that I needed my own room, private space, and personal possessions to function.

Aaron was also concerned about what goes wrong in these communities, but he believed the good outweighed the bad. "I agree completely that these communal ideals only work on a small scale when not coerced, enforced or regulated. I would like to talk very much about ways we could live together in love and unity. I'm looking at buying an abandoned old small house in Philly for a few thousand bucks and moving in, sorta like a squat house that I own and work on slowly as materials and time become available. But I would love for you to be a part of it! Truly, it's not the Bruderhof that I want to show you, but love. There is a tremendous amount of love at the Bruderhof, and kindness and gentleness and wisdom—but there are many problems (they are the first to admit it!). As the scripture suggests, may we cling to what is good and reject what is evil, wherever we find it. G-d is good brother."[145]

The New Monasticism was the cover title of the September 2005 issue of *Christianity Today*, featuring Shane Claiborne on the cover. The article says Shane Claiborne and six other students from Eastern University started an intentional community in Kensington, Philadelphia in 1998 called the Simple Way after they lived among the poor, who were evicted from the abandoned St. Edward's Cathedral two years previous. Their emphasis was on

---
[145] Email 11/29/05.

encouraging comfortable, suburban, materialistic Christians to give up their cushy lives and take the poor seriously by moving into impoverished neighborhoods to bring life to them.

In June of 2004, many of the communities Aaron mentioned in his email—Reba Place, Rutba House, and Bruderhof, among others—attended a conference which gave them definition, discipline, and structure. As Rob Moll explains:

> A June 2004 conference officially marks the birth of the new monasticism, and participants wrote a voluntary rule for the many and diverse communities. New communities and academics met in Durham, North Carolina, with older communities like the Mennonite Reba Place Fellowship, Bruderhof, and the Catholic Worker. Drawing from church tradition and borrowing the term new monasticism from Jonathan R. Wilson's book *Living Faithfully in a Fragmented World* (Morehouse, 1998), participants developed 12 distinctives that would mark these communities, including: submission to the larger church, living with the poor and outcast, living near community members, hospitality, nurturing a common community life and a shared economy, peacemaking, reconciliation, care for creation, celibacy or monogamous marriage, formation of new members along the lines of the old novitiate, and contemplation.[146]

As a result of the conference, a book was written expanding on these ideas, called *Schools for Conversion: 12 Marks of a New Monasticism*, edited by The Rutba House.

Rather than Jesus merely taking away the sins of the individual, they see the Christian life as a collective that takes on societal ills. In the same *Christianity Today* article, Scott Bessenecker said many young Christians today are looking to commit themselves to something far more radical than the suburban

---

[146] Rob Moll, "The New Monasticism. A fresh crop of Christian communities is blossoming in blighted urban settings all over America," *Christianity Today*, September 2005.

evangelicalism of their parents. For many, giving up their lives and taking vows, committing themselves to communities and missions, seemed the answer.

What defines these communities as monastic is that they are counter-cultural and revolutionary. They go to the margins where the abandoned and forgotten are, countering the idols of nationalism and American Christianity. They also bring unity and an ecumenical spirit between fragmented Christian denominations.

The New Monasticism is pacifist, using non-violent protest and obstruction, opposing unjust laws and wars. These groups often share their belongings and depend on dumpster diving, donations, and growing food in local gardens.

Many drawn to a movement like this practice freeganism. Freegans believe we waste so much and throw so much away that we could live entirely on trash. You could squat on abandoned property and furnish it fully, including appliances and entertainment, and you could find an entire wardrobe and fully stock your kitchen with food just by collecting it from the trash. Dumpster diving—or bin skipping—is a way of life. It is meant to expose our culture of excess in light of a world where thousands die daily from lack.

Just like monks—hermits who eventually gathered in monasteries—individual homeless people banded together to squat, often bartering and sharing expertise. They ride bikes and hitchhike to get around. They go to big cities and frequent the dumpsters of chosen restaurants and grocery stores.

Some do this out of necessity, some out of statements against consumerism and waste, and some simply because they like it. Often they are proud of their bum-cheek fashion sense and mismatched thrift store décor.

Aaron and I hoped to partake in this vision of living as urban monks.

31
Beef 'n' Brandy

"I asked my parents about you staying with us until we can find a place for you, and they seemed pretty laid back about it," Aaron wrote.

"Well, Borders hasn't called, so I guess we should set a date."

MewithoutYou was on the Invisible Children tour with Underoath, The Chariot, and As Cities Burn. All proceeds from those shows went to Habitat for Humanity, Invisible Children, Teen Challenge, and Samaritans Purse.

"How does the 20th sound, the day after you get back from tour? Is that cutting it too close?"

"No, man. Not at all."

"Very kind of you guys to let me stay with you. I promise not to overstay my welcome."

I had lunch with my mom, and we apologized to each other for arguing and saying things we didn't mean. We then went to see my uncle who didn't seem very upset about my note disowning him and my grandma. He actually chuckled at it.

"I didn't tell you to leave, you left on your own. I never would have put you on the street."

"But you kept telling Mom that Grandma wanted me out of the house and I was making her sick. Then I got home and the door was bolted and my stuff unplugged."

"She doesn't remember any of it. She doesn't remember saying you had to leave, she doesn't remember bolting the door, and she doesn't remember unplugging your stuff. When I asked her about telling you to put your mattress in the back seat of your car, she cried, saying that doesn't make sense and she'd never say that."

We didn't know it, but my grandma was entering the early stages of Alzheimer's.

My family had enough stress in their own lives without having to worry about me. Happy we were now getting along, I needed to get out of their hair and see what awaited me in Philadelphia.

The night before leaving, I went to Beef 'n' Brandy to sip coffee and write down a few thoughts. I began writing a letter to Aaron. After a few random thoughts about the God of the Old Testament, Thomas Merton, Soren Kierkegaard, and Christian existentialism, I started to write about the heaviness of existing and the burden of each moment.

I looked at the pack of butter on the table and wondered about its production, packaging, and shipping. I looked out the window at a Jiffy Lube advertisement and at an airplane flying by, thinking of a recent mid-air collision overseas where hundreds of journalists and children died. A plane had just skidded off a runway and crashed through the gate at Midway airport and crushed a car on Central Avenue, killing a six-year old child returning from a family celebration. He was in the back seat with his siblings eating chicken strips and singing "Santa Claus is Coming to Town."

I smelled the tires on the trucks as they passed by. I felt the cold of the sidewalk. I was afraid of how dark the sky was. Physical reality was extremely heavy. Everything seemed so empty and meaningless. I wanted to be light and free, a spirit in another world.

As I looked around the restaurant, I couldn't find anything not fashioned by humans: the paved streets, the paint on the streets, the curbs, the lawns and sidewalks, the street lights, the signs, the paint on the signs, the cars and trucks passing by, the clothing everyone in the restaurant wore, the buildings and parking lots, and the very window I was looking through. I gazed around the restaurant at all of the architecture, the design, the tables, the carpet, the dishes, the register—all stuff fashioned together by us.

I imagined the trees being cut and the cement being poured, the pigments for paints being found and mixed with binders to paint the walls that were measured and cut, using invisible things that only exist in our heads—information, numbers, and letters. Once, this all might have been forest before it was developed into a city, and one day it would no longer exist. It would be like looking at a picture of a crowded circus from the 1800s and knowing that every person in that picture is dead and the circus is no more.

I heard people talking, the usual hum in the background of the restaurant, and became acutely aware of the fish bowl atmosphere we exist in which carries sound waves—rippling through a sea of what we wrongly assume is empty space. Our vocal chords will turn to dust and no one will be able to utter a sound. Our eardrums and the signals to our brains will also turn to dust and nothing will be heard. My eyes, their color, my hand in front of my face—everything—was just stuff being magically ordered and held together.

I blinked, and the whole of reality—seen and unseen, people and objects—dispersed into a sea of countless miniature marbles chaotically dancing, expanding through the entire universe, the way the picture on old TV sets turned to snow. Absolutely everything that existed or held some composition or order, including myself, disseminated into a dance of particles before refashioning themselves into the momentary order they were actually in.

There is an infinite combination of potential universes or realities that could have been actualized, but since we are finite, we are located in one spot per moment in a seemingly linear progression of time. We compensate for these limitations with fantasy, art, movies, and imagination. We escape the trap of concrete reality. Sometimes we use imagination to pad ourselves from a world we are discontent with. Some think this is exactly what belief in God is—the delusion of trading reality for a satisfying fantasy, projecting a sense of purpose and order onto an unpredictable and unsafe world.

If everything that exists and has some size, shape, and weight in the universe can be reduced to a scattering of particles, in what sense can anything physical be said to be real? Only something eternal and unchanging, transcendent to nature and the universe, can be considered real with any integrity, and that necessary being is what we call God.

I wrote this all in the letter and began writing about how my left hand was holding a pen while my right hand was on my bearded face, yet both didn't seem real. I was experiencing what Aaron wrote in "Seven Sisters" when he threw a small stone down at the reflection of his image in the water *and it altogether disappeared. I burst, as it shattered through me, like a bullet through a bottle, and I'm expected to believe that any of this is real.*

I was interrupted from this deconstruction by a man walking by. "You're writing a love letter, huh? It's nice to be in love, isn't it?" He walked away.

He jostled me out of my contemplation and took a moment to say hi, to acknowledge my existence, and to remind me that people are still experiencing the power and reality of love, which seems to bond, unify, and hold things together. I wrote: *This man just visited the jailed and lonely. There is a clue here. We may all be dust, but while we are living, we are people. Dust doesn't say hello and show concern as it passes by. Even the passing and fading world is in some sense real.*

I ended the note saying God is the only real thing in existence because only he is eternal: he can never die and can't be destroyed. My needing him was an all-or-nothing proposition, because everything is meaningless without him. If I didn't find him, I was going to kill myself, and time was running out.

"I know you can't help me, but thank you for your kindness and empathy. I hope I can return the same to you," I finished.

I never gave the note to Aaron, finding it too pretentious and insufferable even for me. But I knew he could handle it, because it took no effort for him to be pretentious and insufferable just the same.

I headed to a friend's house to nap until midnight, when I would finally get on the toll road that takes me all the way to Pennsylvania.

Just before I left, Aaron called. "My old boss at the flower shop offered me a job delivering flowers through Christmas. I told him I wouldn't do it unless he gave you work, too. So I got us some work until Christmas. If you get here early enough tomorrow, I'll tell you how to get to the flower shop. Otherwise you can wait for me at my place. Can't wait to see you. Very exciting, brother!"

I still couldn't understand why he was being so kind and thoughtful to me.

As I got on the Chicago Skyway towards the Indiana Toll Road, I told myself that I was going with no expectations and would do my best not to burden him. I didn't know what to expect, but it meant something just to be invited and to keep moving. The longer I sat still, the more I wanted to die.

Halfway through the journey, I stopped at Hardee's for a cup of sludge they told me was coffee. I slept at the table until morning, finally getting back on the road and arriving in Upper Darby at 4:00 that afternoon.

32
Upper Darby

"What a dump."

This was my first impression of Upper Darby. Each block was packed with row homes and storefronts, looking somewhat dilapidated. The traffic was congested on the way in. There wasn't one well-dressed person walking the streets. Philadelphia towered in the background, cold and concrete. Upper Darby reminded me of Bridgeport back home, with the Chicago skyline in the background.

I parked my car in front of Aaron's house and left him a message, letting him know I'd arrived. He called back and said, "I'm just leaving the flower shop and on my way home. I'm riding my bike so I'll be there shortly."

He arrived five minutes later wearing a green bomber jacket and gray paint-stained pants, one leg rolled up higher than the other at the ankles. He greeted me with a warm embrace and a big smile. I smelled the musk from his beard when he didn't let go. I was very happy to see him.

When he invited me inside, my reaction upon entering his parents' house was little different than my thoughts about the town. *What a dump.*

Before I could get my coat off, Aaron's dad, Elliott, greeted me, sporting a mustache and do-rag. "Do you have a car, Paul? Do you think you could give me a ride somewhere?"

I thought it was a strange request to make of someone he hadn't even been properly introduced to yet, but I gave him my keys and told him to take the car. By the way he carried himself, I could tell that something was off.

Aaron took me aside. "I guess I should have warned you about my dad. He's not dangerous, but he's got a lot going on. Sometimes he thinks the FBI is after him or that George Bush has the phones tapped." I would later find out he'd been diagnosed bipolar and had suffered from paranoid delusions.

Aaron then took me upstairs to his room, which he was giving me for the duration of my stay. He would sleep on the couch downstairs or on the floor as he sometimes preferred.

His room was quaint. It had a hardwood floor, and one of the walls had exposed brick. The window above the radiator looked out onto the alley. There was a lone dresser and a few books lying on top, but no band posters, CD collection, or tour memorabilia I'd imagined I would see. It was quite minimalist.

Elliott had returned from his errand and was now drinking diet soda from a stack of plastic cups filled with ice. "Paul, do you believe in God?" he asked.

"Yes."

"Would you like to join the Brotherhood? Do you know who Norma Jean is? They're members. So is Dan Pishock." I wasn't clear what the Brotherhood was, but if those guys were members, I wanted in.

"Write down your address and phone number, Paul." He slid a pen and a piece of paper my way. He opened a manila folder and began handing me sheets of paper with Jewish, Christian, and Muslim prayers printed on them.

"Think only of God, all the time." Elliott started an endless stream of encouragement and quoting of scriptures. It wasn't a conversation, but a monologue that wouldn't stop unless someone interrupted him. It took a dark turn when he mentioned the Bawa Muhaiyaddeen Fellowship. "They tried to turn my wife against me. They tried to run my boys over right outside the house. They tried to kill Mike and Aaron." His voice began to rise. "They are going straight to hell without judgment, and so is George Bush!"

"Dad." Aaron interrupted. "You know you're not supposed to talk about people that way."

"I'm sorry," he said, now sitting calmly.

Aaron encouraged him to let go of bitterness and judgment, to be graceful and forgiving. "Here, play us a song." Aaron handed him the acoustic guitar from the living room. Now Elliott was smiling and singing folk songs.

Elliott at one time had been sending out mail, identifying himself as working for the FBI. This, of course, invited a visit from the FBI, who were lenient when they found out he was mentally ill. Since then, Elliott believed they were tapping his phones, watching him from helicopters, and passing by his house. When his deodorant went missing one morning during my stay, he was positive George Bush had taken it while he was out.

"How did Elliott fall out with the Bawa fellowship?" I asked Aaron.

"I'm not completely clear on what happened. My dad allegedly threatened to kill Bawa. I seem to remember hearing something about an ax. I think what he was getting at was he had just listened to a message about killing your idols, you know, putting nothing before God. You'll notice that my mom has pictures of Bawa all over the house. At one time he ripped them to pieces. He was trying to say that we should focus on God alone. After an outburst at the fellowship that they interpreted as a physical threat to Bawa, they expelled him from the community. He's been bitter about it ever since. My dad is really lonely and has a hard time making friends, which is probably why he started the Brotherhood. Wait until you meet my mom. She's the sweetest woman in the world."

Bitsy came home from work and took off her coat.

"Mom, this is my friend Paul from Chicago."

"Hi, Paul." She smiled. "Aaron tells me you're a kindred spirit."

"Well, his lyrics really resonated with me, and we had a good talk at Cornerstone. On the last night of the fest, I prayed and asked God if I could see him one more time. I'm really reluctant these days to say it was supernatural, but I ran into Aaron moments later while he was picking up trash, and we exchanged information. Since then I've been living in my car and really trying not to kill myself. So he invited me here, hoping we might start a community."

"I think you're a godsend. You're exactly what he needs."

Why in the world would he need me?

"Aaron!" she shouted, opening the fridge. There was no room in the refrigerator or the freezer because it was packed with food he'd found in dumpsters. She asked him to keep it all in the basement—especially anything containing ham. Aaron apologized and started taking food downstairs.

"I don't know how he can eat from the trash like that," she said, making a *blech* sound. "I tried to explain to him that some things have to go to waste, like apples falling from the trees and rotting on the ground, but he has this obsession where he just can't see food go to waste. It will run its course. I'm not worried about him. He has a genius level IQ and is three steps ahead of the rest of us. No one is going to talk him out of anything. He'll know when he's ready to stop."

Some of the guys in the band felt the same, growing weary of smelly bags of trash being dragged onto the bus when they were on tour.

Aaron kept some of the food out to cook. He opened a package of wasabi rolls and offered me one. I declined. "They are so good," he said as he read aloud the price and the ingredients from the label on the package. "How many animals died to make these rolls? Where did the pigment for the ink used to print the labels come from? Who manufactured the plastic containers? Who farmed all day for low wages and grew the vegetables they put in here? Who drove these components to the factory to be assembled? Who drove the trucks to bring them to the store? Who put them out at the market to sell? How many hands and how much labor did it take to produce this, only to be thrown in the trash just to make room for new product, when it's perfectly edible? Meanwhile, so many people in the world are starving."

I warned you that Aaron could be as pretentious and insufferable as I am.

Aaron began cooking. "I should let you know, everything I'm cooking was found in the Trader Joe's dumpster. You don't have to eat it."

I was hesitant, but after chopping vegetables and mashing tomatoes into sauce, I couldn't resist the smell of the spiced sausage and mashed potatoes. We sat down to eat and it tasted amazing. Perhaps this dumpster diving thing wasn't so bad after all.

After eating, Aaron picked up the acoustic guitar and began

singing "We Three Kings" in a very familiar "Son of a Widow" vocal style. I was starstruck for a moment, but I didn't let him know that. I couldn't believe I was in his house, sleeping in his bed, and had him all to myself.

Given it had been a long drive and we had to be up early the next day to work at the flower shop, I gave Aaron a hug goodnight and went up to his room.

I noticed *Rumi: The Book of Love* by Coleman Barks on his dresser. I turned it over and read: "A thousand half-loves must be forsaken to take one whole heart home" and "Lovers don't finally meet somewhere. They're in each other all along." I recognized reworkings of these lines in Aaron lyrics. A peek inside revealed many more.

Coleman Barks described a dream he had in 1977 in which Bawa Muhaiyaddeen appeared. When he went to the fellowship and visited Bawa in person the next year, Bawa gave him his blessing to continue translating Rumi's poetry. "It must be done."

There was another book on Aaron's dresser called *The Desert Fathers* by Helen Waddell. It contained stories of the early Christian monks and mystics. Flipping through it, I was put off by the obviously fanciful and superstitious stories, the neurotic fleeing of all temptations of the flesh, and the purposeful mortification of the body. I wasn't sure the desert fathers had anything to teach me.[147]

I turned out the lights and got into bed, feeling guilty that I was so needy and that Aaron was put out on the couch downstairs. I sighed deeply.

"I'm gonna hate it here."

---

[147] Jean Paul Sartre wrote: "Mysticism suits displaced persons and superfluous children. To push me into it, it would have been enough to present the matter to me by the other end; I was in danger of being a prey to saintliness. My grandfather disgusted me with it forever. I saw it through his eyes. That cruel madness sickened me by the dullness of its ecstasies; terrified me by its sadistic contempt for the body. The eccentricities of the saints made no more sense to me than those of Englishmen who dived into the sea in evening clothes." Jean Paul Sartre, *The Words*, (New York: Vintage, 1981), 100.

33
Flower Shop

I came downstairs the next morning to wake Aaron up. He sat up, groggy and with bed head, and put his arms around me. "I love you, brother," He said. Just like greeting him the previous day, it was a tight embrace and he didn't let go.[148]

We went to the kitchen and made steak, egg, and cheese sandwiches on multigrain bread, loading them with spices and Sriracha sauce. We then rushed out to the flower shop so we wouldn't be late.

The owner of the flower shop, an older gentleman, struck me as bossy and cantankerous. Any time something went wrong as he put the bouquets together, he'd yell, "Ah, shit!" Soon I started to laugh every time I heard it. He barked orders to his partner who took it in stride. "Pay no attention to him," he said with a smile. "He's just a crabby old man."

My workstation was at a countertop where they would pass the bouquets to me and I'd wrap them. Aaron would then load them into the van and make the deliveries. Guarding the access to my counter were two large Macaws perched on either side. "Just don't put your hand near them. They'll snap your finger right off," the boss warned.

Lying in a miscellaneous box on the wrapping table was a beat up copy of *The Selfish Gene* by Richard Dawkins. I found myself thumbing through it on break.

A cute petite girl came into the shop to help out and started talking to Aaron. "Paul, this is Amanda, the girl I've been telling you about." After their on-and-off relationship, this was their first time seeing each other again since they'd decided to be off, so Aaron was slightly uneasy. I thought they looked good together

---

[148] "Most who've met him say you haven't felt a real hug until you've experienced his bone-cracking embrace." Matt Fink, "Busted: me without You. Busted Halo talks conversion, pride, and holistic faith with the leader of indie rock's would-be revolutionaries," *Busted Halo*, 4/27/07.

and was rooting for them to work out after all.

"So what happened between you and Amanda that you didn't end up getting married?" I asked Aaron.

"Amanda and I dated for two years, then I broke up with her because she wasn't Christian enough. That's when I started feeling suicidal. We were on and off for a while, so I proposed to her to stop that cycle, but she saw that this was an act of desperation to keep us together, so she wisely gave the ring back." He paused. "I am the most prideful person I know. I'm in love with myself, and honestly, I always thought I was too good for her because she wasn't as spiritual as I was."

He was frustrated with his own arrogance.

The following day, Aaron took me with him to the sheriff's auction to bid on properties for the community we were planning. We arrived at the auction house to find families outside picketing with signs, begging people not to bid on their repossessed homes. This immediately saddened Aaron, so he felt more comfortable bidding on destroyed properties.

There was a particular burned out shell Aaron picked, knowing no family had been living there, but he balked on the bidding. It sold for less than $600. He found the high bidder afterwards and asked her what she planned on doing with it. Of course, she was flipping it. We estimated it would cost $20,000 to $30,000 to refurbish. Aaron didn't want to get in that deep. We headed to the flower shop for another shift.

Being an anxious driver who is terrible with directions, I didn't envy Aaron's job of driving around the city dropping off flowers. I brought flowers out to the van only to see Aaron standing there with a large map of the city open before him.

As I came out the side door and down a few steps, I accidentally tore a button off of my black pea coat. I paused outside the door, staring at the button on the cold cement step, holding back tears as if it were finally the end of the world.

34
Carols

On the way home from the shop the following day, we stopped at a rehabilitation center that helps get the homeless, addicted, and poor back on their feet. Aaron asked them if they accepted cooked foods. They did. Now he couldn't wait to get home and gather as many ingredients as he could from his dumpster finds to put into stews.

He brought trash bags up from the basement until the kitchen was covered in meats and vegetables. The cutting board and knives were out. Large pots of water boiled on burners. Aaron stirred while I cut vegetables and mashed potatoes.

We heard singing outside. A few members from the predominantly black congregation from the church across the street were singing Christmas carols in the churchyard. They were horribly off-key. Aaron put his spoon down and picked up his coat and scarf.

"Mom, do you want to join me?"

She put her coat on.

"Are you coming, Paul?" Aaron asked.

"No, it's too cold for me, I'll stay here and watch the stove."

They were like children, so excited to go outside and sing. "I hope they don't sing 'Jesus is the Reason for the Season,' because I don't know that one," Bitsy said. As soon as they made their way across the street, the small choir sang "Jesus is the Reason for the Season." I laughed, looking from the window.

After a few more songs, Aaron came back in and got his guitar, hoping to keep everyone on key. I watched as he tuned his guitar and led the next song. They were so proud of themselves for being on key that they laughed and gave each other applause. Aaron and Bitsy came back in with big smiles on their faces, and Aaron returned immediately to the stove, not missing a beat.

Once the pots of stew were ready, we took them to the rehab center. When we returned, Aaron cooked our dinner—spiced oriental chicken and vegetables with mashed potatoes—from the dumpster, of course.

35
Dumpster Diving

Aaron wanted to hit the dumpsters after dinner, both for food and for Wendy's cups. Wendy's was running a promotion with AirTran in which you got a coupon on every large or extra-large soft drink cup. Thirty-two coupons got you a free one-way flight, and sixty-four got you a free round-trip flight. Two round-trip flights a year per person were allowed.

We hit three different Wendy's dumpsters sometime after midnight. The smell was horrendous. Everything you touch is slimy, caked with mashed potatoes, chili, ketchup, soda, and piles of uneaten food. I stood outside the dumpster, hanging my arm over, gingerly shifting around the bags on top.

"You gotta get in there," Aaron said, getting in there.

It's called diving for a reason. He dug deep, tearing bags open and emptying them out, shifting the trash elbows deep, with no regard for what he slopped on himself or his clothes. "When you see what we come back with, it's worth fifteen minutes of this," he said.

Next we went to Trader Joe's. Their dumpster was surrounded by a barrier and gate, but the gate was unlocked. Dumpster diving is legal except where prohibited by local regulations. Some places pour bleach on their food before dumping it and destroy items before throwing them away to deter dumpster diving, which they consider theft.

Aaron hopped in and pulled out bag after bag until there were about ten to sift through. One bag had bananas and oranges, and another bag had mixed vegetables for stirfry. Another bag was filled with bagels, pitas, various breads, and condiments. We found an assortment of cheeses and two roasted rotisserie chickens, fully sealed in their packages with the expiration date being the following day. There were mixed nuts, potatoes, and about six containers of fresh green beans. Aaron even found some flower bouquets to take back with us.

We sorted our find and spent the rest of the night washing out and cutting coupons off of Wendy's cups, nearly three round trips of AirTran flights.

36
Christmas Party

Christmas Eve brought our last shift at the flower shop. We got in early and were out by noon. The boss finally smiled, paid us in cash, and wished us a merry Christmas.

We rushed home and immediately began cooking for Elliott's Christmas party, which was starting at 1:30 that afternoon. We put the mixed vegetables into a stew and tore apart the rotisserie chicken to add to it as we went along. We then boiled the green beans and put them in a casserole dish with garlic, butter, and spices. One of the loaves of bread we found had cheese and tomato in it, so Aaron made a basil sauce to spread on it. He experimented with the strange cheeses we found by putting them together on a pizza and hoping for the best. We made a big pot of mashed potatoes with garlic and seasonings, then followed that with fruit smoothies made from the fruit we found at Trader Joe's.

With guests arriving, we spread the food out on the table just in time. Aaron got everyone's attention and informed them that most of the food was retrieved from the trash, but no one minded. Not content, Aaron made another pot of stew with what was left to bring to the rehab center that evening.

I was introduced to everyone in the band but Rickie, who couldn't make it. As I stood in the kitchen stirring the stew, Chris Kleinberg asked me how I knew Aaron.

"I met him at Cornerstone this year. I've been living in my car and have been kind of lost all year, and for some reason Aaron offered to help me. Aaron inviting me here is saving my life, just his friendship alone. This family is amazing."

I broke down over the stove and started crying. "I'm sorry," I said, wanting to run and hide.

Chris hugged me.

"This really is an amazing family," one of the girls standing there said. "They call Bitsy 'Saint Bitsy' because of her patience with Elliott."

Embarrassed that I was draining the room with heaviness, I apologized, excused myself up to Aaron's room, closed the door and collapsed on the bed. I covered my head with a pillow and sobbed, for some reason, missing Natalie.

On Christmas day, the family went out of state to visit Aaron's grandmother. Though I was invited, I thought I could use the quiet and rest of having the house to myself to unwind.

When they retuned, Aaron showed me a really sharp looking shirt he'd received as a gift and asked me if I wanted it. He held it out in front of him as if it were a dirty diaper.

Bitsy scolded him that he should appreciate the thought. "Maybe you could tear it, pour some paint on it, and take it dumpster diving a few times," I added.

As we got back to cooking more food for the homeless that night, I reminded him that in all of our conversations the five days that I'd been there, we hadn't once talked about the band.

"Good," he said. "That's exactly the way I like it."

37
Thursday

The day after Christmas, mewithoutYou set off for a string of sold out shows in New Jersey with Circle Takes the Square, The Blood Brothers, and Thursday. Aaron invited me to come along.

On the way to the House of Blues in Atlantic City, an acoustic guitar was passed around the bus. Anyone could sing whichever songs they wanted while the rest of us sang along. Rickie played energetic renditions of "Knights in White Satin" and "Hotel California."

We brought some unsold Christmas trees from the lot the bus was parked in as well as the flower bouquets Aaron found in the trash to use onstage, but we were not allowed to bring them inside due to the fire hazard they posed.

Thursday's vocalist Geoff Rickly came up to the green room to meet the band. "I thought you guys were just one more Christian band, so I wasn't really willing to give you a chance. But I read the lyrics and was blown away. I think you guys are so amazing. I can't wait to finally see you live."

I agreed, tongue-in-cheek. "I thought the music was terrible. It took me a long time to get into these guys. It was the lyrics that drew me in, too."

Mike, stringing his guitar on the floor, pretended to be offended. "Hey! What's wrong with our music?"

As mewithoutYou performed, Aaron thanked the guys in Thursday for being so kind and for sharing their catering with them. When Thursday played, Geoff asked, "How amazing was mewithoutYou?"

After the show, I lingered in the lobby of the casino, waiting for Aaron who had wandered outside to the beach for some alone time. There were a handful of fans waiting to meet him for pictures and autographs. When he came in and met with the fans, Aaron didn't crack a smile. He looked overwhelmed.

Mike and his wife Sarah asked me if I wanted to join them to get a slice of pizza in the casino. "Aaron, we're gonna get some pizza, do you want to come eat with us?" I interrupted him as he was signing a T-shirt.

"Ah, you know me, Paul. I'll just find something," he said, pointing to one of the lobby trash cans.

Mike, Sarah, and I walked through what seemed to be miles of twinkling lights and slot machines before finally finding the food court. Over mediocre pizza, I asked them what they thought of Aaron's eccentric behavior, troubled that he would rather eat from the trash than join us.

Mike said he saw the change in Aaron literally overnight. "He used to really be into the band and cared about fashion. Then, one day, he was in ragged clothes, oversized T-shirts, and started eating from the trash. He seemed to care less and less about the band, even to the point that he lost his vocals and couldn't scream anymore. Rickie and I are really dedicated to this band, and we can't imagine doing anything else. It's hard to get excited about writing songs to bring to Aaron when he isn't interested. Just once, I'd love for him to come up with a great idea or show some excitement for the band. But then he comes back with these lyrics and we're all blown away. He's definitely the genius in the band."

Two nights later, mewithoutYou played another show in New Jersey. Aaron slept in his bunk until we woke him up for show time. He took the stage unkempt, straight from his bunk. When the set had ended, Aaron came directly back to the bus. His pastor, Joshua Grace, and Scott from the Psalters joined the band onstage and hung out on the bus afterwards. When Aaron was told there was a group of fans outside waiting to meet him, he wasn't interested. "I have enough friends right here I don't spend enough time with."

With their final show sold out in Philadelphia, Aaron used his guest list spots for his dad and for another friend who had come to visit. His mom didn't go to the shows because she didn't care for the music or "all that yelling and shouting he does," but she was proud of him anyway. Overwhelmed from the travel, noise, and company the past few days, I was happy to spend that evening alone in Aaron's room.

As I enjoyed the peace and quiet after traveling just a couple of days on the bus, I realized how difficult it would be for me to endure touring in a band. A bulk of the time is spent driving, loading in and out, doing sound checks, and finding things to do with hours of downtime. The actual performance is such a small part of it. Just two shows were enough that I was tired of being in a moving vehicle with no privacy. How so many people can function together in such close quarters for weeks on end I'll never know. I was content to never be in a touring band.

38
Kensington

After the shows, Aaron took me on a walking tour of the poorest neighborhoods in the area, like Kensington, to show me the abandoned factories. "Hundreds of thousands of people lost their jobs when these factories shut down. Now the people in this town collect aluminum, glass, plastic, scraps, and anything they can find on the street to sell. The main sources of income in these neighborhoods are welfare, drugs, and prostitution."

Christianity Today wrote:

> Kensington was once one of the most productive areas in America. It is home to hundreds of factories and thousands of row houses built a century ago for the workers. Residents used to say that job hunters walking down "factory row" on American Avenue would have a job by the time they reached the end. Huge stone churches, including St. Edward's, testify to a once-prosperous community. But over the last 30 years, the neighborhood lost more than 250,000 jobs as factories moved overseas, became automated, or simply went out of business. Families moved too, leaving 25,000 abandoned homes. Today it is Pennsylvania's poorest neighborhood. All the manufacturing is gone, leaving 700 crumbling, empty brick factories—often home to the replacement economy of prostitution and drugs, and sometimes, like abandoned churches, shelters for families with no better place to stay.[149]

Aaron then took me to see blocks of abandoned lots surrounded by the artwork of Isaiah Zagar, who created mosaics of angels among other mediums in an attempt to bring beauty to

---

[149] Rob Moll, "The New Monasticism: A fresh crop of Christian communities is blossoming in blighted urban settings all over America," *Christianity Today*, September 2005.

abandoned places.

Walking tours like these were suggested by Shane Claiborne to promote awareness and to encourage social justice and action on behalf of the poor. But the more Aaron showed me, the more depressed and overwhelmed I became. I didn't catch the vision of helping the poor or meeting the needs of others. I needed every bit of energy I could find just to keep myself alive. I felt compassion fatigue before I had an ounce of compassion to spend.

Still, Aaron wanted to take me to the Bruderhof to see love and community in action.

39
Bruderhof

After being on the road for close to four hours, and me learning that you can't pump your own gas or make left turns in New Jersey, a group of us arrived in Rifton, New York. Entering the property of the Woodcrest Bruderhof, we were met with a breathtaking view of the Appalachian Mountains. The property was so clean and pictureque it looked like a small paradise.

We arrived just at dinner time and entered the large communal dining area where we were separated to open seats at long tables. Every man wore blue jeans and a plaid shirt, while every woman wore a blue dress and a head covering. Most of the food they served was homegrown from their gardens or their own livestock.

As dinner ended, their pastor, Heinrich Arnold, led prayer in a heavy German accent. The entire gathering then erupted into a hymn from where they sat. I'd never heard so many voices harmonizing so beautifully. It was so powerful I was moved to tears.

During a previous visit, Aaron recalled that an elderly member was dying. It was customary for the people to gather around that person and usher them into heaven by singing. "It sounded like heaven on earth," he said. I now had a glimpse of what he was talking about.

After dinner, I was introduced to the family that was hosting me. Ben and Daphni showed me to my room where a plate of cookies and chocolates were awaiting me, accompanied with a homemade card from their daughter and newborn. The apartments inside were just as clean and ordered as the grounds looked outside. This was not JPUSA.

They sat down with me and offered me tea, welcoming any questions I had. Knowing very little about communal Anabaptists, I expected the conversation to be awkward. Given their separation from mainstream culture, I wasn't sure we'd have much to connect on.

"Everything looks so clean and pristine, and everyone seems so nice and peaceful. Is it difficult to live in a community like this and not have the freedom to explore the culture outside?" I asked.

"Oh, we're far from perfect," Ben said. "Living in community can be difficult just like living with any family can be difficult, but we humble ourselves for the greater good. We have the same problems here that anyone else has."

"I didn't want to be with the community," Daphni added. "I had a job in Florida and enjoyed my freedom. But I started to realize what a dangerous place the world was and wanted the safety and familiarity of community life."

"Do you miss being able to dress however you like? Do you get bored with the uniform clothing here?"

Daphni lit up. "Oh, no, I love this. It's such a relief to wake up every day and not have to compete with others for attention or promote myself or worry if I'm pretty enough or if my hair is done right. We don't dress to draw attention to our bodies because we want to pay attention to each other in ways that matter."

"I stayed for a few months at a place called Jesus People USA in Chicago but found that in micromanaging my every move, I felt too suffocated and had to leave. People worry that places like this are cults because the leaders overwork the people and control every aspect of their lives. What it is like here?"

"When you are baptized into the community," Ben started, "you are making a life commitment to God and to each other. You trust the godly character of the leadership and are willing to humble yourself to do whatever they ask, knowing it is God's will and for the good of the others."

"If I was asked to give up my baby to do the work of the Lord, I would," Daphni said, holding her newborn. "We trust each other with our children here, knowing they are in good hands, and we trust that our leaders hear from God. There are women who have given birth and were sent off on months-long mission trips, having no fear or worry about leaving their babies with others." Some were sent to start communities in extremely dangerous cities, like Camden, New Jersey.

"How do people date and marry here? Is there a courtship model, or does the leadership choose spouses for one another?"

"We write letters." Daphni said. "We find it's the best way to communicate, share thoughts, and get to know each other. When you choose a person to begin writing letters to, no one knows but your parents. Nothing is made public until you announce that you are engaged. That way, if someone decides not to pursue someone further, there is no public humiliation."

Our conversation began to wind down, and it was almost time for bed. "I was worried that I would have a hard time connecting with you guys, but it wasn't awkward at all. I thought, 'I wonder if these people have ever heard of The Simpsons.'"

They laughed. "Of course, we love The Simpsons."

The next day, I went with the men to work in the factory, making equipment for disabled people. They also made high quality wooden toys and furniture under the name Community Playthings. After I helped assemble a few trays for scooters, I was given a tour of their very clean, organized, and impressive factory.

At break time, we all gathered into a room around a large table for coffee and donuts. A man read announcements over a microphone, then passed it around for others to share thoughts and prayer requests.

When the mic came to Aaron, he said, "I don't know if this is too personal or the wrong time to be doing this, but the Bible says to confess our sins to one another, and I've been carrying such a heavy burden of guilt." Aaron began confessing personal sins.

"Well, this isn't normally what we use this time for," said the man who made the announcements, "but let's pray for our brother." With that, we bowed our heads and prayed.

New Years Eve was the biggest night of the year for the community. Everyone gathered in the communal dining room where all of the chairs were arranged in a large circle. In the center of the room stood a huge tree adorned with hundreds of unlit candles. After singing hymns and listening to a message from Heinrich Arnold, each person approached the tree one-by-one to light a candle, repenting for the previous year's sins and stating something in the way of a resolution.

Young and old alike came forward to light candles for more than two hours. The most common prayer was, "Lord, forgive us for our good intentions." As this continued, many in tears, I began to think they were beating themselves up for nothing, taking a masochistic posture in berating themselves and groveling.

This is all bullshit. I want to go home. I want to die.

I saw through everything, thinking it was all so absurd. I dissociated again and had the sudden urge to run out the door as fast as I could and find a way to kill myself.

The room started to become jubilant as they passed around the spiked coffee and baked goods. I welcomed the terrible taste of alcohol and let the coffee run hot down my throat. I tried to drink enough to get drunk, but to no avail.

Now paralyzed with social anxiety and unable to look anyone in the eyes or even fake a smile, I excused myself, went back to my room, and sobbed myself to sleep.

Knowing we were leaving by noon, I woke the next day and visited the famous Muir House, a straw bale house the kids helped build out of recycled materials, and it runs on alternative energy. From there, I toured their museum which displayed an impressive history of the Bruderhof throughout the centuries, starting with the early church, moving through the Radical Reformers and Anabaptists, their persecution in Germany, their communities thriving in different parts of the world, and the birth of the Community Playthings business.

On the way out, I browsed the books on display from their publishing company, Plough. With so many titles to choose from, like *The Gospel in Dostoyevsky: Selections from His Works*, it was *Provocations: Spiritual Writings of Kierkegaard* that stood out. I bought two copies with Aaron in mind. After leaving the museum, I gathered my belongings, said goodbye to our hosts, and met the others at the car.

I sat next to Aaron in the back seat on the way home. I took one of my copies of *Provocations* out of my backpack and handed it to him. "I got one for you and one for me."

"I picked one up, too." He took out his copy. His cover featured a blue profile of Kierkegaard on a black background, and mine had a penciled drawing on a yellow cover. "I liked that cover better, but they didn't have any left when I bought my copy. It looks like you got the last one. Would you mind trading?" I traded with him, and we read snarky quotes to each other, laughing at Kierkegaard's brazen wit.

After a while he took out his book of Rumi poems and began browsing through it. He tapped me on the shoulder, held the page open, and with a smirk on his face, pointed silently to a selection:

I am so small I can barely be seen.
How can this great love be inside me?

Look at your eyes. They are small,
but they see enormous things.

I looked back up at him. He was shaking his head in shame. "I'm such a thief." These lines are reworked in "Four-Word Letter (Pt. 2)."

We pulled into a rest stop that happened to have a Wendy's. Aaron went straight to the trash can by the entrance and rummaged for food. A man approached the trash bin to throw away the rest of his ice cream cone, and Aaron took it off of his hands. When he had finished eating it, he headed around back and jumped into the dumpster, collecting another flight or two in empty cups. I sat in the back seat, watching and laughing as he approached the car with a bag of dirty cups to cram into the trunk.

Circle of Hope was having a service that night. Despite being tired from the ride back, we voted to attend. When we got to Philadelphia, we stopped for gas. Aaron ran over to the bin behind Dunkin' Donuts and returned with two large, sealed bags of donuts and muffins, smiling big. He excitedly named all the flavors he'd scored. When we got to the service, he spread them out with the rest of the snacks and made sure everyone knew where they had come from.

While mingling over snacks and dumpster donuts, I spotted

Amanda and walked over to say hello.

"I'm trying to get Aaron to write a song proposing to you on the next album. He's constantly talking about quitting the band, so it's now or never."

She waved her hand dismissively. "Oh, he's been threatening to quit the band for years."

40
Dumpster Diving (Pt. 2)

Aaron came downstairs from his shower completely clean-shaven, which he thought his mom would like. He looked in the mirror and sighed. "I look like an eleven-year-old boy. I'm letting it grow back as soon as possible, that's for sure." He went to his room and looked through his dresser drawers for a nice pullover shirt.

"You look sharp, man," I said. "You clean up well! Mike said you used to dress fashionably, then just stopped one day without warning. What happened?"

"I was at Cornerstone wearing nice stuff and dancing around onstage. A fan approached me with tears in his eyes, saying he wished that he could be as cool and attractive as I was, that girls would look at him the way they look at me. That did it for me. I felt terrible."

We took my car through the rain to the lot where the bus was parked so Aaron could drive it to the practice space the band rented in Fishtown to start working on the new album.

When the bus wouldn't start, Aaron thought some filters needed changing. He found a piece of cardboard to lay under the bus, emptied an apple and an orange from his pockets, then slid underneath and went to work. When he came out, he was covered in grease and water, his hands and face and nice shirt stained. He just couldn't stay clean for long. When the bus still didn't start, he plugged it in to charge it, and we returned to his place, cold and wet. As we drove off, I noticed his apple and orange still sitting on the ground by the bus.

A few days later, a group of his friends came over, and we went to a mom-and-pop restaurant for cheese steaks. Aaron didn't buy anything, but he took a bite of mine. On the way out, he couldn't resist the dumpster of the grocery store across the street. He and his friends filled my trunk with Trix yogurt and cheesecake bars, only to come home and find they were expired.

"Can we take your car to get more Wendy's cups and maybe stop at Trader Joe's to see what we find?" Aaron asked.

"Sure, I'll sit this one out," I said, not wanting to go back out in the rain.

They returned a few hours later with so many bags, it took over an hour to sort everything out. We piled and inventoried everything they found, taking up the kitchen floor, counter space, and tabletop. There were 27 bags of various gourmet salads; 8 packages of pork chops; 8 packages of angus beef rib eye; 9 packages of kosher rib eye steak; 5 roasted chickens; 10 subs and sandwiches; 10 packages of broccoli and cauliflower; a carton of eggs; 8 packages of garlic potatoes; 2 packages of uncured beef hot dogs; 10 bags of baby spinach; a package of spiced chicken sausage; an assortment of 35 cheeses; 7 loaves of various breads; 3 packages of whole grain muffins; 5 packages of wasabi shrimp; 2 shrimp party platters; 3 shrimp California rolls; honey Dijon salmon; and an assortment of fruits, vegetables, and cakes.

To celebrate their catch, Aaron picked up his guitar and sang some Neutral Milk Hotel, Bob Dylan songs, and Christmas carols in his scarf and poor boy hat while we sat on the couch and sang along.

41
Conversations

Up until this point in our time together, Aaron and I spent hours nearly every night discussing God, philosophy, and theology and their relation to our hopes, doubts, and struggles with depression, suicide, and relationships.

In of one of these discussions, I handed him my copy of *The Myth of Certainty*. "Aaron, this book has really helped me. Daniel Taylor basically says that we cannot be certain that Christianity is true. Despite our best efforts, we have to live with our doubts and frustrations. He concludes that we have to risk faith."

He opened it to the first chapter, which began with some words from T. S. Elliott's poem "Ash Wednesday" in which he asks God for mercy and to forget matters he discusses and explains too much.

"Did you even read the first page, Paul?" Aaron asked, in light of our endless discussing and explaining. We understood that all of this ruminating and speculating about God was probably useless, but we couldn't help ourselves.

"I feel much more at home in Sufism than Christianity," Aaron started. "Sometimes I think God is truth, or love, or the ground of all being; you who give us our being, the beginning and the end, reality itself. Sometimes I will say, 'Thank you, Father,' and other times, 'Thank you, Mother.'"

"Brian McLaren talked about our metaphors for God, saying that the ones we use the most often tell us more about ourselves than God," I said. "If you are an artist, you emphasize his creativity. If you are a scientist, you emphasize his mind and ability to design and create order. If you're a philosopher, you emphasize his wisdom. If you are in the military, you emphasize his strength and might. If you are an ecstatic, you talk about him in romantic terms as a lover. Is God really a mother or a father, a husband or a wife, or a judge or a king? These are all metaphors and anthropomorphisms—God relating with us on human terms.

At the end the day, I think he's more than we can ever conceive, understand, or speak of. In a certain sense, he is forever elusive and mysterious."[150]

"Yeah," Aaron agreed. "We're just using words."

"But man, I need God to be personal. I need him to know my name. I need him to know me and love me. I need to be significant to him. I need a universe that is made for a purpose, with him in control. I need him to say everything will be alright in the end. That's the only thing that gives me peace. But if I want him to be a person with feelings towards me, I have to accept that he has all of the limits and vulnerabilities of a human person with emotions, which doesn't make sense. He then looks all too human. I can't have it both ways."[151]

"Maybe we don't understand the Trinity, and maybe we can't defend the inerrancy of scripture, but we can understand what it means to love our neighbor, feed the poor, and not take revenge on our enemies," Aaron said. "Jesus told a parable of a man who had two sons. He told one of them to work the vineyard that day. His son said he wouldn't, but changed his mind and did so later that day. The man told his other son to work the vineyard and he said he would, but didn't. Jesus asked which one did what the father wanted, the one who said the right thing, or the one who said the wrong thing but obeyed? Jesus then warned the religious leaders that the tax collectors and prostitutes were getting into the kingdom before they were."

"Some Christians might keep others out of the kingdom, telling them they're not saved because they have incorrect doctrine or for not being able to formulate the Trinity correctly," I added.

"Never mind figuring out the Trinity or the deity of Christ," Aaron said. "I can't even figure myself out."

"I've often found the arguments of skeptics and atheists much

---

[150] This is called negative, or apophatic theology, which describes God by what we can't know, rather than cataphatic theology, which emphasizes what can be known about God. Mystics err on the side of negative theology, systematic theologians on positive theology, and others try to find the balance.

[151] For more on this, look at discussions on the openness and of impassibility of God.

more convincing than those of Christian apologists," I added.

"There are good reasons to be an atheist," Aaron responded, "but also plenty of good reasons to believe. John Lennon wrote a song called 'God' where he gives a list of things he doesn't believe in, you know, Jesus, the Bible, Buddha, Krishna. He gets through all of these religions and historical figures and ends up basically saying that he only believes in himself. I remember thinking, 'God, even though sometimes I don't believe in you, one thing is certain—I will never believe in myself.'"

"When I was in high school and all of my fundamentalist beliefs crumbled, I lost my faith. The only hope I had was that God was bigger than my fundamentalist theology and maybe any of our religions. To be completely disillusioned, then have God show up outside of my expectations, is both scary and hopeful at the same time," I said.

"Yes, in that order," Aaron replied.

"I can only hope he shows up in some unexpected way again. I wonder if any of what happened the past few years really was God."

"But you don't have to wait for something supernatural. You can give a thirsty person a cup of cold water, can't you? You can visit a lonely person, can't you? The Bible says we are the body of Christ, being God to the world. But Jesus also identifies himself as being in the oppressed we are reaching out to. God is in all of it."

Aaron's emphasis on the practical and accessible—rather than being paralyzed by weighty abstract theology or rare supernatural encounters—was refreshing, much like Brian McLaren's advice to simply follow the teachings of Jesus, but I was looking for what I once had and lost. I knew that one ecstatic touch from God could heal my pain, make me alive, and close the black hole in my chest in an instant.

I apologized to Aaron for visiting in such bad shape. I had a hard time making eye contact with him and was still continually holding back spontaneous tears.

"Sometimes I think maybe if I just had good sex with a beautiful woman, it would help me come back to life. Maybe I should stay single and just sleep around for a while. It's a lot easier than trying to find the right one and make a relationship work," I suggested.

"Oh, it will be lots of fun, but you'll want to kill yourself even more," he countered.

"Well, maybe I should just stay single and enjoy porn the rest of my life. Maybe I just want the beauty of women to nurture me, like art at the museum, or like looking at the beauty of a sunset."

Aaron laughed. "I had a friend who tried to pull that one on me before, that looking at naked women was like looking at a sunset. I asked him, 'Oh yeah? When was the last time you were caught jerking off to a picture of a sunset?"

42
Conflicted

Throughout the week there were a number of potlucks and gatherings filled with warm and friendly people. I sat with Chris Kleinberg for a while at one of these gatherings. In many ways, he sounded just like Aaron.

"I'm conflicted about being in this band, too. I don't know how much longer I'll do this. Jesus never said to go play in bands. I want to buy property and open it to low-income families and make beds available for travelers passing through, something closer to the mission of Jesus than being in a rock band and playing songs."

"I tried to convince Aaron that the body has many parts, and people are called to do different things, so there is no shame in one being called to play music and the other being called to feed the poor. I wouldn't feel guilty about being in a band. Aaron feeds the poor *and* plays in a band."

Like Aaron, Chris wasn't satisfied with that.

While Aaron was content to refurbish a burned out shell and squat, Chris's wife Nikki had a vision for something much nicer that sounded more like a bed and breakfast. She imagined having rooms she could decorate with flowers to give people an aesthetic experience. This was a vision of communal living I could definitely get behind.

Chris randomly picked up *Breakfast of Champions* by Kurt Vonnegut and opened the page to a drawing of an asterisk. With a boyish grin, he pointed. "That's a drawing of an asshole." I turned the pages and was immediately sold on Vonnegut's dark humor. "You can keep it if you want it." He gave me the book.

On the way back, Aaron put in a demo CD of music the guys had come up with. We didn't say anything while listening to it. The track ended as we pulled up to his house, and Aaron groaned. "This really bores me. I'm not interested one bit in being in this band. I absolutely hate going away to write and trying to come up with something profound to say. But somehow, in the end, I'm happy with the finished product."

"What would you like to do that you wouldn't be bored with?" I asked. His friend had turned him on to an indie artist called Devendra Banhart. We were particularly taken with a folksy acoustic song called "Little Yellow Spider."

"I'd love to do a whole album just like that, but Tooth & Nail would never go for it."

Aaron echoed Chris' sentiments, saying again he wasn't sure how much longer he could keep doing this.

"Aaron, right now some suicidal kid in France who you have never met is listening to your lyrics, and it might be the only representation of God or hope he will ever get. Isn't that visiting the jailed and lonely in some sense? If it wasn't for the band, I never would have met you at Cornerstone, and you never would have invited me here to keep me alive."

"Thanks, brother," he said.

Still, like Chris, he was conflicted.

43
Goodbye

I knew I had to give Aaron space and that Philadelphia wasn't going to be my home, but I didn't know where to go next. Aaron sent out an email to friends asking if anyone could help me couch hop for a while.

"How much longer are you staying, Paul?" Elliott asked now that I'd been there over a week.

"Just one more week. I'm making plans now. You guys have been really kind to open your home to me like this."

"They must really like you. They've never let anyone stay this long before," Aaron confided. Bitsy ruffled my hair and said she thought of me as her own son.

But Elliott was still skeptical. "Are you really from Chicago? Are you sure you're not from the FBI?"

I showed him my driver's license. "You can go outside and look at my plates if it helps." This pacified him for the time being.

"Don't think you have to show me around or be responsible for me. Don't let me get in the way of the band. If you need time to yourself to write lyrics, I understand."

"Thanks, Paul. I appreciate you saying so. I'm not usually a very talkative person to begin with, and I tend to get overwhelmed easily, but I enjoy our conversations. When it comes time to write lyrics, I disappear with a stack of books and try to come up with something to write about. I absolutely dread it."

"Really? You come up with great stuff though!"

"I'm a thief. I steal all of my lyrics. I'm just a dirtbag, man. I'm sorry, I don't know what you expected when you came here. I don't even know why I'm telling you this." He laughed. "I'd much rather do tangible things, like work on the bus. I put up drywall in here for my mom, and I'd like to put in a new countertop. I like to work with physical things where you can see tangible results. You can't get that from writing lyrics and putting out albums."

"Wow, I'm the opposite. I have always been somewhat

terrified of the physical world. I find it scary and suffocating, especially because my body is in so much pain. I spend a lot of time thinking about God, transcendence, and spiritual things. I'm freed by imagination, creativity, and escapism. I'd rather read and write and make art."

"It's such a luxury, all of this sitting around, thinking and discussing," Aaron said. "I've always wanted a homestead like Thoreau's where your whole day is spent working with your hands, and you don't have time to sit and think."

I got the walking tour of the run down neighborhoods in Philadelphia. I visited the Bruderhof. Aaron bid on properties for our community upstart but didn't win them, and now he had to turn his attention to the band. We explored different philosophical and theological solutions for my despair. If that wasn't enough, Aaron was generous with his time and affection. Still, nothing helped.

"I'm sorry I brought you here for nothing." Aaron was exasperated, standing in his kitchen. "I wish I could give you the hope I have. I'm sorry I don't have any answers for you. All I know is I have a deep love for you, I'm glad you're here, and I'm glad you didn't kill yourself."

He hugged me.

In *Dark Nights of the Soul: A Guide to Finding Your Way Through Life's Ordeals*, Thomas Moore wrote, "You can let the people you trust know a little about what is happening. Just don't expect any brilliant revelations or resolutions. It is the friendship, and not the help you get from friends, that is important."[152]

It was at this moment that Aaron's friendship was a turning point for me.

My chest tightened when I realized we had just said goodbye and it was time for me to decide where I would go next.

---

[152] Thomas Moore, *Dark Nights of the Soul: A Guide to Finding Your Way Through Life's Ordeals*, (New York: Gotham Books, 2005), 266.

44
Rocket Cat

I called family in Florida and asked if I could drive down and stay with them while I looked for work and an apartment. They said yes and asked me to let them know when I would be arriving.

It was now the sixth of January, my last day in Philadelphia. We drove that morning to Rocket Cat Café where Aaron and I would part. He would go across the street to band practice, and I would be on my way to Florida. I was doing all I could to avoid an emotional and sentimental goodbye.

On the way there, Aaron handed me a $100 bill. He borrowed $20 from me to buy a pile of T-shirts from Circle Thrift. He planned to sew mewithoutYou patches on them and sell them as mewithoutYou merchandise. He let me keep the extra $80 to help me out.[153]

"I feel kinda bad that I brought you all the way out here for nothing. We didn't get the property. I feel like I let you down. I don't have anything for you."

"You did more than enough for me. Your friendship, your empathy, and your understanding were exactly what I needed. I'm just sorry I'm so broken, desperate, and clingy. I wish I could have met you in a healthier state and had something to offer you. You know, if you needed me, I would stay in a heartbeat."

We got to Rocket Cat and met the other guys in the band there. They went to the practice space across the street while Aaron talked with a friend for a few minutes. A customer came in and asked Aaron what he did for a living.

"Well, I'm frequently impatient with my dad. I'm often selfish and prideful," Aaron began confessing his sins. The man smiled, but Aaron didn't.

"You're in a band, aren't you?" he asked, perhaps recognizing Aaron or overhearing him talking with the other guys.

---

[153] Sorry, brother. The world now knows. There goes your reward in heaven.

"No, I'm unemployed at the moment," Aaron answered, then walked out the door to band practice. I couldn't help but laugh from my table.

I sat there at a table with my laptop, writing out directions to my grandmother's house in Florida. It was past noon and I wanted to get on the road, so I called her to confirm that I would be leaving shortly and arriving in two days.

"Now is not a good time. My back is out, and I'm not well. We have company coming, so there will be no room for you. Maybe some other time," My grandma said.

What was I going to do now?

I looked up Borders in Clearwater and saw that they were hiring. I called and told them I had history with the company. The assistant manager interviewed me on the spot over the phone. "I don't see any reason we wouldn't take you on. I'll talk to your former manager, and she can send us your information. You won't need to fill out an application. Just call us when you get here and we'll tie up loose ends."

Excited to have a job before I arrived, I found a hostel off of Clearwater Beach that was cheap enough for me to stay in until I saved up enough for an apartment.

When Aaron stopped back in the café later, I told him my situation and asked if there was somewhere I could stay for one more night. Chris, Nikki, and their roommate, Matt, welcomed me into their home for the evening.

"I have a bit of film left on my camera. Would the guys be okay with me taking a few pictures of the band practicing?"

Generally they weren't fond of things like this, but they agreed to let me in the practice room. While snapping pictures in the cramped space, I stepped on one of the cords, and the stringed lights flickered mid-song. When the song finished, Rickie said, "Did you see the lights flicker? What was that?" I thought I'd better get out of there before I did something worse.

Staying with Chris that night, a group of us watched *Devil's Playground*, a documentary about the Amish having a period called rumspringa where they can leave the Amish, experience life among the "English," and decide whether or not to stay Amish.

Chris continued to print out listings of properties he wanted to look at for his communal home. "If you don't find a place to stay and you end up homeless, you are always welcome back to stay with us," he offered.

"That's kind of you, thanks. I hope I won't need to take you up on that."

I woke up the next morning, my thirtieth birthday, to an empty apartment. On the counter was a homemade birthday card, drawn on the back of one of the realtor printouts. It had a cake with candles on it, drawn in red pen:

Happy birthday, Paul! Help yourself to whatever you like . . . cereal, milk, eggs. Coffee is in the white and green glass thing next to the coffeemaker, cream in the fridge, sugar in a little bowl. I put out a coffee filter, too. Maybe you will still be here when we return? Peace . . . enjoy your drive (and journey). Nikki, Matt, and Chris.

45
Parting Reflections

Sitting at Rocket Cat, I reflected on my time with Aaron. Was moving on a sign of failure because I wasn't establishing myself in Philadelphia and we didn't start our community?

No, just like my homeless experiment, I realized that I thrive best living by myself, having control of my own apartment and possessions. I also liked a good middle-class life in a nice suburban neighborhood rather than squatting in a poor neighborhood. Rather than taking on the world's problems, I needed simplicity and enjoyment. If that made me a bad Christian, I was willing to say so.

I recognized that for all I had in common with Aaron, I couldn't live his lifestyle with him. I worried for Aaron's safety on the streets. I worried for his health as he ate from the trash. I worried for his mental and emotional health. I worried when he wandered on trains and hitchhiked. He was not online except when checking emails at the library or on a friend's computer, he had no cell phone, and he was notoriously difficult to get ahold of. Leaving Philadelphia, I felt I would lose access to him.

I still had a strong desire for a monastic life—a structured life focusing on God, doing good works, and being a hermit—but I wasn't as focused on the social justice issues and activism that seemed in the forefront of the new monastic movement.

Just a few weeks after I left Philadelphia, Shane Claiborne published *The Irresistible Revolution: Living as an Ordinary Radical*, which told the story of the Simple Way and living as an "ordinary radical." He and a spate of other authors—David Platt, Francis Chan, and Kyle Idleman—were grouped together in a 2013 *Christianity Today* cover story: "Here Come the Radicals!" What they had in common was the goal of making comfortable middle-class Christians uncomfortable, often making them feel guilty and even questioning their faith because they weren't involved with those on the margins of society.

For all of the good this movement did, it wasn't without criticism. Matthew Lee Anderson pointed out that it is hard for many Christians to read these authors and walk away feeling like a Christian. If you were living a normal, middle-class suburban life and were involved in any number of Christian projects, this wasn't enough. "These teachers want us to see that following Christ genuinely, truly, really, radically, sacrificially, inconveniently, and uncomfortably will *cost us*."[154]

The insinuation was that if you weren't radical, subversive, and suffering, if your faith didn't cost you, if you were too busy enjoying your life, you weren't really following Jesus. This message resonated with relatively bored Christians who wanted more risk and adventure in their faith. But Anderson offers balance:

> By contrast, there aren't many narratives of men who rise at 4 A.M. six days a week to toil away in a factory to support their families. Or of single mothers who work 10 hours a day to care for their children. Judging by the tenor of their stories, being "radical" is mainly for those who already have the upper-middle-class status to sacrifice.[155]

The article further points out the tension between message and medium. The message of giving up all you own, leaving behind worldly comforts, and being among the poor was coming from wealthy celebrity authors often speaking in megachurches, using expensive equipment to spread their platform, and making plenty of money selling their books:

> The really radical path for a megachurch pastor these days would be to refuse to publish, to take a smaller church, to not podcast sermons, and to embrace a more monastic witness.

---

[154] Matthew Lee Anderson, "Here Come the Radicals! David Platt, Francis Chan, Shane Claiborne, and now Kyle Idleman are dominating the Christian best-seller lists by attacking our comfortable Christianity. But is 'radical faith' enough?" *Christianity Today*, 3/15/13.
[155] Ibid

The irony is that if they tried, we'd probably turn them into larger celebrities and laud their humility. The desert fathers had a similar problem. But if the message is going to critique the American dream for the people in the pews, then we may need pastors willing to show us the path of downward mobility with their lives.[156]

The more Aaron tried to be like Jesus, live homeless, shun the band, and put others before himself, the cooler it made him, the more fame it brought him, and the more people he influenced.

Anderson went on to wonder if the new monastics acknowledged their need for institution and the money needed to sustain it:

> The urgent rhetoric of preaching the gospel to the billion unreached and helping the poor right now leaves little space to create the institutions and practices (art, literature, theology, liturgy, festivals, etc.) that can transmit such an inheritance to the next generation, and to form belief in deeper and more permanent ways. Buildings cost money, and beautiful buildings even more. Universities don't feed the poor or win souls, yet they promulgate knowledge in the church and around the world. These are the gears of a transgenerational movement. Yet it's not clear whether radical Christianity has any room for them. Most of the stories that are told in these books clearly do not.[157]

Finally, he reminds us that Christians can be of service in all walks and strata of life:

> For us in the pews, testing ourselves must include deliberating about our vocations and whether we are called to missions, or to a life of dedicated service to the poor, or to creating reminders with art and culture of the gospel's

---

[156] Ibid
[157] Ibid

transcendent, everlasting hope. Discovering a radical faith may mean revisiting the ways in which faith can take shape in the mundane, sans intensifiers. It almost certainly means embracing the providence of God in our witness to the world. The Good Samaritan wasn't a good neighbor because he moved to a poor part of town or put a pile of trash in his living room. He came across the helpless victim "as he traveled." We begin to fulfill the command not when we do something radical, extreme, over the top, not when we're really spiritual or really committed or really faithful, but when in the daily ebb and flow of life, in our corporate jobs, in our middle-class neighborhoods, on our trips to Yellowstone and Disney World—and yes, even short-term mission trips—we stop to help those whom we meet in everyday life, reaching out in quiet, practical, and loving ways.[158]

"If Aaron feels called to live the way he does, to sacrifice comfort and live among the poor, that's fine," a pastor friend advised me. "But don't let him make you feel guilty or like less of a Christian if you don't. Christians in the New Testament enjoyed homes, possessions, and families too."

Dave Donaldson wrote an article for *Relevant* magazine called "Overcoming Compassion Fatigue" which was about the stress and burnout we feel when we spend our lives working to make a difference for the suffering but never step back for rest, relaxation, and enjoyment for ourselves.

Many found that the radical life of dropping out of school, selling their homes, and moving their families overseas to help people was not all it was cracked up to be. The romance and adventure of it turned quickly to the long grind and burnout. It was no more fulfilling than serving in their suburban churches. Seeing the impracticality of living a life of intentional suffering, they returned back to the middle-class life they left behind.

Warren Perry wrote an article for *Relevant*: "Have We Made

---

[158] Ibid

'Adventure' an Idol? The dangers of always searching for the next big experience." In it, he reminds us to slow down and make room for the ordinary.

With any luck, I would get this job at Borders, set up a nice studio by Clearwater beach, stabilize my life, and try, for once, to be ordinary.

46
Trinity of Desire

WELCOME TO FLORIDA: THE SUNSHINE STATE said the sign. I took off my coat. I soon found myself crossing the Gulf to Bay Bridge to Clearwater Beach. Nestled a block off of the beach was a small hostel.

Green potted plants and lawn chairs surrounded a small yard with the blue water of a quaint swimming pool completing the tropical setting. The hostel was set up like a small motel: the boys' dorms on one side, the girls' and couples' dorms on the other, the common dining area and office dividing them.

I paid to stay for one week and checked into my dorm, which included four bunk beds. I got the last bunk available. I was warned of the possibility of bedbugs, ringworm from the shower, that any of my belongings could be stolen by dorm mates, and that I could be accused of theft at any time. With the room cluttered, I kept my belongings with me on my bunk, under the covers. When I wasn't there, I locked them in my car trunk.

I took a shower in the egg-scented water and tried to sleep through all of the noise and activity in my room. Before going to bed, I emailed Aaron, telling him I was thankful for his friendship and our time together.

I went to Borders for my interview the next day. They hired me full time as a member of the morning shelving team. "We'll call you in a few days with your hours." I drove home, elated.

The next morning, the assistant manager called to tell me the store manager changed his mind. "I fought for you, but we had a meeting last night, and he liked another applicant better." They passed on me.

With only enough money to stay one more week and no money to repair my car, which now would not move when I pressed the accelerator, I decided to sell it and take the bus back to Chicago, where I would find a couch to stay on.

I scrubbed out the splotches, spills, and stains in my back seat and trunk from the garbage bags Aaron had piled into my car. "Why can't he just eat like a normal person?" I complained. Under the front seat, I found an apple and an orange like the ones Aaron left by the bus that rainy day, and I couldn't help but smile.

Aaron called a few days later and left a long, meandering voicemail. "Please forgive me for being late. I'm calling to wish you a content birthday, not necessarily a happy one, since God doesn't say we'll be happy all the time . . ." On and on he went, qualifying my birthday message theologically as only he can.

He sent a follow up email saying Amanda had dinner with two other girls he had a crush on. "I thought of showing up with a wedding ring: 'Can or will ANY of you marry me?' Lord, help us."

I responded, "I laughed at your long qualification for why my birthday shouldn't necessarily be a happy one. Wow, the Trinity of Desire all in one room? I'm so sorry, dude."

"Trinity of Desire!" he responded. "You are funny! May G-d protect us and have mercy on us."[159]

---

[159] Emails, 1/08/06-1/18/06.

47
Drowning

I was warned not to sleep on the beach at night because there were a number of homeless people being randomly murdered in St. Petersburg. I wasn't worried.

Now past midnight, needing time to myself, I put on my coat and walked to the beach. Leaving the street and moving closer to the water, my surroundings became pitch black. I could hear the waves, but I couldn't see them. I had the entire beach to myself.

I lay back in the cool sand, looking straight up at the dark sky. It seemed to go on forever. I focused on the moon. Hot tears ran down the side of my head and into the sand.

I was now trembling, choking on my tears, screaming at Natalie and God. All the tension in my body pulled together like gravity in my chest and I couldn't breathe.

I got up from the sand, brushed off my coat, and walked towards the sound of the waves. All I had to do was walk in, swim as far as I could without thinking about it, and sink. No one would see.

Now at the edge of the water, the brisk cold snapped me out of my numbness, and I stood paralyzed again, just as I had at Salt Creek in Brookfield.

"You're not going back to that fucking hostel, Paul, just walk in!" I yelled to myself.

A picture emerged in my mind. I saw myself as a dark silhouette walking into the water and disappearing, but there were two orbs of light in my chest. They were living, like fire. One had Natalie's name on it, the other Aaron's. As I imagined going under the water, these orbs crackled and sizzled, then were snuffed out, dying with me.

If you die, so does the love you have burning in you for them.

I imagined having a unique love for them no one else in the world had. They might need me someday, and I would have left them alone in the world.

"But what about me? Who has me burning on their heart? And where are you? Why can't you comfort me?" I asked God.

I turned around from the water and stomped reluctantly through the sand back towards the hostel, one step heavier than the other. "Now I'm gonna have to sleep in that bed and wake up tomorrow wanting to die again."

I opened my eyes the next morning, the world still a nightmare, my body burning, disappointed to find myself alive.

48
Van Buren (Pt. 2)

The drifters passing through the hostel were shady characters. Drunks and thieves, abusers and lost souls, many of them desperate like me.

A bisexual man flirted with me the entire time, saying I was gorgeous, trying to convince me to "flip sides." A former stripper and drug addict wanted to have sex with me and get an apartment together, reasoning that she needed to connect with the "positive energy" she sensed in me with her spiritual intuition. A drunk man bragged that he rented a hotel room and had a great night with an escort, while another bragged and showed everyone pictures of the underage girl he had sex with in Puerto Rico for just fifteen dollars.

More than anything, I wanted my own place again. I needed a bedroom where the door closed and locked for privacy, where I could sleep for days uninterrupted. I needed a bathtub to soak in. I needed the stability of an apartment again, a place to call home.

I applied for jobs at the mall, the hotels, and at the beach stores on Mandalay, but no one called. I worked one day of temp labor, spraying chemicals on the walls of the rooms in an old hotel, then scraping the drywall. I had run out of money after three weeks and needed to decide where I would go next.

Barry and Sarah, who were founding Mount Olive the last time I was in Arkansas, invited me to stay with them in Van Buren and help me find work, so I took them up on their offer.

My brother put $500 in my bank account to get my car fixed so I could make it to Arkansas, insisting that I not pay him back. "Just get a place of your own and get established again. No girlfriends, no roommates, no one else to depend on who might let you down."

The repairs cost almost all of the $500. With the little I had left and the money from day labor, there was just enough for gas to get to Van Buren, I hoped.

The drive to Arkansas would be sixteen hours. I made it as far as Atlanta before pulling into a rest stop for the night. Before leaving the next morning, my brother called me to tell me that my mom sent him a check for $50 to put in my bank account, which he had just finished doing. The timing was perfect. I learned I had just under $3.00 left as I coasted into Van Buren on empty.

Barry and Sarah gave me a warm welcome and offered me the guest room in their house for two weeks before I could either stay with Arthur or sleep on the couch in Barry's church office.

In the comfort of my own bed, behind a locked door, among people who cared for me, I cried myself to sleep in relief.

1/30/06
Email to Aaron

Aaron,

Hey brother. Just wanted to let you know I got into Van Buren last night and am enjoying luxury. I have a wonderful room and bed, privacy, good friends, and it is beautiful here.

I saw Arthur tonight and told him about my stay with you. "Is he weird? Are his beliefs way out there?" Arthur asked. I made you out to be two steps from our good friend Charlie Manson.

I miss you and love you. Hope the writing is going well,

Paul

2/02/06
Email from Aaron

Hey Paul,

I'm at the old library where we checked our e-mail after working at the flower shop that time. Glad to hear you've found your way to Van Buren safely and all that. My love to Arthur. As for the proximity to Charles Manson, I think 'two steps' is a generous estimate!

Peace be with you brother, your friend,

Aaron

2/18/06
Email to Aaron

Aaron,

Hello there. Just wanted to let you know that I have chosen to move back to Chicago in a week or so. I'm gonna stay with Arthur for a week, then head back.

I've learned how little control and understanding I really have over my life and of God. I have a ton of information and can talk philosophy, theology, and beliefs to no end, but they lead to no conclusive answers. So I'm letting go and living freely. It's the only thing I can do to survive. In an odd way, these overbearing suicidal tendencies make it so that I'm not so afraid of suffering and death.

So I will return to Chicago and enjoy the simple things, trying to revive my life. I certainly hope to see you before too long.

Thank you for sharing yourself. Your friendship has saved my life. God bless,

Paul

2/18/06
Email from Aaron

Paul,

I'm glad you've come to have a certain peace, and may G-d continue to help us both. Learning to be content is the real trick, isn't it? I was just reading Sadhu Sundar Singh: "The real victory is not that we should be saved from pain and suffering or death and evil, but that, by the grace of G-d, we may change pain into ease, the cross and death into life, and evil into good." The cross!

This weekend was a good one here in Philly. The Simple Way holds a "family reunion" community of communities sort of gathering. No one from JPUSA or Bruderhof there, but there were a handful of folks from Reba Place as well as quite a few other smaller communities around the country. Very exciting discussions—alternative economics, spiritual formation—and some intense, intense singing and praying. G-d is good brother. I love you.

Your friend,

Aaron

49
April

I started working at Books-A-Million in Fort Smith and got the job. In the meantime, I stayed on the couch in the unfinished house that was being refurbished into Barry's office.

After Church one Sunday, a group of a dozen of us went out to International House of Pancakes. I felt instant chemistry with a girl there, April, who was sitting next to her boyfriend. Every time our eyes met it was as if we were communicating with each other.

A few days later, she ate with Arthur and me at the Waffle House and explained that she hadn't been in love with her boyfriend for months now. She was trying to find a way out of that relationship.

By the end of the week, they were broken up. April and I found ourselves up all night talking in the car after church, and before we knew it, we had our first kiss and started seeing each other every day.

Arthur started a band called Marca, and given that April's ex was friends with everyone in the band, it put Arthur in a tough spot with me.

April and I were compatible with the exception that she was a Christian and my faith was still hanging by a thread. Some of her friends were concerned that I wasn't Christian enough for her and tried talking her out of dating me.

For fun, we went through premarital workbooks to see if we were compatible and started fantasizing what our wedding would be like.

"What are we waiting for?" I joked after a few weeks of dating.

"We could go downtown tomorrow if you want to. I would marry you right now," she said.

"Are you serious?" I asked.

"Yes."

I decided to get an apartment in Fort Smith and continue

dating her until July, making it almost five months. If all went well, I would propose to her at Cornerstone, and we would plan an October wedding.

MewithoutYou was playing Main Stage at Cornerstone that July, so I asked Aaron if he might want to help me propose from the stage. He didn't hide his reluctance. "Don't you think all of this marriage talk might be a little premature?" I tried to assure him that we would have been dating five months by then and many people propose and have happy marriages after dating six months.

My friend Jay emailed me from Chicago. In May, mewithoutYou would be playing the House of Blues with Minus the Bear, We're All Broken, and Thursday. He invited April and me to stay with him if we wanted to visit and see the band, so we planned a five-day trip for the week the band was in town.

"I'm going to make you fall in love with Chicago and move you there," I told April.

"There's nothing here for me—I'll move to Chicago with you. I love it there!" April said, tired of feeling mistreated by people in town and because her best friend lived in Chicago.

We walked around downtown Van Buren holding hands. We went to the park and fed the ducks. We sat at Aroma's over blended coffee, watching Family Guy clips on the laptop. We spent far too many nights at the Waffle House having great conversation. I used my meager tax return to take her out for steak dinner and a romantic movie: *The Hills Have Eyes*.

Through all of this, however, I was still completely numb.

"I love romantic things. I can't wait to see how you are going to propose to me. I want you to love me the way you loved Natalie," she said.

I cringed. The truth was I had lost all of my ability to be romantic. I was exhausted from a year of wandering and was focused on reestablishing my life and trying to curb the endless compulsions to kill myself.

I realized how much alone time I still needed to think and write. I could only spend a few hours with April, then needed to be alone. I began to doubt I could give her or anyone the attention they needed.

April was so light, exuberant, and fun, which is exactly what I needed. When she talked with my family and friends on the phone back home, they adored her and her southern accent, warning me I'd better not lose her. I told them I didn't really care what happened. "Wow, that's not like you," my mom said.

I warned April that this might all be too much for her—my despondency, heaviness, and melancholy. She told me she loved me and that it wasn't too much for her at all.

My old bookstore manager in Chicago offered me a full-time management position at the new store he was opening in Chicago that May, adding that he could give me twenty hours a week immediately to help set it up. Jay offered to let me stay with him until I could afford my own apartment, even offering to cover my security deposit.

"I'll move back now, take the job, and get our apartment set up, then it will be ready when you come in May. How does that sound?"

April agreed. I took the management position, made plans with Jay, gave Books-A-Million my notice, and booked April's flight to Chicago with the Wendy's cups Aaron and I fished from the dumpsters.

Just days before I was to leave, April began having her doubts. "Maybe we should pray about being together and ask God for a sign."

"That won't do any good. I had a dozen signs concerning Natalie."

"Well, then maybe you should be with her."

"She made a choice, just like you are making a choice. Do you love me and want to be with me?"

"Yes."

"Then there is nothing to pray about. We don't need any signs."

I drove to the park where we fed the ducks, and while sitting in my car, I reluctantly prayed for a sign. Given God's silence and the lack of explanation for why things didn't pan out with Natalie, I wasn't optimistic one would come. Praying seemed so absurd that I felt myself becoming an atheist as I drove away.

April met with Barry for advice. He approached me and said he thought it would be best that I stay in Fort Smith for another year. "You have a job, you have a great girl, you have a church full of people who care for you both, and I think she needs that spiritual support right now. Just get an apartment here and you're all set. I don't want to see you go back to Chicago and be back at square one again when you're so close to being established here."

I assured him that we would be fine. Besides, it was too late—I had already quit my job and taken the other position.

My last day in Arkansas, April and I were inseparable. We kissed goodbye with lovey-dovey eyes and big dumb infatuated smiles.

"Don't worry, you're flying in to see me in three weeks. It won't be long," I reminded her.

When my tax forms arrived at Aaron's house, he mailed them to me in a manila envelope he'd decorated with a black Sharpie. Inside was a note on a small scrap of paper:

PEACE BE WITH YOU BROTHER. MAY G-D PROTECT YOU. STAY GRATEFUL – CONTENTMENT EXISTS. AARON.

50
Chicago

Before I'd finished unpacking and settling into Jay's house, my boss told me another manager wanted to transfer to the store he had just offered me, so I needed to wait a few months for him to open the next one.

I reminded him that I was staying temporarily with a friend and needed those hours to get an apartment. I had just quit a job and moved back for this one, so he couldn't leave me hanging like this. Still, he didn't budge.

By the week's end, April called to tell me she was still in love with her ex. Dating me had been a big mistake. She really hurt him and wanted to forget it ever happened.

I held the phone, numb and dissociated, staring at the wall. "It's okay, I'm used to it." And just like that, I spiraled further into breakdown. With no job on the horizon for months, April gone, and nowhere to go next, I lost all hope.

I called my mom and beat around the bush about the meaninglessness of life, trying to say goodbye in the gentlest way possible. "If I end up killing myself, don't cry, Mom. Just go on with your life as usual. I mean, we hardly see each other as it is anyway, and I won't be suffering anymore. It's really no big deal. Everybody dies."

"Don't talk stupid. Are you trying to put me in the hospital?" She was angry. "Just apply everywhere you possibly can until you are hired, and get your life together. You're gonna lose all of your friends and wear out your welcome, staying on their couches, eating their food, and spending their money. People are gonna stop feeling sorry for you."

"I can't work. I can't even look people in the eyes, Mom."

"Just see a doctor and get some help, Paul."

Friends offered to pay for me to see a doctor and get on some kind of antidepressant to curb the suicidal impulses and obsessive rumination over my losses. I refused. I wanted God or nothing.

51
Elliott

"When I talk about my time with you, I tell people we are friends, but it seems we are more acquaintances than anything. I don't really know you well. It's not like we grew up together, and I don't live near you and spend time with you every day, so forgive me if I misrepresent our relationship," I said to Aaron.

"I don't determine my friendships based on physical proximity or the amount of time spent together," Aaron answered. "I spend time with people every day who I can't connect with and who don't identify with me, even in my own band. I connect with you, brother, and that's why I call you my friend."

It hadn't occurred to me that though those guys were friends with one another, a band was a professional relationship, like coworkers in any job, and sometimes you didn't have enough in common with people at work to spend time with them off the clock.

Rickie once said in an interview that when the band is off tour, they might go months without talking to one another. They were each doing their own thing, living their lives, then having to reacquaint when writing new material or going on tour.

"The other guys are gonna take you aside one day and ask you why you're hanging out with that weird guy from Chicago," I joked.

"Aww, no way, man!" Aaron piled on the compliments.

Elliott sent me more prayers in the mail as a member of the Brotherhood and called to say hello. I thanked him again for letting me stay with them, adding that Aaron had been a good friend.

"He's not a good friend to you. You always call him, but he never calls you."

"Well, he's in a band and he's a public figure, so he's busy and has a lot of people to tend to. He gets hundreds of emails. He needs his alone time as well. If it takes him a couple weeks to respond to me by email, he always apologizes, saying he has a couple hundred more waiting and doesn't own a computer."

"That's neither here nor there," Elliott said matter-of-factly.

Elliott was always difficult to get off the phone. There were times in his monologues that he forgot you were there. If you didn't interrupt him and tell him you needed to go, he would just keep talking, always about God, the FBI, Bush, and Bawa's fellowship.

Because I felt rude every time I had to interrupt him to hang up, there were many times I ignored his calls or hoped it was Aaron saying hello instead. I never called him to ask how he was doing. To Elliott, who was extremely lonely and found it difficult to connect with people and maintain friendships, I was a bad friend. But he never stopped checking in on me.

52
House of Blues Chicago

Now May, mewithoutYou was back at the House of Blues in Chicago to support Thursday. It was cold and rainy that day, and I didn't feel well enough to take public transportation into the city. Aaron called and left a message, inviting me to come say hello even if I was late for the show. "This is Mike's phone. Just call this number if you make it, and he'll find me."

I pushed myself, parking on the street near my old studio in Oak Park, then taking the train into the city. I arrived downtown at 11:00 P.M. to an empty venue, the band already out on the town. I called Mike, and soon afterwards Aaron emerged from nowhere, crossing the street with a group of friends. He gave me a big hug.

We went back to the bus, which was parked under an overpass with the other busses in a dark and seedy lot. We watched rats the size of small dogs scamper by and hide behind the garbage cans.

I brought a book of letters by Thomas Merton and a copy of *A Generous Orthodoxy* by Brian McLaren for Aaron. The few of us on the bus discussed what we liked and disliked about the emerging church movement.

When the other guys made it back to the bus and it came time for them to leave, I went out with Aaron and watched him get dirty filling up the bus from a grease bin behind a restaurant. Having a moment of privacy, I asked how he was doing.

"Too well. When things are going this well, you know there's nowhere to go but down. How about you?"

"I'm not as suicidal as I was before, but I'm getting there. I'm still lost and numb. Nowhere feels like home."

"Is coming with us tonight an option? You can finish the tour with us and stay in Philly."

"I really shouldn't. I need to focus on finding work and getting stable somehow. My car is parked by the train station in Oak Park. I didn't bring clothes or even my contact lens case, so

I'm not prepared for a trip. Maybe we'll talk more about it at Cornerstone."

I thanked him for inviting me, though I wasn't up for it, and hugged him goodbye.

"I love you, brother."

"I love you, too."

6/14/06
Email to Aaron

Aaron,

I am looking forward to seeing you in Dekalb, IL and at Cornerstone in 2 1/2 weeks.

I have been overcome lately with such a numbness and sense of meaninglessness that I don't want to do anything. I feel tired simply being awake. I feel like I can see through everything, and there is no substance or hope at the end.

Nihilism is "nothingness" in Latin. The typical atheist-existentialist understanding that life consists of no substance other than finding something to do and immersing yourself in the illusion that it is meaningful seems to ring true. I still say, "I want to die" every morning I wake up.

Every time I get this nihilistic, suicidal view of life and its meaninglessness, there is always this paradox that I love Natalie—as if she is worth something. Besides Natalie, you are the only other person I know who I would stay alive to love and take care of.

There is definitely a part of me that wants to be on an adventure, going place to place and meeting people. It's just that my "gospel" is a gospel of despair. So I'm screwed if I go and screwed if I stay. It sounds wonderful to me at the moment to sell my car and books, hop on the bus with you with $3,000 in my pocket and help out, maybe go back to Philly and help with Chris's Branch Davidian compound and enjoy the time and freedom I will have to do what I am passionate about. Then I think after a few months of that I will complain that I need my own bed, my own room, I'll want Chicago. So I'm torn, Aaron.

Well, thanks for reading, brother. I don't expect answers. I've just been paralyzed with sleeplessness and indecision. Behind it all I want my relationship with God back, and I want Natalie, and I'm afraid I will never recover from this.

Love you brother,

Paul

6/21/06
Email from Aaron

Paul,

I am truly sorry for your sense of meaninglessness. I understand to some extent of course—having read some of the same things and thought about a whole lot of the same things—your leaning that way. You think a lot and are very bright, but brightness is only brightness, and you see where the mind can bring us. I read something in one of Bawa's books the other day. I'll summarize it:

> Do not look at your own problems and weep.
> Look at the pain of others and weep.

Sometimes that helps me and sometimes it does not. The nihilism you describe seems the utmost absurdity, of course, to a certain part of me (what could be called "the heart, the deepest part of me that recognizes G-d as the source of incomparable love and grace"), and perfectly reasonable elsewhere ("the mind") and I see what trusting this or that leads to. All our thinking, our faith in our own reason and power of understanding seems a bit like looking at a map that says there's a road this way to a certain destination, but when we reach the road, we see that it drops off a cliff to certain death. But so convinced of the directions given by this map, we follow the road and down the mountain to our death, blaming the map makers and the road makers and the gravity makers all the while, rather than accepting responsibility for our driving off the cliff ourselves. The map is our mind. The road is the detached-from-faith-purely-intellectual path. The clear light of day that shows us the true danger of the road is G-d. The cliff is nihilism. The inventor of weak analogies is me.

I love you too.

As for your job and living situation, here goes some hard-nosed, light hearted advice:

* Sleeping on the streets can be nice in the summertime. Grow a pair of balls and screw rent, utilities, etc.

* No one needed cell phones 10 years ago and no one needs them now. Grow a pair of balls and throw it in the garbage.

* Riding a bike is better for the Creation, your physical and mental health, screwing the oil companies, and your checkbook. Grow a pair of balls and get rid of your car and ride or hop trains where you're going.

* The food and clothes we're buying for all we know are brought to us at the expense of slave labor—dumpster dive.

* If all this seems like too much physical pain or inconvenience, think of Jesus Christ who was executed in history.

With such a shitty world, is there any wonder we feel shitty? 30,000 children starved to death today. Do we want a parade in our honor? Ice cream cake?

PLEASE NOTE:

I'm smiling, enjoying myself at our expense. I don't know how well that will translate. I'm trying to make you laugh, and of course I somewhat mean what I say, but I'm kind of laying it on thick, I know. After your David Koresh comment, I figured the doors were thrown open wide for ball busting.

I can only imagine the pain of not being with Natalie. My heart has sworn to me I need this and that, Amanda, always a nice looking girl. I'm starting to suspect my heart, but it doesn't make my loneliness go away.

It's late and I'd better go.

Did I mention I love you?

Aaron

53
Paradoxes

Aaron followed up with a phone call to make sure I was okay. Following my theme of love seeming to point to ultimate value, he asked me if that could be a path out of nihilism.

"What if love is just a chemical cocktail, or a delusion that helps us experience life as meaningful?" I asked. The fact that I loved and valued a few people deeply didn't prove that my love mattered in any ultimate sense.

"But even if that's true, it's a profoundly powerful and inescapable delusion. If we are just a product of genes plus environment and free will is an illusion, it's an inescapable illusion. Why spend so much energy undermining it?"

I thought of those optical illusions where still pictures swirl and move, or you see shapes and colors that aren't really there. Scientists can tell you what your brain is doing to misperceive reality and create this illusion and even when you know better there is just no way to break the spell.

"If I have made Jesus my example and have lived my life in love and sacrifice, helping others, then I have lived a very meaningful, fulfilled, and sometimes happy life. If I'm wrong and we're just worm food, then I've lost nothing. If I'm right, and God rewards us according to our actions as the Bible says, then I come out on top. If I live a life not believing in God while undermining the purpose of everything I do, I remain depressed and unfulfilled. If I'm right that life is meaningless, death will be the end of a miserable life. If I'm wrong, I end up having to answer to God. You have very good reasons for disbelieving, and I don't want to minimize them. I'm not trying to pull a Pascal's Wager on you, but pointing out that even if you're right about this all being a delusion, it's much better to put your faith in God and live a fulfilled life of hope in him and loving others. In the end, if you are wrong, you won't even know it. It can't hurt."

Tired of talking about myself and my despair, I asked Aaron

how he was doing.

"A little disheartened. I hadn't been to church in quite some time, so I went across the street to the church where my mom and I sang those Christmas songs. When it came time to take the offering, they left the baskets up front by the altar, then ushered each row up there one by one. Not only did this make a show of who was giving, but it made a show of those who weren't giving. To see that kind of manipulation, my heart broke. I walked out and went upstairs to my room and wept."

My boss said he would have a store ready for me in August. I asked Jay if I could stay with him until then.

"Well I just moved Morgan in and we're building a relationship so we're going to need our place to ourselves soon. I talked with her and we agreed that you can stay until Cornerstone. If it was just me, you know I'd let you stay as long as you wanted, but this is her house too now."

I made plans to stay in my car in Brookfield again.

54
House Café

A couple of days before Cornerstone Festival, mewithoutYou was booked to play The House Cafe in Dekalb, IL with Unwed Sailor. I called Nikki and asked if I could hitch a ride with them to Cornerstone from the show, given I had no gas money to drive there and back.

"Well, the bus is pretty full so if there is any other way you can make it, I'd try that," She said.

I didn't find anyone else to go with, so I packed a couple of black trash bags with what I needed for the fest and brought it to the show with Mark and Jay.

I spotted Aaron passing through the crowd. "Hey, Aaron. I talked with Nikki on the phone a couple days ago, and she said there was no room on the bus to go to Cornerstone with you guys, but I brought my stuff just in case."

"Oh, there's room. You can stay in my bunk with me," he assured me. "I just need to run it across the guys."

"I have to be out of Jay's house by Cornerstone, and I really have nowhere to stay. Do Chris and Nikki have any rooms open at Cambria House?"

"No, they're all full. I have a room there, but I hardly stay. I want to go lower and lower. Jesus didn't have four walls and a roof or a place to lay his head, so I'm challenging myself to be more like him. I don't want to own anything I can't immediately give away. I'll never pay for rent, that's for sure. You're welcome to come back to Philadelphia and stay on park benches with me."

It wasn't the first thing I wanted to do.

After introducing Aaron to Mark and Jay, we found a spot to watch the show. "It looks like I'll be able to go with them to Cornerstone. Then I'll come back and get my stuff and go to Philadelphia, maybe stay in my car or on park benches with Aaron until I can figure something out. I have nowhere else to go," I said to Mark.

"Hey man, if you want to stay with me, you can have my couch for a month or so until you figure something out. I don't want to see you back in Philadelphia living on the streets."

"Thanks, man. I'll keep it in mind and talk to Aaron."

During the set, Aaron placed my name in some of the lyrics and looked over to see if I noticed. "Oh, Paul Harrison, let's go down, let's go down, wont'cha come on down?"

Although he was having fun, Aaron seemed depressed.

"Are you okay?" a fan asked him between songs.

"No," he answered.

"What's wrong?"

"You expect me to air all my dirty laundry onstage in front of all of these people? What kind of a person do you think I am?" The crowd laughed.

Mark and Jay needed to leave directly after the show because they had work early the next morning. I needed an answer from Aaron right away about going with them, but since I couldn't find him, I took my two large garbage bags of belongings from the trunk and laid them on the sidewalk. "If he says no, I'll just get a taxi home or hang out here overnight and call my brother to pick me up tomorrow."

While waiting with my bags, Nikki came out and said hello. "I'm a little upset. I kinda feel like you went behind my back when I clearly told you we have no room on the bus. I'm not mad, but here you are stranded with your stuff, and we're not just gonna leave you here. I just feel a bit disrespected." She gave me a hug and clarified that she wasn't mad.

"No, no, I'm not trying to manipulate you. My friends had to leave right away, and Aaron said there was room, so I grabbed my stuff just in case. If there is no room, someone can take me home."

"Sometimes I feel that I have to look after Aaron because he is so vulnerable and nice to everyone. He has a hard time saying no. I feel like people take advantage of him."

"He offered me a spot on the park bench next to him back in Philly. He said your place was full."

"Yeah, we're full and won't have any more rooms open until we build more in the fall. We're just praying that God gives you a family and a home, Paul—a place where you really feel you belong. Please don't take it personally or feel like we are rejecting you. We'd bring you along if there was room."

Aaron finally came out. "I'm sorry, I gave you the impression that you could come with us when I hadn't talked to the guys first. They aren't too happy because the bus is already full, and there is already tension because of it. Everyone has sorta found their space, and when we try to have devotions, some people only open up when they feel comfortable with everyone. It's taken some of them a long time to open up, and a fresh face might scare them back into their shell."

"It's okay, Aaron. I understand."

"We haven't been getting along. Sometimes I just keep to myself and we don't talk at all. It can get lonely, so it would be nice to have you along."

"I just talked with Nikki, and she was really sweet about it. She said she was praying that I find a true home."

"When was the last time you felt truly home?"

"When God told me to propose to Natalie. She wasn't supposed to say no. I've been off the map ever since. God has been silent, and everything I do collapses. I keep thinking God will make sure nothing works out until she says yes to me and we end up back in his will. I still can't believe she said no. I was never more sure of anything in my life. I keep trying to call her bluff, believing she really wants to be with me, but she says I'm too skinny, I'm not musical enough, and she doesn't find me sexually attractive."

"Well, Paul, I can't vouch for your musical talent, but I find you sexually attractive." Aaron smiled big.

"Are you saying I can't sing? I guess that makes two of us," I said.

He agreed and hugged me. I gave him a kiss on the cheek.

"Can you give me a few minutes? I'll be right back," he said.

He went back on the bus and deliberated further with the guys, finally coming out with an answer. "It's a yes, but it's a reluctant yes. You can come along."

"Am I gonna get the stink eye the whole time?"

Aaron laughed. "Yeah, probably."

"Well, I don't want to cause any trouble, man. I'll just get a ride home. But thanks for fighting for me."

Aaron got back on the bus and they drove off. Justin, who I'd met on the bus back at the House of Blues the previous month, chatted with me, then kindly offered to drive me back to Jay's house.

55
Nervous Breakdown

With my social anxiety came fear of leaving the guest room in Jay's house. I couldn't look anyone in the eyes, including him, so I spent a lot of time hiding. To handle the numbness, I started slapping myself in the face and punching myself in the chest as hard as I could to feel the pain, then adrenaline, and the endorphin rush and calm that followed.

With my health failing again and my need to see a doctor, I went back to the Social Security office to see about getting my disability benefits reinstated. To my surprise, they said yes. I would start receiving monthly payments in September, as well as medical benefits and a substantial amount of back pay.

This was the floor I needed beneath my feet, a light at the end of the tunnel. If I could just hang on for a few more months, I could set myself up in a place of my own, regain some stability, and finally collapse across the finish line.

My eyes were set on somewhere in the middle of nowhere, where I could disappear from people, noise, and movement, where no one knew me or saw me. If I couldn't be a monk, I would be a recluse.

56
Cornerstone 2006

Approaching the main gate at Cornerstone, I was met by protestors from the Pilgrim's Covenant Church. They had signs warning festivalgoers to repent or perish. "Christians don't go to Cornerstone" the signs warned as a man preached through a megaphone that Satan was behind Christian rock. This was proved by the fact that the women at Cornerstone dressed like whores and the guys in some of the bands looked like women. After explaining that everything at the fest screamed rebellion against God, the flyer continued:

> Cornerstone features ungodly, worldly music. Many of the songs have nonsensical—in a few cases, obscene—lyrics. Many of the singers ape the world's ways as they jerk, gyrate, and screech out those lyrics to ear-splitting music. Such musical performances glorify immature, worldly performers and appeal to the flesh, but they are not holy, and they do not glorify God. Those who take part in such sessions are mocking God in an ugly, worldly way rather than worshiping Him in the beauty of holiness.

After parking my car and getting my wristband, I started walking the main path to find a quiet spot to be alone. Then I spotted Aaron walking in my direction, carrying an acoustic guitar that a fan had painted flowers on and given to him. He gave me a long embrace. "I missed you the past few days and wished you could have come along with us."

Being alone at the fest, I was overwhelmed again by an embarrassing need to cling to him.

"How have you been since we last talked?" he asked.

"Oh, brother, I'm completely numb. I can't feel anything, and I don't want to be around anyone. Nothing seems to matter. I can't stop obsessing on suicide."

Aaron opened up the Cornerstone brochure and showed me a man named Art Gish from the Christian Peacemaker Teams standing with his arms spread in front of the barrel of a gun resting on a military vehicle. He was defending a farmers' market from being bulldozed.

"Paul, if you are going to kill yourself, do it like this." He pointed at the picture. "Go out on a mission for good, don't just off yourself in some lake somewhere."

"I don't know how to give you the hope I have in my heart," he continued. "I just know that everything lined up for me at the Simple Way a few years back, and I have a joy I can't explain."

"Did you happen to get a flyer from the protesters at the gate?"

"Yeah, we passed it around the bus and kinda laughed at it. But then I thought, they aren't that far off." He read aloud, "'Many of the singers ape the world's ways as they jerk, gyrate, and screech out those lyrics to ear-splitting music.' Yeah, that describes me. They speak of everything at Cornerstone being in rebellion against God. I'm tempted to go up there, hug them, and tell them they are absolutely right. They have no clue as to the level of rebellion in my heart."

Aaron walked me to mewithoutYou's campsite just off the main path near the Encore tents and offered me some food. "We dumpster dove just before we arrived and found some steak. I thought I'd let you know where I got it before I offered it to you. Would you like some?" He dug a small hole in the dirt to cook the meat in and started a fire. I accepted. As the steak cooked in the ground, Aaron went to speak with more friends nearby.

I sat and stared at the grass, breaking blades one at a time, dissociated from everything around me. I distracted myself by watching Chris work on the bus. I walked over to say hello and saw that he was covered in grease and dirt. Like an excited kid playing in the mud, he explained what he was working on, battery in hand, adding how much he loved solving mechanical issues with the bus.

Aaron returned to the steak, which was now ready, so I went back over and sat next to him. Seeing that I was still despondent, he handed me a plate of food. "Is there any room for lightness or play in your life?" he asked.

"Not lately. I'm just trying not to die."

Our conversation was interrupted as fans approached Aaron for pictures and autographs. Bruce Fitzhugh from Living Sacrifice and guys from other bands stopped by to catch up with Aaron and the others in mewithoutYou.

"I'm sorry, Paul. I'm so easily overwhelmed here. Cornerstone leaves me feeling quite scattered with fans and interviews and all."

"Oh, it's fine, Aaron. I understand completely." I hugged him. "Don't get too overwhelmed."

"Well, you don't get too underwhelmed. I mean, nihilism? Come on, Paul!"

I appreciated the sentiment and smiled. "Have a good show tonight, Aaron."

Closing the Encore Stage on Tooth & Nail Day at midnight, mewithoutYou played some new songs from the upcoming *Brother, Sister* album. The new songs featured more singing and melody, more background vocals, and there were even three acoustic songs about spiders. Scott Krueger and the Psalters came out to add percussion and vocals to some of the songs, but in my despondency, I wasn't enthused.

The following day, Aaron and I went to see Cliff Kindy of the Christian Peacemaker Teams speak about his experiences in promoting non-violence in Iraq. This was something of much more interest to Aaron, so I snuck off to peek in on a lecture about Soren Kierkegaard by Dr. Stephen C. Evans.

I asked Dr. Evans after the lecture if he thought I was wise to call myself a Christian existentialist as Kierkegaard and Dostoyevsky were said to be. He thought the term was too loose and open to too many meanings to do any good as a label or a formal position. Existentialists are renowned for shunning definition, often throwing off the label when applied to them.

I found myself back at mewithoutYou's campsite before their Main Stage set later in the week. "Aaron, are you going to sing your part in "Memphis Will be Laid to Waste" when Norma Jean plays Main Stage?"

"Yes."[160]

"Are you going to be giving a lecture at the Jesus Village tent again this year?"

"Someone told me I am supposed to be speaking Saturday, but I'm not sure."

"Okay, good. This gives me incentive to stay until the end of the fest. I keep wanting to run to my car and leave. I'm not sure how much longer I can be around people."

As we talked, Casey McBride of Cool Hand Luke gathered various scraps of cardboard and garbage, taping them together into a giant makeshift bird.

"Well, I'll let you get ready for your set. I'm gonna head down to Main Stage and find a good spot to videotape."

As I made my way to Main Stage, I passed the lake on my right. I covered my right eye with my hand like a horse blinder and walked fast as the pull to drown myself was almost irresistible.

It was hot and sunny late in the afternoon. The crowd wasn't impressive by Main Stage standards, and seeing the band stretched out on such a large stage, they looked out of place. The set was a good mix of songs from each album. Guest musicians added harp, trumpets, percussion, and vocals.

Aaron invited up to the stage anyone who wanted to dance for the last song, saying it was his favorite because it was happier than the other songs. "Boy, I sure had something real significant planned to say. That's how it goes, I guess." He fumbled.

What started as an acoustic intro to "In a Sweater Poorly Knit" ended with full instrumentation, harp and accordion, and a stage full of hipster-like "dancers" flailing around to a chorus of *I do not exist, only You exist.*

Casey McBride appeared in his white bird costume, dancing in circles with beak and full wings. All instruments quieted to just

---

[160] I recorded the performance and posted it on YouTube. My favorite comment on the video: "Gotta say I love this video/band/song, I just hate when that idiot hipster comes on the song at the end and starts whining into the mic."

Timbre's harp at the close of the song.

Fans talked about how the song moved them to tears. Feeling nothing, I was too despondent to enjoy the set.

57
Aaron Weiss's Message: Cornerstone 2006

On Saturday morning, Aaron spoke at the Jesus Village tent. Just before he took the platform, a group of children took the stage dressed in sheep costumes, singing, "I just want to be a sheep, bah, bah, bah, bah."

After their performance, the man running the stage asked everyone to pray for Aaron, as God had given him a platform to reach so many with the gospel of Jesus.

Aaron sat down on the folding chair onstage in beige shorts and a white T-shirt, with ruffled bed head and an unkempt beard. "Hello, how are you? Good to be here, etcetera. My name is Aaron, as he said. I don't know why you're here, exactly. I don't know why I'm here. I showed up to the festival and my name was written in the program for 1:00 right now, so I said, 'Oh.' I've talked before at this same festival and I talk too much. Forgive me if I say anything untrue. Forgive me if I say anything arrogant or misleading. I don't know what to say. I don't have anything planned."

Aaron "respectfully declined" anything good said about him in the introduction. "I got nothing for ya."

"About fifteen minutes ago there were some younger people singing and dancing onstage, and it was kinda cute and all that. I'm not very fond of kids. I wasn't moved on that level. But I was struck by something they were singing which was—I want to be a sheep, bah, bah, bah, bah. Frankly, at first, I felt nauseous because—you kids, if you're listening, are wonderful performers, very, very good, but somebody else probably wrote that song. But I wanted to address the lyrics, not the performance, it's a wonderful performance."

Taking his cue from the song, he continued, "We all, at some level, are going to be sheep, and I'm gonna talk, I think, about the ways in which that's good and ways in which that's bad. Jesus was considered the Lamb of God. You've all heard Jesus, you're all at

Cornerstone. The Lamb of God who takes away the sins of the world. Now, he was led to be killed like a lamb to the slaughter. That's one way that Paul says to be like sheep led to the slaughter, facing death all day long. There's another passage in the New Testament of the Bible that says, 'I send you out as sheep among wolves,' and so on my heart particularly at this festival also is this question of whether or not Christians should kill other people, and I simply have to wonder out loud: When has a sheep ever killed a wolf? If we are a sheep among wolves, we will be killed, but we will not kill."

Aaron said if you believe in your military or your government, that is nationalism and idolatry. People started clapping, but Aaron immediately stopped them and said he didn't want to start some new group or movement where everyone agrees and ostracizes those who think differently.

"Ultimately, the only thing I want to talk about is love. Never mind talking about it. The only thing I really want is love. The only thing I want to put into practice is love. The only thing I want to be is love. God is love—I am not love. I don't care about any of you. I don't care about anybody but myself. There's also this point in me, or this sense in me, that there's a better way than that, so I'm seeking it. I'm seeking that point. I'm looking for the kingdom of God that Jesus said was within me. I believe that kingdom is one of peace, justice, and unity which—if I may become very practical in my dealing with the world we live in—by unity I mean if you see someone else who's starving to death, that you have extra stuff that you don't need, you pretty readily give up all that stuff to help the person who is starving to not starve to death. This is biblical. This is also a matter of common sense. We're living in the richest culture that's ever existed in a supposed Christian country. Well, I wonder if any of you also have a hard time reconciling those things."

He insisted again that those who agree with him not start a new faction or movement and start pointing fingers at the other Christians. "We are the Christians who understand the gospel of the poor. We are the Christians who understand the simplicity of Jesus and the revolutionary spirit that Jesus came to bring, and that he was not a sheep in that he was conformed to the ways of the world, and that he floated downstream like a dead fish, or just went with the grain. But he was a sheep in that in a world full of wolves, the most revolutionary and radical and dangerous thing to be is a sheep. Not just dangerous to your own life, dangerous to the powers that be. Particularly for us, it may mean some unexpected ones like our country that says God bless America. It says in religious language we want to rid the world of evildoers, a kind of crusade."

He interrupted himself. "Enough out of me. How are you doing? Any questions so far? Particularly I'd rather somebody who disagrees with me say something like, 'You're a heretic and this is why.'"

That statement set the tone for the rest of the speaking engagement as one after another challenged Aaron's views on pacifism.

Aaron advised the Christians present not to enlist in the military and not care about political power and economic wealth. "The radical rebellion of Christ was to go down, and the life of peace, and humility, and servanthood and gentleness, and kindness, and lowliness, in a world full of pride and wealth and power and arrogance and fighting and scrambling, this teaching that we love our enemies."

When someone asked if he was taking his analogy too far, Aaron answered, "I sure don't know. I'm trying to follow after Jesus and what he told me to do—what he told his followers to do when he walked the earth, I should say. I apply it to my life and say I am to be a peacemaker, I am to love my enemy, I am to overcome evil with good, I am to meet curse with a blessing, I am to meet insult with prayer and never violence."

Another person asked about the violent battles in the book of Revelation. "I sure don't know. I'll tell you all, 'This is what the Revelation means?' I don't know. Strange book, that last one."

Aaron didn't buy the idea that Muslims in other nations were evildoers and American Christians were the good guys, or that Bin Laden needed to be converted to Christianity but not Bush. America had a lot of evil to answer for as well, so we should point the finger at ourselves and worry about that.

"The center of the Gospel, what draws me to Jesus again and again, is this teaching that we love our enemy, and once we accept that, there's no more boundaries to that love. While the world thinks in terms of trade and commerce, scratching each other's back, and thinking of what we get out of the deal, the love of Jesus was, 'I'm gonna give and get nothing in return. I'm gonna lay down my life and get mocked for it. I'm gonna serve others, and no return, at least in this life.'"

Aaron clarified that he has no authority to use the language of forgiveness—to tell people to forgive their abusive parents and cheating spouses—but Jesus does.

"Jesus . . . in the Gospel of Luke, after being blindfolded, beaten, spat upon, mocked by the people he came to save, crucified, prays for the ones who did that, and forgave them, asked his Father to forgive them. So may that same spirit be with us. May we all, everybody here, forgive everybody everything they've ever done, if we claim to follow Jesus."

Another person asked how we could just passively sit there and allow evil and violence to occur, such as the United Nations doing nothing about the Rwandan genocide.

"Forgive me, I have the same answer for every question—it's to come back to the gospel and look simply at what Jesus said and try to put faith in that, saying we don't overcome good with evil."

Aaron's friend Chris had just showed him Romans 13 the previous day, in which Paul says governments are agents of Gods wrath, punishing evildoers, but Aaron was still trying to process that verse. Should Christians specifically ever take up arms in government positions as agents of God's wrath? How could we resist our government in legalizing abortion, but not in bombing Iraq? Didn't God also establish Saddam Hussein and his government? Does that mean the violence he inflicts on his people and others is justified?

Aaron said he was exasperated that even at a Christian festival, he couldn't simply point to the red letters of Jesus who clearly taught something without getting so much pushback.

He expressed his ignorance of history, politics, and

economics, saying he had never been near a war and wasn't a very learned person, but how could we justify dropping bombs on the infrastructure of Iraq and killing hundreds of thousands of innocent civilians and their children, yet still call ourselves Christians and tell ourselves this is okay.

"It's such a tremendous and powerful and deep issue that I can't begin to fathom, it's so horrific. I don't mean to belittle it by just talking about it. I was hesitant to come up and even say anything because of how horrible it is and how silly and in some ways shameful it is for me to come to a festival where everybody is rich, and eat food and drink and enjoy myself and play rock and roll music and prance around on a stage. And all the while I was completely out of harm's way and have the audacity to talk about war. To me, if you come here and hear what I'm saying, and you think, 'This guy's a hypocrite,' believe me, you're right. Believe me, you underestimate what a hypocrite I am and how little I understand even what I'm saying, but that we try not to avoid this, but to throw ourselves in the middle of this conflict knowing that like our rabbi, like our teacher, like our leader, we may be killed. Like the apostles who followed him early on, we may be killed. Like countless saints and martyrs, that we may be killed. But the question whether we will ever kill as Christians, I have to just come to the gospel. I'm sorry, I don't mean to make this all about pacifism or peacemaking, but to me it's just such a strangely overlooked, yet so terribly clear in the Gospels, of our call to be killed, our call to be like sheep that are led to the slaughter, but this is not attractive stuff. If you came here for a party, for a fun festival, I'm sorry, I don't mean to bring up anything heavy. I don't want to trouble your life. I don't mean to come after you with this. But you probably knew I was talking and you came here, and so this is what you get when you come talk to me. I'm sorry."

Aaron asked for more questions and hoped for a change of subject.

The questioner reiterated that according to 1 Corinthians 13, love protects, and aren't there appropriate times that we use violence to protect the innocent and those we love? Another person in the audience suggested that God protects our souls, not our bodies. Aaron was overwhelmed and thought he bit off more than he could chew with such a heavy issue.

"God, who is love, does not protect us bodily, obviously . . . in that so many Christians have been killed. Are you saying God has failed to protect us against violence? No, certainly we would not say God has failed to protect us. God has guarded our soul."

Someone asked why, of all of the religions, Aaron chose Christianity.

"There is a way of responding that pleases people where you say, 'I didn't choose Jesus, Jesus chose me.'" This elicited some laughter as he further explained the frustration of choosing a faith at random or going with what you were raised with.

"My mom is Sufi Muslim, my dad is somewhere between a Jew and a Muslim, my uncle is a Buddhist. I've got all this. I came to Christianity out of fear and manipulation. A very fundamentalist, sort of evangelical American church where they told me I was going to burn in hell if I didn't. I was scared of burning in hell. But that's not a very long-lasting and good motivation, trying to avoid the flames of hell. So I left that form of Christianity just a few months later and sort of stumbled through the dark for years until I sort of encountered this radical side of Jesus as a person, as a man in history who was one with God and um, have you read the Gospels? He's quite a character, Jesus. And I guess the beauty of saying Our Father in heaven, hallowed be your name. Father is like this intimate, loving kind of—say, if I was to stay with the Muslim faith, I couldn't call God my father. And yet this—hallowed by thy name, holy be your name—is holy. This entirely, otherworldly sense of our awe and wonder at God to me is also significant. The Gospels have always seemed to have both God as friend, God as mystery, God as brother, God as creator of the universe and the cosmos that we can never begin to understand, God as father, God as a mother hen to the baby chicks, very intimate, very wonderful. But I don't know, I'm still working all this out. Thanks for asking about my personal life, I'm flattered, and thank you for changing the subject, too."

Aaron felt ignorant and unqualified to talk about political

stuff, but brought it up because in the media, Christianity in America is represented by one specific voice of the religious right. Aaron wasn't trying to convince them to his way of thinking. "I believe so many things that are untrue. I don't want to influence anybody in a bad way, but I do want to ask those questions and keep a soft heart myself."

He continued, "Forgive me if you think I've made up my mind and I'm here to persuade you or to manipulate you. It's just that I don't hear a voice for Christian peacemaking or Christian pacifism in the media or even in the arts."

Another person asked if it is important to let people know you are a Christian as you help them. Aaron explained that there is a tendency to say, "God bless you, I'm a Christian, that's why I'm doing this," after a work, but it feels like giving someone a business card for God. St Francis said, "Preach the gospel, use words when necessary."

"We are here to sow seeds of love, and of truth, and of light. Any deed of love and of compassion is in the name of God. Whether you tell somebody, 'I'm a Christian, that's why I'm doing this,' or you do it in silence, I think the truth will be the truth, light will be light, love will be love. God will speak to that person. So I personally don't believe we need to advertise that we're a Christian with a certain T-shirt. I mean, I wear a cross around my neck as somebody gave it to me, but I certainly don't feel it's necessary for my faith."

Someone asked where the spirit of unity in the band comes from. Aaron advised loving, connecting, forgiving, communicating with, and serving each other, but they weren't perfect.

"We're a total mess, and if you knew half the stuff that actually happened within our group, in particular what I was responsible for as far as causing strife and sowing seeds of discord and jealousy and division, you'd throw a rock at me or else just leave and say, 'Well, I'm not gonna listen to this guy.' And you shouldn't, absolutely shouldn't listen to me. Nothing I have to say to you is of any value. I can't even create a string bean. I can't do anything for you. I can't give you any truth. Somebody told me right before this, 'Don't say anything that isn't true.' I should have come up here and sat here for sixty minutes in silence. I just try to get out of the way and let God put that love for others, seeing others' lives as just as valuable as yours. It's all we're ever talking about. The whole religious life is a death of the self and a bringing to life whether it's Buddhism—you're talking about annihilation and enlightenment of nonexistence or something—or Islam maybe becoming better and more and more holy. For Christianity it seems to be something like the crushing up of the grain into a loaf of bread, a crushing up of the grapes into a glass of wine—the bread and body of Christ—that we come together in a community, that we love each other as ourselves and become one body. So just seeing others in that way and treating them with the same gentleness and kindness and consideration that we treat ourselves, Jesus said, 'Love your neighbor as yourself.' You ever heard that one? I got not an original bone in my body. I'm just trying to take it seriously."

A woman said, "It seems that there are a lot of people that look up to you. You seem really humble. Is it a little overwhelming at times to have so many people paying attention to you?"

"Yes, but it's hard to have people not paying attention to me. You know, I come to Cornerstone and all of a sudden everybody's like, 'Hey Aaron!' It's like, 'You know my name?' Then I go back to Philadelphia and everybody's like, 'Get out of the way!' You know, honking at me because I'm riding a bike in the car lane or something. And so it feels really good for about ten minutes. It's like, 'Alright! I'm the most important person in the world!' Then all of a sudden you realize, 'Boy, just like when I thought sexual activity would gratify me and it didn't, just like when I thought storing up money for myself would gratify me and it didn't, just like when I thought getting signed to a label would gratify and it didn't, apparently having people know your name or want your autograph and have their picture taken with you—as much as we are all convinced that it would gratify us—doesn't. So it's just one more of the many lies we're told, that what we want and should desire in some way is to be held above other people. How to maintain the humility of Jesus from the stage? I still don't know, and about always operating at fifty-one percent like, 'Yeah, it's worthwhile for me to be in this band at all because somehow God's gonna use it,' and then forty-nine percent of me is like, 'Boy, just be poor. Shut up. Quit playing music. Quit using your thousand-dollar guitars to talk about how you don't need material possessions and feed people who are hungry.' This is where I am at for the time being. If I warned you that I was a hypocrite earlier—I think I did—I meant it. If you didn't hear me, 'I'm a hypocrite.'"

Aaron was asked, "If Jesus was a police officer and could protect someone with a gun, would he do it?"

"Well, I could only look at his life in the Gospels and see that he did not defend himself against the violence that others brought against him. No, I would have to say he probably wouldn't." He said he saw something of Jesus in our police officers and military and didn't mean to demonize them, "but again, our question is how did our rabbi live, how did our teacher live, and he lived a life of peace and did not ever commit violence against anybody, so how are we to respond as followers of him? Not by speculating about what you would do here or there, but just try to follow simply and humbly which to me is again, trying to overcome evil with good, trusting even if we're killed in the process that that will plant a seed of peace and bring about more goodness in the world than so-called ridding the world of evildoers. This is obviously like an impossibility. If our administration were to rid the world of evildoers, there wouldn't be anybody left. It would be killing six billion other people, then putting a gun in my own mouth. So we are obviously not called to get rid of the world of evildoers."

Aaron continued, saying that we should all ask and beg for mercy from God because vengeance is his, not ours, and it's a conditional thing—we have to show mercy and forgiveness to others if we want it from God. The Lord's Prayer says, "Forgive us as we forgive those who trespass against us." You have to give it to get it. He then implored the crowd to simply forgive everyone instead of "becoming a pacifist" or taking a political stance.

He went on, "Again, to me, the simple question of how we are to live as followers of Jesus is simply that vengeance belongs to God. And as much as it concerns me, I'm going to follow after

Jesus who was poor, who had no place to rest his head, who was hungry, and as to whether or not there can be such a thing as a rich Christian . . . again, coming back to the words of Jesus, 'Woe to you who are rich.' I have to think there is a danger, or there is a problem with being rich when Jesus said that. 'Blessed are you who are poor,' or in his examples of the rich who ignore the poor going to hell when they die. This is part of the teachings of the Gospel."

Aaron clarified that he wasn't pointing the finger. "I can't say 'you're rich' to anybody 'cause I'm rich. 'Cause, I mean, I live in the most privileged and wealthy country in the world, so even to be poor by the standards of America is to be rich by the standards of the world. So forgive me if any of this has a spirit of saying, 'You need to sell your stuff! You need to start making peace!' Of course, this repentance starts within our own heart. Again, 'If every Christian were to sell everything they had, who would take care of the Christians?' always comes back to somewhat practical questions, but, at the same time, ways of putting off this question of, 'What does Jesus demand of me?' . . . I would suggest to you just look at your heart and come to God with no preconceived notions of what it means to be a Christian. Beg for clarity, beg for God's will to be done, beg for that guidance that says, 'I have no will of my own.' It's just such a simple faith. You say, 'I'm going to obey what Jesus told me to do and God's gonna take care of everything else. God's gonna take care of the wars in the world, all the evildoers in the world, all of our need to be fed, all of our need to be protected with shelter, and if I die in the process, then I die in the process. But the important thing is that I followed Jesus. And again, forgive me for having such an incredibly simple understanding. In some ways I consider myself sort of a fundamentalist, but I want to talk about fundamentalism because on one hand of course—'I believe the Bible is word-for-word the inerrant word of God'—that's not what I mean by fundamentalism, but simply just the fundamentals. Like, the core central things of our faith is to me what Jesus taught, how he lived, how his followers lived, and how we should live. Again, just so tremendously simple, a child could understand. And all of us who are educated and sophisticated and wealthy can argue all the details and all the rest. But I want to encourage you—maybe he meant it. Maybe we should just take it for what it is and not worry about how the rest of the world would take it, maybe."

A woman asked how Aaron's family responded to him choosing the path of Christ.

"At first there was a lot of argument. My mom would try to tell me about her faith, and I would try to argue by telling a Bible verse. And for years this went on at a stand still. And about two-and-a-half years ago I first—almost three years ago—I really felt like I was blinded by this beautiful light of love, and ever since then we haven't had any of these arguments. But I just try to honor my mom. I go to the mosque with her and pray alongside Muslims and sing alongside Muslims, and if they sing something that, uh—there's one prayer that says God was not begotten, nor did he beget. I don't sing that one. But I'll sing other things, even blessings to Mohammed, happy to sing that. So I heard about a story about a missionary who went to a Muslim country trying to convert everybody. Nothing. And then he dropped his arms and just started to study the Islamic scriptures and praying for people in silent. It wasn't long before people were drawn to him. 'What are you doing here? What's different about you?' And then he would read the scriptures with them, the Christian scriptures, and there was tremendous movement of the Spirit of God in that. To me, my experience was we fought and we fought to no avail, and then I started to pray with my mom, and she started to pray the Lord's Prayer with me, and my dad started to come to church meetings with me, and we're all seeking God together. We particularly need to not be afraid of other faiths and to demonize other faiths and anybody different than us. 'I'm a Protestant. I'm a Mennonite. Therefore Catholics are from the devil, Muslims are from the devil, and Buddhists—everything else is from the devil.' As far as I'm concerned, falsehood is from the devil, truth is from God. If there is something true in the Koran, it's true. Some of the stories are exactly the same as the Bible. And I can imagine the end of certain positions being, well, when it says it in the Bible it's true, when it says the same thing in the Koran, it's demonic. And you have to sort of question, okay, obviously I don't mean that, but what do we mean when we demonize other religions? Certainly I don't mean to be like a universalist and say everything is true. At the same time I think there is no boundaries to God's love and his demand that we love others, particularly in my case, Muslims. So ever since I started just loving my mom and dad and honoring them, it all became really clear. Just like, let's get all the beliefs out on the table and let the truth be the truth. I started to read the Koran and my dad's reading the New Testament."

He continued, "Ever since I stopped being afraid of these other religions and stopped demonizing other people, it's just a tremendous weight off of my chest. Let God be God, you know? Let's all search together."

Aaron was asked about being a vegan and whether or not that was for moral reasons.

"A question about my diet, me being vegan. Not true." Aaron explained that in an interview with PETA, short clips were used that took him out of context, but he once was a hard-line vegan for six years. "If you want to know about my diet, there's a whole lot of food that gets thrown away in the world, in America in particular. And if you can find a steak in the trash, that's not hurting that cow because it's already killed and thrown away. So as much as I love animals and find beauty in animals and don't want to support factory farming and all the ways in which they're raised up to be hamburger—I don't think that's really the way God intended if you look at the Garden of Eden kinda thing. I don't think it's wrong to eat meat, but I sorta skirt the whole issue by eating out of dumpsters, which is very doable, and to my knowledge I've never really gotten sick from it. Yes, so I would advise you to look in smaller supermarkets that don't have trash compactors, or bakeries, anywhere that's throwing food away, and you can probably find enough food to feed your entire family free, and you're not wasting the packaging."

At this point the crowd clapped, and Aaron laughed.

"Of all the things! Of all the things to clap at. Boy, you talk about peacemaking, loving your enemies, honoring your mother and your father—but if you talk about eating out of dumpsters, everybody's like, 'Yay!' That's cool!' I mean, and this has some biblical backing for those of us who need to hear everything from the Bible. It's like, 'Well, what does it say in the Bible about dumpster diving?' Well, of course, it says about as much in the Bible about dumpster diving as it does abortion or gay marriage. But it does say let nothing be wasted when Jesus fed the five thousand, and Paul did say our abundance should supply for the needs of others. That's just one way of doing it. We have abundance. Rather than buying food, here's an idea, eat the food other people are throwing away, take the money we would have bought food with, and send that to somebody who's hungry, elsewhere. It's just a real pragmatic kinda thought. Thanks for asking about my diet, I'm flattered."

Aaron was next asked what the band does to stay Christ-centered.

"Not much. We are not very united, and we don't have a whole lot of love between us, and we don't have a very strong Christ center. We are in all different places and, again, I think if you saw the way we lived, really, behind closed doors, you'd say this isn't Christ-centered at all. As much as I do that with the other guys in the band—I can't believe they're doing that, I can't believe they're doing that—until you reach a point where you yourself commit something so wrong or cross lines that are so clear. I've just done so many things that are wrong, is what I'm trying to tell you, where I realize I can no longer judge anybody, and then I just start judging again, and then I commit wrong again. I can't really answer the question because we don't have a Christ-centered band, but we're trying."

They started having Bible reading and prayer together for the first time, trying to make a step towards God, but as Aaron explained, "We fail, and we fail again."

Finally, Aaron was asked if he thought God was bigger than Christianity. "Oh boy, I cracked the can, but you're opening the can of worms. I mean, that's a big one that's going to get me in a whole lot of trouble if I start to answer. But I don't mind that, I'll get myself into trouble, but I do tread cautiously and try not to lead anyone astray or anything. But the question is about—he's experienced that God is bigger than Christianity, and how dare we say that God is exclusive to my tribe or to my understanding of God, and this is true in my experience as well."

Aaron spoke of the tangible fruits of the Spirit that we all taste and see. Paul lists them as love, joy, peace, patience, kindness, goodness, gentleness, faithfulness, and self-control. "What can we make of people who claim to be Christian that don't exhibit or possess any of those things, or what do we make of people who don't claim to be Christian of other religions" but do possess these fruits? "What do we make of people who don't claim to be Christian that do demonstrate love? Jesus said that you'd be recognized as my disciples by this—that you love one another. If you take two Muslims who love one another and two Christians don't, who is the Christian? Well, this is a very important question."

Aaron went on to explain that many of the people at the festival call themselves Christians and want to be seen and known as Christians, but the label means nothing because God sees our hearts.

"All of us coming here and saying we're Christians and wanting to be seen or considered as this or that, are we Christians? I sure don't know, God knows that. Are there going to be Muslims in heaven? I sure hope so. The word Muslim means 'one who is submitted to God.' The word Islam means 'peace,' the religion of peace. Are there those submitted to God in that way, living peacefully in heaven? Rather than saying I hope so, I think so. May our prayer be that Muslims be taken into God's arms, and that atheists be taken into God's arms. If he's willing to accept us may he take us, may God take us all into his arms if he's willing."

Aaron finished, "Please forgive me for anything I said that's wrong, and thank you for being here to love each other. Please take care of each other wherever you go in your life. Believe in God and trust in God, don't trust in me or anything I say. Of course, of course, of course. But trust in God, and by God I mean that power of love that is undeniable, and that light that is undeniable, and truth that is true, the beginning and the end, always has been and always will be. Peace be with you, my precious brothers and sisters. Bye, bye."

Before he had even left the stage, I stopped my camera and ran to my car. I didn't say goodbye to him or see the rest of the bands I wanted to see. In a panic attack, my anxiety drove me to get out of the crowd and hide in my car as soon as I could possibly get to it. I hoped no one would see me, talk to me, or force me to look them in the eyes.

Still daylight, I drove four hours to Mark's apartment, ready to begin my stint on his couch.

As I shared video of Aaron's message with friends and strangers alike, the response was nearly unanimous disagreement. "He sounds like a blame-America-first liberal to me," one friend said. "Down with the capitalism that gives you your platform to speak against capitalism and allows you play in a band and sell T-shirts and CDs, comrade!" commented another. "I love Aaron's music, but he needs to keep his leftist neo-hippie ideas to himself," another said. "He doesn't know what he's talking about."

But Aaron wasn't budging. "Paul, quite a list of thoughts, and thank you for giving me the sense that I'm being passionately disagreed with. Makes me feel like I may actually be on the right track!"[161]

---

[161] Email, 7/19/06.

58
If She Comes Circling Back

After dreaming about Natalie, I emailed her mom, asking how Natalie was doing. To my delight, and against the advice of her family, Natalie responded.

"I would like to forgive and forget that this ever happened and feel free to move forward with my life, but I don't feel free. I feel totally and completely trapped in this unidirectional path. For some reason (people have told me my mind is playing tricks on me, or it's the devil, or that you put a curse on me) you have been on my mind lately and I am trying everything possible to figure out what will make this go away."

After complimenting me and listing all of the qualities she liked in me, she explained that she was looking for something different. "Anyway, this letter is not meant in any way to reinstate your hope that you and I are meant for each other but simply to let you know that I don't understand how something like this could have happened anymore than you do. I wish you well in all that you are working on and I hope you find what you are looking for. I hope that we can both just put this behind us and move forward and actually be happy again someday."[162]

Not wanting to scare her away, I prayed and asked God to give me wisdom and guidance, but nothing came. The only thing I could think to do was to reassure her that she was not being punished by God, that I had not put a curse on her, and that it was okay for her to move forward with her life.

I sent her my autobiography, hoping she could see just how absurd our story was and just how much this supposedly supernatural revelation failed to be true. Instead of helping her, she accused me of having a secret desire still to make her mine.

"I really don't see a need to relive the past," she responded, refusing to read it. "I'm creeped out that you recorded every conversation we ever had. I mean, the book is about me and I

---
[162] Email, July 2006.

don't want to read it."

"You treat me like shit. Why would I want to make you mine? I sent you that document to help you. You know that I journal. Why would that creep you out? Why do you keep making me out to be some terrible person? I don't want you, I'm spending all of my energy trying not to kill myself."

She said she needed to break contact with me because her family feared for her safety, advising me to get some medical help immediately. I found myself standing in front of the bathroom mirror slapping myself in the face over and over again, trying to draw blood. This fresh demonization and rejection was more than I could take. Friends on my end told me to stay out of contact with her because I couldn't handle her in my fragile state.

Pictures soon emerged on Natalie's MySpace profile of her kissing her new boyfriend on the beach. After my initial sadness and jealousy, a peace came over me. She deserved to date whomever she wanted and enjoy her life. She liked foreign musicians, and I wasn't that. He was. As I scrolled through pictures of her out with her friends at bars and clubs, I realized how bored I would be in that scene. We were totally different people with totally different interests, needs, and desires. We were in two different worlds, not compatible in the least. I was genuinely happy for her and relieved that we dodged the bullet of straining our lives together into disaster. I was starting to let go. After all, I wanted someone who wanted me and found me attractive. She didn't, and that was okay.

At the end of September, Natalie wrote me and told me she met this wonderful man. "I see now the kind of love that God wants me to have. When you offered me all the same things, I was absolutely not in the right place to receive any of it. For this I am deeply sorry. I know your intentions were pure and that you meant nothing but positive things for me. I know now that the things you did and said were just an attempt to protect me from the abuse I was suffering. I am sorry I didn't see that then, but this is now. This is the problem: I feel a great responsibility for the pain I have caused you. I internalize a lot of regret and I see now that God placed you in my life to help me and I rejected that gift because of my lack of understanding. It is just totally fucking with me that I am beginning to understand this now and put it all in prospective just as I begin to enter into a healthy and promising relationship. I felt the need to contact you and once again ask for your forgiveness, truly coming from my heart. I am sorry for the cruel ways that I treated you. I wish you all the best life has. I know you are creative and bright and I will continue to pray that God amplifies these gifts for his glory. I guess my sole purpose here is to make peace with you and feel like I am free to turn the page of my life; to get 100% right with God and to let you know that I will continue to pray for your mental and physical health and that God brings great love to you!"[163]

I read Natalie's message numb on antidepressants. I didn't know I was crying until I reached up and felt warm tears running down my cheek.

---

[163] Email, 9/27/06.

7/16/06
Email to Aaron

Aaron,

Hello brother, I hope you are well. Things are great here. I returned from Cornerstone to find an email from Natalie that put us in dialogue, but things got tense quickly. We talked on the phone for fifteen minutes and apologized to one another for the past. We have decided not to be in one another's lives, but to say hi every few months. Either way, a weight has been lifted and I feel like I have a new vitality.

I miss you already and hope to see you soon. I left immediately after your message because I was numb the whole fest and could no longer take the wall of noise. I hope you are safe tonight wherever you are laying your head. I love you brother,

Paul

7/19/06
Email from Aaron

Paul,

Remarkable that you're back in touch with Natalie and how intense it can become so quickly. Not surprising I guess, as we have a way of picking up right where we left off with stored up pain. Very happy that you both sought forgiveness. Very beautiful. May G-d heal your hearts and fill you with that good forgiveness and peace and non-worry, contentment with whatever comes, right now, always.

I am very happy to hear from you. May G-d protect our hearts while we're apart and have mercy on us. Tell me what I can do to make anything better. And I love you—no, I am you.

Peace,

Aaron

8/26/06
Email to Aaron

Aaron,

Your dad gave me an Arabic name for the Brotherhood. One of Muhammad's sons—Hussein! Man, might as well have given me Bin Laden! I'll take it though.

Happy touring, brother. I'm really looking forward to the new CD. The songs have grown on me live. I already hate "A Sweater Poorly Knit" for all of the "if's" and "we'll see's" and "come circling back's." Dude, write a song like Eminem where the girl gets murdered and there is closure. There is too much hope in your complaining.

Love you brother, can't wait to see you again. May God give you peace, rest, and comfort.

Paul

8/27/06
Email from Aaron

Paul,

I'm very happy to hear from you, and as usual, I laughed out loud reading your message.

As for the hope in our songs, can't help it I guess. Out of the overflow of the heart the mouth speaks, and brother, there is hope in my heart. But not for me and Amanda, no, that's long gone, and not even hope that things will get better than they are. More like hope that things ARE better than they are, if you know what I mean.

Glad to see you still using the word "God." Though it's just a word, what's behind it is the source of this hope I've got, and my love. That love, by the way, flows from that source through me to you. Your brother,

Aaron

9/12/06
Email from Aaron

Paul,

My dad's back in the hospital. Don't know if I told you, but back in July my mom had him thrown in the mental ward for almost a month. He was out a few weeks and then back in when he dropped his new meds and started experimenting with old ones. Hard to process all this from the road, from a distance. Don't understand what's happening in him, but at the heart of a lot of it, a whole lot of it seems to be unforgiveness.

Do me a favor, will you? While you've still got your wits about you (and you do), forgive everybody. Don't give some excuse or exception, forgive everybody. When you feel angry again, forgive again. And put all your faith in this: G-d is good. I can't prove it, no. But what bad is gonna come of putting your faith in that? Not just believing it, but pouring your life into goodness. Shit, I'm tired of talking about goodness. What can I do to help?

Do you know I'm sorry? Whatever anyone else has done to hurt you, Natalie, your family, anyone who's let you down, I've done the same things and I am them, you know what I mean? And I'm sorry.

I'm tired as can be. Gonna lay down, and odds are dream about Amanda. She's in love with one of my best friends, and he's in love with her. They're moving down that road and I'm trying to forget we ever met. That's how things go in this world. But it's a short life, and love is so very eternal. Here's to patience,

Aaron

59
Brother, Sister

Brother, Sister—a title based on a song by Saint Francis of Assisi called "Canticle of the Sun,"—progressed experimentally both musically and lyrically from mewithoutYou's first two albums.

When asked about the meaning of the title, Aaron said, "I don't know, ask Saint Francis, he's the one that came up with it. Praying to God and addressing all the aspects of God's beauty and the creation of the sun and the moon and, the wind, the rain, the animals. He really loved the physical world—he saw the beauty and nature of it. That's where you see God the most. I mean, you look around and see a tree and notice that God is there. God is in every aspect of nature."[164]

Besides the shouting and yelling prominent on the first two releases, Aaron took vocal lessons and learned to sing. He also bought an old accordion online and learned chords on an acoustic guitar, bringing more folksy songs to the table, allowing the band to branch out into more harmony, melody, and formal song structures.

"I took voice lessons. So I actually learned how to sing, which I never knew you could do. I thought singing was just, you're born with it or you're not. And I think to some extent that's true—the voice you have is the voice you have, but you can take lessons to learn how to use it better. That's what I did. I took five lessons right when we started recording. The guys were laying down their music and I was taking these voice lessons. The guys had been suggesting it to me for a while and I was always pretty reluctant because I thought, 'Well, I do what I do and I don't want somebody telling me to start singing in a conventional way,' so I was pretty hesitant. I probably got defensive and maybe took it personally, you know? 'What, you don't think I'm doing a good

---

[164] Manuel Enrique Garcia. "MewithoutYou Interview," *Driven Far Off*, 9/29/06.

job? You want me to take lessons?' But I realized that just because I learned how to sing it doesn't mean I can't still, you know, speak or holler or incorporate other vocal deliveries than typical pop singing. I'm not trying to sound like I'm trying to be a pop star or anything, but it's nice to just expand your options."[165]

Looking back years later, Aaron said, "I'm not a good singer. I can't sing on key very accurately and I don't have a very pretty voice, but I am physically capable of singing and I prefer it more than shouting."[166]

In another interview, he added, "I don't think of us as a tight band, musically—at least not my contributions. My playing is pretty shoddy, and my pitch is abysmal, especially for a lead singer. But we play with a lot of bravado I think, so that can sort of distract from the technical shortcomings."[167]

With each release getting progressively softer, Aaron told MTV, "We're not getting any younger, and I don't want to be 40, jumping around onstage. We're kind of all into softer music now, and this new album reflects that. There's a tendency to stick with what worked in the past, but honestly, we wanted to avoid that at all costs."[168]

Part of the reason for the music being less heavy was that Aaron had more hope now and wanted to sing about God instead of his failed relationship with Amanda, or as Aaron put it, "It's more about . . . God and what I think about God rather than this girl that I screwed up."[169]

"I want to encourage and give hope, whether it's to people who were born Christian or people who never considered God," he told MTV. "I'm not trying to convert anyone, but I want to tell

---

[165] Drew Ailes, "mewithoutYou interview," *Lambgoat*, 1/14/07.
[166] Joy Ableson, "Ten Years On: mewithoutYou - [A→B] Life," *Alter the Press*, 7/2012.
[167] Dan McAndrew, "Interview with Aaron Weiss of mewithoutYou," *Oh So Fresh*, 6/05/12.
[168] James Montgomery, "Mewithoutyou Confront Rock's Limitations: 'You Can't Give People Hugs In A CD.' New LP *Brother, Sister* might not appeal to Christians or punk kids, but frontman has bigger concerns," *MTV*, 7/12/06.
[169] Manuel Enrique Garcia. "MewithoutYou Interview," *Driven Far Off*, 9/29/06.

people how great I feel. That's why my songs aren't just, 'Oh, my girlfriend broke up with me and I'm jealous of her new boyfriend.' I want to tell people God is love. That's my eternal, unchanging reality."

"There's only one true motivation behind what I do, and that's love for everybody," he said. "And it's difficult to communicate love through songs—you can't give people hugs in a CD—so there's a tension there. And I feel like that's part of why I do what I do. I want to express things that transcend the music."[170]

"I'm not that creative of a person, so I don't make things up out of thin air,"[171] Aaron told *HM Magazine*. "I had a lot less anxiety in my heart about, 'What am I going to say?' But recording the first record, I didn't care what I was saying for the most part. I just wanted to be cool and make out with girls. With the second record, I had an experience where I encountered Jesus in such an undeniable way that I knew I couldn't go back to singing about a broken romantic relationship that I had stepped over; but I felt tremendously inadequate. My faith wasn't strong enough to say anything to anybody. I wasn't sure I actually believed what I was saying."[172]

"But with this record, I wouldn't say I've resolved all those doubts, or that I've come to believe wholeheartedly in all the Christian doctrine of any particular denomination, but Christianity that . . . the love of Jesus embodied, and taught, and lived and the reality of God being the source of that love, and the eternal light and truth—to me, there's no more doubt about that. And so I felt more grounded than I had—an eternal sense of purpose. Not that I was trying to convert anybody to become a Christian and start going to a building on Sundays, but rather inspire people to consider." [173] He added that David said God was too wonderful to be understood.

When asked about the theme of the new record, he said, "I

---

[170] Ibid
[171] Doug Van Pelt, "mewithoutYou," *HM Magazine*, #121, Sept/Oct 2006, 46.
[172] Ibid, 60.
[173] Ibid

would hope that the main theme would be that God is good. I'm tempted to say something about the spider songs, it mentions a spider that gets old and dies. That's kind of one theme, that all things in this world will pass. Then the other theme is—the first and last line of the record is 'I do not exist,' so it's just a loss of the ego. My attempt of a religious pursuit, like trying to lose my obsession with myself and come to believe in God, to love God and care about other people that aren't me. But that has largely been a failed pursuit, so far. That's what I'm doing with these songs, or eating breakfast or going to a church meeting, or whatever it is. It's always the same, trying to forget about myself and love God and love other people. That's the theme of the record and my life. Again, it's not a successful theme."[174]

Aaron was clear that his contentment could only be found in God, and especially not in the band or in finding a woman to marry. He felt he could speak more authoritatively about that.

"I really wish I could see a parallel universe where I was never in this band and where I'll be right now, probably married, probably still with the same struggles. It hasn't changed too many things fundamentality, but it has given me more of a struggle with arrogance and self-importance and egomania. To think that someone wants to do an interview with me right now, for example. You know, five years ago no one ever wanted to do an interview with me, so this is like, makes me feel like I am more important than I am. The fact that someone wanted to pay us to play a show, buy our CD, the fact that we have a CD. Any of the things, like Jesus said 'Woe to you if people think well of you.' And I'm always afraid that, to whatever extent we haven't been successful by most standards, to whatever step we have been, I think it's probably hurtful to me, spiritually."[175]

"I hope people can love God and love other people more, because my experience trying to find happiness in other things— and not relationships or ambition with music or you know, anything I've tried to do like trying to be smart or a good writer, or

---

[174] Manuel Enrique Garcia. "MewithoutYou Interview," *Driven Far Off*, 9/29/06.
[175] Ibid

anything I've always wanted to come out of being in a band—none of it makes me happy. I hope people can see that, take my experience and one man's experience, that nothing makes you happy except for the love of God and the light of God that shines in your heart. And realize that you don't need to be good, you don't need to be together, you don't need to be smart, you don't need to be cool, you don't need to be good looking, you don't need to be confident or you know, successful or rich. You don't need to be any of those things. You just need to be broken and lonely and humble and needy, which all of us are deep down, but we just hide it and try and act confident and together. So we come to God broken and then God is the physician, God is the potter. God is the loving healer, the mother and the father and lover of us all, the restorer, the forgiver, the most patient one, the most merciful, the most kind and gentle one. We'll find all we need in God, in God's provision and protection. Not a religious group or going to a church on Sunday, or joining an organization or something like that. In reality, God is the source of love and light and serving others and forgiving others and praying for others and mediating on good things and humbling yourself and not taking yourself too seriously. All these things, you know, different aspects of it. The one life that I'm trying to communicate or trying to live, is a life of faith and a following of Jesus."[176]

Produced by Brad Wood and featuring guest vocals by Jeremy Enigk, harp by Timbre Cierpke, and musicians from the Psalters and Anathallo, mewithoutYou felt like they had finally matured to the point that they found their signature sound and came into their own. *Brother, Sister* reached #116 on the Billboard 200 and *HM Magazine* ranked it #9 on their list of the top 100 "Christian rock" albums of all time.

---

[176] Ibid

60
Mouse

Once again, with the arrival of *Brother, Sister*, Aaron seemed to have narrated my short-lived reunion with Natalie. Like old times, it took no time for tension to rise between us. *If she comes circling back, we'll end where we'd begun*, he writes in "A Sweater Poorly Knit." He speaks of a *train derailed and two car head on freeway crash each time we meet* in "Wolf Am I! (And Shadow)."

Natalie wondered if I'd put a curse on her, and being in contact with me, she said her family feared for her safety. Though I was harmless, she kept projecting sinister motives on me. I read in "O Porcupine": *And for the past five—almost six years now!—you know you haven't once looked at me with kindness in your eyes. You say Judas is a brother of mine?*

Still, in all of the unanswered questions about exactly what happened between us, Aaron finished: *But sister in our darkness a light shines. And all I ever want to say for the rest of my life is how that light is G-d. And though I've been mistaken on this or that point, that light is nevertheless G-d.*

I believed that whatever happened between us, God was somehow at the center, and my motives for doing everything I did in her life was to protect her, help her walk with God, and heal from pain. Though I wasn't always graceful with our situation, I knew it wasn't Satan who wanted me to care for her, nor was I using God to manipulate her and make her mine. *The truth belongs to God*, Aaron writes in "In a Market Dimly Lit," *the mistakes were mine.*

When Natalie responded to my email, putting us back in contact, I was on eggshells. "Just don't scare her away," I said out loud. But even being as careful as I was, she broke contact with me and disappeared almost as soon as she arrived.

Aaron wrote about a mouse that peeked its head out from hiding beneath the stairs in "C-Minor": *So I scattered some oats in hopes she'd stay and sat still to stop from scaring her away—but she* hurried on her little way, and scurried around my mind ever since, every day.

Just like Natalie told me that she met a wonderful man—and in our time together there was always another man—the mouse came back again with a "friend." *This never ends,* Aaron writes. *The harder the rain, the lower the flowers in the garden bend.*

Still, Aaron wrote that if being alone and remaining a technical virgin the rest of his life helped him love God more, it wouldn't bother him.

All of the relationship drama in Aaron's lyrics were subsumed in the lyrics expressing the idea that "I" do not exist, only God exists. Only God mattered.

And while Aaron moved in this direction, I found that I could no longer believe in God.

61
The Sad Side of a Nowhere Town

Warren, Illinois is one of those middle-of-nowhere small towns where there is nothing to do. A place to watch the grass grow is how my landlord put it. The rent was cheap, and it wasn't too far from Galena, where my mom had moved.

With a steady income from disability and enough back pay to furnish my place with secondhand furniture, I had finally landed on my feet.

I saw a doctor and was diagnosed with situational depression and prescribed an antidepressant that did little more than make me numb.

The stillness now unleashed the fullness of my inner turmoil. Every time I closed my eyes, I saw people's faces melting off and their skulls turning black. As I shaved my face in the mirror, I watched myself fall to the floor in a pile of dust. At any given moment of the day, my surroundings wobbled, crumbled, and faded into sand. When I went out to get the mail, I was terrified of the cold, the dark, and of the trucks passing by on the street. Every step I took felt like the ground would swallow me. I dreamed of horrific car accidents, football players breaking their legs, and I would simply wake from sleep moaning and sobbing, my heart racing.

I'd pace the house, wanting to open the front door and run—but where, I didn't know. I reasoned that I was like a man on fire, trying to escape the pain, but there was nowhere to run. When you're on fire, you're on fire, no matter where you are. I had to keep forcing myself into stillness.

I stared at a green salad bowl on my counter. "You're gonna learn how to make a good salad, Paul," I said out loud, shaking my finger at the bowl. "You're not on a mission to save the world." I lay on the couch, despondent, watching Little House on the Prairie marathons, escaping into another world.

With the arrival of autumn came allergies, and by Christmas

all of my fibromyalgia symptoms had retuned. After what was seemingly a miraculous healing in the summer of 2004, I was as sick as I ever was, lending more doubt to the idea that God had ever healed me at all. Why would he heal me just to struggle for two years to keep my nostrils above the water line, then when I get settled, allow all of my symptoms to return?

The only peace that came was when I closed my eyes and envisioned a hermitage in a monastery. It was a small cabin, surrounded by trees. In it was a bunk, a fireplace, some books, and a desk to write on. It was surrounded by scenic wilderness, behind the safe and protective stone walls surrounding the monastery grounds. I envisioned singing chants, praying on beads, meditating, and reciting prayer and scripture, spending all of my days in transcendence, thinking about God, and forgetting about the world.[177]

For now, I would have to settle for the happy medium of being a recluse in Warren, looking for anything simple, good, and beautiful to focus on.

I bought a digital camera and took pictures of the trees changing into their autumn colors.

---

[177] Reading biographies by monks and former monks quickly sobered me of my idealization of the life of a monastic. I was more likely to experience boredom, frustration with the daily grind, a fellow monk smelling terribly because he won't shower, or irritatingly singing off key before I would experience transcendence.

62
New Atheism

After so many years of praying over every step I took and looking for signs, anxious about whether or not my decisions were in God's will, I was now making decisions by reason and common sense alone.

I concluded that all I had experienced with hearing God's voice, Natalie, and my healing was delusion, and God's continued silence was explained by the fact that he probably had never spoken to me at all. As a matter of fact, I hadn't seen any God or any supernatural power at work in anyone's life, ever.

Reasoning that there was no God to call upon for help or guidance, I said, "Huh. I guess that makes me an atheist." I shrugged my shoulders.

That very week, I went to Borders to buy Christmas gifts and came across the November issue of *Wired* magazine with the cover story: THE NEW ATHEISM: NO HEAVEN. NO HELL. JUST SCIENCE. INSIDE THE CRUSADE AGAINST RELIGION.

Authors Sam Harris, Richard Dawkins, and Daniel Dennett were profiled. Christopher Hitchens would soon join this group in a literary movement under the moniker of the Four Horsemen of the Non-Apocalypse.[178] Though I continued to long for and seek God, I read these authors and agreed largely with their critique of religion.

I had become a reluctant atheist and challenged myself to see if I could live stoically in a meaningless and dangerous world, knowing there was no supernatural help; that there was no God to love me, help me, protect me, guide me, heal me, give me a plan for my life, and lead me into truth. I had to grow up—trading hopes, wishes, and fantasies for the limits of stark reality—and I

---

[178] The new atheist canon consists of *The End of Faith: Religion, Terror, and the Future of Reason* and *Letter to a Christian Nation* by Sam Harris, *Breaking the Spell: Religion as a Natural Phenomenon* by Daniel Dennett, *The God Delusion* by Richard Dawkins, and *God is Not Great: Why Religion Poisons Everything* by Christopher Hitchens.

hated this.

But atheism delivered what many in my life had been asking of me—to just be normal. Heaven and hell, God and Satan, angels and demons, revealed holy books, and all supernatural powers, places, and beings that once occupied the cosmos of my imagination were now banished and placed on probation.

Up was up and down was down. There was no magic. Atheism made me no promises except that life was hard, the universe didn't know I was here, I would continually struggle and suffer, and that there were no guarantees that my hopes, wishes, and dreams would ever be realized. It didn't blow smoke up my behind, telling me I was thought of before time began, created for a reason, that I was unique and given some calling or mission from heaven, or that I was deeply loved by a cosmic Father in whom I could turn to for comfort, solace, guidance, peace, and healing. The world looked exactly as the atheist said it should look if there were no God.

But I felt God's absence with every breath, and I felt the cold indifference of nature. I was trapped and suffocated in the physical world, and it only made me want to leave it more.

I had to get used to a life without God if I was going to be sane, but as Nietzsche said, though God is dead, his shadow lingers long, and I wasn't positive a lifetime was long enough to come out from under it.

63
Emily

While posting in the mewithoutYou discussion boards on MySpace after Cornerstone, a girl named Emily began reading my blogs, in which I told my life story.

She had been diagnosed bipolar for a manic episode years back and struggled with eating disorders. After passing out at the store, she posted that she was going to spend the rest of the day in bed and hoped her Christian friends and family wouldn't judge her. Frustrated with her struggles, she was told over and over by those surrounding her that prayer and Bible study alone should cure her, that there was no such thing as mental illness.

I was despondent, lying on my couch when I wrote to comfort her. "Don't worry, I'm sitting with you in the shadows."

Famished for support, affection, and understanding, she cried, printed this line out, and put it in her wallet. She determined that day she wanted to leave the marriage she was miserable in and be with me.

She separated from her husband and made her attraction known to me. I told her I was in no place for a relationship. I was unavailable, I was suicidal, and I had nothing to give.

"All I need is your heart," she assured me. "You're everything I've been looking for. I have to meet you just to see if we have a chance. I can't believe those other girls rejected you. If Natalie doesn't want you, I'll take you."

I turned her down three more times. Still, she kept sending me poetry, songs she had written about me, and pictures of herself, desperately wanting to love me.

Shockingly, her husband called me and asked me to be her friend, perhaps thinking this might save his marriage. He knew she was attracted to me, but still wanted us to talk. He called many times during their separation asking for advice on how to win her back. Exasperated by October that she wasn't coming back, he gave up.

Worn down by Emily's persistence, and never having experienced anyone wanting me this way, I used the last of my Air Tran cups to book a flight for first week of January.

I wrote her husband at Christmas, who was already dating someone else with the divorce now in process, and he gave me his blessing. Emily had two young children, and if she was going to be with me, she would give full custody to him and move to Illinois. I wanted to sure he was okay with that.

When I picked up Emily at the airport, she kissed me, crying, and rested her head on my shoulder the entire three-hour ride back to Warren.

Against all odds, Emily and I connected instantly and fell in love with each other. The entire week she stayed with me, we cuddled and watched movies, went out to eat, and took in each other's affection.

"I can't help you or heal you," I said. "I can't be a dad to your kids or take care of pets. I can't handle any drama. I need space to focus on trying to heal from my depression. If you want to move in, you can stay here with me and we'll have something nice together, but I can't invest in a relationship. If at any point you want to leave, or if you miss your kids and want to move back to Florida, you can. I'll thank you for the time we had together. Just, whatever you do, don't try to change me or obligate me or ask me to take care of pets or kids or to move. Don't cheat on me or harm me in any way."

With her divorce finalizing, Emily was happy not to think about commitment or marriage. She knew she couldn't be a mom to her kids because of the stress it caused and how it triggered her eating disorders, so she promised she would never ask me to be a dad. Like me, she just wanted us to be together and love each other. She was sympathetic to my physical and emotional suffering because she suffered from her own disabilities.

Even sick people need love, no matter how imperfect the relationship might be. With this understanding, she moved in with me that February.

Still, concerned friends and family sat her down and asked her how she could just leave her young children this way, worried that she would eventually break my heart and leave me. Still, others were angry that I enabled this situation and allowed her to leave her kids.

Emily explained that the stress of mothering triggered her illness and she had always found being a parent difficult, so she needed to think of her health, and that their dad was a great provider and father, so they were in good hands with him. She planned to visit them on their birthdays and Christmas. She asked everyone not to judge her or view her as a bad person because of this.

"All that time you wanted God to pick someone for you, he picked a girl who put you through hell and didn't even want you. Now the moment you become an atheist, the perfect girl for you falls right into your lap with no effort at all," my friend Brandon marveled.

"Life is absurd and full of irony," I answered.

Natalie, however, was breaking up with her boyfriend and expressing regret for not having given me a chance. She felt responsible for my current atheism and asked me to consider opening up to her before moving forward with Emily. I told Natalie I no longer believed that any of what happened between us was from God. In tears and with reluctance, she congratulated me on meeting Emily and wished us happiness while fearing she was resigned to be alone for the rest of her life because God's plan for us was now gone.

As winter turned to spring, and summer was right around the corner, my relationship with Emily was better than I could ever have imagined. We went on dates, cuddled and watched movies, wrote each other love notes in a journal, and took walks together on beautiful spring days. My heart leapt every day for having her.

She still struggled with binging and purging, feeling guilty for burdening me with this, and I still often felt that I needed to be alone or be a monk.

"Oh sure, you'll be a monk when they allow internet and cable, Mark McGwire videos, Flamin' Hot Cheetos, porn, Famous Dave's, and conjugal visits." She rolled her eyes.

Now together six months, we decided to move to Chicago,

back into the old flat upstairs from my grandma and uncle. The rent was cheaper, there were more job opportunities for Emily, my friends were there, and there was much more to do.

Slowly, our love and nurture was bringing each other back to life.

5/20/07
Email to Aaron

Aaron,

I got a call from your dad last week but the message cut off after 20 seconds. Yes, in that 20 seconds he managed to mention your mom, the Sufi group, George Bush, the FBI, and that you all had prayed for me. If that is true, thank you very much. If not, then I don't know who you are anymore.

Call me and tell me how you are you doing when you have a moment. Love you brother,

Paul

5/25/07
Email from Aaron

Paul,

Hello and peace to you! I recently got the sense that if I've ever done anything worthwhile (i.e., pray for you) it wasn't me but the Good Spirit, who I am most certainly not, but who has made a home somewhere in my chest. Do you understand what I mean? I'm not sure I have ever prayed for anyone. That is to say, I don't love you or anyone in the world, yet there is a love in me, a love for you—but the only problem with me saying "I love you" is that when it's actually true, there's no more "I" and "you." Only "us."

Groaning, bewildered,

Aaron

64
Metro 2007

On June 23rd, Emily and I went to Metro to see mewithoutYou with Piebald, The Snake The Cross The Crown, and Manchester Orchestra. Aaron was clean-shaven, sporting his trademark muttonchops. I hugged him and introduced him to Emily.

"Emily moved in with me in February. She finalized her divorce a few months back and gave her ex-husband custody of the kids. We just moved to Chicago, back to the house I grew up in. We've been building a relationship ever since. It's been wonderful."

Aaron didn't look at me. He just looked straight ahead and listened.

"Too much information?" I asked, thinking I had laid too much on him.

"Just enough." He finally looked at me with a sheepish smile.

Still visibly conflicted by all I'd just told him, he pointed at Emily and said, "Okay, you're gonna die one day."

I laughed out loud at his lack of social grace. He was worried that I was now putting all of my stock in a woman instead of God for peace and happiness.

Before leaving, I gave Aaron a book of Rumi's poetry that I'd found in a used bookstore. As we drove back from the show that night, Emily said, "I told Aaron thanks for loving you and saving your life. He said you were easy to love."

Aaron had been thinking a lot about this idea of not being attached to anyone or marrying, but being devoted to God alone. A little more than a week later, while onstage at Cornerstone, someone asked Aaron to help him propose to his girlfriend during the band's performance. Aaron obliged.

"Oh yeah, before I forget. Where is it? There's a somewhat important announcement coming to you. I want to say, first of all, I personally have been considering that maybe never getting married is a good option for our lives. Then we can more devoted to God and not like, rub my feet kinda stuff. Not that that's a bad thing. But it's a good option. Marriage is a good option, too, I'm quite sure. But we can also consider never getting married. But Anna, if you're listening, Mike Stacey wants to marry you. I don't even know this guy. I'm not endorsing him. I don't know if he's gonna treat you right. People change. There's only one who doesn't change, and that's God Almighty, so don't go putting your trust in this Mike guy, and Mike, please don't put your trust in this Anna. For both of you and all of us, maybe we can put our trust in, well, the Truth, do you understand what I mean?"[179]

Two months later, Aaron gathered the courage to voice his concerns and send them to me in an email.

---

[179] Cecil Marshall, "mewithoutYou Cornerstone 2007 January 1979," *YouTube*, 7/29/07.

8/30/07
Email from Aaron

Paul,
Hello and peace to you my friend. I'm sorry to take so long in writing back. To be honest, I didn't feel ready to say what was on my heart, and though I still don't, I figured I'll try.

This might not come as much of a surprise to you, but some of the things you told me about your relationship with Emily made me sad. I don't want to meddle in your business or to tell you how to conduct your life—not at all! But you are very dear to me, so what should I do with my concern that your comfort and happiness may be coming from something passing?

You understand what I mean (that is, everything changes, Emily leaves, dies, something), and I know that you've searched the eternal things for contentment and in some ways have come up empty. But let me butcher some Rumi: "Not until we keep our wanting still for 40 years do we begin to pass over from confusion." (You don't like it? Maybe you shouldn't a given me that book!)

Also, I know you've read Christ's teachings on divorce and have some understanding of the weightiness of sexuality, so I certainly don't need a quick Bible verse to throw your way or a word of detached advice, "You shouldn't . . . you should . . . "

Still, my faith in love (an unconditional and senseless love that exists equally for all lives—that is, G-d) is devout, and if we have sought that love above all else or submitted to that love fully, I do not believe that that love will fail us. I suppose my question is the same for any of my friends who I see finding comfort in the love of one person, particularly in the physical ways—that question being, what do you think?

I felt I needed to say something about this only because it seemed dishonest for me to nod and smile when I saw you while thinking these things. I didn't want to bring it up with Emily there, as you can well imagine, and I've only said some of what I feel, watered down with cowardice or kindness. I don't know, but I hope I love you. What should I be doing differently, brother?

Aaron

8/31/07
Email to Aaron

Hello Aaron,

It is always a wonderful surprise to hear from you. Unfortunately you have no Illinois dates on your next tour. I would ask to tag along and help out but I'm not sure my health could take it, to be honest. Perhaps I can ask your permission just in case?

If I have the priority of your concerns about me in order, they seem to be:

1) Am I finding my happiness in something temporal like Emily or in a human relationship, and does this concern me?

2) Am I concerned that I am living a lifestyle far from the teachings of Jesus on divorce, remarriage, and sexuality?

Before I begin, I want you to know that I am not offended by you disagreeing with me and am happy you feel somewhat comfortable in being honest with me. This reminds me that you care and that our friendship is still one of integrity.

Let me give you my very short answers and then explain:

1) I don't need Emily, nor do I trust in her for an ounce of happiness. My heart and mind are still far from this world and existing in it.

2) I believe I am responsible for moral and ethical decisions in my life and use rational inquiry to decide what is best for me as opposed to following a holy text or moral system from a religion or a teacher. If in fact I claimed to be a follower of Christ, you would have every right to be concerned that I am not living up to his standards. I don't believe I am perfect, but neither are supposedly revealed standards of living from holy books. I believe all of life involves risk and calculated decision-making, so I find rational decision-making better than absolute obedience to a

teacher, religion, or imposed system.

The teachings of Jesus as I have understood them are clearly these:

1) It is better not to marry or have attachments in this world, but to be free for full devotion to God. Paul also taught this in Romans 7. In both cases, the imminent apocalypse was a concern for giving up this world. For those who burned with lust or could not accept this, marriage was a "good" second choice, but added hardship and suffering to your life.

2) The Bible is unqualified concerning divorce—it is always evil to separate what God joins together. Anyone who divorces and moves on, that divorce will not be recognized by God, and they will be charged with adultery. Some later manuscripts have Jesus qualifying divorce in one gospel by saying "except for infidelity," but many scholars see this as a late addition to the text, believing Jesus's teaching in the purest form is against any kind of divorce or remarriage. In the Old Testament, the Jews were pulled into exile and figured the reason was because they married foreigners and were corrupted by their gods, so God allowed them back into their homeland so long as they left their foreign wives and children behind. This obviously has no application for marital and divorce ethics today.

3) The Bible is clearly against cohabitation and sex outside of marriage. A woman who cannot produce blood on a towel from a broken hymen can be returned to her father's doorstep and stoned. There is no prohibition on men having sex outside of marriage as it was a male-dominated culture, but it is implied as wrong by teachings that tell men to beware of seduction and not to give in to lust. Anyone committing any combination of these sexual sins or immoralities is on more than one "lake of fire" list in the New Testament.

Marital customs, sexual ethics, and the relationship between husband and wife change not only over the time which the Bible records, but in the span of time between the completion of the Bible and today. God allows and endorses polygamy in many cases and circumstances in the Old Testament, even allowing the conquesting Hebrews to slaughter everyone in the land and take any virgin they thought was beautiful as their wives after they were allowed to mourn the loss of their family, whom was just killed. If you then are not pleased with her anymore, you can send her away with a certificate of divorce. This is God himself endorsing this, but Jesus later says, "Moses gave you divorce because of your hard hearts." Even if that is so, it shows that God is flexible (at least back then) on sexual ethics.

We also have women being treated as property to be owned. Even God speaks of blessing men with land, women, and cattle. God reminded David that he gave him those wives and concubines, and if there weren't enough, he would have given him more. He was mad that David stole another man's woman. Adultery is always a property crime against another man in the Bible. The most romantic book of the Bible—the Song of Solomon—finds Solomon telling the Shulamite woman that he has wives and concubines beyond number, but she is the prettiest of them all.

We have to keep in mind that marital and sexual ethics in which romance, companionship, and women being treated as equals play a role is very late in history and is alien to the Bible. Even those most liberating verses in the Bible about treating women with respect are interpreted within the framework of a culture in which women had very little freedom. Every Christian dating and marriage book on the market today is a product of our culture and has a spattering of selected Bible verses thrown in to make it look as if modern Christian romantic ideals, marital customs, and sexual ethics are gotten from the Bible. I saw through this even as a teen, Aaron.

No matter how many times I brought up the teachings of Jesus on divorce to pastors, they would qualify, "I'm sure Jesus wouldn't want a woman to stay with a man who abuses her, abuses the kids, who neglects her, etc." After coming up with very rational and common sense reasons for allowing divorce and placing them into the mouth of Jesus, they will follow with, "I'm sure God has another person for this woman and doesn't want her to go unloved and uncared for her whole life—especially with children." Again, this is all good, rational, modern, common sense, but it is far from the standards of Jesus.

When I bring up pacifism I get the same thing, "I'm sure if your wife is being raped or your children abducted you would violently defend them and have a moral obligation to do so." In other words, most Christians, it seems to me, live by reason and common sense AGAINST the radical and nonsensical teachings of Jesus.

My decision was to live a rational life, making my own decisions, and being who I am as opposed to following ideologies, interpreting texts, and (God forbid) following impressions, visions, prophets, and much of the nonsense that destroyed me the first time around.

I evaluated my situation with Emily and believed she had valid reasons for her divorce. This is where idealism crumbles in the face of realism. In the real world, things don't work like we hope on paper. In a sense, if the Bible says to swear by nothing and not to vow anything, but to let your yes be yes and your no be no, why would I bring a woman before God and say, "I vow to love her forever and put up with her even when I don't want to anymore," then have her repeat the same to me?

For all of the bum wrap cohabitation gets, millions have common-law marriages that work just fine while the institution of marriage fails more than half of the time. We have been together since January and I can honestly say it has been nothing but good for both us. We have a deep love for one another and an understanding of each other's weaknesses. She is very graceful, kind, and loving and has honestly been a refreshing break from so much mistreatment I've received from women in my past. I tell her all the time, "If you were to leave me today, your love has changed my life and I'm thankful for that." It is very much like the impact you had on me. I don't need you or depend on you, but am deeply indebted to you.

Emily and I don't pit "perfect divine love" against "flimsy human love." We simply believe that giving and experiencing love means something in-and-of-itself as opposed to being propaganda for God, a religion, or even ourselves. We are doing our best to extend love to those in her family who show us none. We definitely want to be involved in a spiritual community of some sort. As far as finding a woman who loves me and wants to love me, I hit the jackpot.

So although I am far from the teachings of Jesus, I am not far from the spirit of them. I don't endorse promiscuity or sex for recreation, I am not anti-marriage and family. There isn't a codependency or trust in one another to complete each other. I just filmed a friend's wedding this past Sunday and felt it was all so futile. What was important was not the vows and ceremony, but the fact that they continue to love one another and the world around them. The only problem with my way of doing things is that it keeps us from being accepted in Christian communities. In case you haven't guessed, that's alright with me.

We are built as sexual beings. Our biology is created for it, we have puberty, fertility, hormones, beauty, attraction, a need for love, affection, and community, etc. Without lust, seduction, and social contracts we would have no way of keeping the human "species" going. It is the most basic thing any living thing does—reproducing and nurturing offspring. So the teaching that this should be avoided and that we should live single and celibate lives would be the destruction of the human race. Jesus said only those who could accept celibacy should and Paul sees it as a gift from God for some. By all means, sex, infatuation, marriage, and attachment are the rule and the norm. Those who set their lives apart from these very basic needs are the exception to the rule and are abnormal.

You live a very abnormal and eccentric life, Aaron. I don't know how many people I've talked with online who said, "I respect him and wish I could do what he does, but I can't. He's such an inspiration to me." My old pastor said, "It seems to me Aaron does nothing for the poor, but dresses like the poor for show. So in claiming to be humble and helping people, all he's doing is looking for attention and wanting people to look at him."

It's an interesting point to consider, but I answered, "Well, for the sake of his own heart, he wants to identify with the forgotten, the lost, and the poor as opposed to identifying with shallow culture, crass capitalism, and enjoying a good life while others suffer. There is something to be said for setting a prophetic example." Prophets in many ways are actors, props, mirrors, and challengers who must be set apart in order to be noticed. Your main purpose in life as a prophet is to piss everyone off because they are forced to confront their hearts and hypocrisy with just one glance at you. Trust me, you have pissed off many.

Now, with that in mind, I will tell you that as long as your sexual urges are in check and you don't want to build a family, you would be much better off single for a lifetime. Although Emily and I are together, I still need a lot of alone time, reflection time, and would be very happy if we had separate places. I protect my freedom to be eccentric, to let myself be insane when need be, to hibernate away when my health is too poor to function, to find a place for creativity, and many times, I fear, to have the freedom to commit suicide should life become too painful. Because of these things, I stay free of attachments, bonds, and being "necessary and needed" by people. I tell Emily all the time not to depend on me as I still have a fierce desire to leave this world.

I have spent the last year just stabilizing my life and dealing with poor health. It is the first time since childhood that I am not on some deep, eccentric, idealistic mission or fulfilling some transcendent purpose. My goals have been to take the world off of my back, enjoy my personal world, make money, decorate my place, and just live a "normal" life. It is torture, but at least I am not ruining my life like years past. So for now, it will do. With poor health, I can't do much unless it is from home, so I don't have the energy anymore to do a whole lot with my life. I might fight poor health and a melancholy temperament my whole life, but I am trying to make some good out of the limitations I have—such as art, writing, music, having a home group, etc.

I hope this helps explain a little. Obviously we can talk more in person soon enough. Perhaps you can tell me how you are doing these days, brother. Thank you for your love and concern,

Paul

9/12/07
Email from Aaron

Paul, what a joy to hear from you again, what an intense message you wrote me! Thank you for responding, for understanding that I was speaking out of love and respect for you, and for valuing what I said enough to write back in such depth. I always learn so much listening to or reading what you have to say, sometimes it's hard to keep up. I suppose I've been getting stupider, perhaps less rational, but yes, still trying to follow this teacher, Yeshua. Strange, how we assume different things about one another. When I read:

"If in fact I claimed to be a follower of Christ . . . "

I thought:

"Oh!"

Certainly there is no need to hold you to any gospel standard if that's not where you're at. Please forgive me for my assumptions.

Also, much of what you brought up about the Biblical view of women causes me pain when I hold a certain view of the Bible. What gives me life is not Jesus' teachings in the Bible but times when I follow what he taught and times when I'm broken and don't have anything else in the world, so I pray to God.

And I agree with you, idealism has to crumble in the face of realism, if we believe in this world or desire anything in it. But what if we didn't want anything? I have to believe this is possible.

You described Emily's grace and kindness toward you, and I thank God for that. (You'll bear with my religious talk, of course. You do know what you're getting into when you open one of my emails.)

Of course, you're also right that everyone following Christ's example would result in the end of the human race. But brother, we'd sure go out with a bang!

I was grateful to hear of your old pastor's opinion of me. I thought, "Finally, here's someone who understands me!" If the subject ever comes up again, if anything, you can tell him he's mistaken on one account—he far underestimates my phoniness.

You mentioned thoughts of suicide still linger somewhere, and a fierce desire to leave this world. Brother, is there anything I can do?

And you touched on something that I've been thinking about lately, your move from a transcendental, eccentric, mission-minded life to a stable and normal one. Can such a transition be made? I sometimes think I need to do something like that to tame my megalomania, just not sure if I can pull it off. Do you get the sense that the mission is sleeping dormant, or is it dead and buried?

As for coming along with us, I'll bring it up to the guys. As time passes, I'm more and more of a fool, not caring very much about much other than this God, not able to care or relate to any other concerns. I'm not sure I'd be very good company if you don't want to follow Jesus. Deep down, brother, I don't want to do anything else.

I love you (which you make easy) and may the truth become clear to us,

A.

65
Congress Theater

Natalie invited Emily and me to her birthday party. We couldn't make it, so instead we got Natalie a ticket to see mewithoutYou with Brand New and Thrice at Congress Theater on October 20th.

At that time, mewithoutYou put out a call for fans to bring instruments to the shows and play onstage with them. I asked Aaron if perhaps Natalie could play flute that night. "I would love for Natalie to join us. Mike likes to try people out before the shows and can be pretty picky," Aaron responded.

My friend Brandon and Natalie came separately and met Emily and me in line at the show. I went to the bus to find Aaron and ask him about Natalie playing that night. Mike didn't know where Aaron was, so he invited us on the bus to wait when another group of girls arrived with instruments, to audition.

"Sorry, we don't have any more back stage passes to give out," he said, turning them away.

"Aaron said Natalie could play tonight as well. She just needed to audition for you," I informed Mike.

"Aaron's a nice guy. He doesn't say no to anybody, so I have to be the bad guy and turn everyone away who shows up saying Aaron told them they could play. We've already given out our passes, sorry guys."

I apologized to Natalie, who didn't mind, and we got in the now insanely long line.

"Wow, this is a bigger deal than I thought," Natalie said. With a capacity of 4,000 at Congress Theater and the show being sold out, it was a pretty big deal.

Once inside, Emily and Natalie got drinks just in time for the lights to go down as the keyboard intro to "Messes of Men" played to cheers from the audience. As the song kicked in, Natalie asked, "Is Aaron wearing a backpack on stage? Why is he wearing a backpack? He's so quirky."

After mewithoutYou's set, we headed back to the bus where Aaron stood drenched in sweat with his shirt off and a towel over his head. After a hello and a long embrace, I introduced him to my friends.

"You remember Emily, and this is my friend, Brandon. And this is the infamous Natalie you've heard so much about." Aaron shook their hands and said hello, not reminding me of their imminent deaths this time.

Seeing Emily, Natalie, and Aaron standing together before me, I thought my heart would burst.

Aaron invited us back on the bus, and I offered him *The Cloister Walk* by Kathleen Norris and *An Infinity of Little Hours: Five Young Men and Their Trial of Faith in the Western World's Most Austere Monastic Order* by Nancy Klein Maguire.

"I haven't been reading much these days. As a matter of fact, I'm getting rid of most of my books," he said. He pulled out a large suitcase filled with books. "Take whatever you want."

Brandon and I rummaged through and took some Dostoyevsky while Emily found a book of poetry by Rumi.

Aaron grabbed his guitar and led us out to the sidewalk where he sang for whoever wanted to gather and sing along. Passing an overflowing wastebasket outside the venue, Aaron pulled out an almost empty cup of Jamba Juice with a plastic dome on top and a straw in it, took a sip, and handed it to Emily, who didn't hesitate to finish it.

"Why did you drink from that cup Aaron gave you from the trash?" I later asked Emily.

"Because it was from Aaron!" she said.

It was no different than the reason I ate dumpster food with Aaron in Philadelphia. I wanted to share an experience with him.

Natalie couldn't stay—her new boyfriend was playing piano at another venue. "He's a mad genius type, just a brilliant musician and super creative. He's from South America, so he has this whole exotic foreign thing and an accent going on. I thought this was what I wanted, but I don't have peace about it. Tony proposed to me and I said no. I still struggle with a lot of guilt over you. I tried to tell my boyfriend about you and what happened between us, but he just doesn't get it. I feel like I made a mess of our lives, but Emily is gorgeous and seems great. I'm really happy things are working out for you."

Natalie left with a heavy heart. Brandon left immediately after. Emily and I stayed and sat out front with Aaron, listening to him play "In A Sweater Poorly Knit," "Blowin' in the Wind," "How Great Thou Art," and for old-times' sake, I requested "We Three Kings."

When Aaron finished playing, we retuned to the bus to say our goodbyes.

Peter Syoum was touring in place of Chris Kleinberg.

"I noticed Chris wasn't here tonight," I said.

"Remember I told you last time that he likes to disappear and be alone to read his medical books? He quit the band to focus on pursuing his medical career."

"That's bad news. I always look forward to seeing him. So is this it for you guys?"

"Well, this is definitely it for me. After this tour, I'm done. I don't want to do this anymore. I'd much rather talk to my friend Paul, who I love very much." He hugged me goodbye.

But Aaron trying to quit the band didn't go over so well with Mike, leading to a strained relationship between them over the holidays and during their Australian acoustic tour in January.

Speaking at Cornerstone 2010, Mike talked about his strained relationship with Aaron. "At the end of the day Aaron and I never lost any real love for each other, but . . . I was so upset that he wanted to end the band, or he didn't know if he wanted to keep doing it, that . . . I resented it so much. Because the band was gonna break up, I was gonna not invite Aaron over to Christmas. I was gonna get him back, I was gonna sting him real hard, I was gonna get him. And I remember we were in Australia, right Aaron? And I was like *this* close to saying some horrible things and I felt like I was on a cliff. All I had to do was just tell Aaron the nastiest, most horrible thing that a brother could hear from another brother, and it was gonna make everything even. I was gonna get him. And it was because I didn't want the band to break up."[180]

I wanted to write a book about what Aaron meant to me. Thinking the band was about to end, it was now or never. I went home from that show in October and spent every day laboring over the manuscript until it was complete in December.

---

[180]Joel Swanson, "mewithoutYou Interview LIVE on the Anchor Come & Live Stage @ Cornerstone 2010," *YouTube*, 7/15/10.

66
All the Clever Words on Pages

I hoped to write a memoir of my time with Aaron as well as reflecting upon his lyrics, but the more I asked about the specific meanings of some of his lyrics, the more evasive Aaron became. "I'm more interested in reading what they meant to you," he said.

I asked if he would like to contribute a foreword to the book. "All this about the book, as you guessed, seems a bit self-indulgent, yes, for me to be terribly involved in. On the one hand, my ego is inflated and grateful for any attention, while on the other of course I think people should be concerned with G-d, not me. I don't discount the possibility that there could be something worthwhile in my story, like anyone's story, so I certainly don't object to whatever you want to write about, flattering or embarrassing, true or false, I'm certainly not worried. Still, I don't know how involved I want to be. It just seems too weird for me to write a foreword to a book that is, at least in some sense, about myself."[181]

I called the book *All the Clever Words on Pages*, taking a line from "Seven Sisters," and decided last minute to use a photo of Aaron for the cover, knowing he probably wouldn't be thrilled, or perhaps be too thrilled.

I sent the train wreck off to be printed without being proofread, with typos, mistakes, grammatical errors, and names left unchanged.

I called Aaron in January and asked him if he had a chance to read it. "I read some of it, but my mom is now reading it. I believe there is a section where you called our house a dump. I haven't heard my mom laugh that hard in a long time."

Elliott called and said, "Thank you for putting that wonderful picture of my son on the cover of your book."

Doug Van Pelt wrote a review in *HM Magazine*:

---

[181] **Email, 11/13/07.**

This book was spawned by a series of email conversations the author had with mewithoutYou frontman Aaron Weiss. Two such emails adorn the back of the book. The first is Harrison reaching out for help in the midst of struggling with the idea of suicide. The second is the singer's reply, reaching out in compassion, empathy, and a practical "I will literally help you" love that is compelling. This unfolding drama alone makes for a good read. Then the insight and description of perhaps the post-hardcore scene's most charismatic and engaging artist is another great benefit from this book. Any intelligent inspection of Weiss' lyrics and occasional missives will turn into a challenging and in-depth discussion of Christianity's core teachings. In addition to those, the author chronicles a gut-honest and un-flinching journey from faith to agnosticism to revival, and in conclusion of this book (sadly), atheism. Written with prominent parts first-person and anecdotal journaling, often times pausing to write about writing this very book, it nevertheless chronicles an enjoyable, disappointing, contemporary and spiritual trek.[182]

I wrote Aaron, still sick and sad, and asked him if the band had broken up yet.

---

[182] *HM Magazine*, March/April 2008 #130.

3/10/08
Email from Aaron

Bismillah ir-Rahman ir-Rahim.

Peace to you dear brother, my beloved brother. Yes, we're home from Australia. Yes mewithoutYou is over, but we break up between every show and get back together sometimes, so let's keep our fingers crossed for a reunion show or a thousand reunion shows, may God's will be done.

My dear brother, our health, physical/mental/spiritual, is what it is. It's just as you said, we're dying quick, and please, if there's anything I can do to relieve your pain please say so, but brother we're so poorly equipped to help each other, as you've probably learned, I've got nothing to TRULY help, band-aids maybe, but there is a Healer.

If you don't believe in God, alhamdulillah! (all praise be to God), that's alright. What if we come to accept God not as a concept of the mind, but as REALITY ITSELF? Then what need is there for atheism? Or theism?

Please don't worry. As you know, whatever was good or bad about our lives—whatever pain we feel here and whatever craziness in this world—is less than a blip on the radar, very soon to be very forgotten, is it not? But is there not some stamp of the eternal here? Is it not Love? My dear brother, can we expect to communicate these things on a computer screen?

Dear brother, truly God is our only hope. That is to say, Reality. May Reality protect you for a while, then kill you. Let's see what's next. All in good time.

Your brother, your own life.

67
Healing

Still severely depressed in the final months of 2007, I told Emily I might ask Aaron if I could tag along for a few months on tour to see if it might bring me some healing. Not only was she afraid to be left alone that long, she thought Aaron would convince me we were living in sexual sin, and I would come back with newfound faith and ask her to move out.

Emily and I opened 2008 visiting doctors. She still struggled with depression and eating disorders, and I was still in quite a severe depression, wanting to die. I often told Emily she made a mistake and should leave. I would be out of commission the rest of my life and could only hold her back. Still, the thought never crossed her mind. She loved me just as I was.

Emily began to put on some weight and keep it on, filling out and looking more gorgeous than ever. Friends began commenting on how healthy she looked, but "healthy" was a euphemism for "fat" in her mind. She felt uncomfortable with her new body, thinking she was only lovable when she could see and count all of her ribs.

Emily used to say that in her life it was raining all the time, but she struggled for the rare days when the sun came out to shine. Though our struggles were relentless, we deeply appreciated that we had each other.

My uncle suggested that he might foreclose on the house by the end of the year, so we should start thinking about where we wanted to move next. Emily missed her kids and wanted to be near them, and I wanted to move to Florida my entire life, knowing my health would improve in the sun. This was a no-brainer.

When Emily visited her kids, she was pressured by family to leave me and be a responsible mother. The kids were crying all the time missing her and had to be pried from her when saying goodbye to come back to Chicago. She started to feel guilty being apart from them.

One afternoon, I hugged Emily tightly and said, "I've been looking for love like this my whole life and can't believe I've finally found it. There are millions of lonely people out there looking for something as amazing as we have. We have something rare here. I wonder how it goes from being so good like this to one of us having our bags packed and walking out the door forever. Let's make sure that never happens to us."

"That's never gonna happen to us," she assured me.

"No one has ever been as kind to me as you have. I'm starting to think maybe I should marry you, since you aren't going anywhere. We can move to Florida at the end of the year and have a ceremony and reception beforehand. It will be a celebration of the love we already have. We won't have to legalize it, and we wouldn't obligate one another. Nothing would change. We would still be free to let each other go."

She agreed that would be a good idea, especially if we were going to enter her kids' lives together. With those qualifications, we began planning a wedding and a move to Orlando before winter arrived.

While Emily and I talked marriage, unbeknownst to me, Natalie had accepted her boyfriend's proposal on Valentine's Day. In a blur, they were married.

If there was any question left in my mind that I would marry Natalie one day, that had now been put to rest.

12/31/07
Journal Entry

    I never dreamed in a million years that I would meet someone like Emily or that I would even be open to sharing my life with anyone ever again. She has been nothing short of amazing every day that she's been with me and I can't say enough about her. If I lost her today I would be forever changed and thankful to have had her. After a year, I can say I am definitely the luckiest guy in the world. I have not met a kinder woman nor seen a more beautiful woman since. She has been nothing but good, nothing but wonderful, and I still for the life of me can't understand how I got so lucky. I can hardly live with myself, I don't know how she lives with me. Still she glows and gushes and tells me how me she loves me and how loved she feels. What I have is rare, and I feel guilty bragging about it. I have always wanted to love and be loved. I have always wanted a kind and sweet woman. I still look at how beautiful she is sometimes and I think even after a year it hasn't sunk in that she is mine. In the biography of my life, she is allowing me to experience something I imagined I could never experience. She is the star of my story. She has literally changed my life. I have never once regretted having her in my life since the moment I saw her at the airport.

2/14/08
Valentine's Day Card from Emily

Dear Paul,

When you're not making me crack up over something hilarious that you've said or done, when I look at you I become overwhelmed with emotion because you are everything I ever wanted. States away, you took care of me, you read my thoughts and interpreted my ramblings. You not only put up with my baggage, you were my friend and helped me carry it to the curb. You have always been nothing but transparent with me (which is incredibly sexy to me) which has made me feel the most safe to share all that I am with you. You make me laugh, leave me alone just long enough when I'm upset to "cool down" and then comfort me with understanding and love. Every hug, every kiss is from your heart and they are all appreciated. Paul, I always think when we're lying next to each other, breathing each other in, how grateful I am to you. In a world full of chaos, with you, my heart is calm and peaceful. There are a lot of things I'm not sure of, but I knew I found a treasure when I got to know you, Paul. And I know that when I look at you my heart is so full of gratitude for you loving me in return. I can only offer you my hope that I can make you just as happy as you've made me. I love you, Paul.

Emily

4/20/08
Email from Aaron

Bismillah ir-Rahman ir-Rahim
(In the name of God most Merciful, most Compassionate)

Peace be with you my dearest loving brother Paul—all praise be to God for the wonderful joy of hearing from you, and hearing about our plans for marriage, for all good things. What can be said dear brother, what can be said? We did receive your phone message and the whole family was very happy and we still are.

May you be filled with peace, may your wedding go very well, may you have clarity about the difficulties that lie ahead. There is nothing to worry about, ever. My love to Emily, my love to your family, my love is not actually "my" love but "My" love.

Your brother, your own life.

68
Enigma

"Richard Dawkins isn't good for your spiritual wellbeing," Emily would say, holding out her hand to take the book from me.

She had her own eclectic spirituality. After being homeschooled in a strict Christian home and raised an evangelical Christian, she eventually became an agnostic who would visit the Catholic church on our corner to light a candle and talk to her grandmother, or visit the Buddhist temple down the street to see what they had to offer. She had a small sacred space in our room with a crucifix and candles with saints on them. She hung a dream catcher and a chain of angel artwork around the walls in the bedroom to protect her from the dark figures she sometimes saw coming out of the walls.

I was still exploring the idea of emergent Christianity, hoping to start a home group. I put together my influences under the name "Enigma." It was the perfect name for an emergent group, being both pretentious and mysterious. The logo could have been a guy shrugging his shoulders with a question mark over his head.

My hope was to gather friends for food and philosophical discussion, to be a safe place for doubters and seekers who still wanted community and to seek answers together. There would be a heavy influence on Christian existentialism and mysticism and the practice of spiritual disciplines.

When I asked my friend Mark if he was interested, he didn't see the point. "So you want to get together and discuss books and philosophy and eat food?"

"Yes."

"We do that already. That's not called 'Enigma.' That's called hanging out with your friends, you idiot."

Still, I wrote to Aaron, sharing my vision for the group.

5/28/08
Email from Aaron

Bismillah ir-Rahman ir-Rahim.
(In the name of G-d most Merciful most Compassionate.)

My dearest brother Paul, my own life, my beloved friend, greetings again of peace and joy and love. It is a joy truly to hear from you, even to picture your face and your smile or your mannerisms or the sound of your voice.

Very exciting to hear about this community you're planning to start, but even more exciting is starting it right now, with you, this very moment—perhaps this is the inaugural meeting of our little community, albeit a digital one. Certainly we can agree that everything we've experienced and think and ever claimed to know is strange, uncertain, even crazy, enigmatic yes, paradoxical, backwards, upside-down. So very sweet to go poking our noses into atheist books and agnostic books, see what all's out there, and brother if we can find a better reality than unconditional unending Love, please, you'd better let us know, we'll start worshipping that!

As for my world, thanks be to God, right now you are my world, there is nothing else for me, and what a sweet and wonderful world you are. My loving brother, my loving brother, my love to you.

69
Love

While Emily and I were planning our wedding, Aaron addressed the audience again at Cornerstone that summer, warning them to be careful with the thought that romantic love or marriage could fulfill you or make you happy.

He didn't want to talk about God because he believed God was ultimately mysterious, and his thoughts about God would just convolute that. He explained that though he knew nothing about calculus, "I have a better chance at telling people about calculus than telling you about God."

Still, he tried, ignoring classical Christian theism for a much more Sufi-influenced mystical view of God.

"It's so simple, what's in my heart for you guys. It's so simple a child could understand it, but it's so strange and distant that no PhD or professor of any philosophy or religion can contain it. Of course, you know that love is the mystery that we're talking about, that the love that God has for us is what we're talking about. That's the subject of our lives, that's the source of our lives, the beginning of our lives, the current reality of our lives, and the end of our lives."

He continued, "We open our heart to this love. We fall down dead before it. Perhaps another way of putting it—we give up our understandings of it, we give up our intellectual concepts of it, we give up our doctrines of it, we give up our dogmas, we give up our preconceived notions about where it can appear, in what form it will take, who it could come through, who possesses it, and we find ourselves destroyed on some level and yet made alive in everything."

Aaron simplified God to an unconditional love that is available to all of us no matter what we believe. "Well, you don't have to believe in it, it has nothing to do with you accepting my beliefs or my perspective, but it should be interesting to you to say, 'Well, there's a fool who thinks the love of God doesn't know any boundaries. There's a fool who thinks I don't have to do anything at all to earn God's love. I don't have to be anything to earn God's love. I don't have to know anything, I don't have to accomplish anything, I don't have to be smart, I don't have to be good looking, I don't have to be religiously in-the-know, I don't have to be wealthy, I don't have to be poor.'

"We look at the sun and we're given that example of a power that exists . . . this source of light and heat that doesn't care if you're a Christian, or a Jew, or a Muslim, or an atheist, or an anti-theist, or an agnostic, or a Buddhist, or a moral relativist, or a fundamentalist. We've got an example of something in our reality, not this sort of esoteric abstraction of a God, but something that exists, that gives and never asks for anything back. It just gives. That's its nature."

Aaron lamented that human love was fickle and conditional, ultimately selfish and undependable, so God is all we really have.

In the Jesus Village tent, Aaron was about to sing "It Ain't Me Babe," a Bob Dylan classic. "Dylan saying 'It ain't me babe,' we can look deeper into that and say, 'Well, who is it then? If it ain't you, that's good to know, thank you for not pretending.' Think, what if he married the girl saying, 'It's me babe. It's me. I'm the one that's gonna always be there for you. I'm always gonna be strong for you. I'm always gonna hold the door for you. I'm gonna gather flowers for you all the time.' And what, ten years into the marriage, it's not so exciting anymore.

"You people who have been married a long time, you can reflect. Is my spouse quite as considerate to me and as romantic as he or she was when we went on our first date? Are they paying as much attention to me as they were then? Are they gathering flowers for me? Are they showing up as excited as they were that first day? Probably not. In many, many cases that excitement fades.

"That thing that we call being in love, we start to wonder, is that really love if it fades, if it's subject to change, if it's subject to emotion, if it's subject to sexual excitement and all these things that come and go? Is that what we want to call love? Well, if so, that's fine, but we're offering you something that might be a step beyond that, which is that same excitement and that same joy and that same sense of wonder and focus and priority, and willingness to sacrifice and lay down your life for your brothers and sisters. That same spirit, but all the time, and for everyone.

"This is just what we see with the life of Christ. He lived his life pouring it out. He lived as a servant, as a slave to people. Everywhere he went he said, 'What would you like me to do for you?' He went and met the needs of the people. He didn't go and preach the same Bible verse everywhere. 'I'm the way, the truth and the life! I'm the way, the truth, and the life!' He didn't go around saying that to everybody. He said that in one situation to a certain person or a certain audience, and other people he didn't say anything about himself. He healed them. He didn't say anything about who he was. He fed them. He brought someone back from the dead and that spoke volumes. That declared who he was."

Aaron continued, "You have these marriages, people get married. Maybe some of you here are probably married, if not, you're engaged. You have a girlfriend or a boyfriend you think about marrying, or you came here hoping to meet somebody to get married. But we remind each other, with God in our midst, of the folly and the craziness of this world.

Aaron warned the audience to be careful of human promises and thinking you've found the right one, or that you could be the right one for someone else.

"Look around and ask other brothers and sisters who have been married, ask them, 'Has that fulfilled you? Is that the thing that brought an end to your loneliness?' . . . I don't want to be a stick in the mud or something or rain on our parade, but it's a lousy parade, at least with all of my friends who have gone through it. They've been married, and you see either they don't get along so much and they get divorced, or they live together but there is just a great heaviness or a disappointment because what they expected from that other person was, 'they're gonna meet my needs, they're gonna fulfill me' at some point. And where this is leading to is, if you have any expectations on another person to meet your needs or to fulfill you or to take away that emptiness inside, that loneliness, hand it to God within your heart."

Aaron finished, saying even the nicest people can have a bad day. "If your contentment is based on them being nice to you, if your willingness and ability to be loving to them is based upon them loving you, it's not love. Well, you could call it love, but it's not the love that our hearts have tasted and experienced, that one, that unconditional grace of God which exists for us no matter whether we do the right thing or wrong thing. That love is still love. It's still there for us, but it doesn't cease because of our behavior, it doesn't change, it's unchanging. So we need to tap into that. We need to make that our life. We need to accept that what I'm calling love for this person, maybe that's not really love. . . . it's a pleasure exchange. So in that way, we take this burden off of that person to bring us happiness, and we find our happiness in the one who could truly provide it, who is always there for us. Then imagine what would happen if you literally build your house of peace on a rock, on something unchanging, unchangeable, and love him."

While Aaron was at Cornerstone reminding people that God is all any of us really have and that all human love in some sense is fickle, Emily and I had a conversation while planning our wedding.

I gave her one last chance to bail before going through with the ceremony, but she wouldn't think of it. "You're all I've got. You're my everything, and I love you," she said.

"But I can't be your everything, I'm not even enough for myself." I knew enough about codependency to know that when someone depends too much on another, they begin to obligate and control them to meet their needs. I was still looking for time and space to heal my own depression and couldn't carry both of us. She said this made her feel alone and rejected.

Meanwhile, Natalie wrote me to congratulate me for getting married, but asked for my help. She missed me and now had feelings for me, explaining that no one loved her the way I did. She felt she'd ruined our lives and my faith as well her own happiness by marrying the wrong man.

"I know that your beliefs have changed and rightfully so, but it's important for me to let you know that it was me that let you down, not God. He told me from the beginning just like he told you what he was working on with us. I know you are completely past this and I am so sorry for bringing this up to you. I hope you can forgive me. I fought God so hard because of my stubborn spirit. God told me on several occasions to write down my story with you. I should have taken any of the hundred opportunities God gave me to be honest with myself and to trust in Him and reach out to you before permanently altering my path and becoming married. I honestly thought that if I got married that God would just have to leave me alone with all the talk about you and that if I showed him I was sorry he would have to bless this new direction, but instead all I feel is empty within. I feel responsible because if I would have accepted you into my life like God said to that December, you would have been so fired up at the way God came through that you and I both would have been using our gifts and talents for God and you would be helping to influence people towards belief instead of unbelief."

She was crying all the time, sobbing herself to sleep, sorry for how she treated me. She felt like she was being punished by God.

"Now looking back, I can't see how I didn't rejoice when God tried to orchestrate love for me, to give me someone to care for and someone who would support and nurture my relationship with Him. I don't know if I will ever be able to be really happy again knowing that I altered a move of God by my own fear and disobedience. Now I just don't know what to do, how to approach my marriage knowing full well that it is not the right one.

"I'm sorry again. I'm sure you have put all of this far behind you and are eager to forget all about this painful time in your life and focus on the beauty to come, but I don't know where else to turn. I've never felt more dead before. Numb and empty. Filled with regret and alone. Please if you have a moment. Just this one last request."[183]

I sent Natalie a long response once again trying to convince her that God had never brought us together, that we'd never heard

---

[183] Email, 9/26/08.

his voice, and that God wasn't punishing her. I apologized that I believed and encouraged any of this at all in her life. I reminded her of all of the ways we weren't compatible and told her to take hope in the realization that we dodged a disaster. I asked for her forgiveness, reminded her that I loved her and forgave her, and I told her we would always be friends so she should never hesitate to reach out when she needs help navigating this.

She thanked me for my help, but found little consolation in my doubt and unbelief.

70
Wedding

In August, Emily and I exchanged vows and rings, smiles and tears, in a small informal ceremony in a friend's living room with no family present. The few friends hosting us went above and beyond for us, providing music, corsage and boutonniere, a cake, and dinner after. They gave us a large sum of money to help us start our new life in Florida.

I was weak and trembling, sweating through the ceremony, and twitched in pain as Emily drove us home that night. I hit the bed and slept for fifteen ours. She truly loved me at my sickest.

Our reception followed on a gorgeous day at Kiwanis Park in Brookfield. It was a simple gathering of friends and family on a Saturday afternoon, catered with Italian food.

I took a moment to go off alone through the trees to Salt Creek and stand in the same spot I once stood trying to drown myself a few years back. I stood there alive and in love.

Just like our wedding night, it was a great burden to be social. We were both worn out and fell asleep the moment we got back, glad we were both homebodies who just liked being together.

After so many years of searching, I now had a best friend and partner to grow old with. My friends and family were elated that I'd finally gotten married after searching so many years for someone to love me the way Emily did.

Looking at the ring on my finger while imagining our good, long life in Florida, still holding her wrinkly hand in old age, I felt a deeper contentment than I'd ever had in my life.

71
Clearwater

"My babies, my babies!" Emily woke up yelling one night, two weeks after the wedding.

"Hey, are you okay?" I rolled over and hugged her, thinking she had a nightmare.

"My babies come with me, and if you don't understand that, you shouldn't have married me," she said sternly.

I thought she was talking in her sleep, but she wasn't.

"I know you miss them. We'll be in Florida by the end of the year, and you'll see them all the time." I tried to comfort her back to sleep.

"I need my babies and they need me." She was now crying. "I want to fight for custody. I'm tired of having no control in this situation."

Now I sat up.

"But you know we can't handle the kids, and we can't afford them. We talked about this when we met. You told me you would never expect me to be a dad to your kids, especially because you couldn't be a mom. Everyone judged you for leaving your kids and judged me for enabling that, but you explained to them that you couldn't handle them and chose to be with me."

"I don't remember agreeing in the vows to not having my kids. You can handle them, you just don't want to. How do you know you wouldn't like being a dad? You haven't even tried it."

"Emily, it has nothing to do with liking it or not. You know I'm disabled and need my space and alone time. I can't have anyone depending on me. We never discussed you wanting custody, and I don't remember agreeing to be a dad in the vows if were gonna play that game."

"Well, I work all day and come home tired and in pain. I don't see what the difference is. My dad has employees with fibromyalgia and they work, so he says you have no excuse."

"Emily, you've lived with me for almost two years, you've

seen the pain and the symptoms I have. You've been to doctors with me. Why are you pretending all of a sudden not to understand? You're scaring me—I don't know who I'm talking to right now."

"I don't see why I have to go the rest of my life without a dog because you're allergic. They have pills you can take for that."

"Well, I can't take care of a dog right now any more than I can kids. We can live in separate apartments, and you can have your kids and a dog and whatever you want, I don't mind," I said, offering a compromise.

"No, Paul. We're married. We're not living apart. I don't see why you should get everything you want just because you're sick. What about what I want?"

I felt myself sinking through the bed. I had often pinched myself at our compatibility when we were dating, but now I saw that she wasn't really happy. She was sacrificing a lot of what she really wanted to be with me and was pretending to be compatible. She was now becoming resentful. With a ring on her hand, she now felt comfortable enough to vent her frustrations and demand that I do what I couldn't do.

"Why didn't you say any of this before we got married? If I knew we weren't compatible, I wouldn't have proposed to you."

"I didn't know I'd feel this way, and I didn't want to lose you. I don't really consider us married. I still refer to you at work as my boyfriend."

"But wasn't the whole reason we qualified our vows to avoid this? To avoid one of us obligating the other to do what they didn't want to do? So when you want to obligate me to do something, you're gonna hold me to my vows, but the rest of the time, we're not really married?"

"I don't know, Paul. I just miss my kids."

I went to sleep hoping to wake up in the morning and forget this exchange took place.

Concerned, I called friends and family and confided in them that I felt like I woke up next to a stranger and didn't know what to do. "Poor girl," they said, "she's just going through a hard time feeling guilty about leaving her kids. Maybe she should get some help."

"I don't need help. You need help understanding maternal instinct." Emily corrected me. "Don't make me choose between you and my kids. I love you, but I'm doing this with or without you."

We stayed at odds for the next two weeks. We had never been disconnected this way before.

My mom urged me to send Emily home to Florida alone. "That's not a real marriage, Paul. And if she's this inconsiderate to you now, imagine how it will be when you get to Florida and she has all the leverage. Good thing you decided not to legalize it. I know you're embarrassed that it won't work out, but it's better to be embarrassed now than to ruin your whole life and lose everything again."

Emily agreed that she didn't have the ability to be a mother and understood that I couldn't be a father, so agreed not to fight for custody of the kids. We agreed that we didn't want to live with her parents or depend on them in any way. Emily chose Clearwater because it was the only place she could get a job transfer, but it was four hours away from her kids.

"We are moving to Florida to enjoy our life and to get happier and healthier, not to add more stress and drama to it. We can only afford to move once, and once that wedding money is spent setting up, that's our home. If at any point you want to start a custody case for the kids or move us in with your parents, that will be the end of us. I will move back to Chicago alone. If you really want to move to Clearwater, I'll do it, but I only have enough energy for one move, so you have to be sure."

"I don't want any drama either. I just want to start a life and be with you," she said. "Thank you so much. I love you." She kissed me with tears in her eyes. Just like that, the storm had passed and we reconnected.

At the end of October, we packed the 1999 Ford Escort and headed to Florida to the soundtrack of Copeland, Eisley, Lovedrug, Death Cab, and Owen.

We set up our apartment within two weeks of arriving. We decided to have our first date at Clearwater Beach. We stopped at the old hostel I stayed in a few years back. It had been converted to condos. The beach was slightly chilly and windy, but we still walked along the shoreline in our bare feet and picked shells to the backdrop of a breathtaking sunset. It felt like we were in paradise.

Like I'd done at Salt Creek during my reception, I stood at the edge of the water looking at the waves, celebrating life where I had once tried to end my life.

Emily went to visit her kids and had an amazing time until the moment she was leaving to come home. Her ex-husband handed her papers and a pen, asking her to sign them so his new wife could adopt the kids should anything happen to him. Emily called me, outraged and crying, then called her parents, who retained a lawyer.

"I'm not letting him do this to me. We're fighting for custody and if we have to move in with my parents we will."

I kept my foot down. We had an agreement. We were back to arguing every day. She hated her job, hated our town, and started drinking more to get through each day.

After one of our arguments, she locked herself in the bathroom, then came out and showed me her arms, which were scraped and gouged, elbows to wrists. There was no way I would allow her to fight a court case in this state, so I demanded that she move back to Chicago with me and get help. She refused.

We continued to argue almost every day. In March, I realized I was above ground. Not only did I no longer want to kill myself, but my depression was mild. I was getting healthier and coming back to life in the sun. I felt like I had crawled out of a hole or awakened from a five-year coma. The vibrancy of the world around me was overwhelming as I started to feel again. "Oh, shit," I thought. "If Emily and I don't work out, I'm really gonna feel it."

When Emily got fired from her job in April, she insisted on moving in with her parents.

"We have a marriage and a household. We're not moving in with your parents. They think I'm from Satan, they invalidate you, and they don't acknowledge our marriage. We need to keep our life ours without any obligation to anyone else. How can I get you to care about us and our marriage?"

"Really? You'd keep me here even if I was miserable and didn't want to be here? Everyone I talk to asks me what kind of husband keeps a mother from her kids. They tell me maybe I need to find a new husband."

I dissociated again, feeling disconnected from everything in the room. I looked around at the furniture, the apartment, and Emily—none of this was mine. Feeling like I was an intruder in my own home, I put my hands up in surrender.

"You know what? Go. Go fight for your kids. Go move in with your parents. Take the car. I'll sign it over to you, and you can use it to work and pay for a lawyer. Take all the furniture, take everything you need, I'll pay the final bills and I'll pay my way home. But this isn't a marriage. There is no consideration for me, my needs, or my health, and I need to take care of myself. You trample every agreement we make, so our conversations are pointless. I'm begging you not to do this but you're giving me no reason to stay. If you win custody of your kids, we can no longer live together, even if we work out. I'll have to get my own place. And when I get home to Chicago, don't call me from your parents' house every day and tell me you're puking or cutting or drinking or wanting to kill yourself. I'm trying to keep you from all of that and keep us together because I love you, but you're not listening."

"I knew you'd make me choose between you and my kids. You made vows, Paul. I'm not abandoning you, you're abandoning me."

She moved in with her parents and came back with a truck in June to pick up the furniture. I stayed with her at her parents' house for two weeks. She begged me every day to stay, but she wouldn't give me one thing I asked for or needed. It was all or nothing. I couldn't look in the mirror anymore after allowing myself to be so disrespected. It broke my heart, but I had to go.

Emily dropped me at the airport. After I kissed her goodbye, she stood there next to the car watching me check my luggage. She was tiny and still too pretty to look at, her eyes pained, like a puppy abandoned on the side of the road.

My friend Mark picked me up at the airport in Chicago. "Welcome back to normal life," he said as I got in the car, as if I'd just escaped the Twilight Zone. "All you've been doing is hurting and crying and talking about your problems with Emily for almost a year. I want my friend back."

I rang the doorbell to my uncle's house and found myself in the old upstairs flat I'd tried my whole life to escape. I set it back up with the scraps and mismatched furniture Emily and I had left behind, then collapsed, sobbing. I was back here again, alone, starting over, not knowing if I'd ever see Emily again. It was so angry with her, I was hoping to never see her again.

3/04/09
Email to Aaron

Aaron,

Hello, this is Paul. Just wanted to say I love you, I miss you, and I hope you and your family are well. If you need anything, let me know,

Your brother,

Paul

3/21/09
Email from Aaron

Bawa. Bismillah ir-Rahman ir-Rahim
(In the name of G-d most Merciful, most Compassionate)

Bawa. My very precious brother Paul, it is a joy to hear from you, much peace be with you—thank you for your very loving email. I love you too, very much, and yes, for all our family's craziness all in truth is well. Nothing to worry about. May G-d protect you and your family and Emily and her family and grant us peace and grace. Thank you again for thinking of me and for writing me. You are a gift to me, please know this.

Your brother, your own life,

(P.S. "Bawa" means "Father" in the Tamil language and is the name of my family's guru/shaikh. He once said, "Before you do anything, call me," so sometimes I do that—it helps.)

72
Repudiations

Music journalist Steven Wells spent time traveling with mewithoutYou in the summer of 2008. He reports that Aaron spent his time at Cornerstone 2008 as if he were on an apology tour:

> Aaron Weiss takes the stage and spends 10 minutes apologizing for his presence and warning us he has absolutely nothing of interest to say.
>
> And then he talks for two hours without notes and without repetition, holding the 200 strong crowd spellbound.
>
> He trashes fundamentalism and takes shots at atheism. He finishes by dismissing everything he said last year, mocking his image as a modern-day Dumpster-diving saint.
>
> "This same fool was onstage last year telling you the answer was to eat out of Dumpsters, live in communes and be a communitarian anarchist Christian," he says. "Well, this is me taking it back."
>
> He tells the crowd not to turn out for his talk tomorrow but to send Jesus instead and to tell him to bring duct tape so he can "wrap my stupid head up if I say anything harmful."
>
> He'll do a standing-room-only show with the band later this night—and spend three hours afterward quietly addressing a huge crowd on the subject of why they shouldn't be listening to such a "foolish pile of earth": "Forget every word I've uttered. Not a single word will do you any good. Don't say I didn't warn you. If you've come here to learn something, you've come to the wrong place."
>
> "I am a pile of manure," says Aaron. "And my words are dog food."
>
> Afterward I stop a young woman leaving the tent. She's smiling, her eyes gleaming. I ask if what she's just heard made any sense.

"It doesn't need to make sense," she says.[184]

On July 2nd, 2008, mewithoutYou played a show in Nashville, Tennessee at Rocketown. Steven Wells wrote, "After the show, the young Christians will hang around to seek wisdom from 29-year-old Philadelphian Aaron Weiss, the band's incredibly charismatic lead singer."[185]

Steven went on, "Every show ends with lead singer Weiss out on the sidewalk or parking lot with acoustic guitar, glowing with sweat, smiling beatifically, surrounded by grinning, enraptured young people. I've seen hero worship. I've seen lust. This is something different."[186]

What people saw in Aaron was a connection to something transcendent.

In Aaron's world, he walked the line between megalomania and seeing himself as a fraud, vacillating between ego and self-abasement. He sought the counsel of a spiritual mentor at the Sufi fellowship. The sheikh confronted Aaron, telling him he was neither a guru nor a teacher, and it was best that he stop speaking about things he knew little about. As Aaron put it, "He cleaned my clock."

Aaron told MySpace, "I had kind of a spiritual guide for a few years. I would go and sit with him; he was someone who would talk to me about God and about who I am and what I know, and it was humbling because he cut through me in a lot of ways. He cut through my arrogance and showed me how arrogant and foolish I am. It was difficult to sit with him because he showed me all the ways I was and am a hypocrite, and it made it hard to take myself seriously when I tried to go out and talk about God or truths or love or any of these great big concepts without any real authority. But it wasn't just him, there are so many things in life that show me that. Like anybody, I want to understand myself and

---

[184] Steven Wells, "Oh, Sweet Jesus: Philadelphia is either home to the most genuinely Christian movement in America or it's a festering spiritual slum. All depends on how you look at it," *Philadelphia Weekly*, 9-24-08.
[185] Ibid
[186] Ibid

my own motivations and intentions so I try to question those things and I see more and more how my motivation for this band is totally selfish and totally ego-based, so it starts to feel really silly to try to masquerade that I'm trying to do some holy work when really I just like the attention."[187]

When asked about dumpster diving, Aaron answered, "I hope I don't disappoint you, but I haven't been doing it very much recently. The problem with all the dumpster diving and the way I was living for a long time was that it really separated me from everyone else. Everyone else would go to a restaurant, and I would be looking for food in a trash can with a real sense of, 'Look at me. I'm doing this really wild thing. It's radical,' in trying to live simply or not create waste. It really just became a big ego trip. It's weird how you can have an ego trip when you're crawling through a dumpster."[188]

He told *The Mix*, "You would be amazed that you can find enough food that others have thrown away if you know where to look. But recently, that hasn't been such a priority in my life. Yesterday, I ate at a big pizza chain restaurant. The point is I used to make a big deal of what I do and don't do. You know. 'I eat out of trash cans, and I don't have a cell phone, and I don't have an automobile because I ride a bicycle. I don't wear new clothes because I go to the thrift store.' It goes on and on. You can say, 'This is what I do and this is what I don't do, and that's why I'm better than everybody, and I'm living right and everyone else is living wrong.' It was just so crazy for me to obsess over myself in that way. It didn't bring me peace, and I was tired of feeling so separated from everybody because of all these things I did and didn't do. It's much sweeter to say, 'God, this is all your responsibility, and we are all your children, and you are the one who's good. Any goodness is from you.' Nothing I ever do or don't do will make me better than anyone else."[189]

---

[187] Katrina Nattress, "mewithoutYou's Aaron Weiss Opens Up About His Lack Of Spiritual Confidence," *MySpace*, 6/08/15.
[188] Dalia Colon, "mewithoutYou's Aaron Weiss on God, Dumpster diving and quitting the band," *Tampa Bay Times*, 6/04/09.
[189] mewithoutYou Q&A," *The Mix*, 7/07/09.

Aaron was arrested in a die-in on the Pentagon lawn while protesting the Iraq war with Sister Margaret McKenna and others at the end of 2007. He used to blame the rich, the government, and corporations for the state of the poor, "but anymore, that hasn't proved to help anything except to make me feel better about myself. I'm willing to live the poor way and live simply and share my money. It's nothing. Anymore, none of that means anything to me, anything I've done."[190]

Aaron wanted fans to stop turning to him and the band for guidance. "We are blind and with absolutely no wisdom, in no place to guide anyone. What can we do but turn to God for help and mercy? We can ask that anyone who looks or listens to us would not see or hear us but the One who is good within us all."

"The newer songs focus more on religious themes, but I'm not sure that makes them more spiritual (or True)," Aaron said.[191] He had become "increasingly content with irrelevancy, and less and less concerned with 'expressing myself.' Also, less wanting to impact anyone in the world with a message, rather preach to the hypocrisy in my own heart."[192] When Jamie Pham said he was confused about what Aaron really believed, Aaron answered, "We are also confused and so ask God, please, if You are willing, take away what 'I' believe."[193]

He was asked what he hoped people would get out of his music. "You know, nothing really. It's not too much of a concern of mine, because I don't know what people need, you know? So we just surrender the responsibility to God. I have nothing to say to anybody anymore. No inspiring words, you know, no message or no truth to say to anybody. I have to keep asking God, 'You have to do that work, because I have no ability to do that,' and then just trust that it's all taken care of, you know, on a level I don't even know about."[194]

---

[190] Rock for Hunger, "mewithoutyou - Rock for Hunger Interview," *YouTube*, 6/12/09.
[191] Jamie Pham, "mewithoutYou—05.14.09," *Absolute Punk*, 5/14/09.
[192] Ibid
[193] Ibid
[194] Rock for Hunger, "mewithoutyou - Rock for Hunger Interview," *YouTube*, 6/12/09.

Though Aaron would like to be thought of as smart and wise, "the clearer part of me has no interest whatsoever in anyone listening to me, including you or anyone who hears this interview. There's a clarity in me that grants you a sincere blessing to disregard everything I'm saying. Every single word that comes out of my mouth. You say he's just a crazy man, he has no idea what he's talking about, he's an absolute fool, or he's a religious fanatic or whatever, a heretic. But all of that having been said, there is definitely a part of me that wants to be accepted and liked by people. But you keep it in check, and you see it for what it is, and you don't surrender to that."[195]

The sheikh also encouraged Aaron to go back to school and work on his master's degree in education. This was the last thing on Aaron's mind, but he felt it was wise advice, so he started attending classes at Temple University.

Aaron's radicalism, idealism, and zeal were now evening out into something more laid back, quiet, simple, and stable.

Still, there were more changes. Steven Wells writes:

> At a bar in Birmingham, Alabama, stunned parents who brought what drummer Rickie Mazzotta calls their 'cookie-cutter Christian kids' to see a nice Christian band, stare in horror as the puppy-dog-eyed, scruffy, unshaven singer praises Allah. 'In everywhere we look,' sings Aaron, 'Allah, Allah.'[196]

For both Aaron and the band itself, after coming off the successful *Brother, Sister*, this was a period of transition and new direction both lyrically and musically. Not everyone in the band was onboard, and as they'd soon find out, many of their fans were not prepared for the curveball they were about to throw.

---

[195] Luke Goddard, "Q&A with Aaron Weiss (vocalist of mewithoutYou)," *The Blue Indian*, 10/13/09.
[196] Steven Wells, "Oh, Sweet Jesus: Philadelphia is either home to the most genuinely Christian movement in America or it's a festering spiritual slum. All depends on how you look at it," *Philadelphia Weekly*, 9-24-08.

73
It's All Crazy!

Emily and I heard some of the leaked songs from *It's All Crazy! It's All False! It's All a Dream! It's Alright* and agreed that they were terrible. It wasn't what we wanted from mewithoutYou. Like so many other fans since the beginning, we wanted more aggression, more passion, more distortion, and more shouting.

"This is what happens when God takes all of your pain away," Emily joked.

"Can you imagine trying to suffer through these songs live?" I responded.

The songs were stripped down, led by simple acoustic folksy melodies accompanied by more exotic instruments such as harp, accordion, trumpet, and violin. Since Chris was no longer in the band, his signature spacey guitar sounds were missing.

When I learned that Daniel Smith from the unconventional and artsy Danielson had produced the album, the more bizarre sounds and arrangements in some of these songs made perfect sense.

Fulfilling their four-album contract with Tooth & Nail, I figured the band was ending, so cared nothing for their reputation. They could do anything they wanted for their finale rather than make a calculated effort to ride the popularity of *Brother, Sister*.

Starting out as a post-hardcore band, then moving in the direction of a Coachella-style indie rock band, they were now moving into outsider music that goes by new weird America, neo-folk, psych-folk, and freak-folk.

I found the lyrics online and scoured them for anything that might have resonated with my life as closely as the first three releases did. In the spirit of nursery rhymes, fables, and folk tales—complete with talking animals, beetles, fruits, and vegetables—the lyrics were much more poetic and dependent on imagery than on previous releases. Being that it was more difficult to isolate lines, I couldn't find anything I could relate to.

At first, I considered this a sign of mental health for myself. Then I realized I couldn't relate to it because there was little to be found of the old themes of depression, suicide, and unrequited love.

Using the more experimental elements of *Brother, Sister* as a springboard for this release, mewithoutYou made a conscious decision to do something radical. Hearing the final product, some of the band liked these songs better than anything they had done previously. Knowing they might alienate some of their fans, they hoped instead that these loyal fans would grow with them and be as excited about these songs as they were.

"Nobody wants to hear the same record twice, although we could do that. It would probably be easier to write, you know, our first record all over again. It's just, each song, a few power chords, and some distorted guitar, and a whole lot of pain. But to be honest, there's not that kind of pain anymore. We worked through a lot of those difficulties," Aaron said about the emotional turmoil and suffering he once felt. "It wouldn't be sincere, and in fact, sometimes it's hard to even perform those songs, given that I don't feel that hurt anymore."[197]

Aaron explained the fable-like direction in the new lyrics. "Some of the songs sound like . . . children's stories put to music, and we're hoping that our grandparents and our children, if we ever have them, or anyone who listens, that their children will be able to listen to the songs, you know, no matter what their age, and enjoy them and not go to bed with nightmares."[198] He wanted to write songs pleasant enough for his grandma to listen to. "You know, not all the shouting and distorted guitar. Something that was a little easier on the ear. We're getting older, and how much longer do you want to go on shouting about all these dark or depressing things?"[199]

Emily and I were not alone in our ambivalence about this new

---

[197] "Tooth & Nail Podcast 27: Emery, mewithoutYou, an Interview with Aaron Weiss & more," *Tooth & Nail*, 2009.
[198] Joshua David, "Interview with Aaron Weiss," *Joshua David Photo*, 5/23/11.
[199] Ibid

direction. As Rickie reflected, "The reception of the record varies all across the board. There are people that like our first record to [no] end. There are people that love [*It's All Crazy!*] to no end, too. It's opposite ends of the spectrum. Some people love it and some people hate it. I think if another band put that album out, then people would've received it better. I don't think what we do best got captured on that record. I think that record's a moment in time where we changed character."[200]

Greg added, "This felt right at the time, and we were excited about what we had created. It was different for us, and we anticipated mixed reactions to the album, which there were. But when all was said and done, it felt like an honest album that reflected our lives at that time."[201]

In the past, the band would get together and write the music, then give it to Aaron where he begrudgingly labored over the lyrics, trying to find something to say. Now, Aaron was bringing his folk songs to the band. "None of the other guys felt as connected to [It's All Crazy!]," Aaron said. "It was less of a group effort, more like them playing instruments over 'my' songs—at least for a good portion of it. I was specifically trying to move us in that folk-like direction, but no one else was totally on board, so the end product felt less unified."[202]

The result was an album that was unique, playful, and fun, but recording the album was anything but that. Differences in vision and mission, internal rifts and frustrations, and personal problems almost ensured that the album never got recorded.

"We definitely like the album, but it was more like something that needed to be done—it got us through a really rough time. That whole process is like a blur," Rickie shared. "I guess that stuff doesn't always translate when someone puts on *It's All Crazy!* You hear this kind of goofy, acoustic, neo-folk kind of thing, but underneath that there was a lot of despair, for a lack of a better

---

[200] Zack Zarrillo, "PropertyOfZack interview :: mewithoutyou," *Property of Zack*, 8/31/11.
[201] Steven Edelman, "Letting go with mewithoutYou," *The Rapidian*, 9/26/12.
[202] Jonathan Bautts, "mewithoutyou—5.22.12," *Absolute Punk*, 5/22/12.

word."[203]

He added, "Some of us were going through emotional turmoil with one another and other life situations. In the end, we banded together, built a practice space in the basement and tried to cut through all the crap, meeting every day for who knows how long. Some days we wouldn't even play music, it would just be a full blown honesty session, dudes telling other dudes how they feel about one another, dudes trying to comfort and console, sharing food, scraping songs, rethinking why we are even a band. Life felt hard when we were going through the writing/recording process of this album, what you are hearing is the product of what we were going through at the time. I don't think this record could sound any other way."[204]

"We never were a band with a 'mission,'" Rickie told *Absolute Punk*. "At different points, individuals might have had certain agendas they tried to have carried out, be it our vehicle situations or lyrical content, but there was never one unified, we all believe this, goal with the band."[205]

"There were other aspects of our lives that were more dramatic and difficult," Aaron explained to Tooth & Nail. "We'd had sort of a rocky road for a while, and personally. Some of the guys didn't see eye to eye as far as what's our goal as a band and what do we believe spiritually and our ethics as far as money and all kinds of things that every band has to work out, of course. And we just sorta swept it under the rug and everybody did their own thing and tried to present something like a coherent unit or a whole. And usually I'm the one with the microphone so I'm saying things at the show that doesn't necessarily even reflect what the whole band believes. There were a lot of tensions like that where I think, in a lot of ways, we had a disunity, and a real lack of understanding for each other, and a lack of love and respect for each other because of our differences. And all those have been just been crumbling, all those differences and the walls we've had between us have been falling and just throwing them away,

---

[203] Luke Larsen, "Catching Up With mewithoutYou," *Paste*, 4/06/12.
[204] Jamie Pham, "mewithoutYou—05.14.09," *Absolute Punk*, 5/14/09.
[205] Ibid

coming to . . . appreciate the ways in which we're different and to thank God for the fact that everyone's not like me. And to really come to love and accept each other exactly as we are, and then as a whole, kinda work on moving forward and work on learning what it is to love God and to love each other and to forgive the people who hurt us. All our differences were so subtle, but we made them really big, you know? And the things that were common between us and the things that made us one are so big and so significant, so obvious, but we kinda ignored those things. So everything's gotten so much better, I mean, in so many ways. I can go on and on but I'll try to keep it to a minimum."[206]

Aaron told *Blue Indian*, "Interpersonally, we've had our share of drama in the past and have had all kinds of tension and soap operas that have played out within our little circle, but for the most part they sort of run their course as far as the major ones that we've come at that have gone unspoken, or the elephants in the room have been pointed out and all of the walls have come crumbling down between us that have kept us divided from one another or competing with one another. For example, me seeing this other guy as damaging the band's reputation morally, and then that guy seeing me as uptight and judgmental and arrogant, so there is that kind of tension in the past that has sorta been always there and unspoken in most accounts, and it even got to the point at certain times where members of the band were hardly talking to each other. That was tours in the past we've had, but we kept going because each of us had his own agenda and wanted to keep doing it for his own reason, but there was really no unity in the band. And more recently, again, those walls have kinda come down and there's been more of sort of a lightness to it and more of a joy about it and a real love you can sense between us. Even in difficult times there's a real powerful sense of oneness and a great love in our midst as we travel around, even though we have our own craziness. I want to be respected, this guy wants to be a great musician, he wants to be famous, he wants to make money.

---

[206] Tooth & Nail Podcast 27: Emery, mewithoutYou, an Interview with Aaron Weiss & more," *Tooth & Nail*, 2009.

Whatever it is in our group that divides us or that is selfish, all that is sorta the stage of drama, but a beautiful story is being told on that stage that can only really be appreciated when we step off of the stage and sorta watch from the audience, which is what we're trying to do at some level. Not just with the band, but with life in general."[207]

"I think that we've gotten to the point as a band, and I think Aaron as a lyricist and an individual, really started to accept certain truths," Mike told *Buzzgrinder*. "I don't want to get into all the details really. You know, we've had some issues, not just the band guys, but you know it's been a time where in the circle of friendship that surrounds this area and all the people we know, there's been a culmination of a lot of different issues. Some of them are kinda serious and I think, to relate back to Aaron, just since he's the guy that writes the lyrics, he just became a lot more accepting of certain things that he may have seen in the past as wasteful or overindulgent. Just a particular worldview that he used to have that kinda kept us all from really enjoying one another's lives and accepting one another.

"I mean, not to blame it all on Aaron. I've had my own problems that have kept me separated from other people, you know? I think towards the middle of making this album, I started to shed some of my stuff. For example, for me — I'm not gonna talk about anybody else's issues but I'll talk about mine — I've had a real difficult time putting down this band as what makes me a legitimate person in the world. It's been really hard. I've really used the band as an excuse to feel important, you know? When you look at the inevitability that the band is gonna break up and I'm not gonna have it to feel so important about myself forever, it starts to dawn on you. You really start to realize, 'Oh my gosh, I'm 31 now. I'm not gonna be in the band forever.' You start to see the signs that it's gonna end at some point.

"Not that we've made any plans to break up the band. But everybody's life is moving into a different direction, as it should,

---

[207] Luke Goddard, "Q&A with Aaron Weiss (vocalist of mewithoutYou)," *The Blue Indian*, 10/13/09.

and the band is still a part of everyone's life, but for me to see those changes in everybody else, it was jarring and it caused a lot of problems for me, especially for me and my wife and my friends. It really hurt a lot of people."[208]

"As for me, I was largely oblivious to what they were going through, was kind of in my own little world. For all I hear them describe the tumultuous quality of that time, it was probably the happiest period of my life. Maybe I failed to be there for them," Aaron told me.

It wasn't just the musical direction of the band that caught fans off guard. A large portion of their loyal Christian fanbase read Aaron's lyrics and wondered more than ever if mewithoutYou was a Christian band and if Aaron Weiss was still a Christian.

How they answered these questions now had more weight in light of this new album being heavy with references to Sufism, including a song called "Allah, Allah, Allah." Fans wondered if Aaron had abandoned Christianity for Islam.

Many of the songs on this album were influenced by the collected teachings of Bawa Muhaiyaddeen. In the book *The Golden Words of a Sufi Sheikh*, Bawa is recorded saying: "It's all false, It's all a dream, It's all crazy, It's all over, It's all right, Let's see what's next," which was altered for the title of the album.

"The Fox, the Crow, and the Cookie" was adapted from a story in Bawa's, *My Love You My Children: 101 Stories for Children*. Aaron spoke of the coverless, worn out copy of the book his parents read to him and Mike when they were kids. "A fox says some flattering words to a crow who is holding a cookie in his mouth. The fox says, 'Oh crow, please sing for us, your voice is so beautiful,' and the crow starts to sing to impress the fox, but drops the cookie. The fox, of course, grabs the cookie and runs off. The lesson is to not desire the flattery or praise of other people. All the stories are told in a sweet way that will entertain a child without necessarily needing the child to understand the meaning. A bit like

---

[208] Josh Mock, "Interview with Mike Weiss of mewithoutYou," *Buzzgrinder*, 5/04/09.

Aesop's fables."[209]

"King Beetle and the Coconut Estate" is adapted from Bawa's *The Divine Luminous Wisdom that Dispels Darkness*.

"The King Beetle is a story my dad told me," Aaron said. "You don't have a problem. You are the problem. And that's where the concept of 'you' as an 'I' or as a person who's separate from everyone else flies into the fire."[210]

"Fig with a Bellyache" is adapted from Bawa's *The Golden Words of a Sufi Sheikh*. This song was not only the most bizarre on the album musically, having Daniel Smith's stamp on it, but it was thought to be too sexually explicit for Christian bookstores to carry.

"I think we all have a certain faith in a God that exists," Mike told *Magnet*. "There are moments of doubt in everyone's faith. Sometimes that doubt is stronger than others. Seriously, I think that everyone believes in God; they just don't know how to express it. That's my opinion on faith. I believe that it's the voice inside you that is your conscience. We all have that voice that says we shouldn't be doing things, but we do them anyway. But it's the beauty of our lives. It's something that unites us. I feel like Aaron tries to harness that, and there's nothing more glorious to us than when we're on the same page, onstage playing our music. That's our little goal."[211]

Speaking to *Redefine*, he added, "I don't think we're up there putting on a ministry. We're not up there trying to come to your city to have church. We're trying to be a band and are expressing ourselves as artists. That's what every band does."[212]

Mike elaborated on the nature of universal truths that can be found anywhere. "We don't really try to claim that we are the ambassadors of that truth ourselves, or that the Bible, or the Koran, or Bawa Muhaiyaddeen are. These truths just exist, and

---

[209] Emily Zemler, "Book of Fables Inspires New Mewithoutyou Music," *Spin*, 6/24/09.
[210] Joshua Watson, "Aaron Weiss Interview," *The 138 Collective*, 5/23/11.
[211] John Stich, Q&A WITH MEWITHOUTYOU," *Magnet*, 5/01/09.
[212] Vivian Hua, "mewithoutYou Band Interview: Beyond Religious Limitations," *Redefine*, 7/21/09.

everybody sort of has a way to know them, to experience them, to live them."[213] He further stated, "Bawa is not considered to be a Christian by most Christian people, but he was a wise person who loved God and believed in God more than anything else. He devoted his life to trying to bring people to experience that."[214]

Mike tried to explain the delicate balance between emphasizing Jesus while being open to universal truths in other religions. "Right now is sort of a period, especially in Aaron's life, where he's sort of revisiting [religion] and holding himself up to those teachings that there's no one religion that's going to be the only way to God. If you really want to just try to follow a path to God, I don't believe you need anything beyond [Jesus Christ], but it's just the idea that you're fixed on the only way and that everybody else is just completely misguided . . . that is a sort of obtuse attitude that can hurt your own spirit.

"I always imagine that if we're someone worth listening to, and [fans] see that one of the songs is written in Arabic and says 'Allah' three times—that they're listening to that song and reading the lyrics of that song from the perspective that the band that they're listening to believes in [Christianity] and is very Christian-centered.

"Whenever you point a finger at somebody else, saying [he] is not a true Christian because [he] has a song called 'Allah, Allah, Allah,' on [his] record, you have three fingers pointing back at you. If you want to bring Christianity and Jesus into it, I don't think Jesus would ever put somebody on the chopping block for writing a song like that, honestly. [The record is] meant to do nothing but glorify our Creator."[215]

Mike told *HM Magazine*, "It's just as silly or dangerous to like a band because of what spiritual beliefs you think certain members have as it is to dismiss a band because of what spiritual beliefs you think certain members have."[216]

---

[213] Ibid
[214] Ibid
[215] Ibid
[216] Andrew Schwab, "It's Alright in the End," *HM Magazine*, #137, May/June 2009.

Greg, when asked if he felt stuck in the mold of being labeled a Christian band by some, answered, "I never felt like I was in a mold, in a sense. I never felt trapped by certain things that maybe Aaron was writing about or people's perception of the band. You know, never mind really what he was writing about as opposed to what expectations were put upon us because we were associated with a record label that had certain associations with the Christian market, or how people perceived what kind of theology was coming from the band, you know? I mean, I have a lot of issues with identity when it comes to people assuming I'm a certain way because I'm in a band. Not even the cliché rock star partying kinda thing as much as, 'Oh, because you're in this band, you must not own anything, you must only eat out of the dumpsters,' you know? Like, they assume all these things about my lifestyle that they have no idea about. But it's like with any individual, get to know them before you project this image on them."[217]

Mike added, "We're not like a band that has a hard-lined stance on anything, really, let alone a group of things. There seems to be a lot of people that ask us what we all do as a band outside of playing music together, and we're friends, you know? So just take that experience that everybody has in their own life with their own friends and they can answer their own question. I mean, we're just buddies. We all have very different lives that we lead. And you know we don't all live in a house together in a slum or whatever to be intentionally setting any kind of an example. For some reason people just think that we have some house and we don't use electricity. I don't know, I don't get it. It's kinda funny. At the same time, it does get a little bit tiring to just be seen as this weird offshoot of somebody's understanding of mewithoutYou. You know, it's our band, we love to do it. We play the music, we get together and we work very, very hard at it, but we really all have our own lives. For a while though, I think maybe some of us in the band wanted more unity amongst each other than there could be. And, you know, there has been a journey or at least an attempt for

---

[217] "mewithoutYouInterview," *Project SLC*, 2012.

us to be more unified in certain ways."[218]

A fan recalled Aaron at a concert in Louisville saying between songs, "I'm a little weary of having our album in Christian bookstores with a song titled, 'Allah, Allah, Allah.' To them that just says, 'Shit, Shit, Fuck.' I'm sorry," he said to audience laughter.

Aaron was asked if he would hesitate to put this album in the Christian section of the music shop. He answered, "I don't really understand what it would really mean to put out, for example, a Christian CD given that the central call, as I understand it, of Christ was to die. To come and die, to come and give up our life and to give up everything that we are and everything that we cling to and all of our plans and all of our identity and all of our possessions and all of our family and all of our hopes and dreams and all of this—all of our expression and talent—everything, to surrender all of that. And whatever God does with it is fine. But my sense is that, not having done that, we've instead sorta written songs about that and then marketed it. So let's try to put it more straightforward, I think the whole thing is kinda crooked. The whole thing seems a little crooked, but not in a way that I want to take it on or argue with it. But just in a way that I want to acknowledge in sort of an honest and clear way to myself that, okay, why did I get into playing music? Was it done in the wake of surrender to Jesus? Well, no, it was done because I wanted to play music and I wanted people to look at me onstage and respect me as a lyricist and as a dancer, and it was done because I wanted to meet women and kiss them. Then because I wanted to have my name in a magazine and a review of something that I wrote that was flattering. All of these motivations were there at the beginning. So what has grown out of that, it would be entirely inappropriate to put that in the same category or even in the same world as the founder or as the center point of Christianity, of the life that started Christianity. Now of course what Christianity has become in many ways bears no resemblance to the one whose name it bears. So in that respect it's perfectly appropriate to put it

---

[218] Ibid

in Christian music, in the section of a Christian bookstore, or in the Christian music section. Because Christianity has just become something completely different than who Christ was. So in that respect we fit perfectly well in that we can sell things in the name of Jesus, make money at it, and get up on stage and talk about him, give sermons and organize meetings and sell tickets to our concerts and advertise and have a label and a booking agent and a manager. On and on and on, all things that Jesus did not have and did not do. So as long as we come to terms with the fact that Christianity has no necessary connection to Christ, then yeah, it's completely appropriate to put it there. Now is it appropriate to say our music is truly in the name of Christ or to his glory? No, that would not be appropriate."[219]

Concerns about whether or not the band was Christian or this album was Christian bookstore-worthy led to deeper concerns about Aaron's personal beliefs. Aaron's lyrics took a much more Eastern turn towards pantheism and panentheism, the idea that God is everything, is in everything, and that everything is in him. The traditional theism of Christianity differs by saying that God is distinct and separate from his creation.

In "Every Thought a Thought of You," Aaron writes that God wears *a thin disguise, O light within my brother's eyes*, and *there is no one here to believe but You*. In "Bullet to Binary (Pt. 2)," he writes that *the One who looks out from your eyes looks through hers and looks through mine*.

"Allah, Allah, Allah," which Christians worried was a song supporting Islam, reveals an Eastern perspective. God is everywhere we look, in everyone we meet, and in every blade of grass. Influenced by Bawa, the song ends with the Eastern view that all of life is an illusion, including our individual egos and evil and suffering.

In "The Fox, the Crow, and the Cookie," Aaron writes of letting go of all attachments and ceasing all divisions. "Fig with a Bellyache" speaks of not being so sure of separations anymore.

---

[219] Luke Goddard, "Q&A with Aaron Weiss (vocalist of mewithoutYou)," *The Blue Indian*, 10/13/09.

Even in the gorgeous "A Stick, a Carrot, a String," a song about Jesus coming into the world to save it, Aaron writes that Satan was crushed beneath the foot of Jesus not wanting anything, so could not be trapped by all of the worldly attachments Satan tried to tempt him with.

"Goodbye, I!" speaks for itself—ego is an illusion. In "Cattail Down," Aaron writes about his experiences hitchhiking and drifting. Mike is concerned that Aaron is mentally ill, but Aaron reminds him that he is happily in the "forgetting of himself." He uses drifting as an illustration that we don't know where we came from or where we're going, that you are not you, you are everyone else.

In "King Beetle and the Coconut Estate," a professor beetle and lieutenant beetle set out to understand the Great Mystery. The professor dispenses cold and dispassionate data and the lieutenant comes back with his wings burned, struggling to explain what he experienced. The king decides to give up his position, power, authority, possessions, and all he has in this life to fly headlong into the fiery unknown. The other beetles proclaim that their king is not dead, but has been—as the Desert Father Abba Joseph said—"utterly changed into fire."

Aaron told Luke at *The Blue Indian*, "Eventually he realizes 'I can't take anyone else's word for it. This isn't something I can learn secondhand. It's something that I have to experience, to do and to fall into and see what happens. And it could mean the end of me.' It's ludicrous to think I can talk about this in any way that captures it because that's the whole thing, it can't be talked about, that's what my dad would say anyway. Nobody can tell you any of this stuff; it's all inside of you. It's just a matter of your determination to awaken to it. We keep using the word truth; it seems like a fair one. But at the same time, if you're saying you have the truth, you know what's true and everyone else needs to think like you, you just turn into a tyrant. So it seems to be within, you need to let the real work go on there. This isn't something you need to convince anybody of. This isn't something you should go and manipulate or prove to anybody. Whatever that fire may be, we can make it our determination to fly into it and not dance around it."[220]

Luke asked Aaron if he was still a Christian or if he had now become a Muslim. He further asked him if he believed Jesus was the only way to heaven. Aaron responded, "It's hard to answer questions that have such deep meaning, so I can only sorta ask for help with the answer. God, you have to come and answer that, because I don't know the answer."[221]

Aaron clarified that all of his beliefs are false in that they are the beliefs of a man thirty years young raised in a certain time and place. Aaron didn't like the spirit of the question: "Are you one of us or not? Are you in or out?" He didn't like such lofty mysteries being reduced to doctrines and religious clubs where believers are flippant and arrogant, believing they now hold the truth.

"The reality of what all of this is pointing to is so much better than we understand, so much more beautiful and so much more real than that. We've taken very, very holy and high concepts and truth, and turned it into commerce and turned it into a club or a religion. And I've been very deeply immersed in that and steeped in that for a long time now and I'm trying to step back and say, 'Wait a minute, what does this really mean?' and starting to have the sense that it's much, much, much greater than I thought, and much greater than what we say and what we accept, and all the theology and the doctrine that has come in the wake of that occurrence, of our Lord being born to a manger bed. So yes, still believing that but not in the same way as before. In a subtler way and more beautiful way. I don't know how to answer these questions at this point in my life in a satisfactory way."[222]

Aaron was suspicious of what we think and say about God. "So there's almost a sense of just wholesale throwing it all out, of getting rid of everything from our minds. I guess that's my hesitation to address these issues and questions that are so far beyond the mind or of a different faculty within us than the mind. But they're being handled by the mind in a way that seems to me

---

[220] Luke Goddard, "Q&A with Aaron Weiss (vocalist of mewithoutYou)," *The Blue Indian*, 10/13/09.
[221] Ibid
[222] Ibid

irresponsible and, frankly, irreverent and even blasphemous at times, at least the way I've treated this as sort of a way to evaluate other people. Is this person gonna go to heaven? Is this person gonna go to hell to be with God or without God? Are they going through Jesus? We don't know anything about what these words mean, really. We have no experience with them, they're just figments of our imagination. That there's a reality behind them or what they point to, there's no doubt in my heart, but the way these words are used are so far from the reality. These issues are far greater and far more powerful and more beautiful and more precious and special than we have given them credit for being, and they are far more real . . . far more powerful than I have an ability to address in an interview or in any way in my life or in any way."[223]

Aaron reiterated his powerlessness here. "May God open listeners' eyes to the truth, not to what I have to say, or what the church has to say, or to the ideas of any other religion but to whatever is real and true. You're the only one who is real and true and can reveal yourself to these people. Nothing I say will make anyone believe it in any meaningful way."[224]

Aaron told *The Mix*, "Well, God is my life. During my clearer moments, I realize that I don't really have anything else except for God. I have a family and a band and friends and ideas and beliefs and religious groups and all these things, but all of those things are going to be gone very, very soon. Even my own body, it's all passing away. Religion and all my ideas about God, those things don't give me any life. They don't have any importance. But God, the actual power that created me and gives life to all the world — that is the life within everyone — there are no words that I can say about that."[225]

He went on, "I can't talk about God; I can't put it into words. I do have a sense that there is nothing of any value other than God. Including the religions that people talk about and all my doctrines and beliefs that I've associated with — those don't have any value,

---

[223] Ibid
[224] Ibid
[225] "mewithoutYou Q&A," *The Mix*, 7/07/09.

but only God, who I don't even begin to understand. It brings me to a wonderful place of being just like a child in some ways, not understanding anything but just sort of in awe of everything, and being grateful for everything that comes, and waiting for whatever goes, and to let it go. But I wouldn't call it religion."[226]

Aaron's parents raised him to "believe in God, not to believe in this world or even in myself. God is reality and everything we see is not. It's so wonderful remembering him. It's like a rock that is higher than all the floodwaters in the world. Anything that happens, no matter how bad it is, you just accept that and say, 'That is this world. It comes and goes. But there is a love that doesn't and it's in me now.' So I don't really learn more every day. It's something that just comes. You just need to realize it."[227]

Sometimes Aaron keeps his eyes on the world and all that is wrong. Other times he remembers God. "Oh God, you're the greatest, you're the most beautiful one, you're my only friend, you're really my only family, you're the one who is wise, you're the one who is true, who is merciful, compassionate, loving— you're within everyone. You're everywhere. You're within those who believe in you and even those who don't believe in you. You always were and you always will be."[228]

Luke asked Aaron if he could elaborate on the line: *I do not exist, only You exist.*

"Um, no, not right now. That's another part of my upbringing. It's a prayer that was taught, and it's a powerful one. One that I don't understand, and it might not do it justice for me to try to explain. Except that maybe, you know, that it's experiential, something that we can fall into. But there again, the explaining of it might sort of undermine the meaning of it. So you'll have to forgive me if it's somewhat evasive and paradoxical, but nonetheless very real for me."[229]

Aaron was asked further about the line, "You think you're

---

[226] Ibid
[227] Ibid
[228] Ibid
[229] Luke Goddard, "Q&A with Aaron Weiss (vocalist of mewithoutYou)," *The Blue Indian*, 10/13/09.

you, but you're not you, you're everyone else." He responded, saying that "I" is an illusion that allows us the freedom to change and redefine ourselves, just as a person changes religious views or citizenship of countries. If our identities aren't fixed, and if we all die, how real can we be? Who are "you"? Your identity is shaped by your interactions with others—everyone else.

With few exceptions, there were no landmark moments shifting his beliefs. They were slow and gradual, as a result of conversations with friends and family. "I don't think anybody has taken it too hard except maybe someone on the outside—someone who likes our music and doesn't know us personally and has a certain expectation based on what they have read or interpreted. Then, all of a sudden, they read something different. 'Oh, now they believe this?' But really, it seems like we're all on the same journey of searching for what's true and sort of growing in our capacity to understand the subtleties of what that might be."[230]

The idea that the self is an illusion and that we are all connected has been explored from the standpoint of theists, pantheists, and atheists alike.

---

[230] Derek Barber, "mewithoutYou," *Stereo Subversion*, 12/29/19.

74
Metro 2009

MewithoutYou was back on a headlining tour, playing Metro once again with Deerhunter the first week of July. After taking the Halsted bus, I walked to the venue and saw Aaron standing outside talking with a group of guys. He saw me and gave me a big smile. "First thing's first," he said, breaking from the gathering to hug me.

"Don't let me interrupt you," I said, apologizing to the group.

After catching up and offering me water and food from the bus, Aaron asked to be excused. "I know you aren't supposed to tell others when you go to pray, but I've been doing the salat lately, where you pray five times a day, and I don't like to miss it."

"Oh, no problem, I'll be here when you're finished."

"I don't pray towards Mecca or do it out of duty. I just find that it grounds me and gives me peace."

I sat up against the wall of the venue and watched the line form down the block. Aaron came out after praying and sat next to me. I detailed all that had led to Emily and me parting, and he told me his dad hadn't been doing so well lately.

"You know, every time we get together and talk, our exchange is always so heavy. Either I'm thanking you for saving my life, or we're having deep theological and philosophical conversation. I realized in all of these years that I've known you, we haven't ever really just hung out or had anything light. I was just wondering lately, has anything grown or changed in our lives the past four years?"

"Oh, sure, lots of changes!" Aaron answered.

"I mean, if I invited you to stay with me for a week, what would we do? Could we watch movies, or go to the mall, or play baseball, or something like that?"

"No, probably not."

"That's what I mean. I guess I'm looking for a new dynamic in our friendship, not always so heavy all the time. What do you do with your friends back home?"

"I don't have any friends. I spend most of my time at my parents' house alone in my room. I just go inside."

"Don't you feel like you're isolating yourself?"

"Are you kidding me?" Aaron smiled, his eyes lighting up. "The amazing things I experience with my eyes closed in union with God are more wonderful and real than anything I can describe."

I wanted to tell him that atheism and physical reality had grounded me and made life much more rational and practical for me. "He'll just tell me the physical world isn't real," I said to myself, so I bit my tongue.

Just then, he was handed a cell phone. He excused himself to take the call, getting up and walking towards the street. "Dad, you know the physical world isn't real," he started, right on cue. I rolled my eyes.

The last time we talked at Metro in 2007, Aaron was concerned about me moving Emily in and felt he wouldn't be a true friend if he remained silent. Now I was in the same spot, feeling that if I were a true friend, I'd tell him that spiritualizing his isolation sounded like nonsense to me, a cover for loneliness. I gave it a shot.

"These days, atheism seems to make the most sense to me, Aaron. More and more, I just want a practical, no-bullshit life grounded in the real world. I've been trying hard to lighten up and have some fun, especially after all of the stress in Florida."

"I've heard a lot of crazy ideas before, but nothing is more absurd to me than atheism. To say that everything came from nothing and is here for no reason, and to hold this belief that there is no God with the same absolutist certainty as a fundamentalist, to me, is the height of arrogance."

"I agree, but you don't need to be an absolutist to be an atheist. I view it more as a critique of specific religious claims and ideas about God, finding them wanting, without making any absolutist statements about God's existence or dogmatic commitments to naturalist philosophy. It's enough to say, 'I don't know if there's a God, but it sure doesn't seem to be this God or that God."

"Well, if you're just critiquing specific religions and ideas of God, I can get behind that."

"It's strange, when we all close our eyes to pray, we all see a different God. It's amazing how many different worlds exist in everyone's heads," I said.

Just then, a woman in line came over and introduced herself to Aaron. "It's really nice that you are sitting out here greeting fans."

"Do you think?"

"Yeah, it's really nice of you."

"Do you think?"

No matter what she said to him, he answered the same, until with a puzzled look on her face, she said goodbye and got back in line.

"That was rude—you were a total asshole to her," I said, laughing.

"It's amazing how many worlds are in people's heads!" He smiled, looking at the line of people. In this case, the girl misperceived Aaron as out greeting the fans.

As the doors opened and people made their way in, Aaron put me on the guest list. Three songs into the set, I couldn't tolerate much more. It felt old, and I felt disconnected from it all. *I can't stand here and watch him scream and yell about stuff I just don't care about anymore.* I walked out and went across the street to eat a hot dog and fries at Wrigleysville Dogs.

After eating, I went to Dunkin' Donuts for coffee to stay awake, and being near my bus stop, I struggled with whether or not I wanted to go back and find Aaron to say goodbye, given he said he might be tied up after the show. I decided I should at least see if he was outside the bus, so I headed back to the venue.

On the way back I encountered fans having an engaging theological debate on social justice while another man, well-dressed and in a new Cubs cap, asked them if they had any change. *This guy's not even poor, and if he makes it to the bus, I bet Aaron will feed him.*

When I got to the bus, there was Aaron coming out with

leftover catering and bottled water for him. I looked down and shook my head, feeling like Aaron was being taken advantage of. Aaron saw me and offered me food as well.

As he stood talking with a fan, another stood by with an *It's All Crazy* record, waiting to get it signed.

"That thing is terrible," I said, pointing to it. "I read the lyrics and said to myself, 'Thank God, there's nothing here I can relate to. It's a sign that I'm finally mentally healthy."

The guy laughed.

"Man," Aaron said, taking the pen to sign the album, "you're brutal."

Aaron sat back down with me in the same spot against the wall.

"How many people have asked you if you're a Muslim now because of this album?"

"I never give a straight answer," Aaron said, exasperated. "I don't like the spirit of the question. They are asking me if I'm still 'one of them,' and if they should accept me or reject me, and I don't want to feed that attitude."

"Well, before I go, I just wanted to say I worry about you. I always worry that you're going to end up missing while you're hitchhiking and train hopping. I worry that you are going to end up homeless and killed in some park, or wander off to some other country as a hermit and end up dead. I worry when you say you don't have any friends. Man, you saved my life. I'm trying to stabilize my life and just be normal now. But I want you to know, for the rest of my life, if you ever need a place to stay, there is always room for you, and I'll always be your friend. Don't ever be alone, brother."

He hugged me tight and didn't let go for a long time.

"My last copy of *All the Clever Words on Pages* was lost in the move to Florida, so my mom gave me her copy. Would it be too much to ask you to sign the cover for me before I go? I'd like to put it in a shadow box."

"Not at all."

I handed him a metallic silver marker and he wrote:

Bismillah ir-Rahman ir-Rahim (In the name of G-d most Merciful most Compassionate) My love you my very precious brother Paul, forever.

8/1/09
Email to Aaron

Hello Brother.
You're in my heart. I love you lots.
Be well,

Paul

9/5/09
Email from Aaron

Bawa. Bismillah ir-Rahman ir-Rahim
(In the Name of God most Merciful, most Compassionate)

My very dear brother Paul, my own life, much peace to you. Thank you for your open heart and your love. You have been in my heart also, very good to be with you there, with no divisions at all. My love to your family and to Emily.
    Your brother,

Aaron

75
Ashes

Since coming back to Chicago in June, Emily began cutting herself with surgical razors, drinking herself to sleep, and in cycles of restricting and binging and purging, turned to skin and bones. She called often, crying because of how her family was treating her and how alone she felt.

"Isn't this exactly what I said would happen? You're always welcome to move back here with me where you belong, with your husband. It's safe here."

"I'm not leaving my kids again, Paul. You made vows, you should be here with me when I need you most."

We argued bitterly into August. I told her not to say "I love you" anymore until she can treat me like she actually does and suggested we end our relationship to end the daily arguing. This broke her heart. I asked her if she wanted to stay married or move on, given it seemed we weren't compatible since we married.

"Paul, you're a part of me," she wrote. "What are my options but to say I'll try my best to get better? I can't imagine you not being in my life. I'm sorry I trampled you and didn't think about where I was making every careless step. I don't care if you scold me or think it empty—I hope one day that I can prove to you it's not—but I love you."

As September turned to October, we stopped arguing completely and she seemed to be enjoying herself more. Emily wrote positive posts on her Facebook page, saying she was happy and hopeful, everything was nice for a change, her life outside of the court case was great, she was treating herself well, and that she was almost perfectly content.

She called on Christmas saying she lost the custody case and made me promise I'd come back. I promised her I would. I wanted more than anything for this season of our lives to be over and to go back to Florida and be with her again.

"I love you, Paul."

"I love you, too, Emily."

The first week of 2010 was met with heavy snow in Chicago. As is the case most winters, I was sick with a cold and in hibernation mode. Feeling flat, I looked through the photo albums of my time with Emily. There were photos of the week we met, our many dates together, and our wedding and reception. There we were having dinner on the beach in Clearwater. There she was in her bikini, taking in sun at Paradise Beach. There we were enjoying a day at Largo Park. I felt again the resentment of having to be separated and finding myself alone in Chicago without her.

I called her. "Hey, I'm gonna book a flight and come out to see you for a week. We can talk about how we can bring our lives back together."

"Well, I don't know if I want you to come back. I mean, if you couldn't be here for me through all of this, why would I want you now?"

"You just called me on Christmas and told me you loved me and made me promise to come back."

"I know, I know. There's just a lot going on right now. Part of me wants to work things out, and another part of me doesn't think we're compatible."

I hung up, confused. She sent an email that night:

> Unfortunately, I can't tell up from down anymore. I can't make decisions or trust myself to speak at the moment. I heard the distress in your voice last night and it makes my fears of being "toxic" or "contagious" come true and come to life.
>
> I hate the fact that I have caused you so much pain and confusion and have mistreated you. I feel horrible about it. I can't promise you that I'll go from being this messed up and broken to being something that's better. All I can say is I'll try, and even then, there is a fear that I will be trying for the rest of my life, hurting myself and hurting you.
>
> I have been thinking a lot about us and what would be best, ending things, or staying together and trying to make things work. What repeats in my head is what you've said

more than once: "We love each other, but we are incompatible."

I don't know why I am thinking the way I am, why I feel so distant, like I am underwater and numb. You know I have been suicidal, that I have been self harming—I think this is why the distance. I am isolating myself. In a way I am dying and want to be left alone. I feel contagious. I know you know this feeling.

I do not want to feel responsible any longer for hurting you. I have very deep feelings for you. I care about you deeply, there obviously is a very big part of me that doesn't want to let you go, but on the other hand another side of me that's screaming it's the right thing to do. I have put a wall up to you, because you put a mirror up to me and force me to look in its reflection.

I think back to when you left in June, I felt strongly in my heart that you would not come back. I wondered how I would be able to hang onto someone that I was upset at for leaving. I mourned and mourned. I think I will always mourn over you. You will always be a part of me. But all of this is unfair to you. And I hate myself for being the cause of insomnia or tears or pain. I am sorry. I wish you'd be there when the haze over me lifts and I am healthy, but I don't know when that will be. I am not in a good place. It is unfair of me to think you'd wait for that day.

Some would say (including myself) that I am a lost cause, but there are a few souls in this world that I know would not give up, no matter how many times I would bite them in the process. Eventually they will earn my trust and love and loyalty.

I do not expect you to be this person in my life. I wouldn't be. I have spent an hour on just what I wrote above, thinking it through the best I can and all. This isn't about me not loving you, because I do. If you lived up the road from me, I'd suggest we meet for coffee or walk in the park to talk about all of this.

I shared Emily's thoughts with a couple of friends and their response was unanimous: "She's cheating on you. Just ask her straight up if there is someone else. That's probably why you stopped arguing and she seemed to feel so good a few months back."

I called Emily back. "Look, people on my end say the reason you are balking on me coming back is because you're with someone else. If you met someone and you're happy, that's fine, I won't be mad. Just tell me, and I'll cancel my visit and move on."

"Well, it's not a yes or no answer."

"What does that mean?"

"Promise me you won't yell at me or hang up on me," she said.

"I won't. Just tell me."

"When you left, I never thought I'd see you again . . . we had that big argument . . . you told me not to say 'I love you' anymore . . ."

My heart pounded faster. I saw a tsunami on the horizon. I knew when it hit me, there would be no turning back.

"Emily, it's okay, just tell me."

"I looked for no-strings sex on Craigslist."

The wave slammed into my chest.

"No, not you!" I started to shake.

The rest of the conversation was a blur as I asked too many questions, trying to understand. She was looking for escape from her numbness. She was looking for distraction from killing herself. She chose a man she wasn't attracted to and who she was sure wouldn't fall in love with her and ask for a relationship. This was her way of protecting our marriage. She compartmentalized.

"It's okay, I don't love him. You don't have anything to worry about. I was going to end things with him as soon as you came back. I wore our ring the whole time and the perfume you bought me for Christmas when I was with him because I was thinking of you."

The more she talked, the less she made sense. Something was terribly wrong. I didn't know this woman.

"You know I can't take you back after this, right?"

"I know, I wouldn't ask you to."

"So when I write the story of my life, this is how our story ends? We separate, I wait for you, and you meet a guy for sex on Craigslist?"

"No, that can't be our story! That can't be how we end!" she started crying.

She was lost, desperate, suicidal, and rail-thin from her eating disorders. She felt like she had no one and didn't know what she was doing. I couldn't just hang up the phone and leave her in that state. So I did what I always do. I put on my cape.

"If I take you back, will you promise to stop seeing this guy immediately?"

"Really? You'd do that for me? You'd take me back?"

"Just stop seeing him right now."

"You don't understand. I can't. I need him right now. I can't be alone."

I kept asking her questions, trying to understand, but still nothing she said made sense.

"What are you thinking, doing this?"

"I'm not."

"I'm just trying to understand what's going on in your head."

"You don't want to know what's going on in my head."

Both of us now worn out with headaches and adrenal fatigue, every question revealing an answer more bizarre than the last, we hung up. I fell on the floor and sobbed.

I took out our photo albums again. My Emily was no longer there. All I could see now was a woman smiling at someone else, having dinner on the beach with someone else, and giving herself to someone else. I was not the last person to look in her eyes, kiss her lips, and enjoy her beauty. All I could see in these photos was another man. I was erased, and there was no way to undo this. Now there was nothing left of us. We were destroyed. Every photo turned black and she faded to dust in front of me.

Keeping us together had cost me so much, and I spent all of those months waiting for her, only for another man to put in the meager effort of answering an online ad to have to sex with my wife? I felt like a complete fool.

I went to my bedroom—our bedroom—and tried to sleep through the nausea, tears, dissociation, and nightmares. I looked at the window, thinking if I got a running start, I could clear the awning and hit the pavement below.

When I woke the next morning the world was a nightmare all over again.

January 2010
Email from Emily

Dear Paul,

Knowing the pain this is causing you is ripping me up. I fell asleep in tears, and woke up fantasizing me simply writing you a letter and then slashing my wrists right there in bed. I hate myself for what I've done to you and me. I am numb and want to disappear. I am at the end of myself and am desperate to get some help. I will be telling the counselors everything, and will give them your contact information when I get to the clinic. If things do not work out for me being accepted at this treatment facility I will do whatever I can to get help elsewhere. I think, if I cut myself really well, I imagine an ambulance coming and finally, maybe finally, I will get the help I need. I love you. Please forgive me. Please forgive me. I'm sorry. I love you.

I don't want this to be the end of us. I don't want to be without you. Today I am sick with grief, and mourning. I am so sorry Paul, I want to be better, I want to be fixed and I want nothing more than to stop hurting us.

I love you, I love you, I love you, I love you, I love you, I love you, I love you . . .

Emily

76
Renfrew

Emily checked herself into the hospital after cutting too deep with push pins, and she was kept in the mental health ward for a week. Her uncle offered to cover the difference after insurance to get her inpatient care for two months at The Renfrew Center, a reputable eating disorder hospital in Florida.

"They diagnosed me with bipolar 1 rapid cycling, post-traumatic stress disorder, alcohol addiction, suicidal ideation, body dysmorphia, and eating disorders. They started me on medication, and I'm going to be starting therapy and workshops soon," Emily said on the phone after her first few days at Renfrew.

She said she couldn't see her face in the mirror, and when she looked at pictures I took of her, she often recognized them as someone different than the woman she saw in the mirror.

Over the next two months, Emily and I would have weekly counseling by phone and got to talk fifteen minutes every day on personal time. She had daily workshops and homework that allowed her to identify her emotions again and was fed shakes to put weight back on her frame.

I learned that the man she was with asked her for a relationship and she said yes because she needed him to survive and didn't want to lose his affection. She didn't love him, and wasn't much attracted to him, but felt she didn't deserve to be happy anyway.

He took her on dates, bought her expensive things, and bought her kids Christmas gifts. When I learned they were much closer than a no-strings fling, I got upset and accused her of lying, making her upset, and the session ended early. She wanted to break the bathroom mirror and cut her wrists in front of the nurse.

She felt a tremendous amount of guilt for using him and wished she could call him to apologize. "I used him like a pill or a bottle and was going to throw him away when I was done with him. He was a nice guy and he was good to me."

These counseling sessions were painful, but each one was bringing more healing and understanding. The therapist wanted to get us to a place of reconciliation in the limited time we had. Then they could release her to me, and we could continue outpatient care.

Reasoning that we weren't really married because of our qualifications, we decided to mean it and legalize it this time, hopeful for a new marriage and a fresh start.

Before Emily left Renfrew, her therapist called me to interview me, making sure it was safe for Emily to be released to me. She told me I needed to keep up the momentum of therapy and that Emily shouldn't go a week without seeing her therapist, psychiatrist, or doctor. She also needed to stay on her medication and do her daily exercises.

"Her parents are her main triggers. Whatever she does, she cannot go back to their house. We've seen in the past where the patient will act out so they can find a place to give into their disorders. If at any point she paints you black, threatens to leave, and tries to move you into her parents' house, you have to let her go. She won't get better and you'll find yourself in the same situation. Make it a condition of renewing your vows that she has to stay with you as promised and not try to move you back to her parents' house."

I agreed.

"And don't forget, you have been deeply wounded by this and are traumatized. You've been abused. You need to get your own counseling. You can't just be there for her and neglect yourself. You both need others you can count on for support."

With that, she wished us well, and Emily was released in the final days of March, unfinished and split wide open.

The day before I boarded the plane to get Emily, my mom called, begging me not to renew our vows and move Emily back in with me right away. "You know she's not ready, and she's in no condition to be making these kinds of decisions. She's only been in the hospital for two months, she needs a year minimum, and she's never gonna be completely better. If you bring her here, you know she's just gonna leave again, right? She can't leave those kids again. Does she have family or friends she can stay with in Florida for a year?"

"She feels safest with me, Mom, and I have to try. If it doesn't work out, at least I'll know I did everything I could."

My mom began crying. "It's just that you keep getting hurt. Your whole life you've never been allowed to be happy. I think you're just asking for more pain."

Emily and I had therapy, a treatment plan in place, a renewed commitment to one another, and a new vision for our lives that involved healing and getting back to Florida as soon as possible. I loved her and was ready to live a lifetime of support and recovery with her.

I couldn't wait to have her in my arms again.

2/06/10
Email from Emily

Dear Paul,

Hey baby, it's been too long that we've been apart and I know sometimes it seems like an eternity until the time that I will be ready to leave here and come home to you. So I wanted to send you something you could hold and read when you miss me or begin to doubt. I can't wait until you can see in my eyes how sorry I am, and how blessed I feel to have you. I can't wait to hold you, cry on you, kiss you, love you the way you deserve to be loved, care for you the way you deserve to be cared for. I am willing my make my life a life of recovery and healing, management of my disorders. I am willing to do all of the hard work that it's going to take dealing with all of the difficult things I've blocked and avoided. I am so sorry, Paul, and do not take you giving me another chance for granted. The difference about this time around is that I'm in a place where I am ready and hungry to change and get better. Love you with all of my heart.

Emily

2/11/10
Email from Emily

Dear Paul,

Another note to say I love you, miss you, can't wait until we're together again. There are two things I have to say:

"First, when I was apart from you, this world did not exist, nor any other. Second, whatever I was looking for was always you." —Rumi

Paul, you are my treasure, my lover, my angel, my best friend. Thank you for going through the pain that is creating a rebirth in me. I do not take it for granted. I love you with all of my heart.

Emily

2/13/10
Email from Emily

Dear Paul,

You told me just this morning that you had a rough emotional night and morning and asked me to write out what I value about you, what I would miss if you decided to walk out of my life. When you asked me I immediately said yes, because I knew it would be an easy task.

Number one, I value the pure and seemingly endless unconditional love that you have shown me. There were times when I was so overwhelmed by this knowing that my eyes would fill with tears as I thanked God for placing you in my life so that I know what real love is.

Second would have to be your affection and thoughtfulness. You always show me through tender kisses or just making me a cup of tea that I'm of value to you, that I am special.

Third would have to be the endless passion and loyalty you have for loved ones and hobbies. Everyone and everything you love is obvious and you show it in a big way.

Fourth would have to be your spirituality, your wisdom in knowing that the spirit needs to be fed, always wondering, questioning, and searching and allowing me to do the same.

Fifth would be your sense of humor. You are the funniest person I've ever met. It really helps lighten heavy moods when they come and lifts my spirit.

Sixth, that you help me to remember to take care of myself when I lose focus and forget.

Seventh is that you are a homebody like me and your idea of a good time is simply cuddling on the couch and watching a movie, then making love.

Eighth, I love how you enjoy the beauty and peacefulness of animals and nature.

Ninth, that you are super intuitive, that I can ask you for

advice and know it will be good.

Tenth, you are honest and true to yourself.

Honey, I know all of this has been difficult. I am so sorry for making you feel not-valued. Know that you are of value to me, that you are my treasure. I love you, I love you, I love you,

Emily

2/28/10
Email from Emily

For you, Paul.

I am grateful to have Paul in my life, he has given me another chance to live my life with him. I am grateful because I can't imagine living my life any other way. He has always tried to protect me from myself, and my children, he loves me the way I always imagined G-d did, but had never had it demonstrated to me up until our relationship together. He encourages me, loves me even when it's tough, forgives me, looks for and acknowledges the good in me, laughs with me, cries with me—he is my best friend. I feel complete when we are together. I am grateful for him.

Paul, I want to remind you how thankful I am for you to be loving me the way you do through all of this—for being super patient and kind to me. I don't take it for granted.

I love you, I love you, I love you,

Emily

2/28/10
Email to Aaron

Brother,

My precious wife, my Emily, who I love more than my own life, has been checked into an eating disorder hospital in Florida called Renfrew Center. She was diagnosed with multiple conditions and became suicidal after confessing to being with another man while we were apart.

Brother, I am heartbroken and devastated at my deepest level, but I promised her I wouldn't abandon her to the shadows. She is my wife, and I will live and die with her. I have to mourn my own pain and the broken trust, yes, but I can't imagine the emptiness, desperateness, and lostness she has felt, frankly, since long before we met. As hard as this has been, it has renewed our love and passion for one another, our dedication to one another, and it has made her address herself and break herself open so she can be made whole. I'm proud of her for being brave enough to do this. It's much easier to give up and die.

It's been really difficult not seeing my Emily for nine months only to lose her to such obscene tragedy, then gain her back but not be able to see her and heal with her. I have to mourn without her as she has been hospitalized, our phone time is limited, visitation is limited, and she is in another state. When she gets out, we will be back together repairing our hearts and our lives.

It's amazing, brother, how the things that bring us so near to death make us more alive than ever. I've never loved her more than I do right now, and never looked forward to our future together more than I do now.

Rumi is getting her through a lot of her days there and she quotes some of your lyrics in group discussion with others. Right now, our selected Rumi passage is:

A night full of talking that hurts, my worst held-back secrets. Everything has to do with loving and not loving. This night will pass.

Then we have work to do.

    Your blessings and kind words meant a lot to her at Christmastime. If you have any words of encouragement for her or perhaps a note I can mail to her, I think it would mean the world to her.
    And how are you, brother? Are you in need of kind words or a hug? Do you have any close friends or people to confide in? You know Emily and I love you and we are always here for you the best we can be. We think about you often and miss you. If there is anything we can do, say the word.
    Be deeply loved and filled with all things good,

    Paul

3/13/10
Email from Aaron

Bawa. Bismillah ir-Rahman ir-Rahim
(In the Name of G-d most Merciful, most Compassionate)

My very precious brother Paul, all my love and much, much peace to you. Thank you for writing, as it is wonderful to hear from you.

Yes, all of the events, emotions, joys and struggles and despair and sorrow you have mentioned are familiar to us—all inside my heart, or experiences that we have shared. May G-d help us and protect us and guide us and have mercy on us, comfort us in our heartache, our physical and emotional sicknesses, our broken trust and shattered faith. May we find peace and contentment and rest in the very good qualities of mercy and compassion, kindness, gentleness, understanding, tolerance, patience, humility, truth, unity, and love. May we open our hearts and search for the reality of these qualities, for the state of purity in which there is no need to worry about any of what you have said or experienced, no need to worry about Emily but trusting she is okay, learning what she needs to learn through all this, cared for immeasurably; and certainly no need to worry even a moment about any mistakes it seems we've made, or she's made, no matter how hurtful they may be to our emotions when our mind dwells there. We have another certainty—a deeper certainty, that this world and all of its happenings are only, in some sense, a story or a show or a stage of drama on and in which we have been acting, playing a certain part. But we have found a way to step off of the stage, at least momentarily, to take stock of what we have come to call our life, what we have taken for granted as "reality," and we have been able to sit in the audience and watch the story unfold, without particular identification with any one character, or anxiety over any specific twist of the most unpredictable and, at times, unsavory plot. That is to say, we have taken stock, on at least an elementary level, of the fact of the eternal, and we have found that everything that appears will disappear. Here, let me share with you a song that Bawa Muhaiyaddeen used to sing:

> "Whatever comes, let it come.
> Whatever goes, let it go.
> As long as my Primal Father is with me,
> What care have I?"

My very precious brother, certainly we've been through enough together that I know of the persistence of your doubts that any sort of Primal Father/Mother/Lover is with you. This is fine, to be understood and much respected. It may even seem that there is a great virtue in doubting any images or concepts we may conjure of the Primal One. But, you mentioned Rumi, and so let me refer to him also: He spoke of the sweetness that comes when "existence itself becomes the Friend." Here, we find G-d not as a theological construct, or philosophical abstraction, but reality itself. We've certainly talked about this before.

But why all this now, these words, still ringing of the intangible, or at least not so immediate as a razor blade, a vomiting habit, or the jealous memories of a no-string sex affair? Any words my fingers may type this morning, how am I to know that they will have any comforting effect upon you finding yourself, as you may in the sort of turmoil you have described?

My brother, there is no way for me to know what your heart may need, and therefore what to say, except for to look plainly at my own heart, to where you live without beginning or end and without separation, where both you and Emily live within me as One in perfect peace and wonder, praise and gratitude and child-like trust, contentment, mercy and beautiful love—I see you there, inside my own heart, living that way, perfectly, without blemish or fault, and know that to be the reality of you/her Life (yes, as opposed to "lives"), and accept that Perfect Love as who you Truly are, who you have always been and who you will always be, regardless of the current dream, this drama we've conjured up in our ignorance.

It may bring no comfort to you whatsoever, and that will be fine, as there is no need for "me" to convince "you" of the perfection of all that exists, the absolute perfection of your own Life, the absolute lack of any need to worry or to fear, to be ashamed of anything or to judge anyone or anything, including yourself or Emily. There is no need for me to convince you of the goodness and the rightness and the immeasurable healing power of love and forgiveness—to accept that this forgiveness is a real power, that it exists everywhere and at every moment, within us, for us, for one another, without any cost or loss or harm to anyone; that there is no one who is harmed by forgiveness. There is no one who will need to suffer because we accept forgiveness for ourselves and for one another, when we take Grace to be reality and the world to be questionable (to put it mildly), rather than the other way around, as we have typically done.

My very precious brother Paul, you also do not need me to remind you that our sister Emily need not be thought of as "your wife"—or at least, not in any very substantial respect. We speak of things we own, that may define us—my job, my house, my wardrobe, my beliefs, my wife, my family, my haircut, my faith, my lack of faith, whatever. Meanwhile, we know that everything of ours, our bodies, our possessions, our relationships, our families, that we will all return to the earth very, very soon, and that nothing will remain of all that we called "mine."

Furthermore we have seen plainly that even that one possession to which we might most reasonably lay claim—that is, our "self"—is most problematic, ever changing, unruly, not contained or possessed by any one consciousness, formed by forces beyond our control, acting in ways contrary to the best interests of ourselves and those we love. In short, our very existence has become, to our very own mind, as some of your favorite philosophers might conclude, ridiculous and absurd.

Meanwhile, Truth continues to be true, Love continues to be loving, Kindness continues to be kind, Mercy continues to be merciful, Goodness continues to be good, Unity continues to be united, Peace continues to be peaceful, Contentment continues to be contented, Joy continues to be joyful, Childishness continues to be childish, Simplicity continues to be simple, Existence continues to exist, and so on, forever, no doubt. Outside the cage of the human mind or the physical body? No doubt, but do we really take the mind and the body as the gauge of What Was, Is or Will Be? Why would we do such a thing? That is, why would we continue living our lives, building this house of cards, trusting in the untrustworthy, only to find fault with it for letting us down? It is no wonder we want to kill ourselves. But is there another way?

Let me tell you again something Bawa Muhaiyaddeen spoke about—"to die before death." So we have given our lives over to our desires, to our thoughts, our beliefs and intentions, our talents, our ambitions, our sorrows and our regrets, our attachments and relationships. We have learned a great deal about ourselves, about this world, about the nature of our own mind in doing so, so what sense is there in finding fault in any of this? Why do we not rather surrender our lives with every day, every breath when we remember, surrender to all those most beautiful qualities?

This is the heart of the message this morning. This surrender. Paul, you have kindly wished me to "be deeply loved and filled with all good things." This is all I'm now saying back to you. A cynical response to you might have been, "But how can I be deeply loved? This world is full of selfishness—that is all. And good things? What is goodness?" Yes, these thoughts have their own story to tell, but we have tasted enough of that fruit to know to search for another tree. A belief in those things that you wished upon me, a belief in the reality of love and goodness, a reality that no person can create or destroy, can neither give me nor take away—to allow existence, as Rumi says, to be our Friend, existence to be Love, the Reality within existence (no matter what it brings to us) to be Goodness—in short, to have faith in God: may we pay attention to the tastes that accompany our various beliefs, and the states of consciousness that accompany them.

These are many words. Maybe something shorter would be preferred?

A.

3/13/10
Email to Emily from Aaron

Bawa. Bismillah ir-Rahman ir-Rahim

My very precious sister Emily, my own life, truly and literally, all my Love and endless mercy and peace be with you, your thoughts and all those you love and see. May G-d protect you and your children, your family and your heart and grant you very sweet comfort, joy and rest. Please pray for me and my family, as things have been very strange lately, all praise be to G-d. My love you, my dear and precious sister, my heart and my life. Although our bodies are far from one another we are deeply together forever and truly united no matter what—this is very good news to my poor heart.

Your brother,

Aaron

77
Wedding (Pt. 2)

The day Emily got out of Renfrew, she called me from Walmart to say she'd been released. After abruptly hanging up, she called back. She had loaded her basket with candy, then binged and purged in the parking lot. "Just forget about me, you don't need this. It took everything in me not to buy razor blades. Are you sure you want me back? I'm not in a good place right now. Please forgive me for everything."

I reminded her that what she was doing was common for patients after being released from treatment and that we had a long way to go. This wasn't going to be the last time this happened.

I got on the plane to Florida from O'Hare airport the next morning, eager to see Emily after almost a year apart and bring her back home.

I saw her standing at the end of the jet bridge, her Crayola red hair and pink Converse All Stars unmistakable. As I got closer to her, I felt like I began to float, until I finally threw my arms around her and didn't let go. Even after getting into the car, I couldn't stop touching her and looking at her. I was taking her in and making her mine again.

After eating lunch, we went to Diana Beach to exchange vows. Her freckles burst in the sun against the backdrop of the blue and turquoise ocean behind her.

We found the shade of a palm tree and stood in the sand. She placed the tungsten ring on my finger, the inside of which I had inscribed: I DID NOT ABANDON HER TO THE SHADOWS, and read her vows.

"I promise to learn from my past mistakes and fully commit myself to you. Not to let anything or anyone come between us again. I promise to be sensitive to your fibromyalgia and your needs. I love you always and forever, even when things get tough. I promise to commit to and grow in my recovery, which will only better enhance our relationship. I promise to look you every day in the eyes and tell you I love you, to kiss you and hold you and do my best to melt your fears away. I vow to make time for lightheartedness and fun. I promise to love you 'til the day I die and beyond."

I then placed a white gold aquamarine butterfly ring on her finger and began my vows.

"I'm sorry I didn't know what was wrong and how to help you, or I would not have made the decision to leave nor would I have said the things I said. When we first made our vows, we qualified them, but no qualifications this time. I commit myself to you for the rest of my life and promise to love you, to take care of you, and to do everything I can to make things better. I love you, Emily."

We kissed.

"Only me, forever?" I asked.

"Only you, forever," she said.

"Am I enough?'

"You're more than enough."

78
Chicago (Pt. 2)

When Emily was packing to move back to Chicago with me, she came across the gifts the other guy bought her, including an expensive Japanese teapot.

"Whatever you do, don't bring any of that back with you," I said. "I don't want any reminders of him in the house—it will hurt me. Leave it, sell it, throw it away. I just don't want to see any of it. I don't want to see the old ring or the perfume I bought you, nothing that will remind me of him."

"Agreed," she said. "I look at this stuff and think, 'What was I doing?' I actually feel gross thinking about it."

We arrived in Chicago on a cold and windy night. "We'll be back in Florida in no time," I promised her, both of us hating the cold. Sick and worn out, we took hot baths to defrost and went straight to bed.

I woke early the next morning to unload the car, glad no one had broken into it overnight and stolen anything. As I unloaded her bags and items onto the front porch, I was proud of her for not bringing any of the gifts the other guy bought her.

There was just one bag left under the front seat. I pulled it out and opened it. *It was the Japanese teapot.*

I felt like I was holding a bloody knife from a crime scene. I contemplated taking it straight to the alley, but I needed to confront her.

"It's just a teapot. I kept it because it was really expensive. It doesn't make me think of him at all," She said.

"But it makes *me* think of him. That's why I said not to bring it. I can't believe I'm standing here holding this in my house."

"Fine, we'll sell it on eBay." She pouted. "I can never have anything nice."

I couldn't believe she was being this inconsiderate to me. Shockingly, she couldn't understand why she needed to be out of contact with the other guy. "He was a really nice guy, and he's probably wondering how I'm doing. I only broke contact with him because you asked me to, and I'm respecting your wishes, but I don't see why we can't be friends."

I was taken aback. If I even had to explain why this was an issue, all was lost. Adding insult to injury, Emily said, "I've been going along with you, saying I cheated on you and letting you call it an affair because I know that's the way you see it. But we were separated, and there was little hope of you coming back, so I don't think I cheated on you. It was wrong to keep it hidden from you because I didn't want to lose you, but it wasn't an affair. We weren't together anymore."

"I asked if you wanted to stay married, and you said yes, so I waited for you. We were still together."

"But I didn't think you were coming back."

"That doesn't matter. You should have broken up with me if you didn't think I was coming back. What if I agreed to stay married to you but was sleeping with some girl until we got back together? Would you consider that cheating?"

"I'd be hurt and I wouldn't know who you are anymore, but I wouldn't call that an affair. Given our situation, there's wiggle room here."

"Then all of our therapy has been a joke. If you can't admit you had an affair, I can never heal. Every time you take a piece out of me like this, I can't look in the mirror. You need to pack your stuff and leave."

After putting up a fight saying she'd never admit she cheated, she finally gave in. "I'm sorry for cheating on you."

Emily hated being in her body. She complained that she wanted to tear her skin off. It felt like there were thousands of ants crawling under her skin. Only picking at herself and cutting brought relief. Something had to give, so she asked me to allow her Vodka as the least of all evils. It would keep her from cutting and binging and purging.

As friends stopped by to say hello and offer support, they took me aside and said they didn't recognize her; that she had a wild look in her eyes like a caged animal.

"This isn't my home," she said after just two weeks together.

"I don't want to be here. I made the wrong choice. I should have stayed with my kids. I keep seeing them cry as I waved goodbye to them again. I'm moving back with my parents."

"Emily, you can't do that. We made vows. You can't leave. Renfrew warned you to stay away from your parents' house. They are your main triggers."

"Well, I didn't know when I made the vows that I'd feel this way."

"It doesn't matter what you feel, that's the point of making vows. This is all your illness driving you to find a place to act out. You're being impulsive again. Renfrew warned me you might do this. After all of the work we put in, you can't give up now."

"Would you really hold me captive here against my will? I can't get better here, and you're starting to trigger me. I don't feel safe. You keep bringing up the affair. I don't want you to take this the wrong way, but you need to get over it. If you can't, I need to leave. It's in the past, I said I was sorry, and we're together now, so it's done. I don't understand what 'work' we have to do before we can go back to Florida and I can be with my kids."

"Then just fucking go!" I yelled, crashing my cup of water against the kitchen wall. "God fucking dammit!" I tore the light chain from the ceiling.

She yelped, afraid I might hit her. I sat next to her on the radiator and put my hand on her thigh to reassure her that I wouldn't hurt her.

"See, I knew you couldn't handle me," she said sheepishly through tears, breaking the silence.

"Do you want us to end?" I asked.

"A part of me does. I liked it better when we just lived together at the beginning, before we got married. The other guy I was with just took me out and kept things light. He didn't make me do all of this work and therapy. I didn't have to be good enough to be with him. I wasn't watched over all the time. It's too heavy here, and I need something light."

"But Emily, that wasn't a relationship. You told me you called me with all of your problems to spare him, so I did all the work and he got all the dates and sex. That sounds fair. You were just using him like a drug, remember? What you're saying now is you want to get rid of me and go back to using someone again."

"That's what I need, something light, and I miss my kids. I never should have left them again. You can't take care of me, but my dad can, and he won't help me unless I move home. I'd ask you to move with me, but I know you won't live with my parents. I got a call for a job interview in Florida. I think I'm gonna go back and take it."

The phone rang. It was my mom, asking how we were doing.

"Well, Emily's leaving to interview for a job in Florida, so we're over. She can get back together with her ex or find some other guy to use, I don't care," I said passive-aggressively with Emily in earshot.

Angry, she made herself a peanut butter sandwich and a large glass of water to take to the bathroom.

I hung up and ran to block the door.

"Move out of my way. It doesn't matter anymore! Nothing matters anymore!" She began crying.

I didn't move from the door.

"Fine, you'll just have to watch me puke in the trash." She went over to the kitchen bin and put her finger down her throat. I pulled her hand out of her mouth.

"Don't touch me! Leave me alone!" She fought me off.

She went to the living room and sat on the couch. I sat silently next to her, shadowing her. She picked up the candle torch and held her palm to the flame. When I took it out of her hand, she reached for a pop can, pulled the tab off, and began scraping her wrist with the jagged edges.

"Give me that." I forced her into the bedroom, tackling her on the bed and wrestling the tab from her hand.

"Stop! Let me go!" She kept struggling before giving up and lying still. I spooned her in a bear hug.

"You know, you can't watch over me forever." She finally said.

"I know," I whispered.

As she began packing to leave, I collapsed on my bed and sobbed harder than I ever had in my life. I couldn't believe all of this hard work didn't pay off for us.

Emily came in and lay down next to me, putting her arms around me. She began sobbing with me, to the point that we were convulsing and choking on our tears.

"You can't go," I said, trying to breathe.

"I have to go. It's not fair. We're too sick and poor to be together. It's gonna be so hard to say goodbye to you."

Her dad drove to Chicago to get her, and after a final dinner together, I watched them drive off.

I put her ring on her finger before she left and she took our framed wedding photos with her.

I walked up the stairs to my apartment, once again emptied of her clothing and stuffed animals. She was gone.

I was alone again.

Once back in her parents' house, Emily lost all control, drinking a pint of vodka every night, binging and purging multiple times a day, and cutting herself to the point of waking up to dry blood on her sheets. She wrote me suicide notes she would read over the phone: "Sorry, you couldn't save me." I began to have nightmares of the dreaded phone call and flight to the funeral.

Before long, she called me saying I was a bad husband for not being there with her, then ripped our wedding photos to pieces.

I tried everything I could to keep us together. I spent the day downtown in Chicago, taking her on a virtual date, and mailed her the DVD. "That's not my home," was all she said.

I continued to send her notes on bipolar disorder and borderline personality disorder. She finally told me I was wearing her out sending her all of this and using big words on the phone. "You're not my therapist, you're my husband, and what I need from you is affection. Stop telling me what's wrong with me and tell me what you like about me." She suggested we just be friends, adding that there is no way on earth she could ever be good enough to live up to my conditions. What I read between the lines was: I can't be alone and I need to get back online and find someone.

"My mind screams that I should move on from you, and then

that makes my heart ache over the thought of losing you," she wrote in June. "I can't really make a solid decision, like I can't about everything else. I'm emotionally tied to you and I wish there was a way that we could work, but it's not working. What hurts almost as much as losing you is hoping beyond hope that we find a way back to each other. I want to remain friends, I care about you a lot, I haven't been able to get you off my mind, but then I try to snap myself out of it and go through all the reasons you and I don't work. I do care for you, Paul. I think I'll always love you. I love you, but we just don't work."

After sending this email, making our ending permanent, she fell out of her chair onto the floor, crying.

79
Earthen Vessels

While reading books and looking for answers, I learned that most of Emily's behaviors and struggles were explained by borderline personality disorder.[231] This disorder is characterized by depression, impulsive behavior, mood swings, eating disorders, addiction, self-mutilating, suicidal thoughts, black and white thinking, idealizing and devaluing, having an unstable sense of self, poor boundaries, dissociation, and sometimes psychotic breaks, among other characteristics.

As I read books on this disorder and sent the notes to Emily, she was astounded at how well they described her. But only one of her many therapists gave her the diagnosis.

Because borderlines can't be alone and often feel abandoned and dissociated, they will seek sex or impulsively jump into relationships, using sex not for intimacy or love, but as a coping mechanism. Sometimes they use it to escape, other times to feel.

These authors asked if Emily made me feel like the funniest, smartest, cutest, most amazing person in the world. Was there poetry and romance and passion? Did I feel loved, necessary, and needed? Was I everything she was looking for? Were we so compatible that we agreed on everything and had a relationship that was too good to be true? Did it seem effortless? And once I put a ring on her finger, did I suddenly wake up next to a stranger, literally overnight?

Now I was getting answers. People in these books described their experience waking up next to a stranger as *Invasion of the*

---

[231] The books I read were *I Hate You, Don't Leave Me: Understanding Borderline Personality Disorder* and *Sometimes I Act Crazy: Living with Borderline Personality Disorder* by Jerold J. Kreisman and Hal Straus, *Stop Walking on Eggshells: Taking Your Life Back When Someone You Care About Has Borderline Personality Disorder* by Paul T. Mason and Randi Kreger, and *Breaking Free From Boomerang Love: Getting Unhooked from Abusive Borderline Relationships* by Lynn Melvelle. I also frequented the BPD Family message boards.

Body Snatchers. The body was the same, but a completely different person was inside. They said their partner was replaced by a monster, a demon, an alien, or a brat. This new person was impossible to talk to or reason with, suddenly incompatible, and now used fear, threats, obligation, and guilt to get their way. Where you once felt loved, it was now all about them and your needs no longer mattered.

These authors predicted that I probably believed this abrupt personality change was temporary, due to a situational pressure, like Emily missing her kids, and that the old Emily would come back once she was with them. But the news was grim: the Emily I fell in love with, dated, built a relationship with, and married wasn't real. *I will never see her again.*

"Losing a relationship with a borderline is like losing a relationship with a person who never existed," one author made stark. Who is Emily, really? Even she doesn't know. Borderlines typically become whoever they need to be in order to be loved. They are often referred to as chameleons.

I thought about how losing God was like losing an invisible person who never existed. Now I lost a visible person who never existed. I looked in the mirror wondering if anyone in the universe—eternal or mortal—could ever *really* love me, feeling embarrassed that I believed anyone ever really did.

No one who really loves you just wakes up one morning out of the blue as a different person and begins mistreating you, these authors made clear. For the borderline, unconditional love and support is expected, but their love is booby trapped with conditions and obligations. In the end, if you can't meet their needs, they will invalidate you and become inconsiderate, and they will replace you with someone who can meet their needs. Everyone in the life of a borderline is used, and therefore disposable and replaceable.

These authors helped me understand that borderlines are impulsive and make decisions emotionally. When they say something, they mean it. But when their feelings change next week, they really mean that, too. For this reason, it is nearly impossible to come to agreements, conclusions, resolutions, or to hold them to their word. This explained how it was that Emily could make such heartfelt promises, commitments, and vows, then go back on them two weeks later. It also explained why all of my boundaries were trampled.

What was I to do with all of our memories: all of the photos and home videos and poems and cards that I used to nurture me? Emily brought me back to life. Was this all fiction?

I wanted to believe some things were so sacred that they couldn't be destroyed. I couldn't accept that we sometimes just lose and have to let go and move on with very little understanding or resolution.

"Emily could have the best doctors in the world, all the support in the world, all the prayers in the world, and all the money in the world and it couldn't fix her anymore than it could fix your fibromyalgia," my mom said. "Millions of people in this world live with terrible mental and physical illnesses and addictions that can't be helped. That's just the way it is. And no matter how much you love her, you can't take care of her. You're sick and can hardly take care of yourself. Even healthy people can't do for her what is expected of you."

Emily was astounded at how well the books described her, but still maintained that she was not borderline. She was simply a mom who felt guilty for leaving her kids and needed to do everything possible to show them she was sorry for leaving them and try win them back.

I went to Borders and found *The White Knight Syndrome: Rescuing Yourself from Your Need to Rescue Others* by Mary Lamia. White knights were described as tragic heroes—fated to struggle and to destruction, sacrificing themselves to liberate the oppressed and rescue the maiden from dragons.

The author explained that I unwittingly pick needy and vulnerable partners because rescuing gives me a sense of pride and worth, something to offer, to feel needed, to feel irreplaceable. This is often motivated by my fear, insecurity, anxiety, and need for admiration, validation, and love.

Rescuers like me have a history of loss, abandonment, rejection, and unrequited love. We are altruistic, intuitive, sensitive to the needs of others, and vulnerable. It causes us great suffering to not jump in and help others. Having poor boundaries, we give at the expense of ourselves. This taking responsibility for the needs of others and feeling guilty for not helping only sets us up for exhaustion, heartache, and misery. Rarely is the other person helped by our involvement in the end.

This need to rescue is also linked with the need to be an idealized hero from a myth or an epic. If our lives are not lived for some deep, dramatic, intense, and grandiose purpose, we feel like our lives are going to waste. We find ourselves in risky behavior, making these everything-on-the-line grand gestures. We want to be someone's superhero. We just can't be average.

When we find that life will not deliver on these grandiose idealizations and fantasies, we suffer boredom and despair. We simply can't survive in a world where magic isn't real.

This explained my entire life—my need for God, for a big calling and mission, to empty myself out in something intense, and to rescue and sacrifice. It explained why the practical life was insufferable for me. It also explained why no matter how hard I tried, I couldn't be comfortable with the disenchanted world of stark nature and atheism.

A therapist friend advised me to stop trying to understand Emily and to put all of that energy into trying to understand myself—particularly why I don't know how to protect and respect myself. I read about boundaries, codependency, rescuing, and recovering from borderline relationships, but never saw my life laid out more clearly than in *The Highly Sensitive Person: How to Thrive When the World Overwhelms You* and *The Highly Sensitive Person in Love: Understanding and Managing Relationships When the World Overwhelms You* by Elaine N. Aron.

The truth is, for me, somewhere behind all of this pain, there is a guilty satisfaction in all of this risk, trauma, and heartbreak. My savior complex is my own form of self-harm. This book is my own kind of emo song.

We are who we are. We can change very little and can only manage our demons, trying our best to extend love, grace, and forgiveness to one another, which is all I have today for Emily.

7/21/10
Email from Aaron

Bawa. Bismillah ir-Rahman ir-Rahim
(in the Name of G-d most Merciful, most Compassionate)

My dear brother Paul,

It's unclear whether we will be doing the upcoming tour or canceling some/all of it—Elliott is in the hospital after heart surgery, on life support (ventilator—breathing machine). Uncertain if he's going to pull through. I don't mean to burden you at all, just thought maybe you should know. We're off to visit him in a few minutes.

All my love to you, to Emily, and to your family. Your brother,

A.

7/21/10
Email to Aaron

Aaron,

I'm sorry, please keep in touch about this. I wish there was something more I could do for you than offer the generic "I'm here for you." If you need me to fly over there, just let me know.

Love you, too, brother,

Paul

80
All Our Dads Die

MewithoutYou was going to be at Bottom Lounge the first week of August, which provided a chance for me to see Aaron again. I was happy that the band hadn't cancelled the tour. This surely meant Elliott had pulled through.

The day of the show, I felt rather poorly, and as was the usual habit, my group of friends backed out last minute, meaning I'd have to use public transportation to get to the show.

I chatted with Emily that afternoon, letting her know that Elliott wasn't well and that I was too sick to go to the show. "Well, I hope your dizziness goes away and that you can go see Aaron. I think it would be good medicine for both of you. Please do try to go, you'll regret it if you don't," she said.

Reluctantly, I took the Ashland bus to the show and stood in the back, filming. "At least I'll have some *It's All Crazy* era stuff on film," I thought, shrugging my shoulders and not expecting much. But I was surprised by how much I liked the songs. Rickie's drumming gave them a harder edge live. Soon the album grew on me and I appreciated the boldness and audacity of it.

I sat out front on the sidewalk for a couple of hours after the show, waiting for Aaron.

He finally came out and headed to the bus. "Hey, brother!" I yelled. He turned around and stood silent. I got up to hug him.

"Did Elliott pull through?"

"What can be said, brother?" He sighed, looking at me with sad puppy dog eyes.

I hugged him and told him I was sorry.

Aaron was worn out, but found that being on the road was a distraction from the pain.

"It's tough because I usually identify much more with my mom, but lately, I've been identifying much more with my dad. I really miss him a lot," Aaron said.

"My dad died of cancer when he was thirty. I was almost

eight," I shared.

"How did you handle it?"

"Well, I was too young to know my dad all that well. What I remember more than anything was how frail he was. My brother and I sat on each side of him that Christmas for a picture. He was rail thin and so weak he couldn't hold his mouth shut. There were oxygen tanks behind him. All I kept thinking while putting my arm around him was to tell my brother, 'Don't break Dad.' I thought he was brittle, like a dead leaf and that he might fall apart when we touched him. When he died, I didn't cry. I was happy he was in a better place and wasn't suffering anymore. I always wondered where he went when he died, and this started me wondering about God and the meaning of life."

Still, nothing I said was going to be of much comfort.

"My dad was in a lot of pain and he didn't want to live anymore," Aaron added.

I told Aaron all of the drama that occurred leading to losing Emily again, but that she encouraged me to come see him. It seemed we were all hurting.

Nearing 2:00 A.M., Mike Almquist, the band's manager, came out to get Aaron. It was time for them to leave.

Aaron was about to start teaching urban education at Temple University. He was nervous, but excited. I encouraged him, saying I was sure he would do well.

With heavy hearts, we said goodbye.

8/4/10
Email to Aaron

Aaron,

Always in a rush to cram as many thoughts and questions as possible into shortened conversations, I forgot to thank you for putting me on the guest list again. Very kind of you, as always.

I'm thankful that Emily pushed me to go see you when I was tired and friends backed out. She thought we would be salve for each other's hearts.

I'm very excited for you getting your feet wet teaching. I know you'll do great.

Tell your mom I said hello and I'm sorry.

I love you brother,

Paul

8/31/10
Email from Aaron

Bawa. Bismillah ir-Rahman ir-Rahim
(In the Name of G-d most Merciful, most Compassionate)

My very dear brother Paul,
Much peace to you and thank you for letting me know you made it home safely. Yes, was a grace to see you as it always is, thank you for coming and sitting a while. As for the guest list, of course . . .

My mom was grateful to hear from you, told me she was "just thinking about him the other day."

Started teaching yesterday—still nervous about the overall endeavor, but the first day was relatively painless. Started with a song, something "I" don't have to "do" so much as let happen.

May G-d protect you and your family, Emily and her kids, and anyone else in your life or your mind. May we find peace and contentment in an increasing measure and continue in our search for what is true, what will not die.

My love you,

Your brother Aaron

81
Old Habits Die Hard

The day after the show, I was determined to work things out with Emily. I wanted to move down to Florida, get a studio, and bring our lives together again. I called to run it by her.

"My therapist told me my homework this week is to tell you that I met someone and I'm in a relationship now."

"What? Last week you said you weren't seeing anyone. You called me and told me that you loved me and missed me. You lied to me?"

"Last week, I wasn't seeing anyone. I have been in a relationship with someone I really like, and vice versa, for less than a week. I haven't lied to you, but didn't want to tell you because I don't want to hurt you. I guess there is nothing more to say."

She met a man online and was moving in with him that weekend. I told her she was being impulsive again and I feared for her safety. She couldn't possibly be in a relationship with a guy she'd just met days ago.

"I wish you wouldn't chalk everything I do up to mental illness." She was exasperated, adding that she owed me no explanation and wasn't going to be interrogated.

"We're not together anymore, so I don't have to care what you think. You see things the way you see them and I see things the way I see them. You have your truth and I have mine," she said. Not wanting to deal with my questions anymore, she said she had to go and asked me not to call her back.

Her Facebook profile picture soon changed. There she was kissing some guy over drinks in a bar, gushing about how much she loved him.

I defriended her, but not before printing out the picture and taping it to my door so that every day when I left the apartment, I was reminded that she wasn't mine anymore.

9/17/10
Email to Aaron

Aaron,

Brother, I just read a short memoir called *I'm Proud of You* by Tim Madigan. He was a journalist falling into depression with his marriage on the rocks when he was asked to write a feature on Fred Rogers (Mr. Rogers). They developed a deep friendship and wrote letters back and forth, like we do. Mr. Rogers' letters sound almost exactly like yours, Aaron.

He is an ordained Presbyterian minister, a big fan of Henri Nouwen and other mystical and contemplative types, always erring on the side of forgiving everyone and paying full attention to the person in front of him and making him feel special. Tim expresses the joy of sharing each others' struggles, being blessed by each others' friendship, and of praying for and visiting each other.

When Mr. Rogers visited children with cancer who had a dying wish to meet him, he would ask them to do something for him. "Will you pray for me?" he would ask them, especially in their moments of having little to give. I began to wonder if you had read this book or at least his influences. It made me appreciate our friendship all the more.

Well, I have to run. I hope you are well given your loss, your mom and Mike as well. If you need anything brother, I'm right here. I love you very much,

Paul

11/11/10
Email from Aaron

Bawa. Bismillah ir-Rahman ir-Rahim
(In the Name of G-d most Merciful, most Compassionate)

My very dear brother Paul,
    I was moved to write you this morning more than others because Emily wrote me just a few days ago, sounding sad, as you described, mentioning vaguely her eating patterns, kid troubles, and overall depression, also concerned that she was burdening me by writing. I didn't have much to say except that our lives are the same really, and of course that it was no burden to hear from her.
    I do not intend, as I'm sure you understand, to try to "fix" anything about her that she seems to feel is broken. In fact, this impulse to fix, which is typically strong in me and has long appeared a virtue, is beginning to wear out its welcome. Our snake oil remedies may bring in a few bucks, but they don't heal, and deep down we must know it.
    And no, have not heard of that memoir of Mr. Rogers—though I'd heard he was a man of the cloth, that was the extent of it, but it is very sweet to hear about his visits to the kids sick with cancer.
    This request of his, "pray for me," you realize I am tempted to ask the same of you, believing this to be about the best we can do for one another. Of course, I do not intend to put you in such an awkward position, but even if you are not the praying type, the Quakers made some room for the less sentimental among us, with their typically unobjectionable requests to "hold" one another "in the light." Granted, this could mean just about anything, and with regards to your recent experiences, it may be more fitting to ask that you "let go of me in the light," but regardless of the language, I hope you sense, below the flimsy surface of letter-shapes on a computer screen, my own deep love and great affection for you. And I'm sorry for any pain you are experiencing.

You mentioned our loss, Elliott, and it has been very hard. We conclude little, but that things must not be as they have seemed.

Your poor and fortunate brother,

A.

82
Collapse

Now September, I started to plan my new life without Emily and without Florida. I needed to find a part-time job to supplement my disability payments and get my own apartment again. I once again had to be out of the flat by Christmas, my uncle warned, as the house might be repossessed.

I applied for jobs and went on interviews but got no callbacks. I was still sick and quite broken down from a long year. I knew winter was coming, but I had no choice. I had to work.

One afternoon mid-September, I went out for a walk and noticed all the lights were on in my uncle's apartment downstairs and the mailbox was still full, which was unusual. I went in to check on him and found him on the floor of the back bedroom. He had the flu and had fallen out of his bed. The combination of being obese and diabetic meant he couldn't pull himself back up.

He had been lying there facedown on the floor in the summer heat with no air conditioning for hours. I called my brother, and we helped get him up. The ambulance took him to the hospital where he was told he was lucky to be alive. He needed dialysis for his kidneys, his liver was bad, and they were constantly draining fluid from him. Unable to walk, he was moved to a nursing home to rehabilitate. He wouldn't walk again for over a year.

"You need to be out of that apartment by November—they're gonna take the house," he said.

"Why don't you come out to Galena where it's cheap?" my mom suggested. "It's nice out here and there's no crime or traffic like there is in Chicago."

Galena is a scenic tourist town about three hours out of Chicago where Illinois, Iowa, and Wisconsin meet. The last thing I wanted was to be away from my friends and find myself alone in a small town, depressed, in the middle of winter, borrowing money and using credit to establish a new life, but I had no other options.

I took only what I could fit in my car, and just after

Thanksgiving, reluctantly moved into an apartment in Galena.

Almost instantly there was heavy snowfall and I wouldn't see the ground again until spring. Like so many times in my life, I lay there alone in my bed saying, "How the hell did I end up here?"

12/20/10
Email to Aaron

Aaron,

Merry Christmas to you and your family. Is there anything I can do for you? Always thankful for you, miss you. Stay warm, Aaron, it seems we're all sticks of fish on ice.

Paul

1/4/11
Email from Aaron

Bawa. Bismillah ir-Rahman ir-Rahim
(In the Name of G-d most Merciful, most Compassionate)

My very beloved brother,
    Merry Christmas to you also and to those you love. Thank you for writing and for all of your kindness to me. Our house is well insulated, and stays pretty warm, pretty long.
    It is very good to know you, a big gift. Do you know that?

Aaron

1/4/11
Email to Aaron

Well, I'm certainly glad you are warm!

I found the old T-shirt with your dad on it on eBay and mailed it to you a couple of weeks before Christmas, I hope you received it and it didn't get lost in the mail.

More soon, brother,

Paul

1/13/11
Email from Aaron

Bawa. Bismillah ir-Rahman ir-Rahim
(In the Name of G-d most Merciful, most Compassionate)

My dear Paul,
Thank you for sending the very kind and thoughtful gift, the yellow "Elliott" shirt. Please forgive me for not mentioning it or expressing my gratitude—when I opened the package I got awfully emotional/sentimental, looked at the shirt a while, and hid it away in a drawer. Part of me wanted to hang it up or show it to my mom, but didn't have the courage, didn't want to stir her or myself up, so I kind of tucked it away until a later time. His image and our band name together are now of course all too appropriate, and I am still very sad much of the time.

We went out to the grave last week. I broke down as I always seem to there, and my mom asked, "Why are you crying?"; very sweet and innocent. Just a few weeks earlier I came to sincerely believe that I am Elliott, a view that brought me tremendous, tremendous peace and amazement, but which I forgot shortly afterward. We remember periodically that the birth and death of "selves" may not be the full story, that there is an entirely different way of seeing what's "going on" in this world; but to remember a sunny beach is not the same as to lounge on one, drawings of apples don't satisfy our hunger, and so on.

My love you brother. Thank you,

Aaron

83
Thirty-Five

On New Year's Day, Natalie sent me a picture of her smiling face by request and made plans to come visit the following week for my birthday. We had been talking again through November and December as she was separating from her husband and planning a divorce.

We talked on the phone and enjoyed our conversations so much we started to build a mutual attraction for the first time in our lives. She told her parents we were talking again and hoped to win my mom over.

When she arrived on my birthday, she put together a cake for me with whipped cream, sprinkles, and strawberries, delivering it to me with lit candles, singing "Happy Birthday." Then she took me down the street to Log Cabin for a steak dinner.

"I still feel like I ruined your life and that it's my fault you're an atheist. God told me from day one he had a story for us and to write it all down, and I put up a good fight. I thought he would just let me have who I wanted and bring you someone else. I never meant for you to lose your faith. Please don't blame God for this."

I reiterated that I still didn't believe that any of what happened between us was from God and that it wasn't her fault I was an atheist. I was an atheist because all of that seemingly supernatural guidance was false and God hadn't said a word to me since. I chalked it all up to delusion.

She held her ground. "Well, I still believe it was from God."

I was open to spending time with her and getting to know her, this time without all of the signs and supernatural guidance.

After an amazing day together, she headed home. I pinched myself. *Did Natalie just come over and actually enjoy time with me?* I thought this could be a great year after all if something happened between us.

"Thanks for coming out and being so kind to me today, I really appreciate it," I texted her.

"Any time! I think we should be friends right now as I'm still married, and though we are separating, I still love my husband, so I'll need time to sort things out."

"That's totally understandable. Do you want me to wait for you?"

"What? Of course not. If you find someone you have good chemistry with, you should go for it."

"Wait, didn't you spend the whole day telling me you knew I was from God and wanted me to open to this again? I mean, you came all the way out here and made me a cake and bought me a steak dinner."

"Oh, I do that for all my friends!"

Now I was confused.

The following week we talked on the phone and she confessed. "While we're being honest, I don't know what it was, but when I came out to see you last week, I was so sure I wanted to be with you, but I didn't feel anything. I was so disappointed. I couldn't get away fast enough. I'm sorry, the last thing I want to do is hurt you, I just want to be honest with you."

"It's okay, Natalie. This is how it's always been with us."

"I'm just a flakey girl, it's part of my charm," she joked. "I'll be ready for you one day."[232]

---

[232] I thought of a couple of Aaron's lyrics: *The record ended long ago, we go on dancing nonetheless* from "The Cure for Pain" and *she was like wine turned to water turned back to wine* from "Paper Hanger."

4/21/11
Email to Aaron

Aaron,

I hope this message finds you as well as can be. Just wanted to say quickly I've been thinking about you, I love you, I miss you, and if you need anything, I'm here. Things are well as can be for me—stable, single, working, and keeping things as simple as possible. There is a lightness that comes with having to go to work every day and pay attention to the present and interacting with others rather than being alone and getting lost in the weight of yourself, you know what I mean, brother?

I haven't prayed in a long time, but I have made it a point lately to pray for you, Natalie, and Emily every day so not a day goes by that you aren't loved and thought about. I told Emily last time we spoke that it's hard to love three people so much but you are all so far away. Maybe one day not too far in the future I will make it to Philadelphia and say hello to you and your mother. Hope to see you one of these days, sooner than later.

I love you, brother,

Paul

4/28/11
Email from Aaron

Bawa. Bismillah ir-Rahman ir-Rahim

My brother,
Peace to you and thank you for writing and for the loving words. Very good to hear things are stable, and yes, of course I know just what you mean about the good fortune of having a routine, daily responsibilities to keep us from drowning in thought. What good would it do anyone, drowning in thought?
My love you,

A.

84
Galena

I was hired in April at one of the busiest and most popular shops on Main Street in Galena. I hoped to earn a management position, pay off my debt, and head back to Chicago after a year. "Just be normal, don't talk about your past, stay out of trouble, and do a good job at work," I told myself.

While walking to the library one afternoon just after starting my job, my knees buckled beneath me. I wobbled to the brick wall of the church I was passing for support. "Well, this is new," I said, envisioning myself confined to a wheelchair before too long.

Soon I was experiencing a series of involuntary jerks and tremors in my limbs. I couldn't grip well with my left hand. I couldn't turn a doorknob, hold my knife and fork, or hold my teacup. Being left-handed, it was sometimes hard to write. Trying to extend my left arm to reach for things was near impossible.

Even working part time was so exhausting that I spent all of my extra time at home between shifts in bed, my body trembling from fatigue. I couldn't sit up in a chair or concentrate on a book or the TV. Some days I would shower and dress and that took everything out of me, so I'd get undressed and go back to bed. If I made it down the block to a restaurant, I couldn't be social, couldn't cut through my food, and would begin to hunch over the table because I couldn't sit up. My bed became my home.

I was exhausted, but the pain kept me awake, so in times of insomnia I would let go of my sanity and moan, groan, cry, and mumble incoherently, sometimes begging God to help me, sometimes begging God to kill me.

I saw a rheumatologist and two doctors that year, but like usual, none of the treatments or medications helped. They sent me home with the typical advice of getting to bed at a decent hour, walking once a day, eating healthier, and talking to a therapist for depression.

Like so many times before, I lost my job, but was offered a job cleaning rooms and serving breakfast in a small inn. It was still strenuous and painful, but I could go at my own pace. Soon even that became too much, so I only served breakfast for a few hours on the weekends and spent the rest of my time at home in bed.

In the summer, I got a letter in the mail from Social Security. They were reviewing my disability case to see if I was still qualified to receive benefits, sending me to a doctor and a psychologist. It was good timing, given my symptoms were more severe than ever. I'd been seeing a doctor all year who was recording my symptoms and the failure of the medication. My employers wrote notes for my case about my inability to handle an average workday.

I read a book called *How to Be Sick: A Buddhist-Inspired Guide for the Chronically Ill and Their Caregivers* by Toni Bernhard, a woman who lost her career as a professor to a sudden and mysterious pain and fatigue condition like my own. Toni was applying wisdom from Buddhism and mindfulness meditation as a way to live with pain that cannot be treated and limitations that cannot be helped.[233]

The first thing she advised was acceptance. If I tried to live as if I wasn't sick, it would only increase my suffering. Once I accepted my condition and my limitations, I needed to recalibrate my life to live within my means.

This could mean the most important thing in my universe is having a comfortable bed I will spend most of my life in, or to protect my independence and control of my environment by living alone so there are no stressors or triggers to exasperate my pain.

This small space would be my world, and I never needed to expand my thoughts beyond it to what was happening in the world at large. "You are not called for any big mission. The world isn't waiting for you," I told myself. "There is absolutely nothing you are required to do."

I continued to trade a life of productivity, goals, action, involvement, and accomplishment for a life of quietism, where all

---

[233] See also *How to Wake Up: A Buddhist-Inspired Guide to Navigating Joy and Sorrow* and *How to Live Well with Chronic Pain and Illness: A Mindful Guide* by Toni Bernhard.

of my mental and physical energy went to just surviving day by day, enjoying them one at a time.

"I can't believe I'm not going to leave any legacy," I told my mom over lunch.

"Most people don't. They go to work and take care of their families. Not everything has to be a big mission to be a legacy," She said.

After a couple of week of crying and learning to accept a new reality that might not expand beyond my four walls, I accepted what little I had. Just then, my disability ruling came back. They determined that I was healthy and they were discontinuing payments within two months. I appealed and sat in limbo for the next year, wondering if what little I had left would be taken from me. I eventually won the appeal.

Toni reminded her readers about the impermanence and transitory nature of all things. Death and suffering are a part of life, and all of those healthy and happy people I compare myself to, who are living an idealized life, will also endure changes, losses, and tragedies concerning identity, health, career, and marriage.

So many times, I felt cursed and took my disability personally. "It's not fair! This isn't right!" But there is untold suffering the world over on a daily basis. Life surely isn't fair, and no one is entitled to a good life. Rather than resenting others for having what I don't have, I could adopt an attitude of genuine joy for them.

For all I couldn't do in the world, I had access to my inner-life and imagination where I was freer to do more than I could in the real world. I could develop a rich fantasy life to escape into. I could send out loving thoughts to people and pray for them. Or through mindfulness meditation, I could dissociate from my thoughts completely and give my mind a break, paying attention to my breath, physical sensations, and sounds, instead.

Before the year's end, the new atheist writer Christopher Hitchens died from esophageal cancer. He wrote essays for *Vanity Fair* during his illness, which were compiled into a small book called *Mortality*.

"To the dumb question 'Why me?' the cosmos barely bothers to return the reply: 'Why not?'" he wrote.[234] That he would get cancer is "so predictable and banal that it bores even me." He said.[235] He found prayer, complaining, self-pity, and sentimentality a waste of time and energy.

Hitchens thought that every one of us, sick or healthy, was born into a struggle, a losing battle where we fight for our lives every day and are always a moment away from our last breath. He thought it arrogant to think we are somehow special or chosen or that we serve some cosmic calling, finding it insufferable to be told we are being tested like Job or perfected for an afterlife, that our suffering is an anomaly that happens for some good and mysterious reason. Can we not just be stoic and accept reality on its own terms?

Suffering and death are ordinary experiences for every human being. For an atheist like Hitchens, death is as scary as falling asleep. You don't know you're asleep and that you won't wake up again the next morning. It will be just like before you were born. You didn't know that you didn't exist in the billions of years that came before you.

But knowing this is of little consolation. In the end, I couldn't escape the feeling that life was horribly unfair, and if I was going to suffer like this, it wasn't worth living. If the definition of futility is my life of endless struggle and loss, and the definition of hell is pain and suffering day and night without end, then I was living a life of physical, mental, and emotional torture, feeling rejected, abandoned, isolated from everything good, and utterly alone.

Though I wasn't suicidal, I begged God every night to kill me in my sleep and woke up every morning saying, "Oh, shit. Not again."

---

[234] Christopher Hitchens, *Mortality*, (New York: Twelve, 2012), 6.
[235] Ibid, 5.

11/12/11
Email to Aaron

Aaron,

Hello there, brother. As always I hope this note finds you well. I'm eating animal crackers and drinking tea, winding down for the evening and getting ready for work tomorrow. I just ate a horse.

Things are well here. I've managed a stable, simple, drama-free year thus far and consider that a great success. But then I look at my home videos and pictures for the year and they are mostly of trees and nature. That's when you know you have no life—when you film trees, then go home and watch them on your TV.

I have nothing to say but that I miss you, I love you, I hope you and your family are well, and if you need anything from me, I'm here. I hope to come visit sometime in the near future, it's always on my mind.

By the way, there is an Aaron Weiss Facebook page and some people are saying it isn't really you. I couldn't imagine you would go so low as to have a Facebook page, but I thought I'd ask you about it.

Be well brother,

Paul

12/23/11
Email from Aaron

Bism-llah ir-Rahman ir-Rahim

My very dear brother Paul,
Peace to you, it's great to hear from you—you're very funny.
    It is very good to hear about your stress-free year. As for filming trees and watching them on TV, that doesn't sound so bad at all. Our thoughts are often unbearable. My teacher used to talk about wisdom 'cutting the schemes of the mind.' Something nice about looking at a tree, nothing to say to it.
    And no, I haven't stooped to the level of having a Facebook page—I've stooped lower: I use my mom's Facebook page to look at the profile pictures of potential non-hypothetical girlfriends. Then I go visit them in Atlanta, hold their hand, touch their arm, agree we're moving too fast and are both corpses anyway, and take a Greyhound back home. Yes, you're funny, but grace is funnier.
    Love you dearly,

Aaron

12/24/11
Email to Aaron

Aaron,

Well, merry Christmas, brother.

Georgia? You're worse than me! I tried to bring April home from Arkansas. It didn't work. I brought Emily here from Florida. It didn't work. Now I really like this girl in Virginia. It won't work.

You teach in a college, brother! And you're in a band! And you know of all the gatherings in your neighborhood. There's gotta be someone for you.

I find that even when I say I'm happy single, I still care about what women think and I still want to be attractive to them. Given our sexuality is what we are, I think we will always care about being attractive, even if we don't want to do anything about it. It's nice to look at trees, but better to look at trees with someone you love. There are some experiences you want to have alone though, which can be ruined by the company of another.

Given that I do a lot of reading, writing, and drawing, I like being alone. Then when I need a break, I go out to eat and talk with the staff at the restaurant or chat with friends on Facebook. More than anything, I fantasize being able to travel and speak on a book tour and talk about all of these wonderful spiritual things. Paradoxically, we don't become someone unless it's in relation with others. We don't exist in a vacuum, we need others.

As far as the pain and disability, I have my nights of breakdown realizing I've had 20 years of this and can't accomplish my goals. I get jealous of others being allowed to live their lives. But I also know my limits and try to live within them. I'm glad to have four walls and a bed, and much more. Millions have it worse, all things considered.

There are ways to find mental peace in excruciating pain and even have inner wellbeing. You can close your eyes and be happy. But life requires that I have to move—eat, basic hygiene, get dressed, and do stuff. This can get frustrating and overwhelming.

Plus, I'll be 36 next month with no college, car, money, house, savings, health, or career. Not tops on the most-wanted list as far as the ladies go. I need a rich woman who feels sorry for me.

I've been single since Emily left over a year and a half ago, not even a date, and I'm happy with that. I can only hope someone has mercy on me and loves me despite my limitations.

The God I'm not sure I believe in is much more fulfilling.

May the world not take our faith, our hope, our love, and our souls. Be well, brother,

Paul

3/22/12
Email from Aaron

Bism-llah ir-Rahman ir-Rahim

My dear brother Paul!

Thank you for the note right around my birthday and especially for the very beautiful letter you sent at Christmas time. I'm sorry to be so slow in responding—you must come to expect as much by now. Even my winter break this year was not much of a break at all—had tour and then comprehensive exams, then school started the next day. Trying to balance classes and teaching and band stuff has had me busy to an unprecedented degree. Even now, I'm feeling pretty swamped, always scrambling to just barely hang out, skimming or skipping lots of required readings, hoping not to be called on in class.

All more or less a long-winded way of explaining my silence. Ah, but you would forgive me without all these excuses, I just know it!

Thank you also for the encouraging words re: my romantic prospects. I'm open to meeting someone and have been in touch with the girl I mentioned from Georgia, but seems more obstacles/signs pointing in the 'no' direction than to the contrary. I can relate 100% to what you said: "even when I say I'm happy single, I still care about what women think and I still want to be attractive to them." I'm getting older and my hair's falling out and I'm feeling very unattractive, and then on top of that, ashamed of how upset I am about something that I realize is relatively insignificant, 'vain,' etc.

You also said: "The God I'm not sure I believe in is much more fulfilling." This is interesting, reminds me of something I heard a student say while passing a theological argument on campus today: "Why should I believe in God? Where's the proof?" I used to think of "God" this way, as some-thing or super-thing that either may or may not exist. To me, this caused too much trouble, so at some point the proposition switched: rather than beginning with a "concept of the ultimate," then wondering if it exists, it became possible to begin with existence, and let that be the "concept of the ultimate." All of a sudden it began to seem I'd put the cart before the horse in a pretty exhausting way—could entirely accept atheism and theism and reject them both, as after all, we are using w-o-r-d-s.

Oh, and one more thank you also for your beautiful encouragement: "May the world not take our faith, our hope, our love, and our souls." I could not say it better myself, except I may de-pluralize "souls", but not because I have any idea what I'm talking about at all—

My love you,

Aaron

3/30/12
Email to Aaron

Hello Aaron.

Please allow me to add something quickly about the pluralization of souls. I listened to a lecture just yesterday on the illusion of free will by Sam Harris, who recently wrote a book on the subject.

He said the "self" is an illusion, that we are actually moved by input from the world around us rather than being a closed system where we determine our own lives. Rather than that fact being depressing, viewing yourself as an open system susceptible to a myriad of influences makes change and growth possible. You are not condemned to be who you were yesterday. The self is not a stable entity, but a process. The present is a mystery and we don't know how we'll think or feel next. To understand that we are an open process is to take away our egocentric view of life. You can't take credit for your talents, but it matters how you use them. Your weaknesses aren't your fault, but you should try to correct them. We are not truly separate, but linked to each other. Pride and shame that result from egoism make no sense, but love and compassion do, improving your life and the wellbeing of others.

Just think of how many previous events and variables make you who you are right at this present moment; how interaction with others makes and changes us, even shaping our desires and repulsions. It's difficult to say we are a fixed, rigid, stable identity in the world. We're made to change, grow, and adapt.

Sam Harris studied mystical experiences and spiritual practices under masters and gurus in the East—fasting in caves, meditating, taking various hallucinogens, and looking for universal practices that could be stripped of their superstitious dogmas and used to promote peace and wellbeing. He was angry with absolutist/fundamentalist religions in the wake of the September 11th attacks, so he started writing *The End of Faith* the next day. He had no clue he would be considered a spokesman for atheism because of this. Like you speaking at Cornerstone, telling Christians you put no faith in the word "Christian" or the subculture that the festival embodies, Sam Harris spoke at an atheist convention in 2007 only to tell them atheist groups and the term "atheist" were pointless and counterproductive, urging people to live reasonable lives, continuing to critique the irrationalities and dangers in fundamentalist religions without needing a label to do this.

We'll talk again soon and always know I'm here for you, just a call away. I love you, brother.

Paul

5/03/12
Email from Aaron

Paul,

Strange, something inside me has long reacted against those popular atheists, like a cat's fur puffing up when a god (ah, I meant to write "dog", but I'll leave that typo, for obvious reasons) comes near. Nice to see how much I have in common with these fellows. I read a bit from one of Daniel Dennett's books, found a lot of really nice stuff. It's seeming more and more clear that most of our differences are just word-differences. Tired of having *words* to defend—seems like a flimsy thing to worry about. I suppose we've discussed this before, but I'm continually amazed at the stubbornness of the (or at least my) mind, stuck on certain ideas, revisiting old haunts. My mom said Bawa used to tell her to stop replaying old film reels, make some new ones.

Yes, I remember pushing this idea myself: being critical of self-identifying categorical terms, e.g., atheist or Christian, when we had a staunch and well known atheist journalist on the road with us a few years ago. The fellow was Steven Wells. He came to Cornerstone festival, and I remember harping on about how religious fundamentalism and atheistic argumentative zeal were more similar than they appear. Both rooted in division, ego, and typically arrogance. Tried to put them together in one category, and bewildered, nameless joy and grateful wonder in another.

Ah, time to go try to fix my broken headstock—

Love you,

A.

4/20/12
Email to Aaron

Brother,
    I pre-ordered the boxed set and got the download for "Fox's Dream of the Log Flume". The lyrics brought me to tears. Good job. Yeah, it was the getting down on one knee with your grandmother's ring and the subsequent catastrophe haunting you that got the tears out of me. I'm eager to misinterpret the rest of the album to be about me when it arrives.
    Writing prose, I'm used to stringing thoughts together in a clear, explanatory way. I'm horrible at poetry. When I read your lyrics, they seem to be standalone autobiographical snippets next to lines of imagery that create moods and pictures, but not necessarily a coherent story. My brother, Mark, is a huge Bob Dylan fan. He likes a good story in a folk song. So when I send him your stuff, he can't follow it. "Man, his lyrics are all over the place." One line is a philosophical quip, the next some imagery, the next something autobiographical or reflective, then back to painting a mood. I think the lack of seamless coherence makes it easier for more people to apply individual lines to their lives.
    My mom is beeping outside, gotta run, love you Aaron,

Paul

5/03/12
Email from Aaron

Paul

"I'm eager to misinterpret the rest of the album to be about me when it arrives." Yes, I suppose I've been doing the same thing myself. Thank you for kind words, grateful to know that song made some sense. I've thought of you a lot in relation to it.

As for the more straightforward storytelling—it's funny you should mention that, because this newer batch of songs was initially more along those lines. Dialed back the narrative when it started feeling too one-dimensional, made it a bit more abstract, in hopes that, just as you said, it could be more widely applicable or diversely interpreted.

Love you too brother, TOTALLY.

Aaron

85
Cobain

MewithoutYou recorded Nirvana's "In Bloom" for a *Nevermind* tribute CD called *Come As You Are*. They slowed the song down in a haunting acoustic cover, adding accordion and spacey guitar.

While reading *Grunge is Dead: The Oral History of Seattle Rock Music*, an excerpt about Kurt Cobain by Kurt Danielson reminded me of Aaron, so I sent it to him:

> Kurt was like a magpie—he would find bright objects everywhere he looked, pick them up, and feather his nest with them. He was the most skillful thief I've ever seen. And that's what it takes to be a good poet, or a good writer. It was T. S. Elliott that said, "A bad poet borrows, a good poet steals."[236]

"Oh, nice to read about Kurt Cobain," Aaron responded. "I remember seeing a poster of him, a photo and a quote, 'I hate myself and I want to die.' Have thought of that a lot over the years, one of those 'So I'm not the only one!' feelings. Trying to go easier on myself, as I don't think self-hatred and humility are the same thing, and the latter sounds a whole lot nicer."[237]

It was also announced that mewithoutYou was going back into the studio to record a new album, which they would release independently. Aaron was trying to balance writing for the record with schoolwork and teaching obligations.

"Last night I finished the last of the schoolwork for the classes I'm taking—now just boatloads of grading. I will be busy, but not the same pressure as being 'graded.' Oooh, I sure don't like that, graded on papers, reviewed for music quality, assessed however,

---

[236] Greg Prato, *Grunge is Dead: The Oral History of Seattle Rock Music*, (Toronto: ECW Press, 2009), 391.
[237] Email, 4/14/12.

no peace there. Praise and blame, my Lord, what use do we have for either?"[238]

---

[238] Email, 5/03/12.

86
Ten Stories

"The stuff mewithoutYou is working on is so exciting to me. It touches a lot of the things I like about music—spaced out, groovy, entrancing and thoughtful," Rickie said. "We are working as hard as we can to come up with a new identity and place in music. We have been out of the game a while and are ready to bring it back the way we know how. A lot of experimentation and nitpicking, ultimately all leading into the final goal of making a killer record."[239]

Ten Stories was funded and released independently with the old school work ethic mewithoutYou always had in wanting to earn their fans one at a time. Releasing the album on Pine Street, Aaron said, "Our managers, Almquist and Bender have really taken over the reigns with this. I actually wanted to stay with Tooth & Nail, partly because they handled all the business-side of making our records in such a great way. So self-releasing this was kinda scary, stepping into unknown territory—there are so many steps to the process, from booking studio time to mixing & mastering to manufacturing the CDs & vinyl to advertising to web design to album layout to publicity, distribution, royalties, paying everyone . . . so many things T&N used to take care of or oversee that we had to take on. But again, Almquist and Bender really rose to the occasion."[240]

Unlike *It's All Crazy!* where many of the songs were Aaron's, the band serving as accompaniment, this album was more collaborative. The result was a return to their more edgy and aggressive sound with distorted guitars and shouting.

When asked if he thought this album was returning to their original sound, Aaron answered, "Yes, to some extent. Mind you, we've always tried to challenge ourselves and change with every

---

[239] "Rickie Mazzotta mewithoutYou," *Kick Snare Hat*, 6/17/11.
[240] Dan McAndrew, "Interview with Aaron Weiss of mewithoutYou," *Oh So Fresh*, 5/05/12.

record, so I don't think we really have a single sound that we could return to—but some of the stylistic elements we had abandoned with our previous release are revisited on the newest one."[241]

"It's important to remember that *It's all Crazy!*, you know, really did add to basically what our sound is now," Mike said. "Looking back, it's pretty heavily lush instrumentation over acoustic guitars. We didn't abandon that. I love that record, and I love that we're still doing stuff like that on this record, although it's not the predominant thing. I was thinking about this album as really like almost finding our sound. Like a balance that I think we've all come to sort of need."[242]

But this didn't come about without some conflict in direction. "When we were beginning to practice and even talk about it, there was a lot we had to clear up internally," Rickie shared. "During the making of the last record, there were a lot of heavy, personal things going on in everyone's lives. There was a detachment. But with this record, we kind of took all these things into account. We wanted to make sure we were healthy as friends and as a band before we even started writing. We factored in how the last record got made, how it sounded, people's reactions to it, and where we're at now. It didn't dictate the vibe of the [upcoming] album, but it set a tone of 'We have to do something really awesome here—or at least try to—but just satisfy ourselves at the end of the day.'"[243]

"My struggle with the band has always been finding some kind of unity of purpose where we see eye-to-eye about our ideology or morals," Aaron said. "On the whole, we find a way to resolve it and still have a love for each other. It's all very normal stuff when anybody tries to maintain a relationship. For us, it's been 12 years—the fact that we're even still going, to me, is

---

[241] Levi Rogers, "'Ten Stories' Review, Interview with Aaron Weiss," *Levi Rogers*, 7/12/12.
[242] RaPiD, "mewithoutYou - Key Session Interview [22/12/11]," *YouTube*, 1/04/12.
[243] Luke Larsen, "Catching Up With mewithoutYou," *Paste*, 4/06/12.

something of a miracle and I'm grateful for it."[244]

"I remember at one point the guys saying we want to write these kinda heavy songs, and I wanted to write a children's album," Aaron told Yoni Wolf. "And we were working with Daniel Smith at the time, and I thought we're going to kinda determine once and for all we simply couldn't work together anymore because our trajectories were so dissimilar. They all said we want to write heavy songs, I said I wanted to write for kids. Then Daniel said, 'I don't see a problem here—this could be really interesting.' And it was literally that day we decided to do our most recent album."[245]

Aaron was once again asked about how the new album compared to the first one. "I don't think any of us wanted to make music that was that heavy or simple, just in terms of power chords and screaming almost constantly," he said. "I don't feel the same emotions exactly," he added. "[The songs] were all about a relationship that's been over for many, many years now. I can only feel it so much when we've both moved on. All the other [albums] have aspects that are more enduring for me."[246]

Aaron still felt a disconnect playing the old songs. "I think mainly the level of energy and aggression isn't there. I don't feel that way anymore. I don't have this sort of pent up rage and angst towards this broken up relationship with a girl who has since gotten married to a buddy of mine, and to be still singing about her in this way, which is really passionate, about breaking my heart over ten years ago. Get over it, man! Partially for my sake and hers, to not dredge up these old memories—which still have the potential to be painful if I relive them—maybe has something to do with it."

He continued, "It was kind of fun, a little tongue-in-cheek when I wrote it, and that line, 'You better be alone.' I've never been a creepy, threatening, stalker kind of guy where what if she's

---

[244] K.C. Libman, "Aaron Weiss of mewithoutYou on Academia, Band Conflict, and Paramore," *Phoenix New Times*, 2/10/14.
[245] Yoni Wolf, "Episode 74 Aaron Weiss (mewithoutYou)," *The Wandering Wolf*, 9/24/14.
[246] Alexis Sachdev, "Aaron Weiss," *The Temple News*, 4/24/12.

not alone, what am I going to do? When I wrote that line, I wrote it with laughter. It was never a serious like I'm carving this girl's name in my arm! It's a song with a bit of humor, but now even more so because she is married. Literally all of the songs on the album have a reference to her or address her, so I have to sing them not with some degree of attachment."[247]

When Luke Larson asked him the same question, Aaron said he didn't feel a total disconnect from the first album. "A lot has changed since then, but I still see some of the same patterns of mind, the same desires and the same basic concerns. I suppose there was a time a few years ago I would have said 'yes,' as if I'd overcome a lot of the craziness I felt back in those early days—but now I'm not so sure."[248]

After recording *Ten Stories,* he said, "I don't know why people stay within a certain genre. It makes sense to really focus your craft on a smaller area and go really deeper into it and get better at it. Whereas us, maybe we're spreading ourselves too thin by changing so much. I wouldn't mind if we dialed it back and went back to our roots a little, but I don't know if we're going to record anything else."[249]

He continued, "Yeah, on some level it's been natural with us being older and just not wanting to shout and make aggressive kinds of music anymore. Yet on another hand, we're trying to keep things interesting for us and have the kind of songs that we can play throughout our lives, like just alone with a guitar, and can be expressed in other ways, and I think have a more enduring appeal than the energy that we've been relying on for a long time that's just the raw, live, I hate to say, sort of testosterone, like real, 'RRR!' Just youthful and vibrant and frantic, you know? That's hard to maintain, at least without the use of narcotics. [Laughs] Which I don't go near. So unless I'm going to start a cocaine habit, I don't think I can perform the way I did when I was twenty-three."[250]

---

[247] Jon Ableson, "Ten Years On: mewithoutYou - [A→B] Life," *Alter the Press*, 7/2012.
[248] Luke Larsen, "Catching Up With mewithoutYou," *Paste*, 4/06/12.
[249] "mewithoutYou Interview," *Recoil*, April 2012.
[250] Ibid

Ten Stories would become mewithoutYou's first concept album, telling the story of a circus train that is tipped over by an elephant so the other animals can run free. Each story represents the situation in which each animal would find themselves after the crash.

"It's based on an actual event with a train crash with a menagerie, a traveling group of animals on display, sort of a circus," Aaron told Project SLC. "And somewhere in the 1800s that a train like that crashed. According to one news account I read, a tiger could have escaped and did not. It stayed in the cage. And so I thought that was a nice jumping off point to think about what all of the other animals did. Some of them escape from the cage and leave the circus, and others stay with the circus, and all have different reasons for that."[251]

Aaron continued, "Most of the animals are presenting points of views or perspectives I could relate to but didn't necessarily stand behind, you know? 'Cause, like I got to kinda express different ideas or explore different possibilities without it being this one perspective that was sorta autobiographical. So I think they're all kinda parts or things that make sense to me or different options for ways to live or things to pursue. Just the fact that I could put different ideas in different characters' mouths without having to commit to any one of them, to me, made it a little more lighthearted a project."[252]

Aaron reiterated that he was tired of trying to maintain a public persona as a guru, guide, or teacher. "I did need to have this public persona, and I don't have to live up to this false image of myself that I've being trying to put out there, if that's not the reality of the state that I'm in. It would be a great relief to say, 'I don't know, I'm sorry, I'm really a hypocrite. I'm actually a fool. And I don't know about these things I've been talking about. Please forgive me for pretending like I did or convincing myself that I did.'"[253]

"I guess I started to feel my hypocrisy to an unbearable

---

[251] "mewithoutYou Interview," *Project SLC*, 2012.
[252] Ibid
[253] "mewithoutYou interview," *Recoil*, April 2012.

extent, singing about these super lofty concepts (love and forgiveness, renouncing the world, annihilation of ego), all while on a big kind of ego trip on a stage," Aaron told *Absolute Punk*. "Something about selling tickets or CDs to hear someone sing about 'God' seems pretty off-point to me now. This has always been a muddled region to me, and I've always been conflicted about it. It's only been recently that I've been able to stop trying to reconcile the two, and say plainly that I enjoy playing music for my own sake, for selfish reasons, and that as far as I know it has nothing at all to do with God. I'm not proud of the state I'm in, not proud of my ego-motivations or desire for approval. But it is a relief to not feel the need to pretend to be something I'm not, to parade myself as any kind of teacher, or as righteous or holy in any way. I do want to be those things, but the more I examine my own thoughts, the further I feel from the ideals I've long been preaching about."[254]

When asked how he balances Sufism with Christianity in his lyrics, Aaron said, "Unfortunately, I don't really know the answer. I'm not sure I understand what I've been writing about all this time, or even my own intentions or thought processes."[255]

Aaron told me, many times he would often like a fan's interpretation of his lyrics better than his original meaning, so he would adopt it. In some ways, he didn't see the meaning of the lyrics as his, but as something everyone created together.

"I don't know everything that inspires the lyrics, probably a great big mixed bag of all sorts of things I don't understand. One change I can recognize with this latest record is a movement toward openness, of thought or of heart, I don't know, but an openness that is not so concerned with making definitive statements about the way things are but trying instead to look at them from contradictory viewpoints, and to let those contradictions exist side-by-side without clear or explicit conclusions. A recognition of my own massive, massive ignorance, maybe even a roundabout apology for years of conceit, the blind

---

[254] Jonathan Bautts, "mewithoutYou—05.22.12," *Absolute Punk*, 5/22/12.
[255] Levi Rogers, "'Ten Stories' Review, Interview with Aaron Weiss," *Levi Rogers*, 7/12/12.

uttering of bold truth-claims, the arrogance of my endless moral finger-wagging. These recent songs are my attempt to minimize that conceit, unsuccessful though it may be."[256]

"If anything it's such an unusual dynamic to be there and see all these faces looking at me, and I say, 'Well, what do I do? What do I have for them? I have nothing for them,'" Aaron said. "And so I have to say, 'Oh God, help me.'"[257]

In his interview with *Recoil*, Aaron talked about using the band as therapy. "I have seen the audiences and gone, 'Here are people who are going to listen to me and accept me in all my craziness and all my mistakes, and I can put them out there, and I have been extremely direct at times, like in our online journal when we used to keep that, or in between songs onstage, and this is going back quite some years, but I used to see it almost as a chance to vent and air my dirty laundry and to find a place that's a supporting community. But anymore I don't see so much the need for that or think that that's the best or most appropriate forum for seeking therapeutic comfort in your audience or fans or consumers or however you talk about people. There's definitely a weird power imbalance or dynamic there. Like, 'I'm onstage with a microphone, you're going to listen to me. Or I'm writing lyrics and you're buying the CD. It's sort of a one-directional communication, I guess, the way some therapy is, where you can sit on the couch and you can talk for forty-five minutes to your psychiatrist or whatever. Whoever's listening to our music, I don't want to say 'kids,' but they're a little younger, and they're not looking to bear all my burdens."[258]

Just as he no longer wanted to be upheld as a champion for the poor, he now disavowed any concern for the environment gotten from the veggie bus. "If that was our priority, we wouldn't be in a band that tours. We wouldn't have a bus. There are folks who are really turned on by that goal of sustainability and are

---

[256] Craig Taylor-Broad, "Interview: Mewithoutyou," *God is in the TV*, 4/27/12.
[257] Evan Trowbridge, "Review of mewithoutYou's Ten Stories," *Sojourners*, 9/13/12.
[258] "mewithoutYou interview," *Recoil*, April 2012.

really upset by the state of the Earth and the direction it seems that we're going, and that are devoting their lives to it, either by living off the grid or minimizing their footprint in that way, but that's not my top priority by any means. For a while I tried to put that out there, or sort of position myself as a real kind of eco-warrior or as someone who was real compassionate or caring about the Earth, and caring about the core and caring about animals, but then I had to ask myself, 'Does that have more to do with my actual concern for the Earth or the animals, or am I trying to be seen as the guy who cares about the Earth and animals and everything? If it turns out that my motivations are selfish, how much is it going to benefit? I mean, will it really benefit the Earth for me to be driving around in a bus, and then preaching to people about how we're conserving all the fossil fuels?' Meanwhile, most of our fans I know very well are driving to our shows, many times from hours away, so playing a single show will have at least a hundred or so cars that are driving. If I wanted to make a smaller footprint in earning my living, I could probably work for Exxon-Mobil. Or being a woodcutter chopping down the rainforest, or probably any other job I'd be more environmentally friendly. I guess this is a longwinded way of saying I have no right to preach to anybody."[259]

When it was pointed out that the lyrics on this album were more secular than any other album, Aaron attributed this to being in an academic environment. "Being immersed for the past four years in a secular, academic environment, it hasn't been so easy for me to fall back on my old patterns of religious talk—that sorta thing wouldn't fly, so I had to learn to bracket certain language, and to rely more on evidence and/or rational argument to prove a point, rather than scripture or charisma or emotional appeal. Learning to examine whatever 'truth claims' I might so casually make, scrutinize them for unfounded assumptions, parochialism, biases, you know what I mean."[260]

"Even if I got away from using religious language, to me

---

[259] Ibid
[260] Ibid

there are all the questions that religions wrestle with, like, 'What's the truth?' and 'What's the purpose of life?' or 'What's the right way to live?' Religion really tries to get to the core of human experience—the deepest questions we have about death and meaning and identity."[261]

"Maybe being on university campuses for the past four years has kind of had its effect on me," Aaron told *The Temple News*. "I'm more reluctant, I guess, to try to make any claims about the way things are, or try to state my position on something in any kind of definitive way. I'm really not that smart, and not that knowledgeable about those things to certainly talk about those big questions that religion tends to address. In some ways, the newest batch of songs is more modest in its scope. The big questions, so to speak, still interest me greatly, but also I thought it would be better to write about something I can understand rather than speculate about something that's way beyond me."[262]

When asked further about his current beliefs, Aaron said he considered himself a seeker. "To keep on searching, to remain a student, to stay small, humble, foolish in a sense. I've found a lot of peace in letting go of old certainties, attachments, formulas and intellectual doctrines, trying to stay open to whatever comes, and always looking for some point of wisdom or beauty or grace in every encounter. This is something Greg (our bass player) told me about, and it helps me when I can remember it."[263]

The ideas the animals hold in *Ten Stories* are both fragments of many conflicting ideas within Aaron and ideas he doesn't hold, making them the least autobiographical mewithoutYou lyrics to this point.

He told *Absolute Punk* it was easier this way because "I didn't have to worry about being consistent in any ideological sense. There was no danger of contradicting myself, because I didn't identify 'myself' with any particular character all that directly. Though each obviously represents a part of me, there was less

---

[261] "Chillin' Wit' Aaron Weiss, vocalist for mewithoutYou," *Philly.com*, 7/14/14.
[262] Alexis Sachdev, "Aaron Weiss," *The Temple News*, 4/24/12.
[263] Jonathan Bautts, "mewithoutYou—05.22.12," *Absolute Punk*, 5/22/12.

concern with sounding coherent, or wise, or good, or anything. The fox, for example, engages in some pretty fruitless (I think) speculations, which I could explore or express, but without advocating that type of behavior."[264]

Aaron explained to Yoni Wolf, "Even when I think I'm telling these stories and I have all these different characters, it's my own schizophrenia coming out. To some extent I feel connected with all of them, and I identify with each of them even though they're saying things that might be totally contradictory and incoherent when you try to put them into one character or one person, you know. I think, well, I'm not a coherent person, but I contain all these different voices."[265]

"I think Aaron is very deliberately using this album as a way to be a narrator of different characters that represent many different ways to think about those big questions," Mike told *Boulder Weekly*. "Questions like the existence of God, who we are as an individual, and what meaning we draw from our lives beyond the sort of normal, everyday, mundane, meaningless conclusions. I see this album kind of branching off a little bit more into a new area where Aaron is sort of trying to remove himself as much as he can in his own personal musings or own personal conclusions. And he's more trying to just express the various philosophers that he's read, or taking from experiences that he's had at different churches or synagogues or mosques, and expressed those ideas through characters like the elephant, tiger, rabbit, fox, or bear."[266]

Alternative Press asked Aaron about the lyrical themes on this album. "A lot of the same ideas or elements as our old songs had (faith/doubt, freedom/necessity, celibacy/desire, self-as-illusion, world/s-as-dream, unity, depravity, anthropomorphic animals/vegetables, etc.), and I think every song is about death in some way or another. This last point wasn't intentional. Probably

---

[264] Ibid
[265] Yoni Wolf, "Episode 74 Aaron Weiss (mewithoutYou)," *The Wandering Wolf*, 9/24/14.
[266] Sebastian Murdock, "Messes of mewithoutYou, Guitarist Mike Weiss gets philosophical," *Boulder Weekly*, 7/19/12.

the main difference is the regular use of different characters to present, to the best of my ability, utterly conflicting viewpoints in as sincere a way possible, typically without any explicit resolution."[267]

The lyrics on this album were influenced directly by what he was reading in school: pragmatism in American Poetry, William James, Georg Wilhelm Freidrich Hegel, William Blake, and William Butler Yates.

Absolute Punk asked Aaron about post-structuralism—the idea that words have no fixed meaning and are open to various interpretations—in "Fox's Dream of the Log Flume."

"Yeah, that's exactly what I had in mind with the 'signs/signified' line. Although I have to admit, I've read more about Derrida than from him directly. Even that idea—though I attribute it to him—I didn't actually read it from him. But the notion of making a clean break, separating our symbols or perceptions from the realities they represent or perceive, I think that goes back long before structuralism. With language this is especially pronounced, as we can obviously grow attached to certain vocabularies, which can have pretty serious consequences in our lives. As for Foucault, I've read a lot of him this past semester, but this was all after the album was finished—had only read a bit prior to our recording. Still, his sense of the person/subject as a historical construction—that 'man is an invention of recent date,' is definitely in line with a lot of our lyrics from the past three albums. The 'personhood-is-an-arbitrary-illusion' idea that keeps appearing in our songs is probably informed by this same sentiment, whatever its source. Whether we call it poststructuralist or postmodern or mysticism or something else—and whatever authors we might refer to—you're right, these are not new ideas I'm presenting."[268]

Aaron expressed a more down-to-earth agenda for being in the band. "I've always talked a big game about quitting, but it turns out I find more of my self-worth in this band than I would

---

[267] Annie Zaleski, "In The Studio: mewithoutYou," *Alternative Press*, 2/02/12.
[268] Jonathan Bautts, "mewithoutYou—05.22.12," *Absolute Punk*, 5/22/12.

have ever cared to admit—rely on the attention it provides me, to not feel like such a big loser."[269]

"I don't know what keeps us going. All different motivations I guess. Definitely the desire to be liked, to feel important and valuable. For me, definitely that back-of-my-mind fantasy of meeting an imaginary future wife. Some of us have bills to pay. Some have insatiable wanderlust. Some of us don't feel like we're good at anything else. But all that aside, we do really like playing music together, on tour or otherwise, and enjoy being with each other now more than ever. We have a special love I think."[270]

Haley Williams of Paramore contributed guest vocals to "Foxes Dream of the Log Flume" and "All Circles" while Brandon Beaver of Buried Beds contributed guitar and began touring with the band as a second guitar player.

---

[269] Luke Larsen, "Catching Up With mewithoutYou," *Paste*, 4/06/12.
[270] Craig Taylor-Broad, "Interview: Mewithoutyou," *God is in the TV*, 4/27/12.

87
Wild Goose

The Wild Goose Festival, which started the previous summer in 2011, is a festival in North Carolina gathering authors, musicians, and artists who focus on justice, spirituality, music, and the arts. Popular with the spiritual-but-not-religious crowd, this environment is welcoming to all and inviting for progressive, liberal, and emergent Christians who are deconstructing their faith. You can expect to hear messages given on issues like social justice, racism, pacifism, the environment, tolerance, and inclusivism.

While Wild Goose was just getting started, Cornerstone Festival was now in its final year. Unable to sustain the costs of running the festival, they sold the farm. A smaller festival called Audiofeed emerged in Urbana, two hours south of Chicago.

After the mewithoutYou tour, Aaron stopped at Wild Goose before heading home. He played with The Collection, singing acoustic versions of the spider songs and "Allah, Allah, Allah," "Cardiff Giant," "Bear's Vision of St. Agnes," and "East Ender's Wives," complete with fiddles, banjos, and horns.

Aaron sent me an email at the end of June:

> Just arriving back home from a tour, followed by a band errand to North Carolina and stopping by a festival there.
> Imagine Cornerstone with beer, having swapped its 'evangelical' underpinnings for those of the 'emergent' variety, and you'll have a sense of how it was. Still some CCM style 'praise & worship,' which I actually enjoyed. Trying to find the good in things.
> Feel kinda drained after so much travel and commotion. Nice to be back in Upper Darby, see mom and our cat Blizzard. The cat's lounging in a funny way after her spaying operation—ah, and right after I wrote that she jumped up with a big "WARNING" sticker (from a box fan) stuck on her

tail, running in circles and flailing around the room, apparently trying to battle and/or dislodge the thing. Wonderful, animals.

Mom says "hi" and is now hoping to use the computer. Sensible time to go. Love you.

A.[271]

---

[271] Email. 6/25/12.

88
Sometimes

While lying in bed one morning in July, a day before I was to leave for Chicago to see the band, I received a Facebook friend request from Aaron. The profile picture was his dad as a young man, smoking a pipe. Under the religious views section, Aaron chose "sometimes." I knew this account wasn't fake.

I sent him a message, and after preliminary chatting on how to use Facebook, Aaron told me he was currently online looking into PhD programs.

"About ten years ago I wanted to be a philosophy professor and looked into what that entailed," I wrote. "After the master's, it was at least 6-8 more years of school, including needing to be able to read, write, and translate in at least three different languages. Without even a credit of college to my name, I was talked out of it by other professors who came into the bookstore I worked in. 'Philosophy! Why would you do that to yourself?'"

"Ha! That sounds awfully daunting—and yes, for a path that doesn't promise much in the ways of happiness," Aaron responded. "Nevertheless, it seems you've pursued that goal in less formal/structured and expensive ways, no?"

"Well, I really wanted a doctorate in divinity/theology. Yes, a professor of God."

"You know I often have the thought, 'If there's one thing more useless than philosophy . . .' But I'll spare you that sentiment, or at least, distance us from it by quoting myself as having thought it, as opposed to actively saying it now."

"The goal was to use it in ministry and apologetics. Then I realized I could just buy the books the professors wrote and learn from them, all to come to the sad realization that most congregants really don't care at all about any of it. I like to think of theology as the study of our speculations about God."

"Yes, that makes sense, super interesting—if I had my way that's probably what I would've studied."

"I used to think it was all deduction from revealed text—like being an expert in a holy text and what it means, but I later realized there is so much creative induction required that it's more of an art—and we have no clue what we're talking about, even if it's good conversation."

"Amen."

"How are you doing? Are you ready for the road again?"

"Feeling okay. Not the happiest season of my life, but getting along—just about ready to go, yes."

"Is there something pressing or nagging or is it just a general mood or dissatisfaction?"

"Probably more the former—something nagging, which of course contributes to a general mood, makes it so smaller things bother me more than they used to."

"Ah, sexual frustration. I know exactly what you mean."

"Ha! Well, that's not entirely untrue, but not what I meant either."

"If I can be of any help, please let me know."

"Thank you. Maybe when/if I see you in Chicago we could talk a bit more about it. Nothing to worry about, and nothing I haven't mentioned to you before. But it'd be nice to talk face-to-face."

"I got a pretty dark poem from Emily a couple of weeks ago that I believe was sent to both of us. I tried to get her to call and open up about what was going on but she wasn't very open. I haven't talked with her in quite a long time so I'm not sure what's going on."

"Yes, I did receive a poem from her—saw that it was addressed to both of us. I wrote back something brief, and she replied, but that's been all. How are your thoughts these days about her?"

"Oh, goodness, might as well wait until Monday for that conversation! But in brief—I miss her, I love her, I still dream about her, and I have a very hard time dating without feeling like I'm cheating on her. She wrote, 'I miss you as well. If you were here it would be different, but we've gone there before.'"

"Fair enough, yes."

"I asked her what she was doing for the 4th and she said going with her boyfriend to see some bands and that she felt numb and ready to be hospitalized again."

"Dear Lord."

"Any girls at the school asking you out for coffee?"

"One or two, but no mutual interest."

"If you date just to date, you'll find girls. If you date to find a wife, it's a longer, more frustrating process. One I'm sorry we're both in. Very difficult when people married and single alike tell us how lucky we have it that we have complete control of our lives, money, and time, and that it's much better being single."

"Neither prospect—dating to date or dating to marry—quite sits well with me, as I'm sure you understand. Yes, I can imagine not wanting to hear that from someone who has what you might want, though surely there is something to it? By you, of course, I mean—at least to a significant extent—we."

"Yes, I loved being married. I could go down to Florida and Emily would most likely be with me again, and I'll have deep fulfillment, but life will be as horrible and unlivable as it was before because nothing has changed at a practical level. Or, I could stay safe and stable where I am now and hurt really bad without her."

"Horrible and unlivable in what ways?"

"In that she suffers from mental illness that causes her to do very hurtful things to herself and to me, things that no healthy person with self-respect would ever put up with no matter how much they love someone."

"But you've put up with the same out of me for years."

"But you've never hurt me and I don't have to live with you everyday!"

Aaron sent me a YouTube video of sacred harp shape note singing, adding that he'd been doing it every chance he gets. I countered with a video of singing puppets called "Jesus Loves the Little Racist, Stereotyped, Puppet Children."

"Holy smokes. I've never had a cigarette, but I think I need one. There's only so much flagrant insanity I can subject myself to before needing to water my garden. In this case, four minutes and four seconds worth. I've been traveling quite a bit this summer, and nothing's growing as well as last year."

"Might be more constructive than being stuck on Facebook with me."

"Well, it's good to be with you at whatever capacity—but yes, computers are obviously not my favorite means of communication."

"You too, brother. It's a bit surreal to see you here, but good to see you here as well. I have some packing and things to do myself. I'll be leaving for Chicago tomorrow and returning the 24th. Be safe and try to enjoy yourself. I'm not good at lifting burdens, but I sure hope you feel better."

"Thank you. We'll put you on the guest list for the Chicago show and count on seeing you there, L-rd willing. Thanks for spending some time with me here and for your kind words."

I teased him over his growing use of emoticons throughout his messaging, to which he responded, "You're a treasure. If there were an emoticon of a pot of gold, I'd include it here."

89
Bottom Lounge 2012

MewithoutYou was in town with Buried Beds and Kevin Devine. Arriving at Bottom Lounge a few hours early, I sat outside near the dusty, flower-painted tour bus. Aaron finally appeared, and after taking a few pictures with a fan, invited me on the bus where we spent the next two hours in conversation.

"You mentioned not being happy lately. Do you want to talk about it?" I asked.

"I really miss my dad. It's been difficult without him."

"I'm sorry. Do you think you'll make it through the tour?"

"Yeah, but I just feel like an imposter up here these days. I feel like an old man trying to sing and dance to these songs."

"No way, everything still sounds great. There's a loyal fan base who will buy anything you put out and can't wait to hear what you will write about next."

"It's not just that. I used to view myself as kind of a guru or a teacher. I took myself so seriously and went around talking about all of these things I don't even understand myself. Now I'm sorry anyone took me seriously or listened to anything I had to say over the years. I don't have anything to say to anyone anymore. I can sing alright and I can dance, I'm just sorry I thought I was ever anything more than an entertainer."

"I think about how talented and charming you are, how you get to be in a band and travel, touch people's lives and leave a legacy, and I get jealous because I'm not that talented and can't do this. I read your lyrics and they're so good it makes me angry. I'm stuck where I am, often unable to leave my apartment, or I'm sitting at the park with a book, looking at trees. I'm not doing anything significant."

"I travel and play these shows, but like most jobs, I have to be there at a certain time every night to punch in, ready to perform, whether I feel like it or not, whether the guys and I are getting along or not. Lots of times I'm detached from anything I'm singing about. And you know how much I loathe having to come up with lyrics and being critiqued. It's a cool job to have, being in a band, but it's just a job, and it hasn't made me any happier. I'd love to be where you are, able to just sit in a park and look at trees."

Greg came to the bus and told Aaron it was show time. Aaron walked me into the venue, told me he loved me, and gave me a long hug goodbye, then disappeared through a door next to the stage. A few minutes later he emerged on the stage with a bag full of instruments to the cheers of fans. He was no longer my friend Aaron, but Aaron Weiss of mewithoutYou, and I was no longer his friend Paul, but a fan among many, who let ourselves be charmed again as soon as Mike opened the show with the riff to "February 1878."

7/15/12
Email to Aaron

Aaron.

Thank you for your time and kindness yesterday before and during the show. My brother showed up after work to get me around the beginning of "Torches Together", so about six songs in, and was kind enough to take "the long way" there so I could see a few more songs, though he had somewhere to be at midnight. His request, if you are going to learn any new Dylan songs, is "Tangled Up in Blue."

You guys sounded great from where I was standing. Rickie is fun to watch, the songs have much more power live. I was sad to find that I left before you guys performed "Fox's Dream of the Log Flume."

A few things I wanted to add to our conversation:

1) I feel exactly the way you do about getting older, unattractive, and worrying about appearance. I have a receding hairline, wrinkle lines are setting in, I have a belly that's hard to get rid of, I'm balding on top, etc. But I can say you're definitely still young, handsome, and have nothing to worry about. Everyone in the band has gotten older and (hopefully) more mature. Don't feel out of place on stage, you've earned your platform over a decade, and there's no lack of interest or relevance either in your lyrics or your song writing.

2) "Julian the Onion" is brilliant. *If he so much as skinned his knee, the entire schoolhouse moved to tears.* Too funny. I can really see the labor you put into the lyrics on this album. Even in rejecting the identity of a guru, you still have a lot of beautiful things to say.

3) I feel like I dominated the conversation. I'm sorry. It's a habit I've had for quite a long time. My mom often tells me I hold people hostage in conversation by "going on and on and on."

Off to the museum in a minute. My heart is full from seeing you again, but my body is in horrible pain. So I'll carry both with me today.

Also, what's this Ireland talk I'm hearing about? Is this about a girl?

Love you so much, brother. More soon,
Paul

7/31/12
Email from Aaron

Dear brother,

Peace to you and thank you for writing again, and for your kindness, both in our last meeting and your email below.

Yes, "Tangled Up in Blue" is a good one—the only song I recognized when I saw Dylan live, definitely the highlight of the show.

I'm sorry to hear you can relate to my insecurities re: aging. Though for what it's worth, I can certainly reciprocate your reassurances—you still being young, looking handsome, having nothing at all to worry about. That being said, and whatever we are now, there will come a time that neither of us will be young or handsome, and my hope is we can find a way to remain in non-worry even then; stop identifying so strongly with this one body. Easier said than done, maybe.

No need to worry about "dominating the conversation" a couple of weeks back. I like listening to you, inevitably learn a great deal. Re: your mom's comment about holding people hostage, I feel guilty of the very same thing, and so recently have tried to keep my talking to a minimum—ready to answer questions if anyone cares to ask, but increasingly reluctant to insert myself into someone else's mental space—almost a form of trespassing. In our case, you and me talking, you can tell me anything, and though I am a bit concerned that you seem to me somewhat—well, I won't say pessimistic or cynical or bleak—but, hmm...

You are very smart you know, a good critical thinker, and that can be difficult. Difficult for others to follow along, difficult for you to feel the need to analyze and understand everything intellectually. And I think there is a way of leaving room for optimistic interpretations of our worlds that is not flagrantly dishonest or willfully ignorant.

Greg sometimes says "all is grace," and though I'll spare you the religious language, I'd like to suggest that we do have considerable power over the meanings we make of our lives, even circumstances far beyond our control. We have a certain control over them in this meaning-making respect.

And no, believe it or not, my trip to Ireland was not about a girl—just accompanying an old friend, Shane Claiborne, to a speaking engagement there, (all expenses paid). Just a couple days long, a beautiful trip overall, but nothing to do with a girl.

Now, my trip last week to Idaho on a day off from tour—that is a different matter.

All my love dear brother. Miss & adore you.

Aaron W.

8/17/12
Email to Aaron

Aaron,

Did I come across as less than optimistic in our conversation? What do you suggest, specifically? If you could give me a makeover, what changes would you make?

I am going to visit a friend (a girl!) in Virginia the week of October 14th and would love to make a connecting trip to Philadelphia the week of the 21st for a few days. Is your schedule open? Can I stay with you? You will neither have to feed me nor save my life this time, nor will I need your bed. Don't let me impose if your schedule is full.

Love you, brother,

Paul

8/30/12
Email from Aaron

Hello dear friend,

Sorry to be slow in responding. I was on tour without computer and then the young lady I mentioned earlier (Kaysha, from Idaho) flew out for the end of the tour, we left for a road trip ASAP after tour, (on a motorcycle purchased for the very occasion).

OF COURSE you know you're entirely welcome here any time I'm around.

Super exciting, man—will be great to see you again. Might have a bit on my plate during your stay in terms of school work, but will surely be able to pry myself away from it long enough or often enough that we'll have some solid time together.

You asked if I could give you "a makeover" what would I do? I am reluctant to answer such a question, in the state I'm in, though when we get together next maybe we can explore the matter in a mutual way. I obviously have nothing to improve in you, let alone fix, but when we meet up maybe we will both improve in some way. I like this, being eager to examine ourselves and grow, but let's see.

Love you too and excited to see you again brother,

A.

90
Kaysha

Aaron met Kaysha in Boise, Idaho on July 21st while playing Lord of the Rings pinball in a movie theater arcade while on tour. Aaron felt immediately drawn to her.

Right after the tour, Aaron bought a motorcycle and went to see her, beginning a number of visits throughout the summer. "Just returned from Idaho again, where I was visiting my 'girlfriend,' dear Lord help us," he wrote.

But with dating came the insecurity of being evaluated. Some surrounding Kaysha thought Aaron was a good enough guy, but others questioned just how strong a Christian he was, picking apart his theology, advising her to pass on him and find someone more doctrinally correct.

Aaron and Kaysha were coming to the crucial point of deciding whether to take their relationship to the next level and she move to Philadelphia, or decide not to go forward.

In this state of being evaluated, Aaron began to lose his peace, stuck in a limbo with rejection looming. While he once thought Amanda wasn't Christian enough for him, Aaron was now on the receiving end of this same criticism from those surrounding Kaysha.

91
Trinity of Desire (Pt. 2)

The previous summer, Natalie met a man and began a relationship with him. Still, she struggled to let him in, and this was because of the guilt she felt over me.

She finally saw a spiritually intuitive friend who told her that God once had a path for us, but that path is over. We would be friends for the rest of our lives, but she needed to open to this man's love now.

Any time she felt drawn to me, I steered her back to him. By all accounts, he was a good man, a good friend, patient and loving, and a great partner for her. He was foreign, fit, fashionable, a creative and talented musician, he was driven, he brought out the best in her, and he could give her a life I couldn't. He sounded exactly like what she was looking for.

She felt she was missing a spiritual connection with him that she had with me. I reminded her that for a decade now she had not been able to pull the trigger with me. She never found me attractive enough to move in my direction, and that was okay. She would always have me in her life, and our spiritual connection would always be there.

The following year, she accepted her boyfriend's proposal and married him.

I still loved and missed Emily. Her relationship fell apart with the man she had been living with and she ended up back in the hospital.

We talked about the possibility of getting back together somehow, but she was clear that she would be meeting men as soon as she got out of the hospital and couldn't build something with me long distance. "You know I can't be alone."

I turned my attention to Sarah in Virginia, whom I'd known for seven years. Sarah was so pretty, every time she posted new pictures of herself online, I had to close my laptop and go for a walk.

She became my muse as I unsuccessfully tried to capture her in drawings. I fantasized what it might be like to be with her, idealizing our life together. She loved art and books and coffeehouses and photography and nature. She suffered from fibromyalgia, just as I did. I thought we'd be great together, but she was also a tortured soul with many demons to overcome.

Visiting her would give me the opportunity not only to get out of Galena, where I felt mostly confined to a bed for almost two years, but it would give me a chance to forfeit my idealization, spend time with her, and see if in fact there was a chance we might have a spark.

I planned my vacation so that I would take the Greyhound to see her, then head up to Philadelphia to see Aaron. I knew this would be near impossible with my health in the shape it was in, but I needed to get away for the sake of my heart.

Just days before I was to get on the bus, Sarah informed me that she now had a boyfriend.

"Really? You weren't at all interested in seeing if we had a chemistry?" I asked.

"While I would like to think I am an open-minded person, I have never entertained the notion that we could possibly be a couple. I've only ever viewed you on a friendship level," she said. Still, I made the long trip to Virginia.

She took me out for barbeque and sushi, chicken wings and live music, we baked cookies and had great conversation, we visited a messianic Jewish bagel shop and a bookstore. I went with her to work at an artisan center, and every time she looked at me and smiled, I melted. We drove around looking at the autumn colors, shared an amazing sunset, and I wished the whole time we could be together. By the end of the week, it was exhausting trying to keep my feelings in check. I was relieved to be on the bus to Philadelphia.

Between Natalie, Emily, and Sarah, I felt like Aaron years back, wanting to pull out a ring and ask, "Will ANY of you marry me?"

92
Upper Darby (Pt. 2)

"Hey, I know this guy!" I recognized Aaron's voice behind me as I stood outside the Greyhound station. I turned around and there he was, smiling big, sporting his sideburns and mustache. He hugged me.

"How are you, brother?" I asked.

"Oh, what can I say, Paul?"

"You don't have to say anything, man."

Aaron groaned deeply. "Maybe a few groans and sighs will suffice."

"I've been up for twenty-four hours, so I might be a little bit ripe," I said, my pits stinking.

"Oh, wow, I've been down for thirty-three years."

"You look, good, man."

"Well, you too. Welcome to Philly."

We walked around the corner to the parking lot where a motorcycle sat with a backpack and two helmets on the back. Under the impression that he would borrow his mom's car to pick me up, I wasn't expecting this. "I bought it because I thought it would make me look cool, but then I found that it was a lot of fun."

Aaron suggested that we walk a few blocks down to the Reading Terminal Market. Established in 1892, it's America's oldest continually operating farmer's market. A bazaar of over eighty vendors and thousands of patrons overwhelmed us as we walked in the door. It was so crowded this Saturday afternoon that there was hardly room to walk. Buzzing with noise and energy, there were long lines and tables filled with people buying and eating seafood, Thai cuisine, barbeque, Amish meats, poultries, baked goods, cheese steaks, and just about anything else you can imagine.

"If you see something you like and you want to stop, just say something," Aaron said, making his way to one of the many trash cans. "Old habits die hard," he added and began rummaging. "Not everyone is finishing their food today."

He opened a Styrofoam container from the trash that still had macaroni and fish in it. He enjoyed his meal while I continued to browse the market.

Being tired from traveling and overwhelmed with the enormity of this place, I suggested that we go somewhere a little more simple and quiet.

"I can take you to one of my favorite pizza places—it's called Allegro Pizza," Aaron suggested. "Is there anything you wanted to see while you are here this week?"

"No, man. I just want to spend time with you and your mom, maybe revisit some of the places you showed me last time I was here. Do you know of any used bookstores we could browse?"

"As a matter of fact, there's a good one right by the pizza place we're going to."

We headed back to his bike, strapped my belongings on with the bungee cords, donned our helmets, and headed off.

BOOKS NEW & USED said the sign in the garden as we pulled up to a gorgeous brick building. The stairs leading to the doorway were lined with boxes of closeout books. We had to step over a squirrel gate to enter the bookstore.

Once inside, every wall, room, window sill, and nook was filled with books, seemingly from floor to ceiling. Every space was utilized. The woman behind the register found herself boxed in by stacks of books surrounding her. Even the stairs to the second floor, which housed the philosophy and religion books, were stacked with piles of books. If heaven could be experienced in the here-and-now, this was it.

While browsing, I came across *Rapture Ready! Adventures in the Parallel Universe of Christian Pop Culture* by Daniel Radosh. I turned to Aaron. "I think there's an interview with you in this book."

"I heard a rumor to that effect."

"Let's read what you had to say."

After finding the pages containing his interview, I handed him the book and continued to browse.

I came back a few minutes later, wondering if the interview was truthful and up to par.

"That, I don't know," Aaron said, "but it's flattering so far."

"So, did you say anything you regret?"

"No, I'm pretty happy with what I said. Sometimes I regret everything I say, but at least it's clever."

Aaron moved on to flip through a stack of Frederick Nietzsche books he had selected, exuberantly reading quotes aloud. "I've been on this Nietzsche kick lately." He picked out *A Nietzsche Reader,* and we headed downstairs to make the purchase.

"You better ask for a brown paper bag for that, brother. You don't want anyone on the streets to see you with it," I teased.

"Oh, quite the contrary!" He refused the bag and put the paperback in his jacket pocket.

We walked down the block to Allegro and ordered our pizza. Once outside with our slices and one cup of soda (Aaron insisted we share to avoid paying for two cups), he couldn't help himself and peeked quickly through the trash.

"No luck?" I asked, as he came back to the table empty-handed.

"No trash. Luck, but no trash." He sat down and bit into his slice after loading it with spices.

"Well, I'm glad to see that after your visit to Idaho you are still with Kaysha," I began.

"I'm not out of the woods yet," he cautioned.

"Oh boy."

"What did Dostoyevsky say? 'People love the fall of the righteous man and his disgrace.'" He smiled.

"Uh-oh, did you have sex?"

"No, we're still safe there. Let's just say there are a couple of songs I can't sing anymore. The tweaks might be easy to make. I can just say, 'In the past fifteen years there are only *two* girls I kissed.' After a long pause he added, "Then again, that's not me. That's a talking bear."

We laughed.

"This girl is so beautiful it's sickening. She's drop-dead gorgeous. I bought this motorcycle so we could take a road trip, and we had a blast. When we are together, everything is great. But after she goes home and we are apart for a week or so, she starts to have her doubts."

"Did you ever wipe out with her on the bike?"

"Only once, but there weren't any major injuries."

"Well, no wonder she has her doubts."

"The irony is I broke up with Amanda because she wasn't Christian enough. Now Kaysha might break up with me because I'm not Christian enough. Half of her friends at church think I'm worth it, and the other half think I'm a heretic. Her family is still on the fence."

"Do you fear she will dig around online and find your interviews to size you up and see if your theology is kosher?"

"There's certainly enough out there to incriminate me if she's looking for it."

He took a more serious tone. "I don't have any peace. This anxiety has been a nightmare. I was content and so much happier when all I had was God. I'm trying to find that peace again, but if she doesn't call for one night, I'm a mess, thinking she decided to end it and stay in Idaho."

"I was just in Virginia with Sarah. I had a crush on her for a long time, but she told me right before the trip that she was with someone and didn't see anything happening between us. The entire week was a roller coaster of emotions. When we went out, I wished we were on a date. The dinners, the live music, the autumn trees, the sunset. All I kept thinking was that I wanted to be with her, wondering why she didn't find me attractive, checking myself in the mirror to make sure my hair was okay and there was nothing stuck between my teeth. I kept trying to make an impression, maybe impress her with deep conversation. It was horrible. When I'm not interested in anyone, I have none of this anxiety."

"I tried to impress Kaysha with philosophy and theology too, trying to sound deep and insightful," he said with a smile.

"Sarah was in love with a guy who moved all the way from Alabama to be with her, and after a short while, she sent him back home. When I asked her why, she joked, 'I didn't like the way he did the dishes.'"

"Do you remember me saying you seemed to focus on the negative, and maybe when you got here we could help each other out? You're telling me your whole week was ruined by the anxiety of this girl not being attracted to you. That's all you see. What I hear is that you had an amazing week with a girl and enjoyed good conversation, good food, music, and nature. Think of how lucky you are to have experienced that. Think about how wonderful a particular flower or tree was, or how good the food was, or how good it was to have her company."

"Do you ever look at your face in the mirror and say, 'I'm a good-looking guy, I'm fashionable, I'm in a successful band, I'm a teacher and a PhD candidate, I have depth, I'm creative, I'm passionate, and girls all over the world adore me. Why am I still single?'"

"Man, I can't even look at my face in the mirror. My hair is thinning. I wear a hat everywhere I go now. I used to think I was so fashionable and so good-looking. I sometimes see these old videos of myself on YouTube and I can't watch them because it's too self-indulgent. All I see is this conceited little prick who thinks he's the greatest thing in the world. Other times I see someone who's a know-it-all, taking himself too seriously, thinking he's some kind of a wise guru who can bring the sheep into the fold. Even when I dressed from the trash, I was very particular and meticulous about the look I chose. I made sure everything was just so. I have a compulsion to save food from the trash, and I masked it in these lofty ideals of being concerned for the poor and exposing waste and greed. I'm just sorry I took myself so seriously and led anyone else to think I had answers for them. It all seems like such a blur sometimes."

After finishing our pizza, we got back on his bike and started towards his mom's house.

"What does your mom like to be called these days? Elizabeth? Bitsy?" I asked through the ear hole in Aaron's helmet, over the motor and the wind.

"Well, you can ask her, but she has been going by Aziza these days."

"I just remembered, your mom read the section in my book where I called her place a dump. I hope she doesn't remember that."

"Funny you should bring that up. She was cleaning the house and changing the sheets on my bed for you just before I left to pick you up. She said, 'If I remember correctly, Paul has a particular fondness for cleanliness.'"

"Oh no!" I laughed. "I'll apologize first thing when I see her."

Upon walking into their home, I was greeted warmly by Aziza. "You look good! Your demeanor is much more relaxed. You look much healthier than before," she said.

The moment I sat down, their cat Blizzard jumped into my lap, purring loudly.

"Well, I'm not suicidal anymore, so it's nice to visit and be in my right mind this time."

I got right to my apology. "The place looks great. Thanks so much for letting me stay again. I want to apologize for calling your home a dump in the book. It's not that it was a dump. It just that Upper Darby wasn't any better than Bridgeport, is what I was getting at, but I'm a terrible writer."

"Oh, I had a good laugh, I wasn't offended in the least." She smiled, waving her hand.

She took me upstairs to Aaron's room to show me where I'd be sleeping and gave me a stack of towels. The medicine cabinet in the bathroom was open. "Make sure you leave the mirrors open," she cautioned. "Aaron doesn't like to look at his face in the mirror."

When I came back downstairs, Aaron was playing "The River" by Bruce Springsteen on the piano. Every morning and night for the rest of my stay, he sang songs and played music, whether it was "Don't Think Twice It's Alright" by Bob Dylan, "Take Me Home, Country Roads" by John Denver, "(Sittin' On) The Dock Of The Bay" by Otis Redding, "Hurt" by Johnny Cash, "Let It Be," and "You've Got To Hide Your Love Away" by the Beatles, or various hymns.

"Aw man, this is why I find it hard to get schoolwork done, having a guitar and piano. It's all I want to do. I sit down to do schoolwork, I think I gotta' sing another song."

Aziza had coupons for free Blizzards at Dairy Queen. Eager to use them a few days previous, she waited for me so we could all go together. She suggested that I sign up for my own coupon and print it out before we go.

Aaron went to Dairy Queen's website and typed in my information. "Last name: *Harrison*. First name: *Saul*. "Given that you deconverted and are now an atheist, we'll call you Saul until you fall off your horse again."[272]

As we put on our coats, Aaron opened an ottoman filled with scarves and various hats he'd worn onstage over the years. Decked in hats and scarves, coupons in hand, we headed out for pumpkin and Heath Blizzards.

On the way there, Aaron pointed out Upper Darby High School as we passed. On the other side of the street was a cemetery. "I have a joke where I point to one side of the street and say, 'That's where I went,' and then I point to the other side and say, 'And that's where I'm going.'"

As Aaron drove, recordings of Bawa played in the car. I asked Aziza what we were listening to.

"This is Bawa Muhaiyaddeen—Radhiallahu 'anhu, may God be pleased with him—explaining how to pray in the early morning, citing from the Koran. This surah is called the Suratul Ikhlas, the Surah of Purity."[273]

"This was recorded before I was born, in the early seventies?"

"You were still in the world of souls at that time."

When we got back, their cat Blizzard had escaped, but another cat, Emma, came in and was just as friendly. "Bawa used

---

[272] A reference to Saul, who persecuted and killed Christians. He was transformed when Jesus appeared to him and he fell off of his horse and his name was changed to Paul.
[273] "Say: 'He is Allah, the One and Only! Allah, the Eternal, Absolute; He begetteth not nor is He begotten. And there is none like unto Him.'" (Holy Qur'an 112:1-4) This is the surah Aaron said years back he would not recite because it denies that Jesus is the Son of God. It is often used by Christians to point out one of the stark differences between Christianity and Islam.

to say that the whole world is in a cat's eyes," Aziza shared, taking off her coat. "So when they close them, they think no one is watching."

We spent the rest of the evening reading Kierkegaard quotes and talking philosophy and relationships, like we did when I visited before.

"I'm sorry I invited you here all those years back and thought I had what you needed or knew how to help you in any way," Aaron said.

"Aw man, you were standing right there in the kitchen when you told me you loved me, you were glad I was here, and glad I hadn't killed myself. That did it, so thank you." I held back tears.

In spite of our changing worldviews and shifting theological viewpoints over the years, we stood by our love for one another.

93
The Fellowship

"I was thinking of going to the Bawa Muhaiyaddeen fellowship this morning. Does that sound like something you'd be interested in?" Aaron asked.

The choice was between that or a church, and I'd never been to the fellowship, so I said yes. We took the motorcycle.

Before going in, Aaron took me around back and showed me the beautifully ornamented mosque built on the property.

As we entered the fellowship, we took off our shoes and left our helmets in the entryway. A small congregation was seated before a screen, watching a message from Bawa already in progress. We sat near the back, next to the kitchen, where food was being prepared and dishes washed in preparation for the end of the service.

When the video of Bawa finished playing, the president of the fellowship, Emanuel Levin, also known as Musa Muhaiyaddeen, sat on the platform to give a message.

He opened by telling the story of a woman who had met Bawa, wanting him to read her palm. "Tell me what I will become? What will be my title?" she asked. In wanting to know her future, she was anxious about her identity.

This was a worry Musa implored the congregation to let go of. Reality, he said, is the non-elemental, defined in the qualities or attributes of God. "Reality is when nothing the world throws at us affects us. The elemental world is not real—it changes and disappears. Only God is real, he never changes. Anticipation and destiny cause worry, creating volcanoes and storms both on the outside and the inside because this caring about what we become depends upon our attachment to the results."

He continued, "No matter what, we are all right here, right now, in this moment. We are either attached to the desire-dream egocentric self, or we understand that there is a mystery beyond that."

Instead of worrying, he offered, we should find rest in God. "Let go and let the quality of God flow through you. Don't hold on to anything. Let go. Stop thinking. Don't explore with reasons and thoughts, just rest and become still in these qualities. When you are engulfed by the qualities of God, you are at the center of the universe and cannot be disturbed by the commotions of the world."

He encouraged the congregants not to be monks who escape the world. We are to be in the world—though not of the world—with the qualities of God. He concluded his message encouraging us to continue to expand and grow. We are all works in progress. When we think we've arrived, have all the answers, and are godlike, we are deceiving ourselves.

After ending with a song, the kitchen opened and we lined up for spiced rice, vegetables, and bread. Once we sat back down, I asked Aaron if this seemed a bit too much like a personality cult.

"It seems Bawa's name is on everything. His books and tapes are for sale, his pictures are everywhere, we watched a video of him speaking, and he was quoted in the message. His room upstairs is like a museum or a holy place. I noticed there were numerous pictures of him in your mom's house. Why such an intense focus on him instead of God?"

"You know," Aaron started, and I sensed a twinge of frustration, "you ask these very pointed, rational questions, but what can the intellect say but that there is nothing beyond the intellect? Intellect isn't bad—it's just doing what it does. But it's like the eyes saying nothing exists but what the eyes can see. I've grown suspicious of people who begrudge absurdity. Not everything that's real is reasonable or logical."

As I would learn with Sufism, though there are general principles, every fellowship is different, every guru is different, and the beliefs of the congregants are unique to each individual. Direct answers to specific questions are hard to come by. "I've never met a group of people with more diverse views than the people here," Aaron said.

I wasn't familiar with the concept of a guru representing an enlightened being you are supposed to devote yourself to so he could show you the path to God.

A couple of years later, in a podcast interview with Yoni Wolf, Aaron discussed the difficulties in understanding what Sufism is, what its relation to Islam is, and what Bawa taught. Because Bawa didn't write his own books—they were transcriptions of his spoken messages—it was hard to systematize him.

"If you go to the fellowship today," Aaron shared, "there's a lot of folks there who don't even read the Koran or have a Koran or consider themselves Muslims, but they are Sufis without Islam. There's a mosque there on the premises and a lot of people will— say, more orthodox-leaning Muslims would—go to the mosque but not go to the fellowship house. And then there's a lot of folks of who either live at or go to the fellowship house who would never step foot in the mosque. And then there are some folks who manage to reconcile the two. But if you read the Koran, and in my experience with more orthodox or conservative Islam, it's unrecognizable. When you read Bawa's teachings, he claims that it's based on what he would call the inner meanings of the Koran, but it's almost unrecognizable."[274]

Aaron continued, "It's hard for me to understand Bawa because I feel like I'm so close to him . . . but it's hard for me to step back and look at him sort of sociologically, or look at where he came from and how he might have just melded these different religions together and brought a new philosophy. He just kind of feels like my friend and I guess my grandfather or someone who's always with me. I wouldn't even exist without him. He's the one who married my parents together, and all of my upbringing was just so steeped in him and his teachings."[275]

"So you've looked to his teachings more than you do Muhammad?" Yoni asked.

"Oh, yeah. I mean, I'm reading the Koran for an academic purpose. I'm doing a project in my school on Islam, and I'm trying to understand it more in its kinda global, orthodox—with a lower-

---

[274] Yoni Wolf, "Episode 74 Aaron Weiss (mewithoutYou)," *The Wandering Wolf*, 9/24/14.
[275] Ibid

case 'o,' I mean—it's kinda more mainstream context. But even with Muhammad, there is such a disparity between the version of Muhammad that Bawa presents and the version of Muhammad that you either get from the Koran or historically. I mean, according to Bawa and some of his disciples, Muhammad wasn't even a person . . . but it's more a state of consciousness that you reach, or it's like a level within all of us that we can tap into."[276]

This idea that God is within us all and can be tapped into is no doubt the influence of Eastern philosophy on Bawa, perhaps from when he was a Hindu guru in India, showing just how eclectic and idiosyncratic his teachings are.

"Believe me, I definitely don't speak for Islam," Aaron continued. "I don't even speak for Sufism because even that is so varied that, you know, you talk to a thousand different Sufis, you probably get a thousand different interpretations. And I don't even speak for Bawa's brand of Sufism, because even within the fellowship you get probably two hundred significantly different versions of what he was really about. But I have my takeaway from him, and so I'm gonna process all that."[277]

"Was it cultish, sort of?" Yoni asked, just as I did.

Aaron shook his head yes, saying any religious community that is small and irregular enough could be considered a cult, but he meant "cult" in an endearing way.

Now back at the entryway of the Sufi fellowship, we put our shoes back on. Once we got out to the bike, I realized I'd left my helmet inside.

"Better go back in and get it. You'll need that," Aaron ribbed me. "Precious cargo up there." He pointed to my vulnerable head. "We wouldn't want you to have to start using your intuition."

---

[276] Ibid
[277] Ibid

94
The Farm

When we got home from the fellowship, Aziza was outside pruning the flowers in her front garden. She clipped a handful of roses while Emma rolled around on the concrete path, clawing the bushes and chewing on stems.

"We are going to visit Elliott today at the Bawa Farm," Aziza said. "Bawa's ashram is also there. You're welcome to come with us. It's a beautiful place."

Aaron was tired and had fallen behind in grading papers because he was up late talking with me and playing music when not on the phone with Kaysha. He brought his paperwork with him in hopes of making progress during the hour-long drive.

The church across the street was letting out as we got in the car. I noticed a sign directly in front of the building reserving that parking spot for deacons only. "Did you ever say anything to them about that sign?" I asked Aaron.

"No, but I once left a note on a minister's fancy car at another church telling him we aren't called to be big shots. I left my contact information and went away on tour, but as far as I can tell, he never called."

The autumn trees exploded with color against lush green foliage and blue sky as we drove to the farm. We passed a number of farms and Pennsylvania Amish buggies. Aaron fell asleep in the back seat with his laptop and papers on his lap.

We finally arrived and exited the car to the sun peeking through the trees in picturesque beauty. On our way to the welcoming center, we passed an outdoor mosque, a hardwood porch lined with ornamented rugs. "When I visit, I like to do my salat there," Aaron said, and excused himself to pray.

Aziza and I made our way to the welcoming center, which was filled with vegetarian meals, mainly of spiced rice and beans. There was also tea, coffee, cookies, pastries, and sodas. No meat was allowed.

I was enamored with the display of Bawa's books for sale, including *My Love You My Children*, which was a big influence on the lyrics of the *It's All Crazy* songs.

Aaron went to Elliot's grave first. When Aaron returned, I walked with Aziza to the burial site where wooden stakes protruded from the ground with white name tags stapled to them. Once we found the one with Elliott's name on it, I walked away to give Aziza her privacy with him.

I walked over to the domed mazar, which housed Bawa's body. Aziza returned from Elliott's grave and met me there, asking me if I wanted to go in. We took our shoes off and entered. The ornamented casket in the center of the room sparkled. There were folding chairs lining the walls and stacks of books in small bookcases. A few people sat in silence facing Bawa. The light of the sun beamed down from a high window as Aziza sat in silence on the carpet before him.

I thought this would be a good time to see Elliott. I put on my shoes and made my way to his grave marker.

"Hi, Elliott. Funny meeting you under these conditions," I said, trying to be humorous. I imagined him not sick or sad anymore. "Thank you for inviting me to your Christmas party and letting me stay in your home years back. It saved my life. Honestly, I was afraid of you. I have no idea the amount of suffering you've endured in so many ways in your life, but I hope you are better now. You have a wonderful wife and two fine boys you should be proud of. They've touched the world in so many ways. Without them, I'm not sure I'd be here. Thank you for them."

We all met at the welcoming center to eat.

95
The Dump

After leaving the farm and making our way to the Quaker church for shape note singing, we passed a warehouse-sized furniture store called The Dump.
"What do they sell there?" I asked.
Aaron leaned forward from the back seat. "It's just like my mom's house, only bigger."

96
Sacred Harp

With just a hint of sunlight left on the horizon, we made it to the old Quaker house in Douglassville. Built in 1759, it retained its charm.

"Now explain to me what we're doing again," I asked Aaron as we got out of the car.

He showed me his Sacred Harp hymnal. "They take turns choosing a song, which one you're gonna sing, and everybody turns to that page. They sing through the song first by singing the shapes of the notes that are written, so there are four different shapes—a rectangle, a triangle, a diamond, and a circle—and each one has a different sound that corresponds to it."

Aziza added that people are seated in sections according to what types of voices they have. I told her I'd just observe this time.

There were a dozen people or so seated in a small area of benches arranged in a square. The person choosing the song got up and stood in the center. I sat behind Aaron, next to a woman with a large dog sleeping at her feet. She was eager to teach me how to sing the notes in between each song, but I still didn't get it.

Aaron chose a hymn called "At Rest" one of the few times he had the floor.

After a few rounds with a break in between for cider and cake, the woman next to me ended with one I might find easy: "Amazing Grace." As she began, her dog woke up and began howling along. Aaron reached back and pet it, perhaps hoping to distract it.

I looked through some of the Quaker pamphlets up front. One emphasized that God is the Light Within, and that this inner-light of direct revelation from God in a mystical sense meant more than institution, theology, and doctrine. The Religious Society of Friends are pacifists. As the Exeter Friends Meeting pamphlet stated:

As Friends we do not subscribe to a written creed, we emphasize testimonies, a common set of deeply held, historically rooted attitudes and behaviors of living in the world. For more than three hundred years Friends have acted upon sacred concerns and today continue to act on concerns and underlying beliefs similar to those of past generations. Some of these are: equality, simplicity, integrity, social justice, peace, stewardship.

As I looked through the small library of books, I noticed there were some liberal Christian authors such as Bishop John Shelby Spong and John Dominic Crossan and Marcus Borg of the Jesus Seminar, like Matthew Putman and I used to read. And of course, what would a Quaker library be without George Fox?

Once home, Aaron excused himself and went upstairs to his room to pray while I stayed downstairs talking with Aziza. He came back down half an hour later, and in an outpouring of affection, hugged his mom. "I love you," he said. He then came and embraced me, telling me the same.

"You missed it—I converted your mom to Christianity while you were up there, and it only took me five minutes! I don't know why it was so difficult for you to do all these years."

They gave each other reassuring smiles at the impossibility of such a notion. Aaron didn't believe me for a second.

97
Temple

Aaron invited me to sit in on his philosophy class with him and spend the day with him at Temple University.

Before we went, we thought it was a good idea to make breakfast. We scrambled eggs and added cheddar cheese, green bell peppers, spinach, mustard leaves, and beet greens we got from his rooftop garden. We placed the eggs on toasted English muffins and topped them with Sriracha.

Once we got on the train, Aaron began reading aloud from his textbook, *Oneself as Another* by Paul Ricoeur. We discussed that people observe events, but being products of nature, people are events, so nature is observing itself.

Aaron liked that his professor, Joseph Margolis, pointed out that the whole debate between free will and determinism—whether nature is acting through us or we're acting on nature—is itself a historical artifact and a cultural development, so he expects no hard answers and has an informality about it.

"It's truth trapped in language and culturally relative contexts," I said.

"Oh, he's a relativist, through and through."

Once we arrived on the campus grounds, I offered to wear a sign that said THE END IS COMING to start some trouble. Aaron said it would take more than that to get attention as some street preachers attack certain behaviors and get lit cigarettes flicked at them.

Right on cue, we ran into a street preacher.

"Nothing like religion and politics. You don't see that happening at culinary school over how to cook meat correctly," I said.

"No, the steaks are lower there," Aaron punned.

We began a mock heated debate with dueling cookbooks instead of holy books, filled with terrible puns I can't remember.

We sat in small, cramped desks in a room that held perhaps

twenty people as Dr. Joseph Margolis began his lecture. Confirming what Aaron and I were talking about on the train, Margolis explained that causality isn't enough to explain human nature, and that it's difficult to formulate a theory of human agent and personhood. We could only detect action, but not motive.

The lecture was getting dry and difficult to follow, so I started drawing a picture of a Teenage Mutant Ninja Turtle on my notes. Aaron, sitting to my right, tapped my foot and shoved his class notes to the edge of his desk. It was a mostly blank sheet of paper with two words at the bottom: FUCK THIS.

I tried hard to hold in my laughter so as not to interrupt the lecture and get kicked out.

Margolis ended the class discussion by saying, "I think we've gone about this in a very strenuous way."

No shit, I thought, looking at my drawing.

After class let out and we made our way to the elevator, Aaron said, "Now I know what Kaysha must feel like having to listen to me go on all the time."

We went to an area on the roof with a nice view of the city where I asked him about his class notes. "I thought the lecture was getting a little dry myself."

"Oh, that wasn't about the lecture. It's all the anxiety and insecurity I have over this relationship and how much peace has been taken from me. It's taking everything in me not to call her and end it right now just to get my peace back. Everything was easier when all I had was God."

While waiting for the train to head home, Aaron managed to find some pizza crust, cheese sauce, potato chips, and a drink while hunting through just a few trash bins around the campus.

We discussed marriage once we got on the train and sat down, and I told him it was definitely worth it. For all that had gone wrong in mine, I also had the most wonderful experiences in my life being married to Emily.

"Have you ever considered the idea that you weren't really married?" Aaron asked.

"I did. There were enough qualifications there and we didn't legalize it. But I meant my vows, so in my heart, yes, we were married. My friends will say things like, 'Be glad that bitch is gone,' and I don't like when people talk that way about her. She was my wife—I loved her."

I started to cry. "I'm sorry." Before I could even finish my apology, Aaron had tears rolling down his face. He reached over and hugged me.

Once we got back to Upper Darby, he suggested a hoagie from Wawa. When I wanted to go alone a few nights previous, his mom advised against it because the neighborhood was dangerous.

"I had friends who lived in Philadelphia. When they heard I was moving here to start a community with you years back, they said, 'Are you kidding me? They'll slit your throat for a quarter over there.'"

"Some of them probably will," Aaron said with a shoulder shrug.

Because I got ham on my sub, we weren't allowed to bring it into the house. We took our subs, caramel smoothie, and donuts to the playground at Stonehurst Hills Elementary School where Aaron went from kindergarten to fifth grade—cutting his hair every morning to make it look straight before class. As he unwrapped his sub, he pointed to the small ledge where he and Mike had filmed a remake of a scene from *Dead Poet's Society*.

I asked him about his dad's mental illness. "Do you ever fear with both of your parents having been mentally ill that you might have inherited something genetically?"

"Oh, definitely. I'm positive I have something—it's just undiagnosed."[278]

"I think you've been prone to melancholy, depression, and maybe have obsessive behavior with saving things from the trash, but I've never known you to be manic, psychotic, or clinically depressed. For a while I was afraid you would end up a crazy homeless man in the gutter, and I would have no way to find you."

"Me too. That's a very real possibility."

---

[278] Aaron wrote a line in "Mexican War Streets" saying he trembled at the thought of what is often referred to as karma, a reference to the possibility that he might have inherited mental illness from his parents.

"There is a line in "Cattail Down" where you mention Mike being concerned for your mental health. Did he ever say anything to you?"

"Oh yeah, he just told me straight out that he thought something was wrong with me and I needed help."

"Well, I have to say, I'm really happy knowing you are teaching, dressing well, eating from restaurants, and starting a relationship with a woman who I think can help keep you grounded and stable. The more stable you become, the less I worry about you. I'm proud of you. I think you're gonna be alright."

98
Linvilla Orchards

Aaron got home from school in the early afternoon and had a meeting with the band. "We asked Brandon Beaver if he wanted to join the band officially."

"That's exciting. Did he say yes?"

"Yeah. I don't think I said two words the entire time, and the pizza was mediocre,"[279] Aaron said in his trademark disinterest in anything happening with the band.

"Mike and Sarah are at Linvilla Orchards with the kids and already picked up Aziza. Do you want to join them?"

"Sure!" We hopped on the motorcycle and halfway there stopped for oil as the engine was smoking.

Once there, Aaron saw one of Mike and Sarah's boys playing in the playground, then used my cell phone to call Mike and pretend he had abducted him for ransom.

After meeting up and watching Mike and Sarah ride the train with their son, Aaron began looking through the trash, offering me a bite of an apple cider donut he found and described as "dynamite."

I declined. "If I didn't have a germ phobia, I would do it."

"Yeah, it's usually the dissuading factor," he responded, "but I've never gotten sick eating from the trash that I'm aware of."

Before we left, Mike and Sarah bought fresh donuts and offered us one. I didn't decline.

When we got home, Aziza saw the pizza slices, a bag of cheese fries, warm cider, and poultry for the cats sitting on her dining room table. With her face grimaced in disgust, she said, "Did he get that from the trash? I don't know how he can eat that!" She wanted it off her table.

Aziza went to the kitchen and began making a big pot of homemade vegetable soup. Aaron fell asleep on the couch reading

---

[279] Papa John's: because why have frozen pizza at home when you can order out for it?

Nietzsche. When she'd finished cooking, I offered to do the dishes. Halfway through, Aaron woke up and peeked into the kitchen. "You'd better do those dishes properly or I'm sending you back to Alabama."

Aaron made us banana smoothies and began reading *The Essential Sufism*, finding one entry after another that hit home.

"Just like that children's book *Are You My Mother?* I keep asking who my true mother is. Everyone is claiming to be my mother." Aaron held up his Nietzsche book. "Nietzsche says, 'I'm your brother, and we can hang out for a while, but I'm not your mother.' But Sufism," he held up *The Essential Sufism*, "says, 'I'm your mother.'"

As we talked about how much we hated dating but enjoyed the thought of marriage, Aaron read from *The Essential Sufism*:

> *I used to think that love and the beloved are different. I know they are the same.*

"I brought up the one quote while me, you, and my mom were going out to the mazar, about love with no object. Remember that? That phrase really struck me because of all this stuff we get hung up about—about a particular person that we want to love, you know, and how much pain that can cause if it goes wrong, at least, or falls apart. So the idea of having a love that isn't attached to anything but is just a force that's always going out or coming in, but doesn't change with the outside scenery, that's what strikes me about this."

"Even the goodness of *my* love as the lover doesn't matter, like *my* love should be significant to you. So it's not even *my* love that matters, but love itself," I added.

Rumi wrote that there is no greater love than love with no object. If we dissolve into Love itself—which is always here for all of us—and become one with it, we will care far less about the value of "my" love for you, and "your" love for me.

This ultimate Love can also be called God.

I wasn't sure any of this was true, but the sentiment was beautiful.

99
All Circles

Aaron had class the afternoon of my last day there, so he took me to the Greyhound station in the morning. During the motorcycle ride, Aaron pointed out the Philadelphia Museum of Art and the famous steps Sylvester Stallone ran up in the *Rocky* montage. He also pointed out the YMCA the band rented to film the "Nice and Blue (Pt. 2)" video, explaining that they worked with a water ballet instructor for a few hours to choreograph their dance moves in the pool. Finally we pulled into the Greyhound lot and parked almost in the very same spot he had when he came to pick me up.

"Well, brother, it looks like we've ended where we begun," I said.

"Yes." Aaron took off his helmet and hugged me.

"Ah, brother, thank you."

"Thanks for being here, it was great to have you."

"Yeah, it's been great."

"Ah, I love you so much."

"I love you too, brother."

10/28/12
Email to Aaron

Aaron,

I posted photos from the trip on my Facebook page. Thank you again for a wonderful time and for all of your kindness and conversation.

Love you, brother,

Paul

10/31/12
Email from Aaron

Paul

Thanks for posting all those videos and photos. I liked revisiting some of those memories—had such an awesome time with you. Thank you also for coming and for all our conversation and time together. You really helped me, lending such a patient ear with regard to my girl troubles. That was a rough week for me but you were very understanding and insightful as usual. Believe me, your timing was perfect.

Yes! Thank you, Paul. And I-you, no doubt. Think of you often and very fondly,

A.

11/17/12
Email to Aaron

Hello, brother.

Just a quick check in to make sure you are well. Are things any more stable and comfortable for you and Kaysha? Is she taking the plunge and moving there?

Paul

11/19/12
Email from Aaron

Hey dude,

Thanks for this email, super sweet. As for Kaysha, yes, actually things have become much more "stable," to use her word. Way more balanced and reciprocal, no longer do I feel like I'm doing the disproportionate amount of work. Also—she's come around to saying "I love you" in return, so that feels nice.

Speaking of which, I love you,

A. Jonathan Weiss

100
Winter Trains

Mike and Sarah were coming through Chicago to visit Sarah's family for Christmas. Aaron called and asked if there was any way I could make it to Chicago to see him. Given there were blizzard conditions, I had no way of getting there.

"Is Kaysha moving out by you to continue your relationship?"

"Yeah, Mike and Sarah are driving back, and I'm gonna hop trains to meet her. Then we're gonna drive her car back to Philadelphia."

"Wow, that's good news!"

"Yeah, thank you."

"So you're hopping flatbeds in subfreezing temperatures? You're not worried any?"

"Not exclusively flatbeds—they can be boxcars. I'm not too particular. I'll find a way to stay warm."

I worried about him over the next week, then checked in with him the first week of January to make sure he was okay. "How was your trip hopping trains? Did you make it back alive?" I asked.

"Is there some intermediate state I can claim?"

And with the new year came a new step in Aaron and Kaysha's relationship.

101
Ring

On some of my more lonely nights, I looked for Emily online. I'd search for her on Facebook and MySpace. I checked YouTube and searched variations of her name and user names, but all that came up were old, abandoned profiles. She wouldn't respond to any of my texts or emails. It had been nine months since we'd last talked. I wondered if I'd ever hear from her again.

She still appeared in my dreams often. They were different variations of me trying to talk to her, rescue her, or stop her from leaving, but she never heard me or acknowledged me. These dreams always ended with her walking out the door with a guy I couldn't see. I moved in slow motion and was never allowed to touch her. I often woke from these dreams crying, telling her I hated her for this, wondering if my heart would ever heal and these nightmares ever end.

I tried to look through our photos as exposure therapy, and even got the guts one afternoon to put a home video in to hear the sound of her voice. She went through every cell in my being, and I had to take it out immediately. It was too overwhelming.

Like so many nights since she'd left, I opened my desk drawer and took out my wedding ring one night at the end of June. I placed it on my finger, and everything in me transformed. A deep love for her came over me. I decided that tonight, rather than feeling empty, I wanted to feel my love for her, so I wore the ring to bed.

I turned out the lights, got under the covers, and wrapped around my pillows, pretending they were her. "When are you coming back?" I said, twisting the ring on my finger. Tears welled up and my chest tightened. I let myself sob. No one was watching.

"I love you so much," I said. "How in the world did we end? I still can't believe this happened." Not knowing if anyone was listening, I prayed for her. I asked that she be kept safe, or be loved, or stop having impulses to hurt herself. I got mad at God, or biology, or reality—angry at how powerless I was and everyone else was to help her.

It was 2:00 A.M. and trying to storm. There had been lightning and thunder for the past few hours. I was too restless to stay inside, so I walked out the door as it began to rain. It was dark, besides street lights, and I had the entire town to myself. I walked across the foot bridge to Grant Park.

"Lord, I'm not supposed to be here. This isn't my home. I'm supposed to be with Emily in Florida. If you could just have her call me tonight, I will drop everything here and run to Florida in a heartbeat."

I smiled from embarrassment. "I know, I haven't learned anything, right? I'm gonna throw away all of this progress and go right back to someone who will hurt me all over again. And here I am in the rain, praying like you exist."

I went home, got out of my wet clothes, and climbed back into bed wearing my ring, telling Emily I loved her.

Upon waking the next morning, I checked my phone and found a missed call.

It was Emily.

I sent her a text telling her I saw her missed call.

She texted back, "I was just hoping you could send me Aaron's email again, I'm not doing too well. There is a lot of drama, the usual with my medication, and I'm just looking for some inspiration. I'm trying really hard to stay out of the hospital. I would call you, but I don't think it's fair to my boyfriend that I confide in you."

"Well, whatever is going on, I put my ring on last night and spent most of the night praying for you. I worry about you and always wonder if you're safe."

"Aw, thank you. I'm safe. I finally have a great boyfriend. You'd really like him. I have a very supportive new family."

I texted her a couple of weeks later to check up on her, and she called me.

"I never wrote Aaron. It's been really difficult lately, but I have an extremely supportive and loving boyfriend. I have no doubt that the man I'm with now is who I want to spend the rest of my life with. We were definitely put together by God. He's my soul mate. We had a sign between us. I got a tattoo on my chest to commemorate it."

"I didn't think you believed in those sorts of things."

"Oh, I have an altar in my bedroom with my crucifix, a rosary, candles, and all kinds of good stuff. I still read Rumi, too."

"That's pretty eclectic," I said.

"I finally agreed to adopt the kids over to my ex-husband's wife."

"Wow, what led to that?"

"My boyfriend and I can't really start our own life living in his parents' house. We don't have a lot of money so we can't afford to pay child support. We need to get our own place so we can thrive."

"Isn't that all I ever wanted for us?"

"I know, but I had to fight for my kids. I had to try. I don't have any regrets."

"Hi, honey!" she suddenly shouted. "Well, he just pulled into the driveway, so I guess I'd better go."

"Do you want to send me your new email address so we can stay in touch?"

"I don't think it's fair to my boyfriend that we stay in contact. But don't worry about me, I'm loved and I'm safe."

Emily suggested that if saving all of our pictures, home videos, wedding cards, and my ring caused me to hurt, I should throw it all away. I was the only one keeping those memories alive.

I tried to bring myself to do it, but I couldn't. My ring represented more than our marriage. It represented being with her in spirit in the dark. With the demons she has to fight for the rest of her life, she needs all the love she can get. "Never throw someone out of your heart," I'd read somewhere. I put the ring back in my desk drawer and saved the history of my time with her.

I chose to let go of Emily that night and to never wear my ring again. My years of nightmares finally came to an end, and I finally found the closure I needed to move on.

Emily sent me a final text. "There's a Rumi quote that I love that goes something like: 'Don't grieve for what you lose, because it will come back to you in a different form.'"

The next year, Emily and her soul mate were married.

102
Bottom Lounge 2014

In February 2014, mewithoutYou was back at Bottom Lounge with Touche Amore, Seahaven, and Caravels. Once the band's dirty, flower-painted bus pulled up in front of the venue, under the elevated tracks, I went out to film them unloading.

After getting some of the gear inside, Aaron opened the front door and invited me out of the bitter cold. He introduced me to Jack, Nikki's dad, who loved driving the bus and had come along to help out.

"Greg's girlfriend Marlee flew out yesterday to be with us for a few days, and so did Kaysha. Would you like to meet her?" Aaron asked.

"Sure! We'll see if she lives up to all of this hype," I teased. "I promise I won't remind her that she's gonna die one day."

He took me back to the green room and invited her out to meet me. I shook her hand. "It's nice to finally meet you. Aaron showed me your picture when I last visited, saying you were so pretty it was sickening. All week long I put up with him being lovestruck, anxiously waiting for the phone to ring, singing you songs on the piano." She laughed, and Aaron smiled at her.

"Well, I'll let you guys have your time together. I'm gonna be out in the lounge reading if you want to find me later."

"We're headed there to get something to eat, too. Do you mind if Paul joins us?" Aaron asked Kaysha.

"No, not at all," Kaysha said.

We sat at the bar, looking at a menu. As Aaron asked the bartender about their veggie burgers, I flipped through my copy of *The Words* by Jean Paul Sartre.

"Did you get to the part where he was a kid playing with matches, and he burned a rug?" Aaron asked. "He felt God staring at him and yelled 'God damn it!' over and over until God disappeared and never returned."

"Really? No. I don't remember that!" I laughed. "Seems a

strange way to determine that God doesn't exist."

Jack and an exchange student from China he'd brought along joined us, so we moved to a booth. As we ate and watched skiers shoot at targets in the winter Olympics, staff at the venue taped SOLD OUT signs on the doors.

"I didn't buy a ticket. Do you need to use the guest list spot for Kaysha?"

"No, she's part of the crew. Let me text Almquist."

A few minutes later, Mike came out and put my name on the list.

The line of fans had now snaked around the building outside, and the lounge was full. A man approached our table and stopped in front of Aaron. "Do you mind if I just geek out for a minute?" he asked. Aaron didn't know what to say. "Your lyrics helped me through a terrible break up and a tough time in my life."

I smiled, seeing myself in him, wondering how many times Aaron had heard this over the years. I figured this was a good time for me to get my wristband and give them space to talk. I came back and overheard him telling Aaron he was writing a dissertation on where the Holy Spirit was when Jesus was being crucified.

Later during the show, Aaron referred to Kaysha as Sea Witch, the name of the pinball machine he played before the show, joking that she might be his ex-girlfriend by the end of the night if he kept teasing her that way.

103
Idaho Courts

In June, mewithoutYou was playing at Hawthorne Theater in Portland, Oregon, a stop on their *Catch for Us the Foxes* 10th anniversary tour. "Well, it begins about two years ago, right here, with a young lady that I met," Aaron said from the stage. "And that chapter came to kind of an end about one week ago to the day."

The crowd groaned.

"That is to say, we got married."

The crowd cheered.

"Welcome to the club," Mike said.

"Well, first it's sort of an end of a certain time, an end of wondering and certain sorts of mind-drifts and doubts and all that. You finally make a decision and say, well, from here on out, no more of those. But of course it's another kind of a beginning as I get this larger family, a few of which are here. So I wanna first share my love for them and gratitude for them."[280]

I wrote Aaron to congratulate him, telling him I saw the video clip online.

"Ah! Sorry you had to find out I got married via YouTube," he responded. "We eloped on June 10th, decided that day and went to the Canyon County Courthouse in Caldwell, Idaho—so none of our friends were there. And I've only really been telling whoever I happen to see, so still haven't told Kleinberg, Pishock, most of my closest friends."[281]

Soon after, Aaron was a guest on Yoni's Wolf's Wandering Wolf podcast, where he talked, among other things, about being newly married. Given they'd only been married for three months, Aaron still by habit referred to Kaysha as his girlfriend. After eloping on a whim, there wasn't a substantial difference, as they'd

---

[280] MessyRTK, "Seven Sisters pt2 by Mewithoutyou @ Hawthorne Theatre 06/17/14," *YouTube*, 6/18/14.
[281] Email, 7/08/14.

had no wedding and still lived apart. Calling her his wife was mostly an adjustment in language that helped him feel more stable and put his doubts to rest. "I just decided, you know what, nothing's ever gonna seem perfect to me. I'll find fault with anything, it's just how my mind works, but I thought she's a good girl for me and a really good influence on my life."[282]

Like every couple, they were trying to find a balance between closeness and space.

"My wife and I have been asking married folks, or anyone who would care to talk about it—but mostly married folks—about that dynamic. Like, how much do you give yourself over to this other person, or how much do the two become one as the saying goes, as opposed to kinda hanging on to your individuality. And I've struggled. I used to think it would be kind of a compromise to not totally merge your life with your spouse. You know, if that ever happened to me, I thought I'd want to just give everything, but now anymore I feel that less and less.

"Probably more than anything, there was one quote I read by a fella who was talking about marriage as a means of protecting each other's solitude that cast it in a different light. Because I have a feeling no one is ever gonna take away the loneliness that we have. Like, you can be on tour, and all kinds of people will be saying all kinds of great things about you: 'Oh, I love your music, I love your lyrics, you're so great.' But you don't feel happy, you know, something still is empty in the midst of that. In my experience, no matter how many people are around, you can feel totally alone, you know? And I thought it would be a real heavy burden to lay on somebody to expect them to take that away, or even chip away at it. And so I said to my girlfriend at the time, 'I'm not gonna ever take away your loneliness, and I will not let you or expect you to take away mine. But if we can just have kind of a partnership where we can be alone together in a safe way and go through life as in this, I don't know, quasi-monastic kind of way, I've always been drawn to the monk ideals of solitude and

---

[282] Yoni Wolf, "Episode 74 Aaron Weiss (mewithoutYou)," *The Wandering Wolf*, 9/24/14.

silence and simplicity to some extent.'"

"You find comfort in that," Yoni adds.

"Oh, yeah, yeah, hugely. I mean, there's a discomfort in it to some extent, but there's a real rich, almost ecstatic joy that I've tasted, like, here and there in my life. It's been enough to think this is the path I want to go down or this is kinda the treasure I'm seeking."

"How does your wife feel about this together-alone thing?" Yoni later asked.

"Well, I think she had planned on being single and celibate and kinda going a nun-ish kinda way. That was kind of our initial point of connection, because when we met it was a strange— I felt a real conflict because I had this hope to be—not necessarily a monk, because I didn't have any specific religious group to plug into—but I definitely had an intention to be alone and sort of intensely inward and single-minded in my life. And I always thought a wife and a family and a mortgage and all of those things would kinda really water that down or muddy the waters, you know? And so when I met her, I felt a real strong connection and a real kinda magnetic pull. I felt a mutual attraction right away that I never felt with anybody else, but I also said whatever becomes of this, I have this pretty serious pattern in my life. So it was kinda one of the—I don't want to say conditions, because I'm not sure anything would've stopped it, if she wasn't cool with that we might still not be married today—but it was something we talked out like right from the beginning. I said, 'Look, there's a few things you gotta know about me,' and that was one of them. 'I'm not ever gonna give myself to you in the way I think romantic ideas often portray that kind of relationship.'"

Aaron didn't think it was fair to put so much pressure or expectations on another person to make you happy. "So I thought if we go in with sort of counter-intuitive intuitions, sort of like an entirely unromantic and sort of, I don't know, I want to say just pragmatic or something, but in a sense of marrying, or finding a partner as a means of being more determined and single-minded in my aloneness. Because I think even when I thought I was going to be a monk, I had this backdoor plan of, like, no, but I'm gonna meet somebody. And I would go to a show, like, I'd be here and I'd be looking around like, 'Oh, that girl's kinda cute—no, I should be a monk.'"

"Well, we've all done that!" Yoni joked.

"Yeah, but for me I guess I felt like it was to an extent that was sort of distracting me. It became unhealthy. It was just enough that I thought, you know what, when I met—her name is Kaysha—when we met I thought, 'You know what, this is a really good thing for my life.' I've been happier, my family approves of her, and I talked to her family. It just felt like it made sense, and so we had some of those conversations that were pretty deliberately unromantic but sorta, 'Hey, look, I don't think you're ever gonna be like the one for me, and I don't want to be the one for you."

"That's so unromantic."

"Yeah, but we still do romantic things to some extent, but we always have that bedrock."[283]

"[Celibacy] was something I was happy with and willing to maintain for the rest of my life," Aaron told *Phoenix New Times*. "I had no hopes of losing my virginity and no plans of having sex. It wasn't an easy decision [to get hitched], but in some respects it felt like it wasn't even a decision. It felt like it was something I was sort of carried along into . . . When I met my wife, there was strong attraction, a magnetic pull that I felt. And I didn't necessarily decide to go and see her and to talk with her. It almost felt like something was unfolding, and I was a spectator. And so I didn't fight very hard to stop it."[284]

Natalie was now married, Emily was now married, and Aaron was now married. I began asking God if there was possibly someone out there for me too.

---

[283] Ibid
[284] Troy Farah, "MewithoutYou Frontman's Sexuality is an Open Book," *Phoenix New Times*, 5/24/15.

104
Foxes Anniversary Tour

The *Catch for Us the Foxes* 10th anniversary tour with Hop Along and The Appleseed Cast made its way to Bottom Lounge in October.

Before dropping me off, my brother took me for pizza and a quick stop at Half-Price Books in Countryside. I found *The Life of St. Teresa of Avila by Herself* and *The Intimate Merton: His Life from His Journals* for $5.00 each and brought them to the show with me.

I walked into the near-empty lounge and looked for a table where I could sit and read while keeping an eye out for Aaron. I found him standing alone, having just completed second and third place on the Addams Family pinball machine. Without saying a word, he hugged me.

"Hello, brother," I said. "You look good, man!"

"Yeah, so do you."

After small talk, he got back to his game and let me play a ball or two. I was an obvious liability. First place would have to wait.

After setting up and doing sound checks, Aaron came down from the stage to get meal tickets and order his falafel sandwich.

"I didn't get a chance to formally congratulate you on getting married. Congratulations, you did it!" I shook his hand.

"Yeah, thank you."

"I heard your podcast interview with Yoni and thought, 'He's gonna be in big trouble when Kaysha hears this.'"

"Nah, why do you say that? We talked about all of those things. We listened to it together and she was fine with everything I said."

"It reminded me somewhat of the setup Emily and I had. We were like two individuals living together. We made our vows, but Emily said she still referred to me as her boyfriend and didn't really see us as married. I was always wanting my own space and still wanting to be a monk. Looking into it, I realized I wouldn't last two years as a monk."

"Try two months," Aaron said.

"I used to think I was missing out on so many things, but lately I've been finding peace living alone just inside my four walls."

"Thomas Merton called the monastery 'the four walls of my new freedom,'" Aaron added.

"Speaking of Merton . . ." I opened my backpack and showed him the books I'd just bought. "You can take one or take them both with you if you want."

Aaron ordered his falafel burger, and we went out to the bus to sit and talk until his sandwich was ready.

MewithoutYou had been writing and recording songs for a new album. I asked Aaron how that was coming along.

"Some of these songs are the best we've ever done. I generally don't get too excited about our music, but these are already some of my favorites. They have the edge of some of the songs on the older albums and some experimental stuff we've never done before."

"Have you finished the lyrics?"

"Some of them, but I still write every day, then go in and record them in sections at a time."

"Any particular message or theme this time?"

"No, not particularly. A lot of it is stuff I've written about before."

As we talked about songs having messages, Aaron asked, "Have you heard of Ludwig Wittgenstein? He was a disciple of Bertrand Russell. He can be dense and over my head sometimes, but he is also really personable and says some pretty amazing things. Well, he said that words didn't symbolize anything, they were just noises we make in relation to their usefulness in serving our agendas."

"I've been getting through a lot of books the past two years while researching for the *All the Clever Words on Pages* rewrite. Sartre, Camus, books on Anabaptism and Sufism, some emergent stuff and new monastic stuff, Christian mystics, and I just started reading Kierkegaard to try to determine exactly what his impact has been on me, since I've only read selected quotes repurposed by other authors."

"What have you been reading apart from the project, just for yourself?"

"Stephen King and escapism. But going through these books is something I wanted to do for myself anyway. In your interview with Yoni, you spoke of your mom being a quietist. I had insomnia one night and watched Stephen King answer audience questions from the stage on YouTube. They were all moved by him and what he meant to them, yet everything he writes is escapism and entertainment. I can't speak for God, give ultimate answers, solve political and economic problems, or be an activist and save the world, but escapism? That I can do."

"That's how I kinda see what I'm doing tonight. People paid to see a show and I'm here to entertain them, nothing more," Aaron said.

Aaron wanted to take a crack at first place on the Addams Family pinball machine again. With his game face on, he explained his strategy to me, that he was particularly good at nudging the machine without tilting, which I thought was cheating, but he assured me it was a legitimate move. Another fan came to the machine and watched him play as well.

"Hey, are you Aaron Weiss?" he finally asked.

"Sometimes," Aaron said, quickly shaking his hand before getting back into the zone.

"This is it," he said, down to his final ball, still in second place. With that ball, he got top score, his face lighting up like a child's. After a high five, he entered mewithoutYou's initials and took pictures for bragging rights:

1) MWY 194,811,060
2) MWY 158,836,150

I had no energy left to stand up, so I sat down at a table near the pinball machine and put my head down. The lounge was now full and loud. I started to feel claustrophobic and overwhelmed, overcome with social anxiety.

When Aaron was finished playing pinball and chatting with a

few surrounding fans, he came over and sat down, putting his head down, too. He let out a deep sigh. "I'm tired. It's getting harder and harder to do this every night. I'm getting older."

"I apologize, my tank is on empty, too. I only get to see you once or twice a year, and I'm already out of gas. I try not to overwhelm you. I know I only have a short time with you, and I try to take advantage of that. And now that you're here, I have nothing to say, but it's good just to sit with you."

"Tours are overwhelming, especially when there are so many people who want to talk to you," he said.

"If I was in a band and I wrote lyrics, this would be the time I'd like the most—having fans want to talk with me about my lyrics and tell me they were moved by them."

"Yeah, but would you still feel that way after thirteen years of that? I've been trying to find time each night to be alone to write lyrics for these new songs. When I don't do that, I feel off, so I suppose I should go do that now. I'll be around after the show."

I gave him a hug and headed across the street to McDonald's for the padded booth and peace and quiet for the next two hours, preparing for an hour of crowd and noise when mewithoutYou took the stage at 11:00 P.M.

Come show time, I found a spot to film. Opening with the deep, booming toms of "Torches Together," they played *Catch for Us the Foxes* straight through, the audience with them the whole way.

In the middle of the set, after "Paper Hanger," Aaron shared, "So I have a funny story. The funny story involves a young man who was over here a few minutes ago during a relatively quiet moment in between two songs where I had just gotten finished bastardizing a line from Kierkegaard at the end of one of our songs, and he asked me, 'So who is Soren Kierkegaard to you?' Don't lose sight of the fact that this was in the middle of our show. I think I even told him, 'Don't you think it's a strange time to discuss this?' But I think he was the better man than I, because when isn't it? If I were in a clearer place, I probably could have engaged him right then and there. Well, thank you for the good question. This same phenomenon goes for whoever was trying to interact with me when I was playing pinball earlier. I gotta tell you, that's a lost cause. My apologies. But if you notice who has the number one and two score on the Addams Family machine, you'll have some grace with me."

I laughed, given that just before the show I'd brought up reading Kierkegaard, trying to understand his influence on me. Kierkegaard, when he was alive, was not read outside of Denmark and wasn't popular until after his death. Could he have envisioned his name coming up at a rock concert in America over a century later?

After the show, I asked Aaron if he wanted to get some Mexican food with a group of friends.

"I'm always interested in Mexican," Aaron said, "but bus call is 1:30, which is in a few minutes. We have an early show in Detroit tomorrow."

"Okay, just let me know if you go back inside to use the bathroom so I can peek over the stall mid-stream and ask you what Kierkegaard means to you."

Aaron laughed. "Okay, will do."

He was happy to take Teresa of Avila back with him and left me with Merton.

"Well, thank you for the show tonight and for spending time with me. It's a very important album to me, as you know, and it's great to see you perform it live again. The last time you did this was at Cornerstone in 2005 when we met."

"Yeah." He smiled and hugged me. "You're welcome. I love you, brother."

"I love you, too."

I got home and sent Aaron an email, thanking him for everything and apologizing for my tiredness. He responded, "Thanks for writing, old buddy, and for once again braving the Bottom Lounge. No need to apologize for being tired. I've been feeling more quickly run down lately, and feel less need for conversation than I used to. Often Kaysha and I will just sing together, more restful."

He asked if I had any good news. "The good news is, I love you, brother, and if God loves us no matter what, how can there be bad news? It's at least something to hope for."

He responded, "I love you too, and like you. Thank you for mentioning the possibility of 'God loves us no matter what.' Regardless of how much/little you/I believe that, I'm comforted by the words. I remember hearing something about Rilke, that he said it didn't matter if a God exists, because even if not, our belief would create one. I'm butchering it, but you get the point. Even if there is no unconditional love, we can hold that ideal and live toward it, even loving ourselves in falling so short. I'm talking to myself, as usual."[285]

MewithoutYou closed their anniversary tour at the Trocadero in Philadelphia on October 21st. Like so many years back, flower bouquets adorned the mic stands . In "Tie Me Up! Untie Me!" Aaron sang that he hadn't thought about killing himself in ten years. Closing the set with "Son of a Widow," Daniel Pishock and Chris Kleinberg came onstage to play in a beautiful reunion.

---

[285] Email, 10/13/14.

105
Pale Horses

Produced by Will Yip at Studio 4 in Pennsylvania, *Pale Horses* kept mewithoutYou's signature sound while once again changing things up. This album had some of the band's heaviest moments with a return to distorted groves. The song structures were still not pop-friendly, but featured plenty of bright melodies. Brandon Beaver added signature guitar sounds to these songs, bringing a new complexity to mewithoutYou's sound.

It was announced in a one-minute teaser video that mewithoutYou had signed with Run For Cover Records. A clip from "Dorothy" played in which Aaron hauntingly asks a Krishna-follower in a dream if he could shape-shift into his dead father, who would have liked to have met his wife.[286] MewithoutYou assured fans via Facebook that this would be a particularly dark album.

MewithoutYou updated their bio page, painting a picture of what to expect lyrically from Pale Horses:

> The one constant in mewithoutYou's storied career has been lead singer Aaron Weiss' ability to sketch ornate, thought-provoking narratives. Seamlessly weaving his signature holler amidst whispered storytelling and stream-of-consciousness outpourings, his latest offerings vacillate between the emotionally wracked, vibrantly symbolic, and ambiguously metaphysical. His meandering, technicolor vision of a world apocalyptic—populated with werewolves and vulturemen, shape-shifters and apparitions, android whales and an Idaho bride—combines the fantastic opulence of the group's recent albums with the vulnerable personal confessions of their earliest work.[287]

---

[286] Runforcovertube, "MWY / RFC," *YouTube*, 3/25/15.
[287] mewithoutYou, "Bio," *mewithoutyou.com*, 2015.

"We're really stoked. When I listen to it, I don't even believe that's us, and I've never felt that way about an album before," Rickie told *Flip Side PA*. "It's almost like we just de-evolved back to being 18-year-olds playing garage rock."[288]

Mike was asked by *The Aquarian Weekly* what fans should look forward to on this upcoming record. "Well, for one thing, the thing I am enjoying about it . . . the first thing that comes to mind is that I feel like I am kind of reconnecting with Aaron Weiss a little bit—as far as what he is going through in his life and how he is processing certain events and where his mind is. I feel like I am getting more in touch with Aaron as an individual through his lyrics on this record . . . Aaron speaking in his own point of view—and not just that, but also making accounts of certain ideas and certain understandings and certain misunderstandings, or whatever the case might be with where Aaron's at, and just hearing more of his voice in the first person."[289]

In a Run for Cover video promoting *Pale Horses*, Aaron said, "Probably the most concise way to put it is that it feels without a doubt like the most unguarded and the most unfiltered album I've ever been a part of. The themes that are there are subtler and kinda more personal and more dispersed—catastrophe, disaster, nuclear war. And I'm interested in the smaller versions of Armageddon and personal catastrophe. And so with the idea of pale horses being a symbol for that in the end times, just expressing it in different ways. You know, I assume also the world will end one day and it's an interesting fact. But I also wonder, how attached can I be to anything when everything's just gonna die? And I think about that."[290]

As with every new mewithoutYou release, fans pored over the lyrics, eager to find out what Aaron currently believed and what messages he might be conveying. Aaron returned to the

---

[288] Brett Sholtis, "MewithoutYou lands at the Depot Monday night, The Philadelphia-based five piece prepares for new album, tour with Dr. Dog," *Flip Side PA*, 3/19/15.
[289] Ryan McGrath, "An Interview with MewithoutYou: More Stories To Tell," *The Aquarian*, 1/07/15.
[290] mewithoutYou, "Pale Horses - Album Teaser," *YouTube*, 5/04/15.

"very personal, revealing, kinda vulnerable thing I had always been trying to do: writing about my experiences in a pretty direct and unguarded way. I think with *Pale Horses* I tried to go back to that, largely because the guys in the band suggested I do so."[291] Still, these would be some of his most ambiguous lyrics to date.

"This time around with writing I tried to avoid having a single theme that ran across the entire album, simply because I didn't want to repeat the last approach," Aaron told *Absolute Punk*. "I also didn't want it to be a total hodgepodge of nonrelated content, which is what some of our earlier albums were. I tried to split the difference, where I picked a few different themes and separated them. I wrote a bunch of content under each theme and then mixed and matched content from each of those themes to make different songs. There's probably 5-10 different themes on the album, several of which show up in each song."[292]

The Bible, Rumi, Thomas Merton, James Joyce, Fyodor Dostoyevsky, Shakespeare, and Ludwig Wittgenstein were referenced in *Pale Horses*. As if the Rumi well had run dry, Aaron now took to stealing robot whales out of the dreams of his two-year old nephew, Harvey.

Aaron continued, "I like that, being able to change and find new approaches to writing. It keeps it more interesting for me. A lot of my ideas have stayed relatively consistent over the years. I've changed personally, I suppose, but sometimes it feels like I'm not saying anything terribly new. It's a lot of similar stuff that I've said on previous albums, but I need to find new ways of expressing it. I do have new experiences that change my perspective, but I think having a more fundamental shift in the style of writing can create an overall mood or a feeling for an album."[293]

Aaron was further asked about the religious content of the lyrics on *Pale Horses*. "I think there are more critical aspects of my relationship with religion and my sense of trying to incorporate

---

[291] Jeremy Zimmerman, "It's the End of the World, and I Feel Fine: Aaron Weiss of mewithoutYou talks Pale Horses," *The Key*, 6/16/15.
[292] Jonathan Bautts, "mewithoutYou—06/03/15," *Absolute Punk*, 6/03/15.
[293] Ibid

the full spectrum of what I feel, that is the extremity of my emotions and my mental state, which in some respects in the past might have been a little bit embarrassing to reveal the depths of. I had a hesitation to be either too overtly religious or to criticize religion too overtly, or some kind of a feeling that I needed to present some kind of an internally consistent worldview that I'm then giving to people. Basically, I abandoned that with the last album, *Ten Stories*, but I also made the different worldviews different characters. This time around, I tried to own up to the depths of my dissatisfaction with religion, but also the depths of my love for religion. It's kind of inconsistent internally, just in that one respect at least, but also I didn't need to make different animals voicing these different perspectives. I could just say, 'Yeah, that's all how I feel.' It's not clear and it's not coherent, but it's all in there."[294]

Aaron told *HM Magazine* that unlike *Ten Stories*, "I think, more than ever, I tried to let all the characters in my brain come out and be seen and be available, without putting them in the different characters' voices. This is part of what I believe, and this is part of what I think and part of who I am. It might contradict something that's in the next song, but that's who I am in some ways, so conflicted and contradicted.

"I have that certainty, that sense of religion in my Abrahamic roots, as you noticed. It is still very much there. I still very much want for the album to be one of praise, that's characterized by praise and gratitude and faith and worship and love and uplifting things. At the same time, there's this whole dark side I've struggled with, and how much to let out and how much to show people. Do we have other doubts or questions or even animosities toward certain aspects of religion? That's all part of the package for me. It's not a matter of me losing my faith in any way, it's just part of expressing an ever-changing faith and trying to do so holistically."[295]

Aaron told *Digboston*, "We used to draw different conclusions

---

[294] Ibid
[295] Sean Huncherick, "The Evolving Education of mewithoutYou," *HM Magazine*, 2015.

about reality and our beliefs since we're five individuals, especially about how we label ourselves and don't label ourselves. Lumping us into one entity means there's room for error. That goes for a single individual, too. 'This guy is a Christian' or 'This girl is an atheist' allows a margin of error where, at least in my case, there's a person who is internally divided with different beliefs and convictions that change over a week."[296]

Aaron's lyrics were intentionally ambiguous. "Whenever there was a word or phrase that left an idea open to considerably different ways of interpreting it, I tend to go with that phrasing as compared to another way that might even sound nicer but was less ambiguous. I appreciate it, enjoy the ambiguity. I like the idea that people will come and bring their own ideas to a song, and take away from that same song totally different things. I think that is an interesting thing that happens."[297]

As with the band's previous couple of releases, Aaron doubled down on his insistence that no one look to him for help, guidance, or truth. "I would be okay if somebody didn't take anything away from *Pale Horses* in terms of ideas on it. I would be very happy if somebody didn't take anything away from it."[298]

"I've just been thinking and reading more about language and words and how hard their meanings are to pin down—even simple words, let alone complex, lofty ones that I've long since been fascinated with," he told *MySpace*. "So I sort of questioned my ability to communicate anything worthwhile. If I'm not sure that I'm going to say something that's going to help anybody or say anything that's true, then I might as well make it sound pretty. That's an oversimplification, but it came from me being less confident in my power to save anybody."[299]

"I tried to resist the temptation to try to make someone take

---

[296] Nina Corcoran, "Educational Emo: mewithoutYou's Aaron Weiss Returns to School," *DigBoston*, 7/15/15.
[297] Ibid
[298] Sean Huncherick, "The Evolving Education of mewithoutYou," *HM Magazine*, 2015.
[299] Katrina Nattress, "mewithoutYou's Aaron Weiss Opens Up About His Lack Of Spiritual Confidence," *Myspace*, 6/08/15.

something away from the songs," he admits. "There's a juggling act where I'm trying to be precise in what I have to discuss, but very open-ended in what I expect anyone to take away from that discussion. I'm a person born to a certain family at a certain time and place. I only have so many things that captivate my interest. There's a redundancy in the kind of issues I address, and I assume that would minimize our audience. Some people have no interest in religion whatsoever—I wouldn't blame them for writing off the lyrics and maybe enjoying a melody—but the new album is so overtly religious whether it's in favor of or critical of different religious ideas that for somebody who has no interest in that, I can see them finding our lyrics boring. That's okay," he told *Digboston*.[300]

"I don't feel like I'm qualified to tell people what's true about God, the way I once felt like I was," Aaron further told *Phoenix New Times*. "So I like leaving it more open for people because then I feel like I'm less likely to mislead somebody. I'd say there have been times that I've been much more confident, not only that what I believed was true, but also that I was able to communicate the truth of that belief using words. And I've come to doubt both of those things. So I can say certainly there are things I have come to let go of that I once held to be true."[301]

"A lot of this other stuff, writing about God, or love or judgment, it feels pretty deeply out of my league, pretty thoroughly a point of absolute ignorance for me," he told *Absolute Punk*. "To try and write about God and say anything seems almost preposterous at this point, as if I speak from a point of knowledge. Of course I can share my experiences and my faith, but I can't tell people what's true when I don't know what's true."[302]

He reiterated that he had to do away with any illusion that the band was ministry. "Like anybody, I want to understand myself and my own motivations and intentions so I try to question

---

[300] Nina Corcoran, "Educational Emo: mewithoutYou's Aaron Weiss Returns to School," DigBoston, 7/15/15.
[301] Troy Farah, "MewithoutYou Frontman's Sexuality is an Open Book," *Phoenix New Times*, 5/24/15.
[302] Jonathan Bautts, "mewithoutYou—06/03/15," *Absolute Punk*, 6/03/15.

those things, and I see more and more how my motivation for this band is totally selfish and totally ego-based, so it starts to feel really silly to try to masquerade that I'm trying to do some holy work when really I just like the attention."[303]

"There's all this other stuff that comes with me being in this band, like totally superficial ego stuff. I probably have become more arrogant and more pretentious, and I take myself more seriously because more people have paid attention to me as a musician than they ever did when I was the manager of a dollar store in high school. That makes me feel like this sense of importance is probably inflated. I think it probably has all kinds of harmful effects on my sense of self-importance."[304]

In "Red Cow" Aaron alludes to Wittgenstein from *Philosophical Investigations*, "A picture held us captive." Aaron then asks, *What Pharaoh now or Jew/Christian/Muslim/atheist, etc. or picture holds us here?* In "D-Minor" Aaron deconstructs the phrase "God is dead" rephrasing it *capitalized 3-letter sound has died.*

Because words and images carry so much baggage, so many meanings, and so many assumptions, we talk past each other, limiting ourselves and others—being held captive—to labels and their assumed meanings.

Some fans thought Aaron had fallen too far down the postmodern, post-structuralist, deconstructionist rabbit hole into a kind of nihilism where words and ideas couldn't convey anything of substance at all, so all of his answers to simple questions about his beliefs sounded complicated, elusive, and evasive. This is often an overcorrection in response to giving up past certainties.

In "Red Cow," Aaron asks if the story of Moses and the Pharaoh was penned by fiction's hand, adding *to which of us does this not apply?* Even our thoughts of ourselves, others, and how we construct our stories while in the midst of living them out aren't true in any substantive way. Never mind biographical constructions of our histories by others after the fact.

Absolute Punk asked Aaron about his beliefs. He said he

---

[303] Katrina Nattress, "mewithoutYou's Aaron Weiss Opens Up About His Lack Of Spiritual Confidence," *Myspace*, 6/08/15.
[304] Jonathan Bautts, "mewithoutYou—06/03/15," *Absolute Punk*, 6/03/15.

thought his relationship with religion was made up of considerations that were "relatively haphazard, selfish, emotional and superficial. They're untrustworthy." Concerning religion and Christianity, he said, "These concepts are so hard to pin down, so broad and so abstract. For me, they're so difficult to define, there's no way I can even address what it is I have a love/hate relationship with. There's not any one thing called religion or any one thing called Christianity, or even any one thing called Quakerism or Sufism. No matter how specific you get in a worldview, there's still these abstractions that are going to take on totally different meanings for the people that approach them. So I get more reluctant to talk about these things in any kind of universal way. I don't have anything very solid to say because they seem like very slippery concepts. You know that I mean?"[305]

Aaron told Sean Huncherick at *HM Magazine* that he had lost some lightheartedness and happiness after his dad died, but questioning his beliefs also took a toll. "Through studying at grad school, I have also been repeatedly confronted with many different views and perpetually challenged or questioned all my beliefs and learned to let go of things I have held onto. That's difficult, too, to continuously uproot the things you find comfort in, and continuously question them, and continuously try to go deeper and understand more fully basic things about the world."[306]

"I don't have to carry around this set of ideas that then everything else that contradicts that becomes an enemy or becomes a threat in some way. It's a lot lighter of a journey when I don't carry those things, and I stay open and eager for whatever comes today to replace whatever I accepted yesterday. Maybe yesterday's beliefs or practices were appropriate for yesterday, but maybe today there's a deeper place that we can go to. I also think it's important for me to stay flexible and to stay open and to stay humble and to recognize the limits of what I know."[307]

Aaron wasn't afraid to question his beliefs, even down to

---

[305] Ibid
[306] Sean Huncherick, "The Evolving Education of mewithoutYou," *HM Magazine*, 2015.
[307] Ibid

certain assumptions we take for granted. "Things about what we perceive to be true, and the trustworthiness of our perceptions, and the trustworthiness of our reason and our emotions, and things we've experienced and are validated in our beliefs. Those things I wouldn't really know how to even begin questioning. They're just so essential to how I experience the world. Certainly any ideas I have about God or truth or love or eternal things I have to call into question, because I assume, almost as a point of faith, that whatever I have come to believe about those things is bound to be false to some extent, and limited, and so not entirely to be trusted. I try to let go of those things and live more like a child, where I try to maintain a sense of wonder and curiosity than a list of things I can explain and tell people about."[308]

"That's been a big shift for me," Aaron continued. "There used to be a time I would really enjoy spending hours talking to people, telling them all kinds of things about God after the shows or at Bible studies I would lead. Or at festivals, I'd give these talks or question-and-answer sessions. People would bring questions to me, and I would have answers for them about God and about things. Looking at them now, I can't imagine where I'd be claiming to know what I was talking about."[309]

Aaron said being certain and dispensing truth about God feels very empowering. "You can hold people's attention by telling them things that are very important to them. 'I know how you can get your soul into heaven when you die, or go to hell.' These really big ideas. People who think there's such a thing as heaven or hell are going to be interested in, 'Okay, how do I get into one and not the other?' I think it can be a dangerous thing to start throwing around our ideas about those places and those concepts, just based on things that we've read or that we've been told."[310]

Sean asked Aaron if he was more certain of his beliefs earlier in the band's career.

"I definitely felt more certain about a lot of beliefs earlier in our career and felt like I had a lot more to offer people. I was not

---

[308] Ibid
[309] Ibid
[310] Ibid

only willing but I was eager to answer people's questions and talk with them about God. In some ways, I respect the way I was because I felt I was more courageous or more passionate. Today it feels more that I'm cautious, and I'm a little bit more shy and reserved and introverted. That can be difficult, because sometimes people will come to me expecting that maybe we talked before, maybe they saw me at a show and I was carrying on afterwards about all my ideas. Now I don't feel as inclined to do that. I'm a little less outgoing and a little less confident. I don't know if that's a good thing, if it's a good direction that I've gone in, but that's where I find myself. Maybe one day I'll go back the other way and I'll be out preaching again, but I don't think it's going to be today."[311]

Sean asked Aaron what he believed strongly today.

"As far as things I believe very strongly, they are also basic. They're all very basic about the goodness of love and about the beauty of love and about the reality of love and about the importance of compassion. Those are good things, and that goodness is real. Love is real. My life goes better when I remember that, and when I pray, and when I give thanks to God. Even if I don't have a strong idea about who God is, I still benefit from getting on my knees and giving thanks and asking for forgiveness."[312]

"This whole band, my involvement in it, is just something very silly and small and personal," Aaron told *Slant Magazine*. "I have no idea what anyone else gets out of it, or how it relates to God or reality, but I know what it means to me and what it meant to my dad, playing in the band." He continued, "I think that when I quote the scriptures or old hymns, in a sense I'm just using language that I know, that is meaningful to me, or that evokes certain emotions in me, but I don't presume that I'm presenting anyone with the word of God or that there's anything I'm saying that they need to believe or accept.[313]

---

[311] Ibid
[312] Ibid
[313] Caleb Caldwell, "Interview: mewithoutYou's Aaron Weiss," *Slant*, 8/27/15.

By the end of recording *Pale Horses*, Aaron said he was totally drained and had nothing more to say. "I can't imagine two years from now, or whenever this one runs its course, having any desire at all to write another song, let alone an album. Sometimes I've thought it might be a good album to end our career on, one about the end of the world. I have no intention of quitting. It's just that I try to stay open and ready for change and for growth, and that, I know, is going to involve discontinuing my musical career at some point, and I'm okay with that."[314]

He told Yoni wolf, "I never wanted to put out a second album, let alone a sixth album. I'm still touring and not doing so many of the things I dreamt about when I was younger, largely out of a sense of momentum and habit. That I have wedded myself to these other personalities and they have different agendas or different dreams in life, and I get carried along with their dreams insofar as fulfilling their dreams is dependent on me, given that we're in a band together at this point."

"Do you ever resent them for that?" Yoni asked.

"I resent them for everything at one point or another."[315]

---

[314] Ibid
[315] Yoni Wolf, "Episode #106 Aaron Weiss (mewithoutYou) 2, *The Wandering Wolf*, 7/22/15.

106
Fuck

The first show of the *Pale Horses* tour in June 2015 was in Chicago. That afternoon, mewithoutYou played a set for Audiotree that was streamed live.

After performing "Red Cow," someone yelled, "Fuck yeah!" eliciting laughter in the studio.

"In case my mother-in-law is listening, it wasn't me," Aaron said.

The host reminded the audience that mewithoutYou would be at Abbey Pub that night with Lithuania and Foxing.

The set that night included old favorites like "Torches Together," "January 1979," and "In a Sweater Poorly Knit," newer stuff like "February 1878" and "Foxes Dream of the Log Flume," and a bunch from *Pale Horses*—"Pale Horse," "Mexican War Streets," "D-Minor," "Magic Lantern Days," "Blue Hen," "Red Cow," and "Rainbow Signs."

Ending the set before the encore with "Rainbow Signs," Aaron strapped on an electric guitar. "Bob Dylan goes electric," my friend Joel said, sitting next to me. The song started out mellow, the vocals gentle, almost in a whisper, then kicked into a heavy distorted section with screaming vocals, before coming back down to spacey guitars and soft vocals. Aaron playing a third guitar made the middle section heavier.

I hung around for about an hour after the set until Aaron came onstage to pack up his gear. I gave him a hug and asked how he was doing. Tired already, he confessed, on the first day of tour.

A girl was waiting to speak with him, so I brought her to his attention. Within five seconds of introducing herself, she was in tears, telling him how much his songs helped her through a tough time in her life. I walked away to give them time, like usual. Once Aaron was free, I asked him about me maybe coming to visit him in the fall.

"Actually, we're expecting right around that time."

"No way!"

"Yeah, I wanted to wait until I saw you in person to tell you."

"That's crazy! Congratulations!"

"Thank you. So Kaysha is gonna give birth in Idaho, and we'll just bring the baby on tour. But I think we're playing Chicago again this fall."

"Someone was collecting questions from fans for an interview with you this past week. I told him to ask you, 'How much do you love Paul Harrison?' Did that one make the cut?"

"No, I don't think that one made the cut," he said, laughing.

"Well, I still want an answer."

"How far can I stretch my arms?" he asked, stretching out his arms.

Aaron returned to the stage to pack up his gear, showing me his new distortion pedal. "I made a big mess tonight, all these extra cables. I play electric guitar now."

"My buddy Joel up there saw you put the guitar on and he's like, 'Oh, Bob Dylan goes electric.'"

"Oh yeah, sure, I wish!"

Come to find out, it was fifty years ago that summer that Dylan went electric.

Having stopped at the used bookstore again, I offered Aaron a few titles. He took Denis Johnson's *Jesus' Son*, a thin book of short stories about a hitchhiking addict. "I'm reading a lot for school. I better not bite off more than I can chew."

My brother arrived to pick me up. I figured since he didn't come to the show, finally meeting Aaron would be a happy compromise.

"Do you want to meet my brother?"

"Yeah, sure."

We walked out to the car.

"Hey, Aaron, what's up, man?" Mark rolled down his window and they shook hands.

"Paul here says you're a Bob Dylan fan," Aaron said.

"Yeah, man. I love Bob Dylan."

"What's your favorite song?"

"Tangled Up in Blue," Mark said, throwing a song out there

because he couldn't pick a favorite.

"That's one of my favorites, too. I saw Dylan live, and he changed the arrangement to the point that I hardly recognized it."

"Yeah, he likes to change things up live."

"There's no one like Bob Dylan," Aaron said. "He's the best."

"Dylan has a lot of character in his voice, but he can't really sing. You guys both have that in common," I said, busting Aaron's chops.

"Well, that's never stopped me before," he said.

A person on the street now approached Aaron to talk with him, so we let him go.

"Good to meet you," Mark said.

"Good to meet you, too. And thanks for carting this guy around all these years so he can come to the shows."

"No problem."

"I love you," Aaron said to me.

"I love you too," I said, getting into the car.

"Wow, he's really nice," Mark said. "Looking at him, you'd never guess he was in a band. He looks more like a professor."

"You're not far off. He's working on his PhD in urban education and taught at Temple University."

We drove to the old neighborhood, lamenting how crime-ridden it had become, then ate at Huck Finn Donuts before Mark took me to the Greyhound station at 2:00 A.M.

I bought the *Pale Horses* CD at the show, so I passed the time reading the lyrics. I came across the line in "Rainbow Signs" where Aaron sends a mute curse to the Boise sky for his *fucked up Napoleon of St. Helena hairline*, and I laughed out loud. I thought of him trying to save himself from the disapproval of Kaysha's mom earlier that afternoon when the same profanity was shouted during their Audiotree performance. "Well, he can't get out of this one," I said.

Some fans complained about this, but Aaron had been singing, "You'd be well inclined not to fuck with me," live in "O Porcupine" for a decade at that point.

Aaron told *Absolute Punk* there's "some language that I have kept edited out in the past. I don't like to curse a lot, but it's there.

I didn't want to not put it on an album just because I thought maybe they won't sell it at a Christian bookstore or something. That's no reason to change what you're creating."[316]

Earlier in the year, I discovered the Bad Christian Podcast. Run by members of the band Emery, they interviewed Christian musicians, authors, and public figures in often transparent and revealing conversation. Infamous for its extremely lax attitude with profanity and lewd humor, I thought Aaron would make a great interview, given his unabashed potty mouth.

Bad Christian put out a call on Facebook in April, asking fans who they would like to hear interviewed on the program. Aaron Weiss was the top vote-getter.

I asked Aaron if he was interested in doing it and he said sure, because he liked the guys in Emery.

After months of miscommunication and false starts, they finally got the interview.

---

[316] Jonathan Bautts, "mewithoutYou—06/03/15," *Absolute Punk*, 6/03/15.

107
Bad Christian

The first week of December, the Bad Christian Podcast aired their interview with Aaron Weiss.[317] After discussing urban legends surrounding him, they asked Aaron where he was spiritually today.

Aaron said calling yourself a Christian doesn't make you one, so he was hesitant to label himself. "Over all the years that I very confidently considered myself a Christian, I always remembered that, well, I'm not exactly living up to the ideals that I think Christ asked of us or who I think Christ was or is. I don't consider myself to be worthy of that kind of company. So I was always a little bit reluctant. Like, I'm told Kierkegaard suggested it's probably more fitting to say you're *striving* to be a Christian than to say that you are or that you've kind of already arrived at this place. So, I try to dodge those kind of labels, not so much because I don't want people to consider me this or that, but because if I answer honestly, I could recognize that even if I were to say I'm this or that, I might be mistaken, and I would rather err on the side of not making bold claims with high moral implications."

Toby Morrell asked Aaron if he still prayed with people and called out the name of Jesus.

"I don't think I've moved away from faith in God or in reality or truth or love or any of the kind of basic principles that I associate with Christ and with God, but I also have become a little bit more reluctant to put my faith on display, especially when I feel like somebody has an agenda."

Toby then asked Aaron if seeking truth and contemplating faith in God was a big part of his life.

"I sure hope so. I intend that. I also really like playing pinball, and that has nothing to do with the search for truth. It's just more of a way of shutting my mind off and getting a real clear and

---

[317] Bad Christian Podcast #144.

singular and low-stakes focus that kind of, you know, is a break from the heavier things in life that I've wrestled with over the years. So, there again I couldn't say that I in a consistent sense am a seeker of truth."

Concerning the pursuit of truth, he added, "I've been in graduate school for about seven years now and that has changed, for me, what it looks like to search for truth. Where once I could turn to the scriptures or certain parables and wisdom traditions and confidently feel like I was growing in my understanding of truth, in most of my academic courses and in that context, it seems like some kind of combination of rational arguments and empirical evidence is the gold standard—that those are kind of our two major inputs for truth. And I've come to respect that very deeply. That doesn't mean that I've let go of the kind of mystical or ecstatic experiential search for truth or the wisdom in teachings or the faith-based pursuit of truth. But it does mean in some ways that I've sort of started to search for things that are more grounded in the tangible material world and in rational thought. And I've taken those about as far as I could at this point in my life, and I've found that it's pretty exciting and interesting to search for truth in those ways. And what I try to resist is the idea that either we're going to find truth through some sort of faith tradition like Christianity, or we have to turn to science and philosophy, and that's our only means of finding truth when we have all these faculties, whether it's our senses and our intellect and our emotions and our deepest—what you might call a soul—or our sense of will and agency and deepest priorities and moral instinct. We have so many faculties as human beings, and my main strategy anymore in searching for what we are calling truth is to try and let all these faculties have their day in court, so to speak. I want to hear from each of them. I don't want to discount any of them or see them as mutually exclusive or a kind of binary opposition where you're a person of faith or you're a person of science and empiricism or something—I just don't see it that way. So my search for truth has expanded certainly beyond the realm of the religious world, but it hasn't by any means abandoned the religious world."

Toby suggested that it shouldn't be scary to be on a journey and to search for truth, as it's dangerous to say you've arrived, then never change or grow.

Aaron answered, "Well, there's an element of the unknown, of course. I think there can be something kind of on an existential level that's terrifying or dreadful even about not knowing the answer, at least it is for some people, to some of these really massive and important questions like, well—who am I? Where do I come from? How should I live? Where am I going? What happens when I die? Will I survive it? All of these big, lofty questions, that when you sit and wonder about them, in my experience at least, can be unsettling. I think it's a trade off of whether we're gonna start with a clinging to those certainties or points of faith. 'I know the answer to all of these questions, and that is true, my understanding of God or reality is true, and then I'm gonna try to find a way to make reality fit into that or worship that idea I have of the truth.' And I think, of course, a pretty reasonable alternative to that is starting with more of an open-handed position where you don't begin with assumptions about what is true and who God is and what reality is about, but you begin with an intention to seek the truth and to discover in increasing fullness what the nature of reality is in whatever aspect, and then there's less of a fear and there's less contentions. You don't have to start disregarding evidence that doesn't support and that even challenges your worldview. You don't have to start seeking out likeminded people to affirm your belief. You don't have to go listen to somebody repeat the same basic message every Sunday to remind you of what you think you're supposed to believe."

Aaron was thankful to be invited on to talk about these issues, but had to run for sound check. After saying goodbye, he set the phone down as the band played in the background. The guys at Bad Christian joked that he still didn't know how to use a cell phone, wondering earlier if he even owned a computer and knew what a podcast was.

108
Birdie

On August 28th, Kaysha gave birth to their daughter. I wrote to Aaron in the middle of September, telling him that a mutual friend, a "little birdie," broke the news to me.

He responded, asking if that was a pun on the baby's name, given they were calling her Birdie, though Margaret was put on the birth certificate just in case she turns out "serious or religious," Aaron wrote. "Imagine that."

Aaron wrote in "D-Minor" that he and Kaysha affirmed their divorce before their marriage began. I asked him if he resolved fatherhood in the same manner, letting go of Birdie before affirming she was his.

"As for resolving fatherhood, in a sense it was already resolved with the 'affirming divorce before the marriage.' Yes, same logic applies, though sporadically in both cases. Another way to look at it is: having a nuptial attachment, at least outwardly, already disqualifies me from monk-dom . . . might as well get the full householder monty. So far, so good."

Aaron forgot to send an attachment with a picture of Birdie as promised. "Ah, sorry about that—have attached one this time. It's black and white, but one of my favorites of both Kaysha and the baby."

He sent an old, vintage photo of a sailor holding a kitten in his massive beard.[318]

---

[318] Email, 9/14/15-9/15/15.

12/17/15
Note to Aaron

Aaron,

Hello, brother. I really hoped to see you in Chicago and say thank you, given it was 10 years ago this Christmas that you invited me to stay with you. Your friendship and care over this past decade has been extremely valuable to me and your presence such a bright spot in my history. Being sentimental, I thought I should say or do something, so I put together a loose representation of your place in my life through photos. It warmed my heart putting it together. Who knows what's next, and even as the past fades, your presence in this world and in my life will always be a miracle I am thankful for. Thank you, Aaron.

Love with no object,

Paul

12/17/15
Email from Aaron

Dear Paul,

I did receive the photo books—forgive me for not mentioning them. When I first opened the package it brought me to tears but I didn't have time to respond, as I was just stopping home briefly.

Then these past few weeks I've been preparing for and ultimately attending (and passing!) my dissertation oral defense, so I've kinda been in a one-track-mind headspace. This last hoop (the oral defense) was actually the last one to jump through. As of yesterday the final dissertation manuscript is uploaded along with all the other documents needed to complete the degree. So, looks like I'm finished!

Kaysha and Birdie and I are off to Israel/Palestine, leaving tomorrow, then straight to Europe for tour, over 2 months on the road, who knows where exactly. Will be even more out of touch than usual, but my love for you never changes!

Thank you for taking the time to put those booklets together, for sending them along, and for all the love I sense in them. You are truly a wonderful friend and I cherish our relationship. We will try to come back in one piece so I can continue to be a forgetful and ungrateful asshole!

Your affectionate uncle,

Screwtape

Epilogue

I'm listening to the Bad Christian Podcast this morning. The episode title is *Life Is Hard and Then You Die*. Pastor Joey Svendsen complains that the church feeds people "bullshit" about leaving a legacy, teaching that God has big plans for you and that your life is worthless if you don't make a big impact, or as Matt Carter added, if you haven't "stepped into your destiny." Matt offered consolation from the fact that "nobody gives a shit about anybody else's legacy . . . It's only for my significance that I need a legacy."

Your life's story is important. It reveals whether you had goals and lived intentionally or if you merely floated through life event-by-event. It shows whether or not you invested passion and energy and were mindful of who you were, what you had to give, and how your life affected others.

Toby Morrell calls it a lie and a scam, this idea that you have to do something big in life and leave your mark on the world to be remembered, that what you do with your life has to be exciting, make you famous, or make you a lot of money. He suggests that there is a legacy in doing things no one sees or cares about, common trades like being an electrician or a plumber, or being a good spouse and parent. There is even a legacy in trying and failing.

It's been popular of late to categorize memoirs like this one as "spiritual journeys," as if we were being taken through events for a reason to end up in some final goal or destination, coming out the other side with epiphanies and spiritual truths. But my story is one of endless failure and recalibration, of living on side roads and contingencies, of continually being forced off "the path" and trying to make adjustments and grow wherever I'm planted. I can't tell the path from the side roads anymore, so I am forced to create a path.

In *Listening for God: A Minister's Journey Through Silence and Doubt*, Renita Weems writes, "Mystics have been hard pressed to come up with a better metaphor to describe the inner life of growing, stretching, climbing, retreating, scrambling, slumping, and soaring that the soul endures than to refer to it as a voyage, a path, a way, a pilgrimage, a journey. And I am hard pressed to characterize the unpredictability and inconstancy of that journey as anything other than itinerant. Itinerancy captures for me the inner journey, the going with no particular destination in view, no itinerary, and no arrival time, living on the road, traveling from circuit to circuit, along a path that twists and curves from morning to evening, across valleys and plains. . . . It means living every day open, accepting what the journey brings us, relying on nothing but faith in God to get us from one location to the next. It is the hardest thing in the world to get accustomed to: constantly wondering whether you're getting anywhere, never sure if you're where you ought to be, feeling as though you're wandering and cycling the same spot again and again."[319]

Renita used the freed Hebrew slaves wandering in the desert for forty years waiting to enter the Promised Land as her illustration of going in circles. In *The Myth of Sisyphus and Other Essays*, Albert Camus attempted to develop a philosophy of the absurd using Sisyphus as an example. Sisyphus was condemned to the torture of an eternity of hopeless and futile labor in the underworld; of struggling to push a boulder to the top of a mountain only to see it roll back down to the bottom again and again, the "unspeakable penalty in which the whole being is exerted towards accomplishing nothing."[320] Camus imagines this long, mundane droning on measured by "skyless space and time without depth." This is often how I feel when confined to a bed for days, living in a fog, disconnected from time, environment, and other people. Like all of us laboring and suffering through life, Sisyphus knows there is no escape from his sentence.

I have often prayed over the years, "Lord, I'm not afraid of going to hell, I'm already there. I'm afraid of never getting out." If hell is defined as conscious torment day and night forever and

---

[319] Renita Weems, *Listening for God: A Minister's Journey Through Silence and Doubt*, (New York: Touchstone, 1999),118.
[320] Albert Camus, *The Myth of Sisyphus and Other Essays*, (New York: Vintage, 1991), 120.

ever with a pervasive sense of having been banished, exiled, rejected, and kept from all things good with no appeal that can be made to change this, then where can hope be found? Pervasive hopelessness leads to suicide. Camus begins his essay: "There is but one truly serious philosophical problem, and that is suicide. Judging whether life is or is not worth living amounts to answering the fundamental question of philosophy."[321]

Camus imagines Sisyphus rebelling against his sentence. What the gods meant to be torment for him—and even in a world where these gods don't exist—becomes obsolete as he finds something to enjoy in his world. He owns his own feelings and constructs his own meaning. "The struggle itself toward the heights is enough to fill a man's heart. One must imagine Sisyphus happy."[322]

In my record of failure in life, I do gain satisfaction from the fact that I lived passionately and took risks. I went after what I wanted. My losses are deep, my grief is long, and it has taken me a long time to come back to life after each hit because I invested everything into those passions.

These upheavals and disillusionments have created chaos not only of the outside landscape of my life, but the inner landscape as well. Grief and trauma send earthquakes through my past, change how I see myself, and blot out hope for the future. In the wake of lost love and abandonment, the Rabbit in "East Enders Wives" laments: *And as the past and all plans are undone, slowly sank like the shipwrecked sun, bridges and boats, burning them both, burned up the sky.*

These ashes now become the scorched earth on which to build new life.

In her memoir about her husband Richard dying of cancer—*Nothing Was the Same: A Memoir*—Kay Redfield Jamison writes that after grieving the loss of her husband and the life they had together, she took it on faith "that at some point, unannounced, a love for life would reemerge. I had been through so many cycles of

---

[321] Ibid, 3.
[322] Ibid, 123.

darkness and light that I believed to my quick that nature would keep her rhythms."[323]

But as hit after hit weathers you and takes something from you, you never quite bounce back to the same place. Any vibrancy, exuberance, vitality, excitement, joy, or hope you find is now tempered with melancholy. Your bright and vibrant colors are muted and the cracks are seen in a vase glued back together. But these cracks give the vase character and complexity.

Kay speaks of grief as fracturing time to bring awareness to what is being mourned and why. In my experience, the loss of the hope I had for a future with Natalie and what I thought was God's plan for our lives took five years to recover from. The loss of Emily took another five years. I have never bounced back from the loss of my health or the loss of my faith. These have left a permanent cloud over me. And just when I think I am done with the past, I realize it isn't done with me.

In her grief, Kay still saw life happening among her friends. Even in my despondency, I tried to do things that brought life, even though I couldn't feel them. I just needed to know there was still life to be had, to see others feel it. Kay's heart "thawed slowly back into life." She writes that "Coming again to life was a hard but good thing. Life was in front of me now. The glove had been thrown down. I could not back away from the world . . . Life had to be taken up again."[324]

"The future, inevitably became more inviting than the past," she continues. "Sentiment and reminiscence, necessary at the beginning of grief, were now in active competition with life."[325] There is a limit to grief, she writes, and it starts to wear out its welcome. The past, containing memories of things good and bad, becomes old and clutters the space that needs to be freed to experience the present.

Kay quotes Martin Luther saying that if the world ended tomorrow, he would still plant his apple tree. While in Scotland,

---

[323] Kay Redfield Jamison, *Nothing Was the Same: A Memoir*, (New York: Vintage, 2011), 181.
[324] Ibid, 185.
[325] Ibid, 186.

Kay saw the town covered in snow. "In so many places, the students and townspeople had built snowy defiances of time, small tributes to imagination and impermanence."[326] The next day, then snowmen were destroyed. "The creators of the snowmen had placed their joy in the creating, fully knowing the transience of their creations."[327] Don't be afraid to live, as you are alive right now.

When I asked Aaron what his biggest life lessons have been since starting the band and going through so many changes over the years, he said it was learning to let go of life lessons. What he learned yesterday might not apply today, and there was no way to bottle a lesson and present it to another person so that it applies the same way. In this regard, looking for and presenting others with theological answers had worn out its welcome. Instead, he sees the present moment as unique and tries to be in it, learning what it has to teach him now without importing baggage from the past or worrying about the future.

One benefit of reading spiritual memoirs is understanding just how diverse and idiosyncratic our stories are. No two stories are the same, though they might have a lot in common, and epiphanies are often found in the most unexpected, taboo, and unconventional places. It is impossible to systemize the millions of stories out there into a single coherent truth. Despite similarities to others, your story is unique.

Aaron writes in "Messes of Men" of *watching sink the heavy ship of everything we knew*. In "Bullet to Binary (Pt. 2)" Aaron implores the listener to *forgive all the time, everyone, everywhere, everything*. It's in the spirit of those words that I write about these events before sinking them to the bottom on the sea. This includes letting go of Aaron Weiss and of his long and steady love and kindness towards me.

In the words of the great philosopher and comedian Norm Macdonald: "Hope is never good. Don't try it. It never works out." But I figured "life is terrible and then you die" probably wasn't the

---

[326] Ibid, 201.
[327] Ibid, 202.

payoff you were looking for after a 500-page venture through more than a decade of my dizzying misadventures.

Ralph Waldo Emerson said, "Finish each day and be done with it. You have done what you could; some blunders and absurdities have crept in; forget them as soon as you can. Tomorrow is a new day; you shall begin it serenely and with too high a spirit to be encumbered with your old nonsense."

I still fast, pray, and seek God often, unable to shake the sense that he is out there somewhere, or right here unaware. "Lord, I don't understand a thing. If you love me, it has to depend nothing on me or what I think of you." In a world of absurdity, strange events, and unanswered questions, this gives me hope.

The past is gone. All we have is now. Life is not over. Let's see what's next.

One day the water's gonna wash it away
And on that day
Nothing clever to say

Wolf Am I! (And Shadow!)